...ndre que le Président ait passé aux ...icaux, car il a annoncé qu'il n'ac...derait plus de pardons, à moins que ... pardons ne soient approuvés par les ...icaux. Le même correspondant pré... que la convention de Philadelphie ... a un fiasco, car les délégués de l'In... ont reçu, de leurs constituants, ...dre de se retirer si les Etats du Sud ... sont pas représentés par des unio...tes purs.

Le révérend Horton existe encore ; ...s on n'a aucun espoir de le sauver. Le docteur Dostie a passé une nuit ...s tranquille.

M. S. S. Fish et le docteur Hire ...t mieux.

Le révérend M. Jackson, quoique ...s une condition critique, se sent ...nmoins un peu mieux.

...MITE CENTRAL EXÉCUTIF.

SÉANCE DU 2 AOUT.

La séance est ouverte à l'heure or...naire. Le secrétaire ayant procédé ...'appel nominal, il est constaté que ...semblée n'est pas en nombre. Une ...tion d'ajournement est mise aux ...x et adoptée.

...TES POUR SERVIR A L'HIS- TOIRE DU MASSACRE DE LA NOUVELLE-ORLEANS.

II.

Tandis que les journaux rebelles de... ...andaient à grands cris que leurs ré... ...sentants fussent admis au Congrès, ...us, les unionistes, étions attaqués, ... eux, dans nos droits les plus sacrés ... droits que nous avions de nous réunir ...bliquement. Lorsque la liberté de la ...scussion n'existe plus, toutes les liber... ... du citoyen sont en danger.

Les émeutiers en furie s'emparèrent ... Mechanics' Institute où s'était as... ...blée une Convention qui avait reçu ... sanction de l'Exécutif. Les émeutes ... New York ont été honteuses et ...ieuses à l'extrême ; mais le nombre ... personnes tuées à New York durant ... émeutes, n'est pas aussi grand que ... nombre de nos morts. A New York ... émeutiers s'étaient répandus dans ...tes les parties de la ville ; ici, ça ... un massacre en gros. Des citoyens ... offensifs, des femmes, des enfants ...me ont reçu des coups de feu ou ont ... assommés jusqu'à la mort de la vic...

Des noirs, sur la rue Baronne, ... été si cruellement assommés avec ... "clubs" et des pierres, que leur tête ... représentait plus qu'une masse in... ...me.

---

dit que le lieutenant-gouverneur Voo- rhies avait laissé croire au général Baird que la Convention ne devait siéger qu'à 6 heures du soir. Chacun peut voir maintenant quel avantage les émeutiers pouvaient tirer de cette as- sertion. La ville restait au pouvoir des émeutiers qui avaient grandement le temps d'accomplir leur dessein. Nous espérons, néanmoins, pour l'honneur du second magistrat de l'Etat, que la ru- meur n'est pas fondée.

Quoiqu'il en soit, trois heures de car- nage ne suffirent pas à nos ennemis. On entendit deux policemen dire- comme il le sera prouvé devant la com- mission d'enquête : "Où est donc X...? (parlant d'un de nos unionistes les plus respectables), où donc est-il ? Je ne le rencontre pas ici ; mais je saurai bien le trouver ailleurs."

L'exaltation des esprits parmi la po- pulation déloyale n'est pas encore pas- sée. Mercredi dernier plusieurs noirs ont été assommés dans différentes par- ties de la ville. On nous rapporte que dans la soirée de mercredi un noir a été poursuivi par des "ruffians" rue du Camp, près Thalia.

LES ÉMEUTES DE MEMPHIS.

Le comité spécial du Congrès, char- gé de faire un rapport sur les massa- cres de Memphis, après avoir raconté avec impartialité tous les crimes com- mis par la populace et la police de Memphis, disait, en terminant son rap- port, que tous les témoignages recueillis prouvent combien les sentiments de la population de Memphis sont peu fa- vorables au gouvernement des Etats- Unis. L'exaltation des esprits est aussi évidente qu'avant la rébellion Les sécessionistes, tout en affectant parfois une certaine modération, sont toujours prêts à persécuter les hommes qui n'ont pas, comme eux, combattu le drapeau fédéral. Il serait impossible à un unioniste, blanc ou noir, de se croire en sûreté à Memphis si les trou- pes étaient rappelées. Le Comité ajoute, du reste que la situation est dans tous les Etats du Sud, la même qu'à Memphis.

Les massacres qui ont eu lieu dans cette ville se renouvelleraient probable- ment dans le Sud, si le gouvernement cessait d'occuper militairement l'inté- rieur du pays. En présence des dispo- sitions hostiles de la population de Memphis, les noirs ne sauraient obtenir justice auprès des autorités civiles. Le comité propose donc que le gouverne- ment fédéral fasse arrêter et punir mi- litairement les coupables, et qu'une taxe spéciale soit levée dans la ville pour indemniser les victimes de l'é- meute.

Après les scènes sanglantes de lundi dernier, personne n'osera dire que les prévisions du comité n'étaient pas fondées.

...eur procès serait instruit, le 14 ... ...raient l'audace de déposer en justi... Quand le magistrat, M. Dix, vou... procéder à l'examen de l'affaire, il ... menacé des dernières violences s'... donnait suite. Les motifs qui s'op... saient à l'action de la justice fur... alors, par les soins de M. Dix, co... gués par écrit et envoyés au ma... French, agent du Bureau des aff... chis, qui vint sur les lieux et enga... les hommes de couleur à retourner tr... quillement chez eux. Ils écoutèr... docilement cet avis de conciliation, se disposèrent à se retirer. Mais ... dénouement aussi pacifique ne fai... pas le compte des esclavagistes. ... étaient dix contre un, et, de plus, ... armés. L'occasion était trop belle ... ne pas en profiter, et ils en profitè... Les affranchis furent poursuivis, bat... traqués par cette lâche meute blanc... On ne sait où se serait arrêté le co... de ses exploits, sans l'apparition s... daine des troupes. A leur approc... ces tristes chevaliers se dispersè... prestement, et, de poursuivants deve... poursuivis, disparurent de l'horizon.

—On dit que le jour où est a... vée à Paris la nouvelle de la défa... subie par ses compatriotes, Mme ... princesse de Metternich, ambassadr... d'Autriche, a pris deuil et ne l'a ... quitté depuis.

Le monde de la Bourse accue... avec faveur une petite fable due ... méditations d'un de nos grands fin... ciers :

Notre Bourse ayant haussé
Tout l'été
Se trouva fort dépourvue
Quand la baisse fut venue.
Elle alla crier famine
Chez la banque sa voisine,
N'ayant plus d'obligation
Pour juer aller la maison.
La banque n'est pas prêteuse,
C'est là son moindre défaut :
—Que faisiez-vous au temps chaud ?
Dit-elle à cette emprunteuse.
—Chaque jour, à tout venant,
Je haussais, ne vous déplaise.
—Vous, haussiez ? j'en suis fort aise.
Eh bien ! baissez maintenant.

TEMPÉRATURE PRISE AU THERMOMÈ... DE C. DUHAMEL OPTICIEN.

2 août 186...
                                    Fahre...
6 heures du matin........81
Midi........................87
3 heures du soir............90
6 heures du soir............77

Mulet Egaré.

AFRO-CREOLE POETRY *in* **FRENCH**
from **LOUISIANA'S RADICAL**
CIVIL WAR–ERA NEWSPAPERS

Qu'importe si le canon gronde

AFRO-CREOLE POETRY IN FRENCH
— FROM —
LOUISIANA'S RADICAL CIVIL WAR–ERA NEWSPAPERS

A BILINGUAL EDITION

Translated and introduced by **CLINT BRUCE**
Transcribed by **JR RAMSEY**
with a foreword by **ANGEL ADAMS PARHAM**

THE HISTORIC NEW ORLEANS COLLECTION

The Historic New Orleans Collection is a museum, research center, and publisher dedicated to the study and preservation of the history and culture of New Orleans, the lower Mississippi Valley, and the Gulf South region. The Collection is operated by the Kemper and Leila Williams Foundation, a Louisiana nonprofit corporation.

Library of Congress Cataloging-in-Publication Data
Names: Bruce, Clint, translator author of introduction. |
 Parham, Angel Adams, author of foreword.
Title: Afro-Creole poetry in French from Louisiana's radical Civil War–era
 newspapers : a bilingual edition / translated and introduced by Clint Bruce;
 transcribed by JR Ramsey; with a foreword by Angel Adams Parham.
Other titles: Union (New Orleans, La. : 1862 : Triweekly)
Description: New Orleans : The Historic New Orleans Collection, 2020. |
 Includes bibliographical references and indexes. | In English and French. |
 Summary: "Original French text and English translations of Afro-Creole
 poetry published in L'Union and La Tribune (Civil War–era New Orleans
 newspapers established by free people of color), with a scholarly introduction
 and brief biographies of the poets"— Provided by publisher.
Identifiers: LCCN 2019048785 | ISBN 9780917860799 (hardcover)
Subjects: LCSH: French-American poetry—Louisiana—New Orleans—
 Translations into English. | French-American poetry—Louisiana—New Orleans. |
 French-American poetry—Creole authors—Translations into English. |
 French-American poetry—Creole authors. | French-American poetry—
 19th century—Translations into English. | French-American poetry—19th century.
Classification: LCC PQ3937.L8 A37 2020 | DDC 841/.8080976335—dc23
LC record available at https://lccn.loc.gov/2019048785

© 2020 The Historic New Orleans Collection
533 Royal Street
New Orleans, Louisiana 70130
WWW.HNOC.ORG

Project editor: Margit Longbrake
Director of publications: Jessica Dorman
President and CEO: Daniel Hammer
Design: Nathan Moehlmann, Goosepen Studio & Press

First edition
All rights reserved
Printed in Firenze, Italia, by Conti Tipocolor.

24 23 22 21 20   1 2 3 4 5

ISBN: 978-0-917860-79-9

The endpapers reproduce details from the 3 August 1866 issue of *La Tribune de la Nouvelle-Orléans / New Orleans Tribune*; courtesy of American Antiquarian Society.

An early version of the translator's preface appeared in the Winter 2018 issue of *64 Parishes* as "Discovering the Lost 1866 Issues of the *New Orleans Tribune*."

Contents

List of Illustrations	xii
Foreword by Angel Adams Parham	xiii
Preface	xvii
Acknowledgments	xix
Introduction	1
Note on the Text	65
Note on the Translation	69

POETRY AS PROPHECY

Les tyrans au tribunal de l'histoire / Tyrants before the Judgment of History ANONYMOUS	82
Stanza [À M. A. P…] / Stanza [For Mr. A. P——] ADOLPHE DUHART	82
Le poète / The Poet ADOLPHE DUHART	84
Hommage au poète / Homage to the Poet HENRY LOUIS REY	90
La poésie / Poetry JOSEPH MANSION	94
Poésie ! Vox Dei ! / Poetry! Vox Dei! ADOLPHE DUHART	96
Fiat Lux ! / Fiat Lux! ADOLPHE DUHART	98
L'astre s'est levé ! / The Star Has Risen! ARMAND LANUSSE	100
Espérance / Hope ADOLPHE DUHART	102
À toi / To You "ASTER"	104

THE WAR AND RECONSTRUCTION

La guerre et l'avenir / The War and the Future 110
    "L. de P."

Le capitaine André Caillou et ses compagnons d'armes /
Captain André Caillou and His Comrades-in-Arms 116
    Émile Honoré

Votre temps est passé ! / Your Time Has Passed! 118
    Anonymous

Le 13 avril / The 13th of April 124
    Adolphe Duhart

Washington et Lincoln / Washington and Lincoln 128
    Henry Train

La rébellion du Sud en permanence /
The South's Unending Rebellion 128
    Henry Louis Rey

Combat de l'Aigle Républicain et du Copperhead /
The Clash of the Republican Eagle and the Copperhead 132
    "A." [Victor Eugène Macarty,
    copying text by Alexandre Soumet]

Aux conservateurs / To the Conservatives 134
    Joanni Questy

Ode aux martyrs / Ode to the Martyrs 136
    "Camille Naudin"

Pot-pourri / Potpourri 140
    Jean-Sylvain Gentil

LIBERTY, RACIAL EQUALITY, AND FRATERNITY

Étrange coïncidence / A Strange Coincidence 146
    Armand Lanusse [probable]

Le triomphe des opprimés / The Triumph of the Oppressed 146
    Anonymous

Le chien et le chat / The Dog and the Cat   *148*
   Adolphe Duhart

Stanza [À M. Th. J. Durant] / Stanza [For Mr. Th. J. Durant]   *150*
   Adolphe Duhart

Communication d'outre-tombe / Message from beyond the Grave   *152*
   "J. B."

Pour les incendiés de Saint-Domingue /
For the Victims of the Saint Domingue Fire   *154*
   Adolphe Duhart

Le droit de suffrage des noirs / Blacks' Right to Vote   *158*
   Émile Honoré

Un cri de l'alcyon / The Halcyon's Cry   *160*
   Adolphe Duhart

Au Père Chocarne / To Father Chocarne   *164*
   "Pierre (l'Hermite)"

La Marseillaise noire : chant de paix /
The Black Marseillaise: Song of Peace   *166*
   "Camille Naudin"

! / !   *168*
   Adolphe Duhart

THE WORLD OF IDEAS

L'Ignorance / Ignorance [1862]   *176*
   Henry Louis Rey

Maris Stella / Maris Stella   *178*
   Adolphe Duhart

Le moqueur / The Mockingbird   *180*
   Adolphe Duhart

L'Ignorance / Ignorance [1865]   *180*
   Henry Louis Rey

Résignation / Resignation   *184*
   Henry Louis Rey

Épître familière / A Familiar Epistle   *186*
    Henry Louis Rey

Le saule pleureur / The Weeping Willow   *188*
    Adolphe Duhart

Une page de Hebel / A Page from Hebel   *192*
    Adolphe Duhart

Il est / He Is   *194*
    "Antony" [probably Victor Eugène Macarty,
    copying text by Hortense de Céré-Barbé]

Il n'est pas / He Is Not   *196*
    Armand Lanusse

La fleur et le papillon / The Flower and the Butterfly   *200*
    Ernest de la Valette

À Théodule Delassize / For Théodule Delassize   *202*
    "Antony" [Victor Eugène Macarty,
    copying text by Henri Blaze]

Les trois perles / The Three Pearls   *204*
    "Antony" [Victor Eugène Macarty,
    copying text by Amédée Pommier]

Tristesse / Sadness   *206*
    Adolphe Duhart

Sonnet / Sonnet [1867]   *210*
    "Pierre (l'Hermite)"

Le souvenir des morts / Remembrance of the Dead   *212*
    "Camille Naudin"

Deux novembre / The Second of November   *214*
    Adolphe Duhart

L'avenir / The Future   *218*
    Lucien Mansion

Lettre à Nath / Letter to Nath   *220*
    Joanni Questy

La vie en rêve / The Dream of Life   222
  AUGUSTE GIROD

MATTERS OF THE HEART

Hommage au sexe / Homage to the Fairer Sex   228
  LUCIEN MANSION

Des baisers / On Kisses   236
  ADOLPHE DUHART

Pensée / Pansy   240
  ADOLPHE DUHART

L'échelle de l'amour / The Ladder of Love   242
  ADOLPHE DUHART

Sonnet / Sonnet [1865]   242
  ADOLPHE DUHART

Guzla / Gusle [1865]   244
  ADOLPHE DUHART

Étoile du soir / Evening Star   246
  ADOLPHE DUHART

Rêve / Dream   248
  ADOLPHE DUHART

À une enfant / For a Child   250
  ADOLPHE DUHART

La fleur blessée / The Wounded Flower   252
  ADOLPHE DUHART

Guzla / Gusle [1866]   254
  ADOLPHE DUHART

Le Jasmin / Jasmine   256
  ADOLPHE DUHART

Amaritudo / Amaritudo   258
  ADOLPHE DUHART

Ange du ciel / Angel from Heaven　262
ADOLPHE DUHART

Souvenir / A Memory　264
ADOLPHE DUHART

La fleur indiscrète / The Indiscreet Flower　266
"ANTONY" [VICTOR EUGÈNE MACARTY,
COPYING TEXT BY HENRI BLAZE]

L'amour / Love　268
ADOLPHE DUHART [POSSIBLE]

Berthe!... Lucie!... Marie!... / Berthe!...Lucie!...Marie!...　270
ADOLPHE DUHART

Au cimetière / At the Cemetery　274
ADOLPHE DUHART

Vision / A Vision　278
JOSEPH MANSION

Méditations / Meditations　280
JOSEPH MANSION

La sensitive / The Sensitive Plant　284
LUCIEN MANSION

L'ange en exil / The Angel in Exile　286
ADOLPHE DUHART

Idéalisme. — Matérialisme. / Idealism. — Materialism.　288
ADOLPHE DUHART

Une dépêche télégraphique / A Telegraphic Dispatch　290
JOANNI QUESTY

La couronne d'amour / The Crown of Love　290
LUCIEN MANSION

Dors ! / Sleep!　292
JOANNI QUESTY

S... à L... / S—— to L——　296
"STÉNIO"

Biographical Notes on Known Authors

Adolphe Duhart	*301*
Jean-Sylvain Gentil	*303*
Auguste Girod	*304*
Émile Honoré	*305*
Armand Lanusse	*306*
Victor Eugène Macarty	*308*
Joseph Lucien Mansion	*310*
Lucien Mansion	*312*
Joanni Questy	*313*
Henry Louis Rey	*316*
Henry Train	*318*

Notes	*319*
Bibliography	*329*
Lists of Poems by Title	*341*
Index	*345*

List of Illustrations

Figures

1. Louis Charles Roudanez, one of the founders of *L'Union* and *La Tribune*   *9*
2. *Échelle de progression / Ladder of Progression*   *16*
3. Inaugural issue of *L'Union: mémorial politique, littéraire et progressiste*, 27 Sept. 1862   *20*
4. Jean-Charles Houzeau, editor-in-chief of *La Tribune*   *22*
5. *A Negro Regiment in Action*   *24*
6. *The Escaped Slave in the Union Army*   *24*
7. *Our Colored Troops at Work: The First Louisiana Native Guards Disembarking at Fort Macombe, Louisiana*   *26*
8. *Our Colored Troops: The Line Officers of the First Louisiana Native Guards*   *26*
9. *Pickets of the First Louisiana "Native Guard" Guarding the New Orleans, Opelousas and Great Western Railroad*   *27*
10. *Funeral of the Late Captain Cailloux, First Louisiana Volunteers (Colored) — Sketched by a Native Guard*   *29*
11. 527 Conti Street, as it appeared in 1962   *30*
12. 527 Conti Street, as it appeared in 2011   *31*
13. *The Copperhead Party — in Favor of a Vigorous Prosecution of Peace!*   *34*
14. Two illustrations of the Mechanics' Institute massacre, from *The Riot in New Orleans*   *36*
15. Four illustrations of the Mechanics' Institute massacre, from *The Riot in New Orleans*   *37*
16. Issue of *La Tribune de la Nouvelle-Orléans / New Orleans Tribune* published four days after the 1866 Mechanics' Institute massacre   *40*
17. Portraits of delegates to the Louisiana Constitutional Convention of 1868   *43*
18. The poem "Les tyrans au tribunal de l'histoire," as it originally appeared in the 20 Dec. 1862 issue of *L'Union*   *64*

Foreword

I AM DELIGHTED TO WRITE THIS FOREWORD for Clint Bruce's excellent volume *Afro-Creole Poetry in French from Louisiana's Radical Civil War–Era Newspapers*. Through a combination of painstaking labor and beautiful, thoughtful translation, Bruce has done readers the tremendous service of re-presenting the poetic work and social commentary of a group too long concealed beneath the shrouds of history. I invoke the image of the shroud intentionally here, because despite their centrality to the nineteenth-century fight for civil rights for people of African descent, Afro-Creole intellectuals and their contributions too often remain buried and forgotten. They have yet to attain even marginal presence in mainstream US history textbooks, syllabi, and popular narratives that describe who we are as Americans.[1] In concert with other scholarly efforts to resurrect these histories, this volume provides an excellent, accessible introduction to Afro-Creole writers and activists who crafted a sophisticated civil rights movement that spoke clearly and powerfully to the struggles of black people locally, nationally, and throughout the Atlantic world.

The poetry Bruce collects in this volume was originally published in two newspapers established by free people of color — *L'Union: mémorial politique, littéraire et progressiste* and *La Tribune de la Nouvelle-Orléans*. He divides the poetry into sections that organize the reader's experience and introduce the writers' social, cultural, and political worlds. The first section, Poetry as Prophecy, emphasizes the social and political power of poetry engaged in a critique of racialized injustice. Bruce is careful to explain that by "prophecy" he refers not to the practice of divination but rather to the biblical tradition where the prophetic voice "serves just as much to warn of divine judgment on humanity for its sins as to herald future changes." The poetry in this section holds true to this charge. It begins with a powerful piece entitled "Tyrants before the Judgment of History" ("Les tyrans au tribunal de l'histoire"). Published just a few months after Union forces successfully claimed New Orleans, the poem serves as a snapshot of a moment when there was reason to hope that justice and freedom would triumph but when victory was far from certain. The anonymous author does not mention slavery explicitly but speaks in more general terms of wickedness and crime, lamenting that "merit is oppressed, while crime is honored, and virtue is suppressed" ("le mérite opprimé, / Et la vertu proscrite, et le crime honoré"). In this time of struggle and peril, the writer of "Tyrants" reminds both the oppressed and the oppressors that "there is an avenger whose unrelenting hand shatters the tomb and makes the guilty stand" ("Il existe un vengeur, dont la main implacable / De sa tombe ébranlée arrache le coupable"). As is common in the prophetic tradition, the poet paints a portrait of judgment filled with hellish visions and tortured nights and days worthy of Dante's *Inferno* ("l'image épouvantable / Qui, tourmentant ses nuits, empoisonnant ses jours"). As is also common in this tradition, however, the focus is not only on the judgment of the wicked, but also on the triumph and ultimate flourishing of the righteous. Our anonymous poet concludes with a note of hope and encouragement, urging that "all the oppressed take heart in this idea" that the oppressor will be vanquished ("Ô! que les opprimés embrassent cette idée!").

In the section Liberty, Racial Equality, and Fraternity, we see Afro-Creole writers engaging in the complex task of situating themselves racially and politically in ways that allow them to be allied locally with newly freed black people — many of them culturally Anglo-American — as well as with members of a larger francophone Atlantic world. Bruce notes in his introduction that the editors and writers publishing in *L'Union* and *La Tribune* made a conscious decision to side with the black majority, seeing the realization and preservation of their own freedoms as ineluctably linked to the fate of this long oppressed group. These poets' decision to position themselves with the black majority was neither automatic nor unanimous within the larger Afro-Creole population.[2] Even within the newspapers' pages, we see initial hesitance on the part of some Afro-Creole writers to be equated with an Anglo-black community that, only recently freed, had long been denied education and social advancement.[3]

Despite the social and political risks of throwing their lot in with the newly free Anglo-black population, the poets featured here clearly position themselves as black. Consider, for instance, the poem "The Black Marseillaise: Song of Peace" ("La Marseillaise noire: chant de paix"), which issues a call for the "Sons of Africans" ("Fils d'Africains") to arise and which condemns the infamous lash ("le fouet infâme") that has carved its marks and broken "us" ("De ses sillons nous a brisés"). The use of the collective "nous" in this line demonstrates that the writer identifies not only as a person of African descent but also as one in community with the black majority that only too recently endured the cruelty of the enslaver's lash.

At the same time that these poets position themselves locally alongside the Anglo-black community, they also embrace and build bridges with others in the francophone world beyond US borders. Many among their number could trace their lineage back to Saint Domingue (or Haiti, its post-independence name beginning in 1804), and they did not forget these connections, even one or two generations out from their parents' and grandparents' migration to Louisiana in the late eighteenth and early nineteenth centuries. The strength of this memory is manifested in Adolphe Duhart's poem "For the Victims of the Saint Domingue Fire" ("Pour les incendiés de Saint-Domingue"), published in May 1866. The Port-au-Prince fire, which occurred in March 1866, was devastating, wiping out about fifty percent of the city's buildings.[4] Duhart's poem calls on readers to listen to the cries of Charity, who stands mourning in the streets, and to refrain from standing aside, "cold as the stone" ("aussi froid que la pierre"), in the face of such a tragedy. Instead, the community is encouraged to give generously to those suffering the loss of their homes and loved ones. Although Duhart's poem is the only one in this volume that directly invokes Haiti, many articles in *La Tribune* and *L'Union* make reference to Haiti and to progressive writers and activists in France who labored on behalf of people of African descent.

Three additional sections round out the volume: The War and Reconstruction, The World of Ideas, and Matters of the Heart. Each reveals additional nuances in the Afro-Creole writers' lives and politics and helps make clear their central and powerful role in articulating the complex situation of black people seeking to harvest and enjoy the fruits of freedom both in the US and abroad.

I conclude by underscoring how important it is that these poets and their sociopolitical project be recognized and re-presented to the US public and to all students of the nation's history. Among the many contributions of this francophone Afro-Creole community to US history and politics are the first anthology of poetry published by writers of African descent (*Les Cenelles: choix de poésies indigènes*); the first broad-based civil rights movements (active from the 1860s into the 1890s); and the *Plessy v. Ferguson* case, which, though unsuccessful, was organized to further the civil rights of all black people and whose legal legacy was monumental. At a time when black Americans continue to fight for and defend their civil and political rights, and when the specter of white supremacy casts an ever larger shadow over the painstaking gains of the last fifty years, it is more important than ever to remember and learn from the cultural engagement and political legacy of New Orleans's Afro-Creoles.

ANGEL ADAMS PARHAM
New Orleans
June 2019

Preface

Lost documents sometimes reveal themselves when we need them most.

Preparation of this book began initially for me by building on the efforts of JR Ramsey, who compiled most of the poems featured in this volume. As I worked on editing and translating the poems, I realized that they provide a new perspective on the two bilingual newspapers founded in the 1860s by Louisiana's French-speaking *gens de couleur* (people of color), *L'Union* (1862–64) and its successor, *La Tribune de la Nouvelle-Orléans* (1864–70). Further research led me to untapped sources in archival repositories as near as next door — the Williams Research Center at The Historic New Orleans Collection (THNOC) is on the same block as *La Tribune*'s offices — and as far away as New England.

L'Union and *La Tribune*'s approach to race has sometimes been reduced by scholars to a classist monolith, based on the papers' publishing a number of editorials highlighting the purported divide between free-born *gens de couleur* and formerly enslaved African Americans. The poems, however — written by some of the same people who wrote the editorials — place strong emphasis on *fraternité* and *égalité* among black people and humankind in general, an emphasis that demands readers recognize the papers as sites of a wide range of positionings. The poetry and the historical discoveries I present in this volume increase both the body of Louisiana francophone literature and our understanding of the troubled times in which these authors took up their pens.

Complicated and evolving perspectives on the part of the writers are hardly surprising: the papers' journalists and poets courageously covered and commented on events during and following the Civil War, providing crucial counterweights to mainstream English-language (and primarily white) news sources, in real time.

One such event was the pivotal and tragic Mechanics' Institute massacre of 30 July 1866. On that fateful day, when a constitutional convention gathered in New Orleans to extend the right to vote to men of African descent, nearly fifty advocates of black suffrage were murdered by racist reactionaries, including police officers. Frustratingly, the issues of *La Tribune* from the days surrounding the massacre were believed to be lost — until now.

My decade of research yielded several fortuitous findings, often in unexpected places. It was in New England that, in 2016, I located several of the "missing" issues from July and August 1866 at the American Antiquarian Society (AAS), a research center and learned society in Worcester, Massachusetts.

Nearly twenty years ago, I visited the AAS as a research assistant to Dana Kress, professor at Centenary College of Louisiana. Kress and I spent a week combing through the AAS's mammoth collection of Louisiana French imprints and manuscripts donated by Edward Larocque Tinker (1881–1968).

I distinctly remember, after asking to view the folders containing issues of *La Tribune*, the staff's apologizing for the small quantity and poor condition of their offerings. Little did they or I know, as I flipped hastily through them, the worth of those folders' fragile contents.

In the summer of 2016, while I worked on this book for THNOC, the 150th anniversary of the Mechanics' Institute massacre weighed heavily on my mind. I wished more than ever for *La Tribune*'s account. One afternoon, I recalled my first trip to the AAS. It occurred to me that those folders I glanced through so briefly years earlier might contain some of the "lost" issues of *La Tribune*.

They do. Several weeks later, breathless with anticipation, I traveled to Massachusetts to view them.

La Tribune's articles provide a gripping account of those tumultuous days from the summer of 1866, as the paper worked hard to prevent the racist press from controlling the narrative. One piece in French, "Notes to Serve in the History of the New Orleans Massacre," opens thus (my translation): "While the rebel newspapers were requesting, with great cries, that their representatives be admitted to Congress, we, the Unionists, were being attacked by them in our most sacred rights — the rights that we possess to gather in public. When liberty of discussion no longer exists, all liberties of the citizen are in danger."

THNOC, the AAS, and other institutions devote themselves to preserving the many voices in the discussion as it evolves over time and, in so doing, help preserve those sacred rights and liberties championed in *La Tribune*. The chance to reintroduce this key nineteenth-century source to accounts of the Mechanics' Institute massacre and its place in the history of race and rights in the United States is a privilege and a thrill.

That particular finding is but one of the surprises awaiting readers of this bilingual edition of the radical poetry of Louisiana's Afro-Creole activist writers. This project has been for me a labor of love and awe. It is my hope that the fruits of my research and translation will allow others to experience similar awe, admiration, and inspiration.

CLINT BRUCE
Lafayette, Louisiana
October 2019

Acknowledgments

CREATING THIS BOOK HAS BEEN a decade-long journey, and the roots of the project go back even further. Over that time, the contributions of four individuals stand out.

To my mentor and lifelong friend, Dana Kress, professor of French at Centenary College of Louisiana and *parfait magicien ès lettres franco-louisianaises*, this book is humbly and admiringly dedicated. His vision as founder of Éditions Tintamarre has shown the way for this publication and others like it.

My gratitude is likewise owed to JR Ramsey, who laid the groundwork for this edition while still an undergraduate at Centenary College, by transcribing the majority of the poems from *L'Union* and *La Tribune de la Nouvelle-Orléans*.

My wife, Chantal White, at Université Sainte-Anne, has not only provided loving encouragement along the way but, as a scholar of Haitian and North American francophone studies, has also fully understood the worth of my late nights spent working.

The role of Margit Longbrake, senior editor at The Historic New Orleans Collection, cannot be overstated. From our first meeting over coffee ten years ago, she has believed unwaveringly both in my potential as a literary translator and in the research undertaken to present this corpus of Afro-Creole poetry. Her thoughtful, discerning guidance makes this book hers as much as anyone's.

In addition to its holdings and public initiatives, THNOC's strength resides in its brilliant and dedicated staff. From the publications division, I thank Jessica Dorman, director; Cathe Mizell-Nelson, editor; Dorothy Ball, senior editor; and Siobhán McKiernan, associate editor, for their expertise. At the Williams Research Center, Alfred E. Lemmon, director; Robert Ticknor, reference associate; and their colleagues in the reading room provided invaluable assistance. The volume's nuanced and conceptually *à propos* design was created by Nathan W. Moehlmann, at Goosepen.

The introduction and biographical notes have benefited from a variety of libraries and archival institutions. I wish to express my appreciation to the staff of the American Antiquarian Society, especially Lauren Hewes and Marie Lamoureux, and to the staff of the Boston Athenaeum, particularly Stanley Ellis Cushing and Patricia Boulos. Greg Osborn and his colleagues at the New Orleans Public Library are to be commended for their service to professional researchers and to the general public. I am also indebted to the staff of Mantor Library at the University of Maine, Farmington, and to the folks at the Bibliothèque Louis R. Comeau, at Université

Sainte-Anne. Repaying that debt has often taken the form of paying late fees!

Research travel was made possible by the Canada Research Chairs, and my efforts have received welcome support from Kenneth Deveau, vice president of academics and research at Université Sainte-Anne. Réanne Cooper, student assistant, helped with this project on several occasions.

Among the scholars whose work has informed my own, some have become true interlocutors. Five must be identified by name: Caryn Cossé Bell, a guiding spirit in many ways; William Horne, whose research and conversations about Victor Eugène Macarty provided crucial information; Angel Adams Parham, whose foreword graces this volume; Nathan Rabalais, an ever-invigorating intellectual presence; and Robin White, who asks all the right questions. Anne Malena and Chris Michaelides offered helpful insights at an early stage of the project.

Numerous others from the Louisiana Creole and francophone communities have influenced my approach or otherwise spurred my thinking: Brian Gabriel Comeaux; Michael Dardar, of the United Houma Nation; Albert Devall Dumas, Jr.; Joseph Dunn; Robyn Joseph; John Lafleur II; Christophe Landry; Jonathan Mayers; Elizabeth Rhodes and Pat Schexnayder of LA Creole; and, last but not least, Tiffany Guillory Thomas. Mark Charles Roudané's efforts to spotlight *La Tribune*, cofounded by his ancestor, have been inspiring. My personal perspective is also grounded in a former life in the Bronx, where I had the privilege of knowing Leo W. Curry, pastor at Fordham United Methodist Church; and my dear, departed friend Phyllis Yvonne Reed.

For media coverage of my findings related to the massacre of 1866, thanks are due Laine Kaplan-Levenson, at WWNO; Erin Greenwald, at the Louisiana Endowment for the Humanities; Guy Taillefer, at *Le Devoir*; and at *Astheure*, Marie Hélène Eddie and Luc Léger.

To my parents, Michael Bruce and Gloria Williams, who did not attend college but always insisted that I would do so: please know that this book, like any accomplishment I may realize, stems from your unflinching belief in education.

During the decade I spent researching and translating these nineteenth-century progressives, I was continually energized by courageous people combating enduring injustices in new ways. Key to addressing the wrongs dealt to black people in the Americas is understanding how dominant narratives of the past prop up the structures of the present. The dedication of twenty-first-century activists including Bree Newsome, those involved in the Black Lives Matter campaign, and many others has sustained me. *Merci à vous toutes et tous*.

CLINT BRUCE

Introduction

> Qu'importe si le canon gronde,
> Si partout s'entrouvre un tombeau:
> C'est le départ d'un mauvais monde,
> L'aurore d'un autre plus beau!
>
> What matters it that cannons roar,
> That all around an open tomb yawns:
> For 'tis the end of one bad world
> As another, much more beautiful, dawns!
>
> — Henry Louis Rey, "L'Ignorance"
> (*L'Union* 27 Sept. 1862)

ON 24 APRIL 1862, BARELY A YEAR AFTER the outbreak of the American Civil War, Union naval forces under the command of David G. Farragut stormed past Confederate fortifications near the mouth of the Mississippi River. The fleet continued toward New Orleans, where it encountered paltry resistance, and in a short time, the South's largest, wealthiest, and most culturally variegated city had fallen under the control of United States authorities. While the war would rage on until 1865, the Crescent City and surrounding areas of southeastern Louisiana soon became a testing ground for policies designed to reshape Southern society and institutions: thus began the ambitious, even revolutionary experiment known as Reconstruction, intended to ensure the US Constitution's "more perfect Union" after centuries of race-based slavery and four years of bloody conflict.[1]

The seventy-nine poems featured in this volume bear witness to the contributions of Louisiana's francophone *gens de couleur* — people of color — to the struggle for a just social order during and after the Civil War. Steeped in French culture, Louisiana Creole mores, and Caribbean heritage, the most progressive of this cosmopolitan minority boldly embraced the Union cause; though free before the war, they ultimately cast their lot with the population of people formerly enslaved, now newly emancipated. Their primary vehicle for political mobilization took the form of two radical newspapers: *L'Union: mémorial politique, littéraire et progressiste* (*The Union: Political, Literary, and Progressive Record*) — founded in late September 1862 by Louis Charles Roudanez, a physician trained in Paris and at Dartmouth College; his brother Jean-Baptiste Roudanez; and the educator Paul Trévigne — and

La Tribune de la Nouvelle-Orléans, which succeeded *L'Union* in the summer of 1864. In the pages of *L'Union* and *La Tribune* the poetry of more than twenty activist writers, mostly Creole *gens de couleur* but also a few white allies, appeared over a period of seven years.

The urgency of the poets' verse comes into stark relief when set against its immediate historical backdrop. Writing in 1937, Charles Barthelemy Roussève, a Creole historian of Louisiana and great-grandson of one of the papers' poets (the wealthy cigar maker Lucien Mansion), summarized the impact of *La Tribune* as follows:

> The influence of *La Tribune,* the only important Republican organ in Louisiana during Reconstruction, was immense. Copies were sent to every member of Congress. The official organ of the Radicals, it vigorously championed universal suffrage [...]. In its columns, friends of the Negro's cause both in the North and in Europe found a weapon with which to fight the battle for the black man in the state. (120)

The legacy of *La Tribune* continues to inspire a current-day avatar, the *New Orleans Tribune,* a monthly periodical founded in 1985.[2] In *La Tribune* of the 1860s, poetry marched alongside editorials, reprinted speeches, official reports, and letters from special correspondents. In poems penned by Adolphe Duhart, Armand Lanusse, Joseph Mansion, Joanni Questy, Henry Louis Rey, and other literary comrades, the reader will discover ample commentary on issues surrounding the so-called "battle for the black man" during the civil rights struggle of the 1860s. These issues include matters of national import, such as the emancipation of the enslaved, the involvement of black troops in the war effort, the assassination of President Abraham Lincoln, and the legal recognition of racial equality.

This stirring body of work brought the Creole poets' francophone worldview, refracted through a local intellectual tradition, to bear on the turbulent but promising circumstances of the Civil War and Reconstruction. A universalist vision appears throughout the texts, highlighted time and again through explicit references to the French revolutionary motto: *Liberté, égalité, fraternité.* As the walls of slavery and state-supported white supremacy crumbled, the effulgent idealism expressed in these texts gave voice to the hope, as Henry Louis Rey's poem "L'Ignorance" proclaimed in the first issue of *L'Union,* that a new, more beautiful world was dawning.

True appreciation of these poems requires critical awareness of their particular sociohistorical origin and standpoint. The idealism expressed in these texts is part of a strategic attempt by the Creole *gens de couleur,* a tight-knit society quite distinct from the vast majority of African Americans in the region (who were or had once been enslaved), to claim political leadership among the whole African American community. Attaining that position of political power required not only the articulation of ideology and policy as well as committed involvement in the political arena but also, as one scholar has put it, "choosing to become black," and thereby emphasizing one aspect of a multifaceted Afro-Creole heritage, as "a means of communal liberation" (Thompson 215). In this light, these French-language texts perform and enact racial identity in a changing American context: in and through them, race functions as a sociopolitical construct.

The significance and aesthetic quality of the poems published in *L'Union* and *La Tribune* have been increasingly acknowledged by scholars. By and large, however, the poems remained unavailable for general readership until now. English translations, few and far between, have generally served as subjects of historical analysis rather than texts in their own right, to be read for enjoyment. Also, though most of the poems have been available on microfilm to researchers, a few lay hidden in archival collections outside of Louisiana.[3] This bilingual edition thus fills a major gap in Louisiana studies, in black literatures of the Americas, and in ideological perspectives on the francophone Atlantic world.

A Note on Creole Identity in Louisiana

As an ethnoracial and cultural descriptor, the term *Afro-Creole* is used by scholars more than by members of the community themselves. As is frequently pointed out, the word *Creole* has been subject to various and contested interpretations for more than two centuries. Beyond the recognized existence of actual Creole languages (of which Louisiana Creole is one), debates erupted in the late nineteenth century over the term's racial implications. Many Louisianians who identified themselves as white claimed it as a badge of pure European ancestry (some continue to do so); their definition marks an ironic contrast with the term's current connotations of cultural fusion and multiracial heritage. In keeping with colonial-era understandings of Creole persons as having been born in the Americas of non-indigenous parents, whatever their racial background, the New Orleanian author Sybil Kein asserted in 2000 that "[t]his inclusive definition is as it should be," for "Creoles are the New World's people, and [...] the term should not exclude anyone based on color, caste, or pigmentation."[4]

To specify as Afro-Creole is to emphasize both the reality of black African ancestry — to varying degrees — and the African element in Louisiana Creole culture, whether in music, cuisine, folkways, crafts and trades, or patterns of resistance to colonialism. In her pathbreaking study *Africans in Colonial Louisiana:*

The Development of Afro-Creole Culture in the Eighteenth Century, Gwendolyn Midlo Hall forcefully demonstrates the decisive, even defining, impact of that element. Hall argues elsewhere that, despite the official racial hierarchy, colonial life in the lower Mississippi valley was characterized by a "permeability extended to relations among peoples of all races, classes, and nationalities in New Orleans, producing a culturally open and profoundly Africanized milieu" ("Formation" 82–83).

This volume's application of the term "Afro-Creole" to the poetry of *L'Union* and *La Tribune de la Nouvelle-Orléans* flows more directly from Caryn Cossé Bell's notion of an "Afro-Creole protest tradition" (in which she places the two newspapers). Like Hall, Bell explores attempts to challenge the racial order, but Bell approaches the efforts as a coherent ideological tradition. "Rooted in the egalitarianism of the age of democratic revolution, a Catholic universalist ethic, and Romantic philosophy," a "republican idealism" evolved, she claims, between the outbreak of the French (1789–99) and Haitian (1791–1804) revolutions and the US Civil War, into "a well-developed philosophy of political radicalism" informed by the experience of race-based oppression (*Revolution* 3–4). Notably, white allies could be and were full participants in the Afro-Creole protest tradition. The radical newspapers of the Civil War era are a case in point: for most of *La Tribune*'s existence, the editor-in-chief of the paper was Jean-Charles Houzeau, a Belgian whose dark complexion led many to mistake him for a mulatto,[5] and a few of the contributing poets featured in this volume were white, such as the lawyer and judge Henry Train, a native of Martinique.

While the category "Afro-Creole" usefully underscores the poems' ideological orientation and historical grounding, it cannot be taken uncritically. For one, it was not used at the time. More crucially, an overenthusiastic insistence on radical idealism can obscure the complexities of material and social life in a three-caste enslaving society, rife with intractable contradictions — a system in which, paradoxically, many free black people and *gens de couleur* had a stake.[6] To grasp this context, it will be useful to revisit the historical development of the *gens de couleur libres* in tandem with the intellectual tradition reflected in the poetry of *L'Union* and *La Tribune*.

Louisiana's *Gens de Couleur* and the Development of an Afro-Creole Intellectual Tradition

On the eve of the Civil War, the population of Louisiana included 18,647 persons classified as "free colored" by the US government, alongside 357,629 (free) whites, who barely outnumbered 331,729 enslaved people. More than half of the free colored persons resided in New Orleans, where they composed slightly more than six percent (10,689) of the 168,675 inhabitants of the city, a growing metropolis home to French-speaking native Creoles, increasingly dominant Anglo-Americans, and immigrants from France, the Caribbean, Ireland, Italy, the German states, Latin America, and elsewhere, as well as 13,385 enslaved people who, in this vibrant urban setting, experienced the institution of slavery differently than did those on rural plantations.[7]

"Our free colored population form a distinct class from those elsewhere in the United States," noted the *Daily Picayune* in 1859. The paper expressed admiration, albeit tinged with racial condescension, for this "sober, industrious and moral class, far advanced in education and civilization." In highlighting the dynamic role of "creole colored people" in various economic sectors, particularly as artisans and skilled workers, the authors conveyed dismay that some had responded to overtures by the government of Haiti to leave the oppressive conditions of the southern United States ("Hayti and Immigration Thither"). Though the emigration movement did not meet with great success, its appeal did speak to a shared identity — black, francophone, and Afro-Creole.

Enslaved Africans had been present in Louisiana since the early eighteenth century. From ten individuals among the fledgling colony's population in 1712, their number would begin to grow around the time of the founding of New Orleans. In late 1718, two French slave ships, the *Aurore* and the *Duc du Maine*, sailed from Ouidah, in today's Benin, with 451 African captives, arriving in Louisiana a few months later.[8] By 1732, the enslaved, most of whom had origins in Senegambia and the Bight of Benin, numbered almost 3,500 in the colonial settlements along the lower Mississippi River — three times as many as the free population. As in other French colonies, the Code noir provided a legal framework for the status of free persons of African descent, either emancipated or born free.[9] After slow growth during the French regime, it was under Spanish governance (1769–1803) "that free persons of African descent in New Orleans made their greatest advances in terms of demographics, privileges, responsibilities, and social standing" (Hanger, "Origins" 2).[10] Spanish law and customs opened new avenues for emancipation (such as self-purchase [*coartación*]), for economic betterment, and for limited participation in official institutions.

For men, participation in free black militias allowed *hommes de couleur* to prove their worth, instilling pride even as it aligned their interests with the established order; free black militias had been used to fight indigenous peoples, hunt down fugitive enslaved persons, and put down revolts. However, shows of prowess and authority could also be perceived by whites as a threat. When the United States officially took possession of Louisiana in December

1803, three hundred black militiamen paraded during the ceremonies, causing some alarm to American officials. At the end of the War of 1812, two battalions of free men of color were summoned in response to General Andrew Jackson's call to defend New Orleans from the British.[11] Jackson's vague promises to improve free black people's standing in exchange for their participation in the Battle of New Orleans would ultimately go unfulfilled. The bitter disappointment felt by *gens de couleur* is expressed in the poem "La campagne de 1814–15" ("The Campaign of 1814–15"), penned by a pseudonymous veteran of the battle and preserved for decades in family notebooks before its 1911 publication in *Nos hommes et notre histoire* (*Our People and Our History*), an important Creole community history written by the civil rights activist Rodolphe Lucien Desdunes (1849–1928), who came of age during the struggles of the 1860s and 1870s. The "La campagne" poet, who signed with the pseudonym Hippolyte Castra, recalls that, despite his valiant contribution, he remains, because of his race, "nothing but an object of scorn" ("je ne suis plus qu'un objet de mépris"; qtd. in R. Desdunes, *Nos hommes* 9).

Suppressed during the prewar decades, free black people's martial tradition would be revived during the Civil War. Having at first offered their services to the Confederacy — a move that can seem contradictory to us and was controversial at the time — the *hommes de couleur* wasted little time, once the federal occupation (or liberation) of New Orleans commenced (1 May 1862), in forming the Native Guards, the Union army's first black unit, which mustered on 27 September 1862, the same day the first issue of *L'Union* was published.[12] The paper enthusiastically supported the effort, now directed toward the fight against slavery and for racial equality.

A full appreciation of the dynamics of race in Creole Louisiana, with the attendant considerations of class and ideology, requires that we adopt a much more expansive frame of reference. New Orleans, much recent scholarship has insisted, constituted a zone of cultural convergence: a "nodal point of the French Atlantic" (Marshall 219), the city was also a "circum-Caribbean cosmopolis" (Roach 179) with transamerican connections across Latin America (Gruesz 108–60).

No event brings that reality more into view than the Haitian Revolution, which vanquished slavery in the French colony of Saint Domingue and gave birth to the world's first black republic.

An event of transatlantic impact, the Haitian Revolution sprung in large measure from the French Revolution, begun in 1789. Once the first article of the *Déclaration des droits de l'homme et du citoyen* (*Declaration of the Rights of Man and of the Citizen*) had declared that "men are born and remain free and equal in rights" ("Les hommes naissent et demeurent libres et égaux en droits"), the genie was out of the bottle. Revolutionary ideology spread seeds of revolt across the colonial Americas — including in Louisiana[13] — but especially in Saint Domingue, France's most prosperous colony and home to half a million enslaved people. Open revolt erupted in 1791, quickly turning into a revolution led by Toussaint Louverture, formerly enslaved himself. By 1804, the revolutionaries had defeated three European powers, obliterated slavery, and founded a new country: Haiti. Thus, Napoléon Bonaparte resigned himself to sell Louisiana to the expanding United States, after only recently recovering the colony through a secret treaty with Spain (see L. Dubois).

As momentous as the Haitian Revolution proved, and even though its first ripples reached US shores quickly, its ultimate consequences would not be felt in Louisiana until several years later. Starting in the 1790s, a steady stream of refugees had relocated from Saint Domingue to the lower Mississippi Valley; however, many more — white and *libres de couleur*, often with the individuals they enslaved — had settled in nearby Cuba. Then, in 1809, in reaction to the French invasion of Spain, authorities in Cuba expelled all French citizens. Within a few short months some ten thousand former Saint Dominguans landed in New Orleans, nearly doubling the city's population. "In a word," wrote one distraught American official in February 1810, "we are at this moment a French Province" (Brown 454). In the context of a nascent rivalry between the *ancienne population* and the *Américains*, the massive increase in the francophone population would stave off linguistic assimilation, thus buttressing French Creole social life, institutions, and political influence for decades.

Beyond this numerical fact, the Saint Domingue influx had two major long-term effects on southern Louisiana's social fabric. First, it reinforced the three-tiered racial hierarchy of Latin Catholic cultures, at odds with the American racial binary of black/white. More specifically, the number of *gens de couleur libres*, of whatever complexion, jumped dramatically: the population of free people of color experienced a ninety percent increase, after which it constituted approximately one third of the free population (Lachance, "1809 Immigration"). Second, the refugees and their descendants, white and *gens de couleur*, injected extraordinary dynamism into a variety of sectors, from journalism and education to the arts, commerce, and politics. The composition of *L'Union* and *La Tribune*'s staff and contributors, including the poets, reflects this background. Take, for example, the educator Adolphe Duhart, the papers' most prolific poet by far: his father, Louis-Adolphe Duhart, was born in Havana and his mother, Françoise Palmyre Brouard, in Saint Domingue; moreover, the poet grew up in the company of the elderly Pointe-du-Jour Daragneinte (perhaps a relative), also of Saint Domingue, and the Haitian themes in some of his works can be traced to that early influence.[14]

While mainstream America feared the specter of Saint Domingue and most white exiles harbored bitterness at having lost their possessions in the country that became Haiti, progressively inclined Afro-Creoles maintained and cultivated ties with the island. When southern Haiti was devastated by a hurricane in 1831, Numa Lanusse, brother of the future educator and pioneering writer Armand Lanusse, spearheaded a fundraising committee whose members included other families associated with the activists of the 1860s, such as the family of Victor Eugène Macarty.[15] Some *gens de couleur* traveled to Haiti despite legal restrictions. One such example is the family of Pierre-Aristide Desdunes (brother of the aforementioned activist Rodolphe Desdunes). Pierre-Aristide was a student of some of *La Tribune*'s poets, several of whom were teachers, and would go on to become a Native Guard soldier (Bell, Introduction). Desdunes's father, in fact, was appointed immigration agent in New Orleans by the Haitian government in the late 1850s, while Lucien Mansion, author of four poems in *L'Union* and *La Tribune*, financially supported emigration to Haiti and Mexico (R. Desdunes, *Our People* 65, 112–14).

The radical newspapers of the 1860s reveal ongoing exchanges with Haiti: the young nation appears regularly in news features and special correspondence and receives thematic treatment in literary pieces. Though such an interest was not uncommon in the black and abolitionist press (just as, conversely, Haiti's recurring political turmoil became fodder for proslavery apology eager to point to the failures of the so-called black republic), *L'Union*'s and *La Tribune*'s attention to Haiti reflects a profound bond.

An Afro-Creole egalitarian ethos was further nourished by contact with France. Despite maintaining slavery in its overseas colonies until 1848, metropolitan France was by long-standing tradition a *terre de liberté*; indeed, some enslaved persons from Louisiana were able to sue for freedom based on temporary residence there (Schafer 15–24). Over the nineteenth century, a number of elite Afro-Creoles emigrated to France for good; others went to study, often with the support of white French fathers. As Michel Fabre explains, "Temporary or lasting, their expatriation expressed their dissatisfaction with the prejudices that limited their aspirations and cut them off from the American cultural mainstream" ("New Orleans Creole Expatriates" 181).[16]

Those who returned had experienced life under a different sociopolitical model and felt that a more just United States was possible. The cofounder of *L'Union* and *La Tribune*, Louis Charles Roudanez, born upriver from New Orleans, in St. James Parish, to a French merchant and a free woman of color, had studied at the Faculté de médecine de Paris in the late 1840s under the

FIG. 1. Louis Charles Roudanez, one of the founders of *L'Union* and *La Tribune*. Image from *Nos hommes et notre histoire*, by Rodolphe Lucien Desdunes; Arbour and Dupont, 1911, p. 65.

mentorship of an ardent advocate of progressive republicanism (fig. 1). When the French Revolution of 1848 broke out, Roudanez had joined his classmates "before the barricades in Paris" (New Orleans *Crusader,* 22 Mar. 1890 [qtd. in Bell, "Common" 20]). The composer and actor Victor Eugène Macarty (1821–81), who published as the poet "Antony" in *La Tribune* — though, as we will see, these texts involved a literary hoax on Macarty's part — had studied at the Conservatoire de Paris, thanks to a recommendation from the French-born politician and diplomat Pierre Soulé. An activist with the Louisiana Republican Party in the 1860s and 1870s, Macarty would sue the New Orleans Opera House in 1869 for racial discrimination, based on the opera's segregated seating (Horne).

Sending shockwaves throughout Europe and the Americas, the leftist uprising of February 1848 overthrew the constitutional monarchy of Louis-Philippe and established the short-lived Second Republic (destined to be dissolved by Louis-Napoléon in his 1851 coup). Throughout the United States and especially in Louisiana, the so-called February Revolution was hailed with great fanfare, by pro- and antislavery constituencies alike. Two months later, on 27 April 1848, France's provisional government ended slavery in all French territories. The fact that the decree was promulgated by the poet-politician Alphonse de Lamartine, a founding figure of literary Romanticism and longtime abolitionist, was in keeping with the Romantics' claim to a dual commitment to creative freedom and human freedom.[17] Moreover, France would expand on the example of British emancipation (1834) by granting universal male suffrage, leading to the election of African-descended political representatives from the Antilles. During Civil War–era debates over these issues, *L'Union* and *La Tribune* would point forcefully to the integration of nonwhites into French political life.

Transnational experiences and international awareness further augmented the *gens de couleur*'s foundational sense of worth and dignity in Louisiana society, which endured in spite of entrenched discrimination and inferior political rights. Looking back on the prewar years, Charles Gayarré, a nineteenth-century white Creole historian, would later affirm that "it is always to be remembered that in their contact with white men, they did not assume that creeping posture of debasement — nor did the whites expect it — which has more or less been forced upon them in fiction."[18] Observers of the time were also quick to point out the prejudiced attitudes of light-skinned *gens de couleur libres* toward black people and the enslaved. Inherited from the racial structure of colonial Saint Domingue — which, as the anthropologist Michel-Rolph Trouillot (109–38) and others have shown, has to the present day dogged Haiti's cohesion as a nation — such biases were real but not universal. They were also viewed by the radical Afro-Creole activists as an obstacle to political empowerment.

Owing to the appearances of an anomalous "colored aristocracy" in prewar Louisiana, a great deal of supposition, often verging on legend, has arisen around the *gens de couleur*. Much of it has revolved around sexual mores, notably the infamous so-called quadroon balls where young women of color were supposedly contracted to wealthy white men as concubines (aka *placées*), a model known in later parlance as *plaçage* (though evidence suggests this understanding of *plaçage* is a titillatingly sexualized and racialized reduction of a complex practice with a long history outside New Orleans).[19] More generally, observers marveled at the socioeconomic conditions some of the *gens de couleur* were able to achieve, including possession of enslaved people. Even among scholars, a persistent perception has long maintained that the *gens de couleur* enjoyed the status and trappings of a "privileged" caste.[20]

There can be little doubt that francophone *gens de couleur* had access to certain opportunities less available to free black people elsewhere. It is also true that some families attained impressive assets — which, along with their transnational connections, they could parlay "into moral capital and political power in Republican Louisiana" of the 1860s and 1870s.[21] Empirical data, however, reveal that such advantages were merely relative. Paul Lachance has examined assets declared on marriage contracts and property inventories, concluding that "even free coloured property owners were demonstrably less wealthy than whites in antebellum New Orleans" ("Limits" 439).

Moreover, enslaving practices among *gens de couleur* cannot be considered monolithically. Many free people of color bought relatives in order to free them: for example, André Cailloux (sometimes spelled Caillou), a once-enslaved cigar maker who became a Native Guard captain and died on the battlefield (a sacrifice celebrated in Émile Honoré's poem "Captain André Caillou and His Comrades-in-Arms," in this collection), purchased his own mother in 1849 for that purpose.[22] For women, investments in human property could provide financial security. According to Elizabeth C. Neidenbach, the case of the African American philanthropist Marie Justine Cirnaire, a formerly enslaved woman whose will granted a bequest for the foundation of a free school for poor children of color (which would eventually become ground zero for Afro-Creole intellectuals), shows "how a free people of color community insulated itself through property ownership and institution-building" (par. 25). Born in Africa and enslaved in Saint Domingue before migrating to Louisiana, Cirnaire (also known as Marie Couvent, widow of Bernard Couvent, a financially successful free man of color) owned, employed, and manumitted enslaved people for reasons ranging from bonds of kinship to her own material advancement. The complexities of an enslaving society were such that, even as she took measures in favor of her community, thus preparing the ground for radical Afro-Creole protest, Cirnaire certainly "considered owning slaves a legitimate financial investment" (Neidenbach, par. 16).

In many ways, measures taken by Afro-Creoles to improve their position in the existing order reflected the real oppression and precarity they endured before the Civil War, whatever their condition or complexion. Persons of known African descent could not vote, of course; they were also required to append to their signature the initials indicating their status — *h.c.l.* or *f.c.l.* in French, *f.m.c.* or *f.w.c.* in English. Other restrictions limited their rights to bear arms, to exercise certain professions or own certain kinds of businesses, to move freely within the state or return to Louisiana from the Caribbean, to reside in New Orleans without express permission, or to congregate or engage in certain activities with the enslaved.[23] With regard to freedom of speech, an 1830 state statute imposed a sentence of death or hard labor for life on "whosoever shall write, print, publish, or distribute any thing having a tendency to produce discontent among the free coloured population of the State, or insubordination among the slaves therein." Other stipulations in the act prohibited bringing into the state any written material "having such tendency as aforesaid," speaking to such effect either publicly or "in private discourses or conversations," and, with much broader intent, teaching enslaved persons to read or write (*Acts Passed at the Second Session* 96).

Though never executed in full force, the law had a chilling effect on Afro-Creole literature and political discourse.[24] Its text implied white people's fear of common interests between enslaved people and *libres de couleur* — common interests and perhaps an alliance, as had happened in Haiti. Such an alliance would indeed characterize the political thrust of Reconstruction.

Toward Afro-Creole Radical Discourse

The 1840s witnessed a flowering of Louisiana French literature. Though some literary works had been written during the colonial era, and real talent began to emerge in the 1830s, the following decade, a time of economic prosperity, brought both cultural maturation and a desire to affirm Louisiana Creole identity, in the broadest sense, in the face of the inexorable dominance of the Anglo-Americans. "Published works began to multiply," observes the literary historian Auguste Viatte. "For a time, this literature, prematurely ripened, outstripped those of Canada and Haiti" (243), where francophone literatures also developed.[25] There is a transatlantic dynamic to this emergence: several young Louisiana Creoles published in France (Adrien Rouquette and Alfred Mercier, for example, published works while students in France), and, more important, Louisiana attracted hundreds of French immigrants, many of them political liberals fleeing France's oppressive environment. The French-language press in Louisiana blossomed.[26]

The French Romantic movement had also reached its ascendancy. Louisiana francophone literature would develop through a complex relationship with the literature of France, in a climate of "interaction, influences, creation, and recreation" (Amelinckx 29).[27] Broadly speaking, Romanticism valued authentic expression — of the self and, for many writers and thinkers, of cultural identity as a cornerstone of nationhood. On the ethical plane, many Romantic writers took an interest in the marginalized and the oppressed. For some, like Victor Hugo and Lamartine, this interest dovetailed with strong antislavery convictions. Francophone writers of the Americas absorbed and creatively appropriated these influences, especially in Haiti. Pioneering Haitian authors of the 1830s and 1840s took to heart the "French Romantic poets' assertions of individuality and universality" in shaping their own poetic vision for their nation (Kadish and Jenson xxxiv), thus offering to their Louisiana Creole cousins one model of transatlantic reimagining.

In the summer of 1843, Armand Lanusse and Joanni Questy launched a literary journal, *L'Album littéraire: journal des jeunes gens, amateurs de littérature*, with the support of the French immigrant Jean-Louis Marciacq. The tone of the writing in *L'Album littéraire* was often scathing. Several texts denounced in vague terms the rampant injustice of Louisiana society. An anonymous essay ("Aux Louisianais," published 1 Aug. 1843) called for education for all — the unspoken but clear context being the exclusion of children of color from New Orleans's nascent public schools. A few pieces broached the race question explicitly. "Un mariage de conscience" (15 Aug. 1843), a short story by Lanusse, tells of the desperate suicide of a young woman of color abandoned by her white lover, an effect of the racial hierarchy. *L'Album littéraire* did not last long.

Two years later, the anthology *Les Cenelles: choix de poésies indigènes* (*The Mayhaws: Selected Indigenous Poetry*) — considered by the literary scholar Henry Louis Gates, Jr., to be "the first attempt to define a black canon" (24) — marked a significant step in developing a Creole poetics appropriated from French Romanticism. Edited by Lanusse, the book brought together eighty poems by seventeen writers, all *hommes de couleur*. The acerbic tone of *L'Album littéraire* had yielded to melancholy. The recurring themes of exile and abandonment in *Les Cenelles* evoke the subordinate condition of the *gens de couleur*, but only subtly.[28] An unknowing reader could certainly mistake the authors for white French writers (or white Louisiana Creoles), a subversive effect Gates describes as "[a]n apolitical art being put to uses most political," carrying the implicit message, "We are just like the French — so, treat us like Frenchmen, not like blacks" (25).

Of the themes that are treated in *Les Cenelles*, the only one that explicitly concerns race is, perhaps unsurprisingly, *plaçage* (that is, *plaçage* as it was understood by Lanusse — namely, the practice of contracting young women of color as concubines to older white men). Lanusse's poem "Épigramme" offers the most pointed example. The short piece chides the hypocrisy of a mother who asks her priest if she can wait to confess her sins until after she has the chance to "place" her daughter. Lanusse, as Emily Clark points out, stands out as "the first New Orleanian to use his literary gifts to shine a spotlight on the plight of the quadroon" (*Strange History* 157). At the same time, the male poet's perspective, throughout *Les Cenelles*, is conditioned by a sense of gender propriety, according to Shirley Elizabeth Thompson, who perceptively notes, "In a strong sense, *Les Cenelles* serves as a form of prescriptive literature for pubescent girls, emphasizing propriety and chastity over maternally sanctioned *plaçage* and the promise of property and wealth" (190). Such a push for a normalized patriarchal structure also permeates the poems of *L'Union* and *La Tribune*.

Lanusse's avowed cause in the mid-1840s, however, was education. "From all quarters a great need for instruction is being felt," he wrote in *Les Cenelles*'s preface, as "a shield which dulls the arrows cast upon us by disdain and calumny" (13). The bequest of the aforementioned Marie Justine Cirnaire provided help. Cirnaire's will had designated a plot of land to build a free school for poor children of color. After being held up for a decade by legal restrictions, the plan to build such a school was validated by an act of the legislature in 1847. A group of Creoles of color set up a committee to incorporate the Institution catholique des orphelins indigents. Barthélemy Rey (father of the poet Henry Louis Rey) presided over a board that included Lanusse and Louis-Adolphe Duhart, Adolphe Duhart's father (Bell, *Revolution* 123–37; Daggett, *Spiritualism* 15–17). After opening in 1848, the school would unite, in one way or another, most of the activists who would later work with *L'Union* and *La Tribune*; in turn, the papers would advocate for the Institution in the 1860s. The school initially opened in temporary quarters, where its first principal was the educator Félicie Cailloux (wife of the future Civil War hero André Cailloux). In 1852, the school moved to its permanent home in the Faubourg Marigny, and three of the poets featured in this volume served in succession as its principal: Lanusse, Questy, and Duhart. Trévigne taught there as well (R. Desdunes, *Our People* 14n4, 104).

Dedicated to providing, as described in its prospectus, "une éducation pratique, morale, et religieuse" to even the poorest children of color, the Institution catholique harnessed the finest intellectual talent the Creole community had to offer (qtd. in Mitchell 19). Social and political consciousness inflected the curriculum. The historian Mary Niall Mitchell has studied English-language compositions from the Institution catholique and observes that otherwise typical school assignments also encouraged pupils "to think about the possibility of living in a nation without racial oppression." Setting their community's history within the framework of world events, the Creole teachers cultivated "a political awareness and a sense of allegiance to other free people of color in the Atlantic World" (19). Such a perspective sowed the seeds of future activism, watering the soil with a deep reverence for literature and the arts.

The situation of free people of color became dire in the 1850s as the clouds of the sectional conflict over slavery grew ever darker. The abolitionist bent of the newly formed Republican Party (founded in 1854) antagonized proslavery Southerners. Armed struggle broke out in "Bleeding Kansas" over the status of slavery in US territories and new states, while the Supreme Court's *Dred Scott v. Sandford* decision (1857) definitively denied free black people the rights of citizenship. The rights of free people of color in Louisiana eroded. By 1855, a revision of the Code noir of 1806 by the state legislature imposed drastic restrictions on the manumission of enslaved persons ("An Act Relative to Slaves" 387; Schafer 72–73). Other statutes curtailed freedom of assembly and restricted freedom of movement within the city by requiring *gens de couleur* to carry passes certifying their status. In other parts of the state, free people of color fell victim to vigilante violence intended to intimidate and to suppress any sign of resistance to white supremacy. There also existed the very real threat of being kidnapped and sold into slavery.[29] These conditions prompted hundreds of people to migrate to Haiti and Mexico.

Faced with an assault on their rights in the 1850s, many Afro-Creole radicals who remained in New Orleans found a powerful source of inspiration and ideological sustenance in a new religion sweeping through mid-nineteenth-century America. Known as Spiritualism, the religion was based on communication with the spirits of the dead, and its belief system combined the pseudo-scientific healing practices of Franz Anton Mesmer; the utopian socialism of the French philosopher Charles Fourier, especially his concept of social harmony; and the mystic theology of Emanuel Swedenborg, who claimed to have conversed with beings from the spirit world. Though condemned by the Catholic Church, the movement soon attracted a number of Afro-Creole activists and writers who already had a contentious relationship with established Catholicism, their traditional religion. They had and would continue to support rebellious priests in New Orleans and were drawn to progressive Catholic thinkers like Félicité Robert de Lamennais, a French priest and political theorist whose 1834 book *Paroles d'un croyant* (*Words of a Believer*) was described by Lamartine as the "évangile de l'insurrection" ("gospel of insurrection"; qtd. in Guillemin 747). Many also practiced Freemasonry, with its similar reconciliation of rationalism and mysticism. Spiritualism's central tenet, "the Idea," "a concept that meant equality and brotherhood," appealed to dissidents and social reformers of all stripes (Emily Suzanne Clark 23).

Spiritualism came to New Orleans in the mid-1840s under the influence of the French immigrant Joseph Barthet. By the early 1850s, its converts included the white radical author Charles Testut and two renowned Afro-Creole spirit mediums: Valmour, a blacksmith whose real name was John B. Averin; and a medium known as Sister Louise (Emily Suzanne Clark 24–27). According to Melissa Daggett, Henry Louis Rey, then a clerk at a hardware store in the Tremé neighborhood, joined their ranks in 1858 (*Spiritualism* 39, 46). Recalling visions experienced by his mother and deeply affected by his father's passing, he became one of the movement's most influential practitioners (fig. 2). Séances held by his group, later called the Cercle harmonique ("Harmonic Circle"), brought together other future poets for *L'Union* and *La Tribune*, namely Duhart and Questy. Messages believed to be dictated by the dead were recorded in handwritten registers kept during séances, and their content expressed hope for a better world. As Emily Suzanne Clark summarizes,

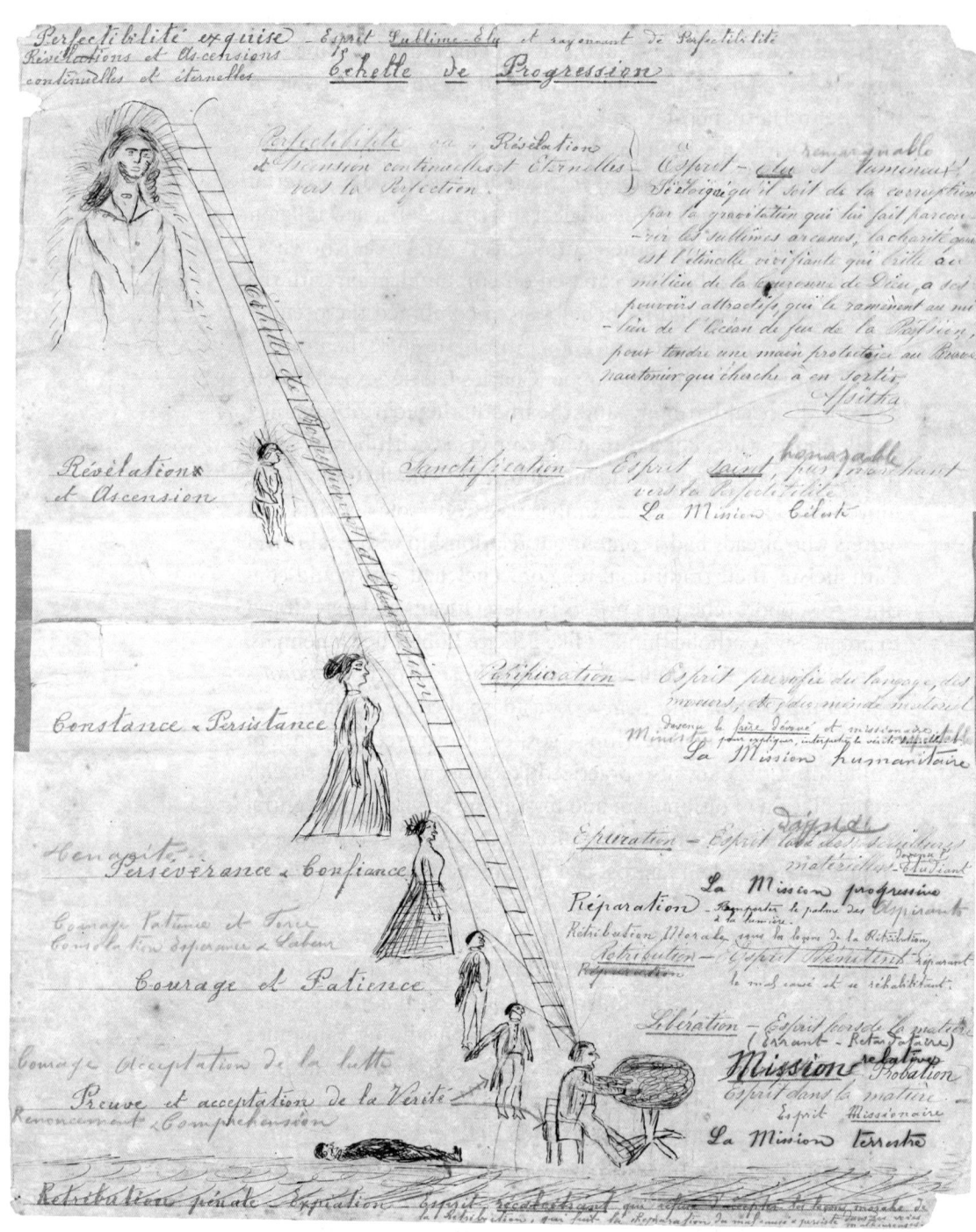

FIG. 2. Henry Louis Rey's drawing *Échelle de progression* (*Ladder of Progression*) depicts the Spiritualists' understanding of the process by which the human spirit undergoes purification and perfection. *Spiritualist Registers*, vol. 40, between pp. 2 and 3; René Grandjean Collection; courtesy of Earl K. Long Library, University of New Orleans.

> Afro-Creoles could hear their social and political goals echo in the messages from the invisible world of the spirits — the call for harmony, desire for progress, the triumph of humanity, the need for moral and just leaders, the fight against despotism, fair political representation, and a voice for the people. The French revolutionary motto "Liberté, Egalité, Fraternité" resonated in the recorded messages. (150–51)

Over the coming years, communications were reported to arrive from deceased family members, such as Adolphe Duhart's father; spiritual figures, including Jesus, Muhammad, and St. Vincent de Paul; revolutionaries, such as Maximilien Robespierre and Toussaint Louverture; and political leaders, including Napoléon Bonaparte and Abraham Lincoln. The majority of spirit messages would remain confined to the séance registers.[30] However, a number of them were published — most in Spiritualist periodicals, such as Barthet's short-lived *Le Spiritualiste de la Nouvelle-Orléans* (issued from 1857 to 1858), but also in *L'Union*. In the latter paper's seventh issue, a communication from Napoléon expresses the dead French emperor's regrets for not having used his might to combat oppression: "Oh! Si je pouvais encore revenir sur cette terre que j'ai remplie du bruit de mon vain et triste nom [...], [q]ue de tyrans je renverserais par des moyens plus humains, que d'esclaves à qui je ferais rendre la liberté!" ("Oh! If only I could return to this earth that I filled with the sound of my vain and sad name [...], how many tyrants I would overthrow by more humane means, how many slaves to whom I would have freedom restored!"; "Pensées d'outre-tombe," 18 Oct. 1862).

The language of the Spiritualist messages informs mightily the poetics of the Afro-Creole writers of *L'Union* and *La Tribune*. Rey's "L'Ignorance" (1862) evinces this explicitly, naming Swedenborg, along with Galileo, Jesus, and Joan of Arc, among a pantheon of persecuted apostles of truth. The poem "Communication d'outre-tombe" ("Message from beyond the Grave," 5 Nov. 1865) is in fact presented as a spirit message: it is attributed to "J. B." — namely, (Pierre-)Jean de Béranger, one of the era's most popular songwriters, who had been imprisoned by French authorities for the political content of his lyrics and had died in 1857. As in the recorded communications, the republican values of *liberté*, *égalité*, and *fraternité* recur often in the poetry. A more important fundamental connection, however, lies in the intention of the poetry, much of which, like messages from the dead, is called upon to function as prophecy.

Prophecy is understood here in its Biblical sense and is not to be confused with divination or merely telling the future. For these poets, prophecy functions much as it does in the Hebrew Bible, from Elijah to Ezekiel and Malachi: namely, it serves just as much to warn of divine judgment on humanity for its sins as to herald future changes. Many texts from this corpus do both.

Several poems declare this mission openly. Lamartine had written in his 1834 essay "Des destinées de la poésie" that nineteenth-century poetry would henceforth act as "sung reason"; verse would no longer reflect an image of humankind but would become "man himself":

> It is [poetry] that hangs over society and judges it, and that, showing man the vulgarity of his deeds, ever calls him to go forward, pointing with its finger toward utopias, imaginary republics, cities of God, and breathes into his heart the courage to attempt them and the hope to attain them. (58)

In a similar vein, the anonymously penned "Les tyrans au tribunal de l'histoire" ("Tyrants before the Judgment of History"), published in *L'Union* in December 1862, attributes to the poet the power of retribution for injustices gone shamefully unpunished. Though "Les tyrans" does not make direct mention of slavery, "Le poète" ("The Poet," 4 June 1865), by Adolphe Duhart, does. Shifting rhythmic patterns and rhyme schemes as it addresses various aspects of the poetic experience, the poem exhorts the "archange-poète" ("poet-archangel") and "oiseau-prophète" ("prophet-bird") to sing "des chants pour la patrie, / Des chants qui réveillent les cœurs" ("songs for our country, / Songs that rouse the heart"), at which "tyrans" will tremble.[31] This allusion to the overthrow of the enslaving class comes into sharper focus when we read that "l'esclave qui dans les chaînes / Gémit sur les rives lointaines" ("the slave who, in his chains, / Still groans on distant shores"), hearing these songs of liberation, now "espère la liberté" ("for freedom now does hope").

"Le poète" was written in June 1865, shortly after the assassination of Abraham Lincoln. Nearly three trying years of war, upheaval, and uneven progress had passed since Rey proclaimed the coming triumph of reason against prejudice, yet Duhart's message ultimately does not waver: there is a brighter future ("Il est un meilleur avenir").

Poetic practice thus partakes in a larger project of historical transformation, indeed, of revolution, shining the light and showing the way through the troubled and uncertain days of the war and Reconstruction.

L'Union and *La Tribune* during the War and Reconstruction

The inaugural issue of *L'Union: mémorial politique, littéraire et progressiste* came off the presses, then located on Jackson Square at the corner of Chartres and St. Ann Streets, on Saturday, 27 September

1862 (fig. 3). The front-page editorial by Trévigne proclaimed, "Sans crainte et sans trouble, nous inaugurons aujourd'hui une ère nouvelle dans les destinées du Sud" ("Without fear and without anxiety, we initiate today a new era in the destiny of the South"; "Au public," 27 Sept. 1862).

Consisting of one sheet, front and back, in French, the paper featured a lengthy denunciation of slavery in Louisiana, thus taking a local stance on the major issue of the war; an exchange of letters between Victor Hugo and the Haitian newspaper editor Eugène Heurtelou, situating the enterprise within the revolutionary Atlantic context; and, on the second page, the first articles of the Constitution of the United States translated into French, thus framing the work to be done within the bounds of the American nation and its political traditions. Henry Louis Rey's poem "L'Ignorance" followed the first installment of the constitution.

Although the Emancipation Proclamation would not take effect until 1 January 1863 and slavery would not be abolished throughout Louisiana until 1864, there was no doubt in the minds of Trévigne and his colleagues as to the stakes of the war: "La lutte se trouve maintenant engagée entre l'esclavage et notre pays" ("The struggle is now under way between slavery and our country"; "L'esclavage," *L'Union*, 27 Sept. 1862).

Over its two-year existence, *L'Union* would advocate for emancipation, voting rights, and the full participation of black troops in the war effort. The paper criticized labor policies by federal authorities that kept formerly enslaved workers in a state of near servitude. Initially appearing twice a week, *L'Union* became a triweekly in late December 1862. It added an English-language edition in July 1863. *L'Union* would henceforth remain a bilingual endeavor, offering separate pages in French and English with overlapping but not identical content, and *La Tribune* would follow suit. This choice represented a dual strategy. On the one hand, Afro-Creole leaders sought to assert their claim to speak for black people as a whole and strove for influence on the national scene; on the other hand, a forum was needed to affirm Afro-Creole cultural specificity and to engage with the francophone world — which, in nineteenth-century America, included a vibrant French-language press in many parts of the country.[32]

The paper would test its political muscle in the national arena when, in March 1864, *L'Union*'s publisher Jean-Baptiste Roudanez and Arnold Bertonneau, a wine merchant and former captain in the Native Guards, traveled to Washington, DC, to meet with President Abraham Lincoln. The two men presented a petition, backed by some "thousand signatures of the free colored citizens of Louisiana" — including a number of veterans of the War of 1812 — asking that "all the citizens of Louisiana of African descent, born free before the rebellion" be "admitted to the rights and privileges of

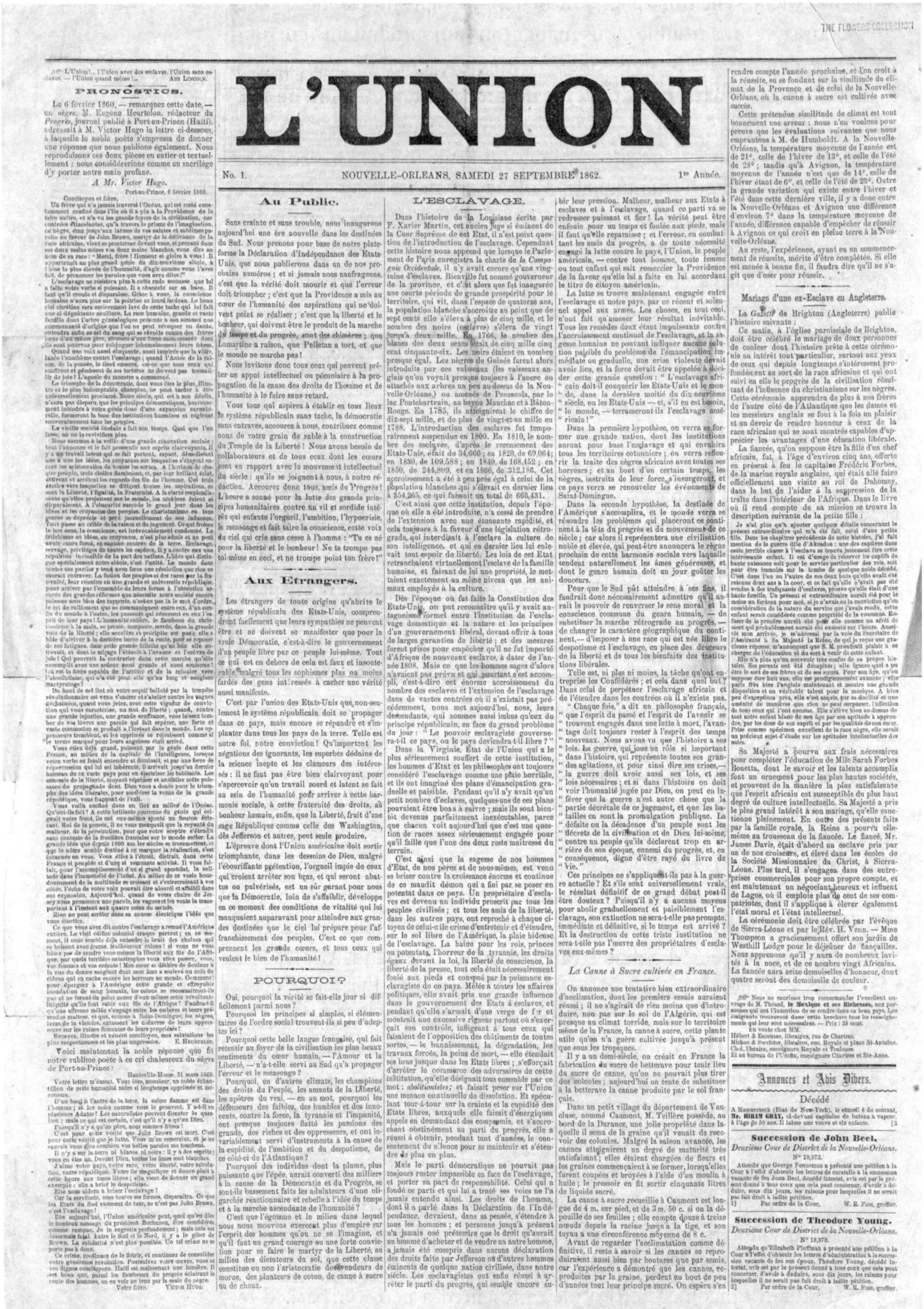
L'UNION

No. 1. NOUVELLE-ORLEANS, SAMEDI 27 SEPTEMBRE 1862. 1re Année.

PRONOSTICS.

Au Public.

Aux Etrangers.

POURQUOI?

L'ESCLAVAGE.

La Canne à Sucre cultivée en France.

Mariage d'une ex-Esclave en Angleterre.

Annonces et Avis Divers.

Succession de John Beel.

Succession de Theodore Young.

FIG. 3. Inaugural issue of *L'Union: mémorial politique, littéraire et progressiste*. 27 Sept. 1862; courtesy of David M. Rubenstein Rare Book and Manuscript Library, Duke University.

electors." An appended memorandum by Roudanez and Bertonneau urged that "the right of suffrage may be extended not only to natives of Louisiana of African descent born free, but also to all others, whether born slave or free." Lincoln was impressed; though he did not immediately embrace black suffrage, the encounter moved him in that direction.[33]

Following threats against Trévigne's life, *L'Union* shuttered its windows on 19 July 1864. Two days later, "a new paper devoted to the principles heretofore defended by the *Union*" hit the streets (Leavens 48). Thus was born the *New Orleans Tribune / La Tribune de la Nouvelle-Orléans*, soon to become America's first black daily and, as W. E. B. Du Bois later observed, "an unusually effective organ for the Negroes" (456).

In undertaking their work, New Orleans's Afro-Creole leaders were able to count on a brilliant, eloquent, and tireless ally in the person of Jean-Charles Houzeau (aka Jean-Charles Houzeau de Lehaie [1820–88]), a Belgian astronomer, journalist, and liberal republican activist. Like many of his generation, Houzeau was drawn to the radical revolutions of 1848; after his political leanings cost him his job at the Belgian Royal Observatory, he wandered around Europe before heading to the southern United States in the late 1850s. Racial prejudice — and the Confederate cause, more pointedly — appalled him. He felt solidarity with the colored Creoles, and in fact his naturally dark complexion often led to his being mistaken as such. Fleeing the war first to Mexico, then traveling to Philadelphia, Houzeau corresponded with *L'Union* as "Cham." Then, in November 1864, he accepted Roudanez and Trévigne's offer to take up the position of editor-in-chief of *La Tribune* (fig. 4).[34]

The Belgian scientist's presence at the helm of the newspaper would prove decisive. Though historians have not agreed to what extent his vision dominated *La Tribune*, it is clear that his perspective shaped its stances and strategies on crucial issues including suffrage, free black labor, land distribution, and economic development. He penned hundreds of editorials, in terms more pragmatic and in a style much more direct than Trévigne's. In keeping with Houzeau's socialist outlook, labor policy and coalition-building received emphasis. The paper's motto, printed under the masthead, proclaimed in English: "To every citizen his rights — universal suffrage, equality before the law! — To every laborer his dues — an equitable salary and weekly payments — eight hours a legal day's work." And in French: "Suffrage universel! Égalité devant la loi — à tout citoyen ses droits — à tout travailleur justice — salaire équitable, payé chaque semaine —journée legale, huit heures de travail."

Seeing *La Tribune*'s potential as "the organ of five million black and brown-skinned men of the United States," he ventured "to transform a local newspaper into a newspaper of national importance"

FIG. 4. Jean-Charles Houzeau, editor-in-chief of *La Tribune* for much of the paper's existence. From *Deutsche Rundschau für Geographie und Statistik* 11 (1889), p. 140; courtesy of Universitätsbibliothek Trier.

(Houzeau 79). And so it happened. A turning point came in January 1865, when *La Tribune* was quoted and lauded in a widely published speech delivered in the US House of Representatives by Congressman William D. Kelley of Pennsylvania (Kelley 19–20; Rankin, "Introduction" 86–88); Houzeau later exulted, "This was a sort of baptism for the *Tribune*. From this day on, we stood before the nation" (87).

Additional seals of cultural approval followed. On 27 October 1865, *La Tribune* reprinted a letter written by the eminent social reformer Frederick Douglass to its publisher Jean-Baptiste Roudanez, in which Douglass said of the paper, "I see it and read it with very great pleasure. I am proud that a press so true and wise is devoted to the interests of liberty and equality in your Southern latitude." In the paper's heyday, it was dispatched to members of Congress, the head of the Freedmen's Bureau, and state capitols across the North. References to and excerpts from *La Tribune* appeared in major Northern newspapers such as the *New York Times*, the *New York Herald*, the *Philadelphia Inquirer*, the *Chicago Tribune*, the *Liberator* (William Lloyd Garrison's abolitionist newspaper), and scores of others.[35] Fighting for the civil rights guarantees that would eventually be enshrined in the Fourteenth Amendment (conferring citizenship, in 1868) and Fifteenth Amendment (ensuring universal male suffrage, in 1870), the paper gained the federal designation of "Official Journal of the United States Government" in April 1867. It may very well be true, as Rodolphe Desdunes claims, that *La Tribune* and its leaders "acquired a prestige that made them as powerful in Washington as in New Orleans" ("ces chefs avaient acquis un prestige qui les avait rendus aussi puissants à Washington qu'à la Nouvelle-Orléans"; *Our People* 133; *Nos hommes* 176). Reactionary parties came to despise the "impudent and shameless radical sheet," as one Louisiana paper fumed (*Opelousas Courier*, 13 Oct. 1866).

La Tribune's readership extended beyond the United States into the international public sphere, especially in the French-speaking world. Upon publishing a letter from Trévigne to the Guadeloupe-born politician Sainte-Suzanne Melvil-Bloncourt (1825–80), the editor of the *Revue du monde colonial, asiatique et américain*, based in Paris, remarked that the journal had quoted *La Tribune* on numerous occasions (Noirot 486). An English-language newspaper in France, the *American Register*, printed a letter from an African American reader claiming that *La Tribune* enjoyed "a successful circulation [...] not only in the United States, but in most of the principal cities of Europe" (qtd. in "Colored Editors in France," *New Era*, 25 Aug. 1870).

Dissension would arise in 1868, over a hotly contested gubernatorial election. In the course of a disagreement between Houzeau (who sided with the rest of the Republican Party in supporting the twenty-six-year-old Illinois native and Union veteran Henry C. Warmoth) and Roudanez and other members of the Afro-Creole elite (who backed James G. Taliaferro, a former plantation owner but staunch Unionist who had been imprisoned by Confederate authorities), *La Tribune* would become a casualty. Houzeau soon left the paper, which shut down temporarily in the spring of 1868. Though subsequently revived by the Roudanez brothers and purchased in the summer of 1868 by Paul Trévigne and fellow journalist J. Clovis Laizer, a printer by trade who passed away soon afterward, *La Tribune* ceased publication for good in October 1870.[36] It was not to take part in the battles that awaited during the remaining years of so-called Radical Reconstruction (1868–77).

There is no doubt today about *L'Union*'s and *La Tribune*'s mighty contributions to the civil rights struggles of the 1860s, each functioning both as a platform for advocacy and, by widening the public sphere, "as a rhetorical tool that used self-representations of blacks' literacy practices to construct an African American discourse community that was worthy of citizenship and suffrage" (Melançon 24). To understand the particular function of poetry in that larger project, we must look first at two matters of import faced by the Afro-Creole leadership during the time the war overlapped with Reconstruction: namely, involvement in the military effort and the burgeoning political movement for racial equality.

The arming of free black people, enslaved people, and freedmen represented a major issue throughout the war (figs. 5 and 6). Many white people — in both the Union and the Confederacy — doubted whether black people were up to the task. Calling themselves Defenders of the Native Land in the spirit of the Battle of New Orleans volunteers of 1814–15, Creoles of color formed the Louisiana Native Guards under the banner of the Confederacy. Several notable Afro-Creoles, including Lanusse and Henry Louis Rey, expressed enthusiasm for the cause. Some may have hoped for

FIG. 5. *A Negro Regiment in Action*, by Thomas Nast. *Harper's Weekly*, 14 Mar. 1863; courtesy of Metropolitan Museum of Art.

FIG. 6. *The Escaped Slave in the Union Army*, by Thomas Nast. *Harper's Weekly*, 2 July 1864; courtesy of Dickinson College Archives and Special Collections.

a strategic alliance with the ruling class, especially under intense pressure to support secession. Editorials and letters in the first issues of *L'Union* would later explain certain *gens de couleur*'s allegiance as either loyalty to their home state or due respect to the ruling government, "whether or not by their choice, and whatever may have been its form or character."[37]

Whatever their original motivations, the Native Guards remained in the city when Confederate forces evacuated in late April 1862, and a delegation of four officers, including Henry Louis Rey and his brother Octave, approached the Union commander Benjamin F. Butler to offer their cooperation. By August, Butler decided to "call on Africa to intervene" in case of a counterinvasion (qtd. in Hollandsworth, *Louisiana* 15). Though Northern units like Massachusetts's Fifty-Fourth Regiment have enjoyed more staying power in the national memory, Louisiana's Native Guards, eventually reorganized as the Corps d'Afrique, became the first black units in the Union army (figs. 7–9). *L'Union* would throw its energy behind the recruitment campaign, urging former Confederate militiamen of color to rally behind the Union banner.

The paper would likewise follow the reformed Native Guards' progress with zeal. An editorial by Duhart, who did not join the federal units, expressed excitement about the opportunity for *hommes de couleur* to demonstrate that "nous avons les mêmes aptitudes, la même conformation" ("we have the same aptitudes, the same makeup") and that "nous pouvons prendre place régulière dans la société" ("we can take our rightful place in society"; "Un mot des Natifs," 25 Oct. 1862). In Louisiana as elsewhere, black troops endured discrimination, grueling manual labor, and inferior pay — pay that often did not materialize, eventually resulting in desertions. Rey, a captain in the First Regiment (until a medical discharge in April 1863), sent frequent dispatches from Gentilly Station and Bayou Lafourche with the aim of "faire comprendre à mes malheureux compatriots qu'ils doivent, comme un seul homme, se lever et se ranger sous l'étendard du progrès et de la liberté" ("bringing my unhappy compatriots to understand that they must, like a single man, rise up and line up beneath the banner of progress and freedom"; "Correspondance," *L'Union*, 18 Oct. 1862). In late spring 1863, the country's eyes would be riveted on the Native Guards' assault on the Confederate stronghold of Port Hudson, twenty miles north of Baton Rouge on the Mississippi River. The stakes involved more than victory or strategic advance: decades later, the retired white commander Thomas J. Morgan would argue that "the share borne by colored soldiers in the war for the Union," though sidelined in official history of the time, was "a silent, but most potent factor in influencing public sentiment, shaping legislation, and fixing the status of the colored people in America" (qtd. in Wilson 305).

FIG. 7. *Our Colored Troops at Work: The First Louisiana Native Guards Disembarking at Fort Macombe, Louisiana.* Harper's Weekly, 14 Feb. 1863; The Historic New Orleans Collection, 1974.25.9.6.

FIG. 8. *Our Colored Troops: The Line Officers of the First Louisiana Native Guards.* Harper's Weekly, 28 Feb. 1863; The Historic New Orleans Collection, 1974.25.9.7.

FIG. 9. *Pickets of the First Louisiana "Native Guard" Guarding the New Orleans, Opelousas and Great Western Railroad. Frank Leslie's Illustrated Newspaper*, 7 Mar. 1863; The Historic New Orleans Collection, 1974.25.9.293.

The campaign at Port Hudson stirred the poets' pens. Butler's successor, Nathaniel P. Banks, more politician than soldier, displayed much more reticence about black troops and especially officers. Although many of Banks's policies provoked protest from *L'Union*, his decision to send the Native Guards into battle inspired the rousing "Votre temps est passé!" ("Your Time Has Passed!"), composed by an anonymous author as federal forces prepared to besiege the Confederate fortifications on the Mississippi. Though the initial attack on 27 May 1863 did not bring an immediate victory, the engagement would "settl[e] the question that the negro race can fight with great prowess," as the *New York Times* concluded a few days later.[38] The battle also brought attention to the valor of one formerly enslaved man in particular, the aforementioned Captain André Cailloux of the First Regiment, slain as he was pressing his men onward.

The poem "Le capitaine André Caillou et ses compagnons d'armes" ("Captain André Caillou and His Comrades-in-Arms") — most likely by the future politician Émile Honoré, whose plantation in Pointe Coupée Parish was located only a few miles from the battlefield — was penned in the weeks while the unrecovered bodies of Cailloux and other Native Guards, monitored by Confederate sharpshooters, still lay rotting under the summer sun. Printed on the Fourth of July, the ode urges fellow citizens not to weep, for "when he fell on that naked plain, / He laid to rest a vile suspicion" ("en tombant sans abri dans la plaine / Il abattit un indigne soupçon") of racial inferiority. Having braved death, Cailloux thus set the example for "a hundred thousand Caillous" to rise up in his stead.

Poésie engagée, or politically committed poetry, was hardly exclusive to the Afro-Creole newspapers. Cailloux's funeral, a public event that drew thousands of mourners in New Orleans and attracted the attention of the national and international press (the *Times* of London, for example, featured a letter from New Orleans on the "extraordinary funeral" [22 Aug. 1863]), generated a significant poetic response (fig. 10).[39] The French-language poets thus "participated in the rich interplay between news and poetry that characterized nineteenth-century verse culture and politics" but in ways consonant with their Afro-Creole background and singular status in Louisiana society (Hankins 529).[40]

It is imperative to situate poetic Afro-Creole protest in relation to the shifting grounds of the 1860s, against which the newspapers' positions acted and reacted. The historian Justin Nystrom has cautioned against "the teleological model that lends grand design and idealistic purpose to the politics of Reconstruction." Ambiguous moral and political realities affected diverse allegiances, from partisan positions to class loyalties, and even ethnic identity itself. As a result, "'radical' alternatives blossomed not so much because they were morally or ideologically just but because they satisfied a broad range of the Civil War generation's societal and political needs" (2–3). Tunnell has likewise commented that the Afro-Creoles' defense of and alliance with the freedmen "reflected in part a genuine awakening of liberal conscience, but even more they resulted from a realistic perception of class interest" (91).

The urgent need for race- and class-based solidarity with "every laborer [. . .] whatever his color" ("chaque travailleur [. . .] qu'importe sa couleur") in the pseudonymous Camille Naudin's "La Marseillaise noire" ("The Black Marseillaise," 21 July 1867) soon became crystal clear. Under President Lincoln's conciliatory approach to readmitting Louisiana into the Union, the "Free State" Constitution of 1864, drafted largely by conservative delegates, brushed aside calls for black suffrage to accompany formal abolition of slavery. As the war ended, conservative Unionism paved the way for increasingly reactionary elements, including recent rebels, to (re)gain power. By the end of 1865, Lincoln's assassination had left President Andrew Johnson to implement an indulgent version of so-called Presidential Reconstruction, generally unfavorable to "radical" racial egalitarianism and social integration. The

FIG. 10. *Funeral of the Late Captain Cailloux, First Louisiana Volunteers (Colored) — Sketched by a Native Guard. Harper's Weekly*, 29 Aug. 1863; The Historic New Orleans Collection, 1958.43.3.

Louisiana legislature, supported by Governor James Madison Wells, had enacted oppressive "black codes," statutes whose strictures against the formerly enslaved recalled the earlier Code noir, while rising violence against freedmen and freedwomen went unpunished. Elections in early 1866 would formally return many former Confederates to power. Decried by Rey in "La rébellion du Sud en permanence" ("The South's Unending Rebellion," 24 Sept. 1865), these dire developments provoked "a critical shift in the history of black thought and action during Reconstruction" (Tunnell 65).

The rebel sympathizers' rise to power galvanized the opposition and prompted the formation of the Republican Party of Louisiana, in which *La Tribune*'s team and affiliates had an active hand. The first step was the creation of the Louisiana branch of the National Equal Rights League in January 1865, following which a convention of the Friends of Universal Suffrage of Louisiana convened that June. In September, members of the suffrage group met to form the Republican Party, at which point the Central Executive Committee of the Friends of Universal Suffrage would become the Central Executive Committee of the Republican Party of Louisiana. The committee proclaimed, "The battle of bullets has been fought [...]. The battle of ballots has commenced and will surely gain the victory" (Republican Party of Louisiana, *Proceedings* 1).

FIG. 11. The leftmost of the three townhouses pictured above is 527 Conti Street (formerly 21 Conti Street), site of *La Tribune*'s offices from July 1864 to November 1865, as it appeared in 1962. Photograph by Dan S. Leyrer; The Collins C. Diboll Vieux Carré Digital Survey at The Historic New Orleans Collection.

Delegates to one or both meetings included Roudanez, Trévigne, and Houzeau, among *La Tribune*'s management, and the poets Lanusse, Macarty, Rey, and Train. The choice of "official organ" of the party went to *La Tribune* (Republican Party of Louisiana, *Proceedings* 21), whose offices were by this time located on Conti Street between Chartres Street and what was then Levée Street (now Decatur) (figs. 11 and 12).[41] Thus, the *républicanisme* of French revolutionary tradition and the stated aims of the Republican Party came into alignment.

More than simply reflecting hyperbolic idealism of the revolutionary Atlantic, the Afro-Creole poetry incorporates specific language used in political debates of 1864–68. In nearly identical language, opposing factions "described the war against slavery as a revolutionary struggle — and each saw itself as revolutionary," often resulting in positions quite far from meaningful social equality (McCrary 16). The major question at hand concerned the degree to which Southern society would be transformed through policies favoring racial justice and the political and socioeconomic

FIG. 12. 527 Conti Street, as it appeared in 2011. Photograph by John Watson Riley; The Collins C. Diboll Vieux Carré Digital Survey at The Historic New Orleans Collection.

aspirations of people of color. In the poem "Il n'est pas" ("He Is Not," 9 Sept. 1866), Armand Lanusse alludes mockingly to an 1864 speech in which President Andrew Johnson had proclaimed himself the "Moses" of the freedmen, intending to lead them, like the Biblical prophet, to a promised land of true freedom. Joanni Questy's poem "Aux conservateurs" ("To the Conservatives," 12 May 1867) denounces the Reconstructionist politicians dangling a promise of suffrage to Louisiana's *gens de couleur* in order to entice them to the conservative camp and thus drive a wedge between them and the freedmen. A number of poems thus partake in the heady political give-and-take of the period. Moreover, this body of radical poetry offers concrete examples of discourse conjoined with action.

The poems in this collection that appear under the pseudonym "Antony," associated with Victor Eugène Macarty, offer a peculiar case of oblique political commentary: they involve, in fact, a literary hoax. "Combat de l'Aigle Républicain et du Copperhead" ("The Clash of the Republican Eagle and the Copperhead"), "À Théodule Delassize" ("For Théodule Delassize"), "Il est" ("He Is"), "La fleur indiscrète" ("The Indiscreet Flower"), and "Les trois perles" ("The Three Pearls") were presented in *La Tribune* as works written in 1866–67 by a Louisiana poet, but research for this volume has uncovered the fact that they are actually plagiarized from various French Romantic authors, who wrote them decades earlier. The term "hoax" applies because the versions in *La Tribune* not only change author names and titles but also add plausible dates of composition, dedications to Louisianians, and even, in one case, a local site of composition.

Whether anyone at the newspaper was in on the hoax or whether the secret was known only to "Antony" is unclear. Also unclear is how much, if any, deceit was intended. While it would have been safe to assume a general readership would be unfamiliar with the original poems, Macarty knew the editors and readership of *La Tribune* to be extremely well read: it is difficult to imagine his assuming no one at all would recognize any of the texts. (Difficult, but not impossible—the hoax has, after all, flown under the scholarly radar for over a century.) Unless additional evidence surfaces, the motivations, expectations, and number of people behind the hoax must remain a mystery.

In many respects, no poet in this collection better embodies the *artiste engagé* — the politically engaged artist — than Macarty (though Rey is perhaps his equal).[42] The scion of a powerful and eccentric Creole clan, son of the white financier Eugène de Macarty (who kept several enslaved people[43]) and Héloïse Croy, a free woman of color from Saint Domingue (also a slaveholder during Victor Eugène's childhood), Macarty (1821–81) was one of New Orleans's most esteemed composers, vocalists, and actors. As the historian William I. Horne has demonstrated, Macarty's creative endeavors complemented his radical activism begun in 1865. That activism included intense involvement in the Republican Party and also the bold move of suing the New Orleans Opera House for removing him, on account of his race, from a performance he attended in January 1869. Despite his very light complexion, Macarty suffered discrimination due to mounting insistence by postwar white supremacists on separation of the races; the segregationist campaign aimed to combat social equality with black people, who by 1869 had won guarantees for political and legal rights. "As a highly accomplished and engaged person of color," writes Horne, Macarty "illustrates the outer limits of equality following emancipation" (497).

The pseudonym "Antony" has long been identified with Macarty.[44] One of his numerous benefit performances featured him as the protagonist of Alexandre Dumas's *Antony* (1831), the role that likely inspired the poetic pseudonym in *La Tribune*. As will be discussed in more detail below in the context of Duhart's poem "Pour les incendiés de Saint-Domingue" ("For the Victims of the Saint Domingue Fire"), the French writer Dumas *père* hailed from a mixed-race family from Saint Domingue, and his physical features made him the target of occasional racist jabs and caricatures in the French press. Dumas's background undoubtedly added to the appeal of choosing a pseudonym from one of his plays, and *Antony*, which dramatized an adulterous love affair sealed by a tragic murder, had provoked a *succès de scandale* that heralded Macarty's own willingness to brave social reproach — or worse. (In 1875 Macarty suffered a brutal beating at the hands of two white reactionaries [Horne 520–22].)

In the light of my discovery of Macarty's poetic hoax (a finding sparked by Horne's article), the poems pose an interpretative enigma.[45] All five have been included in this book because, despite the plagiarism, they genuinely partake in the constitution of the Afro-Creole poetic community and its discourse, and the implications and effects of their publication in *La Tribune* prove rich ground for study (the poem republished as "Il est," for example, elicited a number of texts in response).

The pseudonym "Antony" and the other added features all work together to recontextualize and reinvent French works that the "poet" found thematically relevant to Reconstruction-era Louisiana. The four poems attributed to Antony bear fictional dates of composition (1866 or 1867). Three of the poems are explicitly dedicated to acquaintances of Macarty, important members of the Afro-Creole community: the schoolteacher Nathalie Formento ("La fleur indiscrète"), the inventor and Republican activist Théodule Delassize ("À Théodule Delassize"), and Armand Lanusse ("Il est"). Indeed, the plagiarized text "Il est" prompted Lanusse to respond directly to Antony with "Il n'est pas," a moving and original poem that also offers a reaction to one of the most horrific events of Reconstruction, the Mechanics' Institute massacre of 30 July 1866. The lone Antony poem that does not add a person's name ("Les trois perles") purports to have been written at "Grand Lac," in the lower Atchafalaya Basin. The poem attributed to "A." ("Combat de l'Aigle Républicain et du Copperhead") does not add a date of composition or a person's name but is explicitly dedicated to *La Tribune*.

The appropriation through plagiarism constitutes an intriguing example of the dynamics of transatlantic literary relations: all the plagiarized poems invite the reader to think about what affinities the "poet" found between Romantic-era France and Reconstruction-era Louisiana. Horne points out that "Combat de l'Aigle Républicain et du Copperhead" is excerpted from a patriotic

THE COPPERHEAD PARTY.—IN FAVOR OF *A VIGOROUS PROSECUTION OF PEACE!*

FIG. 13. *The Copperhead Party — in Favor of a Vigorous Prosecution of Peace! Harper's Weekly*, 28 Feb. 1863; courtesy of Library of Congress Prints and Photographs Division. In the editorial cartoon, snakes representing the Copperhead party threaten an allegorical figure representing the United States.

French drama, Alexandre Soumet's *Jeanne d'Arc: trilogie nationale* (1846), which had been performed during the time of Macarty's studies at the Conservatoire de Paris. The "serpent" of Soumet's text (also described as a "reptile" and a "dragon") is specified as a copperhead snake in the excerpt's new title. In the United States in the 1860s, the Copperheads were a faction of Northern Democrats who had wanted immediate peace with the Confederacy (fig. 13). Horne argues, "For Macarty, who reframed the passage from Soumet's work, the conflict between Radical Republicans and conservative Copperheads was a struggle for the survival of the nation that mirrored Jeanne's heroism on behalf of France" (511). The other Antony texts also lend themselves to localizing reinterpretations.

The poem "Les trois perles," copied from the French writer Amédée Pommier's 1832 poem "Les trois perles, élégie," affirms an egalitarian worldview commonly shared by the Afro-Creole radicals. Pommier's poem likens unrecognized human talent and beauty to a pearl hidden at the bottom of the sea; its condition resembles the tragic insignificance of "[t]he man without crown, of greatness unrefined" and "the doe-eyed virgin, poor, simple, and kind," hidden from view by "the Ocean," here representing "an invincible barrier" of ignorance and social prejudices ("Le grand homme qui vit sans gloire et sans couronne, / Et la vierge aux doux yeux, pauvre, naïve et bonne"; "le grand Océan, invincible rempart"). The poet prays to be granted "sharp enough eyes to see / The treasures that hide in the dark abyss of the sea" ("Oh! qui me donnera d'assez bons yeux pour voir / Tout ce que l'océan cache en son gouffre noir") — and the courage to dive down and retrieve them for all to appreciate. Darkness serves here as a metaphor for various kinds of prejudice, a common trope in French Romantic poetry though an equation perhaps as uncomfortable for nineteenth-century Afro-Creole poets as for today's reader. (Beyond Antony's plagiarized poems, the use of color throughout the corpus warrants further analysis.) This egalitarian ideal, holding that each person should be recognized for talents, qualities, and contributions all too often obscured by discriminatory preconceptions, guided Macarty and his fellow artist-activists as they tackled issues that remained (and in some cases, still remain) problems into the civil rights movement of the mid-twentieth century and beyond: school desegregation, integrated public transportation (the object of protests in 1867), equitable treatment in employment, fair political representation, interracial marriage, and more.

In the national arena, *La Tribune de la Nouvelle-Orléans* reached "its pinnacle of prestige and influence" in the months following the so-called "riot" of 30 July 1866, perpetrated to prevent Louisiana's freedmen and *gens de couleur* from acquiring the vote (Leavens 70). In an attempt to halt visible retrogression, a group of radicals from the 1864 constitutional convention — which had failed to extend the franchise to people of African descent — reconvened that body on a technicality, with the goal of granting universal male suffrage. A rally held the evening of Friday, 27 July, drew hundreds of supporters, many black, and stirred the ire of white conservatives. Officials who met on Saturday washed their hands of the matter. Shortly after the 1866 convention opened on Monday at the Mechanics' Institute — which at the time was the state's capitol building — confrontations in the street between supporters of black suffrage and white opponents (particularly irked by the presence of a parade of black Union veterans) exploded into an all-out armed assault on the hall, then escalated into a brutal manhunt of black people throughout the neighborhood. Among the assailants were police and auxiliary officers dressed in Confederate uniforms (figs. 14 and 15).

Officially, the violence claimed some forty lives, though scholars estimate at least forty-eight deaths, and another two hundred were wounded (Hollandsworth, *Absolute* 3). It was not until six o'clock that military authorities arrived and martial law was declared.[46]

Returning from a trip to Texas, Major General Philip Sheridan, military commander of the region, sent a telegram to Ulysses S. Grant, asserting, "It was no riot. It was an absolute massacre by the

THE RIOT IN NEW ORLEANS—THE FREEDMEN'S PROCESSION MARCHING TO THE INSTITUTE—THE STRUGGLE FOR THE FLAG.
[SKETCHED BY THEODORE R. DAVIS.]

THE RIOT IN NEW ORLEANS—SIEGE AND ASSAULT OF THE CONVENTION BY THE POLICE AND CITIZENS.—SKETCHED BY THEODORE R. DAVIS.
[SEE PAGE 535.]

FIG. 14. Two illustrations of the Mechanics' Institute massacre, from *The Riot in New Orleans*, by Theodore R. Davis: *The Freedmen's Procession Marching to the Institute — the Struggle for the Flag* and *Siege and Assault of the Convention by the Police and Citizens*; *Harper's Weekly*, 25 Aug. 1866; courtesy of Library of Congress Prints and Photographs Division.

FIG. 15. Four illustrations of the Mechanics' Institute massacre, from *The Riot in New Orleans*, by Theodore R. Davis: *Murdering Negroes in the Rear of Mechanics' Institute* [top left], *Platform in Mechanics' Institute after the Riot* [top right], *Interior of Mechanics' Institute During the Riot* [center], and *Carrying Off the Dead and Wounded — Inhuman Conduct of the Police* [bottom]; *Harper's Weekly*, 25 Aug. 1866; The Historic New Orleans Collection, 1974.25.9.308 i–iv.

police."⁴⁷ Compounded by similar incidents across the South, the event would produce "an unusual moral aftermath," in Du Bois's words, by drawing attention to worsening conditions in the former Confederacy (466). The national backlash contributed in no small measure to the defeat of President Andrew Johnson and the onset of Congressional or "Radical" Reconstruction, heralded by the passage of the Reconstruction Amendments.

Though *La Tribune* did not fully endorse the convention (because of its dubious legality), the paper had been on the front lines of this tragic event. In his memoir and in a letter to his brother, Houzeau left a harrowing account of his escape (126–35, 155–60). As the first shots were fired, a convention member, William Henry Hire, sought Houzeau out, presumably to witness and report on what was happening. According to Hire's Congressional testimony, "[A] colored man came in and began to talk to me on the subject of that first shot; I said 'Stop a moment,' and I went and called one of the editors of the Tribune, and said to him 'Take particular notice of this, will you?'" (Select Committee 64).⁴⁸ A historian of the 1866 massacre has pointed out that "[t]he *Tribune* was the only outlet for disseminating the Convention's side of the story" (Hollandsworth, *Absolute* 142).

For over a century — in fact, until my research for this volume yielded the discovery — the paper's version of events just before and after the 30 July meeting and massacre was not known, because scholars believed that no issues from the surrounding weeks had survived. Thus I was gratified to unearth a few extant issues that had been lying unnoticed in the Edward Larocque Tinker Collection of Louisiana History and Literature at the American Antiquarian Society in Worcester, Massachusetts.⁴⁹ These "lost" issues of *La Tribune* allow us finally to understand the paper's role and reaction in the wake of the events of late July 1866, and they also shed new light on the poems composed in remembrance of the massacre (fig. 16).

Contrary to what researchers initially believed, *La Tribune*, it appears, did keep its press in action in the immediate wake of the "riot." The first extant issue, from 3 August, explains (in English) that the "issues of yesterday and day before have been exhausted, notwithstanding the large number of copies that had been struck off," further specifying, "Thousands of *Tribunes* have been taken by our Unionists to be sent at the North." The magnitude of the situation elicited an immediate comparison from French history: the St. Bartholomew's Day Massacre of 1572, a wave of mass killings of Protestants across France, tacitly sanctioned by King Charles IX. "Les rebelles sont tellement surpris, tellement effrayés de l'effet de leur St. Barthélémy, qu'ils essaient de persuader aujourd'hui que c'est nous qui l'avons faite" ("The rebels are so surprised, so frightened by the effect of their St. Bartholomew's, that they are now trying to persuade that we are the ones who did it"), begins the French-language editorial.

The paper's immediate concern was twofold. Not surprisingly, *La Tribune* published urgently needed updates on the condition of various wounded victims (some would survive, others would not). But the paper also wanted to ensure that reactionary voices would not minimize the extent of the violence or blame it on antiracist demonstrators and delegates to the convention. With an eye to the political fallout, *La Tribune*'s journalists waged a battle to control the narrative of the occurrences, contradicting other city papers and reporting incoming information to fuel its own interpretation. For example, the *New Orleans Bee*, a pro-Democratic paper, set the "riot" at the feet of "reckless and unprincipled organizers of sedition and revolution" while describing the police's conduct as exemplary ("Lessons from the Events of Last Monday," 1 Aug. 1866). Faced with such apologist spin from other outlets, *La Tribune* featured a two-part article offering "Pages for a Narrative of the New Orleans Massacre" (2 and 3 Aug. 1866).[50] The main points raised in that report and others — the participation of police officers with the concerted premeditation of the authorities — formed the crux of a major Congressional investigation later that year. (Historians to this day continue to debate the massacre's causes.)[51] *La Tribune* would persist in bringing attention to the events of that fateful day: "Mais notre cause cette fois sera portée devant le monde entier. Car les événements du 30 juillet auront un retentissement universel" ("But our cause will be brought this time before the entire world. For the events of 30 July will have a universal impact"; "Vive la liberté!" 5 Aug. 1866).

The 1866 massacre makes a number of appearances, subtle and overt, in the writings of the Afro-Creole poets of *La Tribune*. On 2 September, "Il est" ("He Is"), signed "Antony," was printed just beneath a testimonial from Octave Breaux, a former Native Guard soldier who claimed to have overheard on the morning of 30 July a conversation substantiating premeditated action by the police. Dedicated here to Armand Lanusse, likely in response to previous in-person discussions between Lanusse and Macarty, Hortense de Céré-Barbé's 1832 poem (originally titled "L'existence de Dieu" ["The Existence of God"]) offers a meditation on the self-evidence and ongoing self-revelation of God, whose ultimate plan is unknown to humankind. Whether unaware of Macarty's plagiarism or perhaps in the know about the hoax, Lanusse countered the following week: "Il n'est pas" ("He Is Not"). Though not a profession of atheism, Lanusse's reply holds that God's benevolent power is limited to "the very few / Whom passing passions never do obsess," while "Satan reigns o'er others with despotic hand" ("un petit nombre / Qui ne

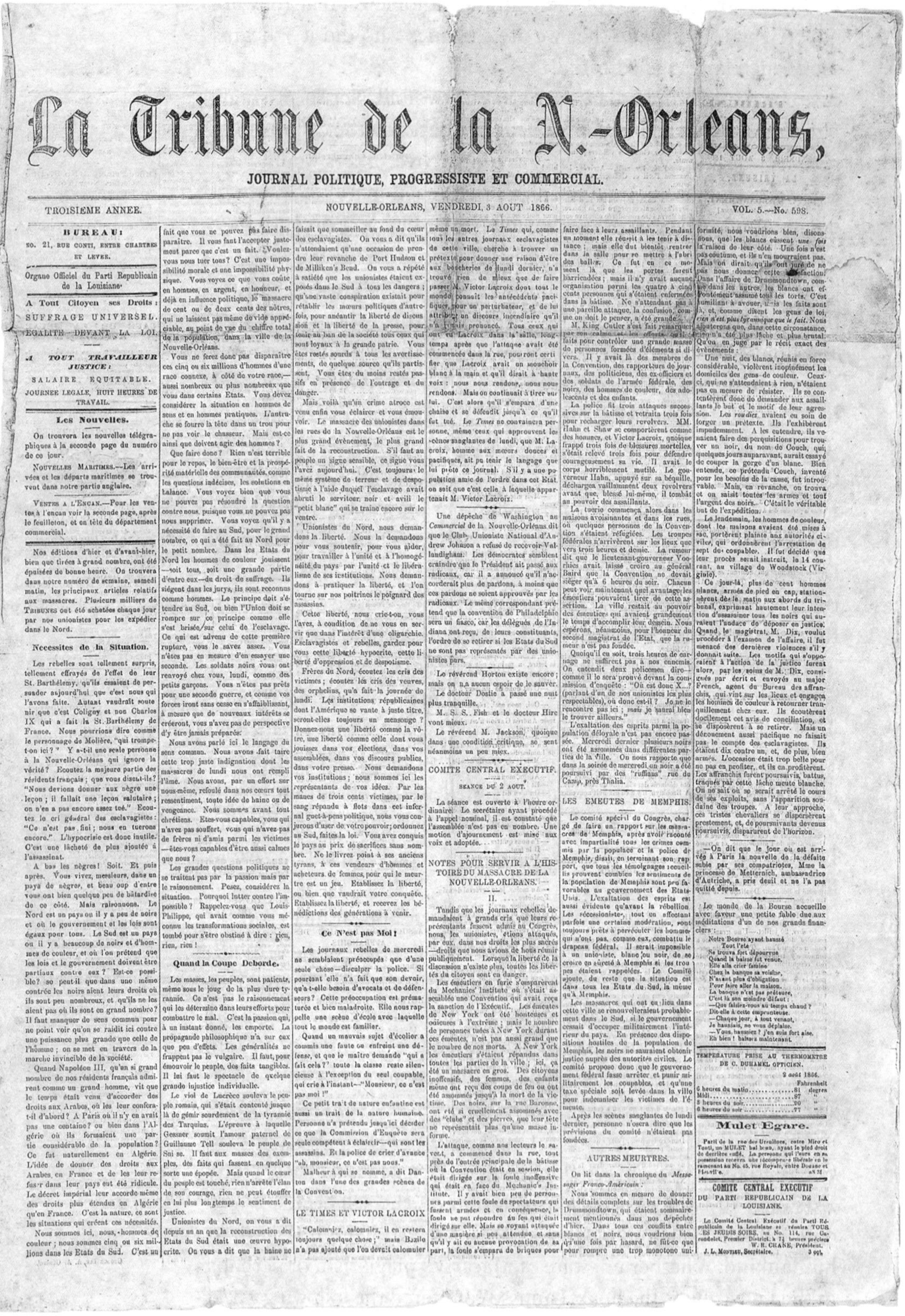

La Tribune de la N.-Orleans,

JOURNAL POLITIQUE, PROGRESSISTE ET COMMERCIAL.

TROISIEME ANNEE. NOUVELLE-ORLEANS, VENDREDI, 3 AOUT 1866. VOL. 5.—No. 598.

BUREAU:

No. 21, RUE CONTI, ENTRE CHARTRES ET LEVEE.

Organe Officiel du Parti Republicain de la Louisiane.

A Tout Citoyen ses Droits: SUFFRAGE UNIVERSEL. EGALITE DEVANT LA LOI.

A TOUT TRAVAILLEUR JUSTICE: SALAIRE EQUITABLE. JOURNEE LEGALE, HUIT HEURES DE TRAVAIL.

Les Nouvelles.

Necessites de la Situation.

Quand la Coupe Deborde.

Ce N'est pas Moi!

LE TIMES ET VICTOR LACROIX

COMITE CENTRAL EXECUTIF.

NOTES POUR SERVIR A L'HISTOIRE DU MASSACRE DE LA NOUVELLE-ORLEANS.

LES EMEUTES DE MEMPHIS.

AUTRES MEURTRES.

Mulet Egare.

COMITE CENTRAL EXECUTIF DU PARTI REPUBLICAIN DE LA LOUISIANE.

FIG. 16. French and English front pages of the only known physical copy of the issue of *La Tribune de la Nouvelle-Orléans / New Orleans Tribune* published the Friday immediately following the 1866 Mechanics' Institute massacre; courtesy of American Antiquarian Society. The French and English versions were published together on one sheet, folded in half. The two front pages form the outside of the folded sheet: the French front page on the front cover, the English front page on the back. The reader opens the sheet to see page 2 of the French on the left inside page, facing page 2 of the English on the right.

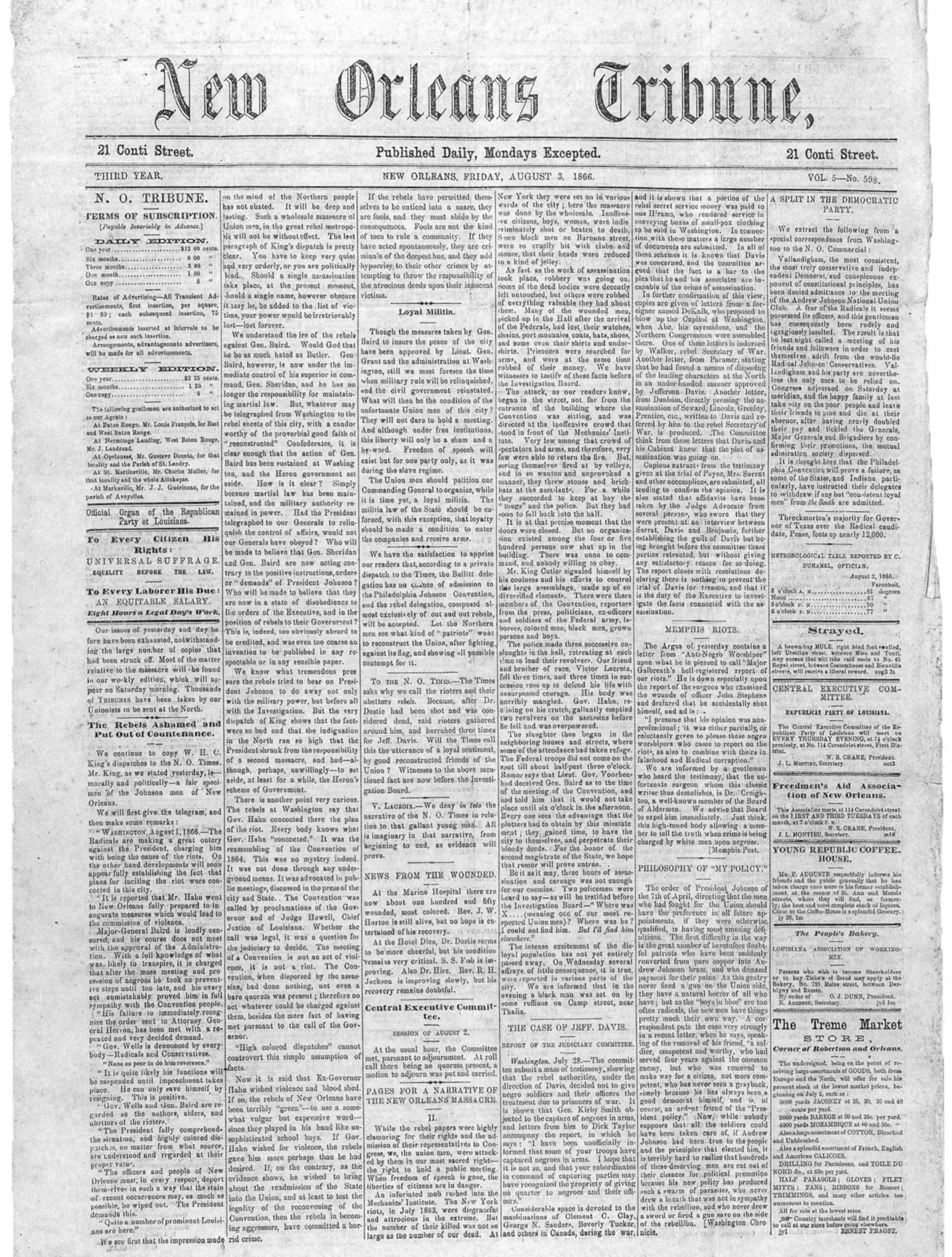

New Orleans Tribune.

21 Conti Street. | Published Daily, Mondays Excepted. | 21 Conti Street.

THIRD YEAR. | NEW ORLEANS, FRIDAY, AUGUST 3, 1866. | VOL. 5—No. 598.

N. O. TRIBUNE.

TERMS OF SUBSCRIPTION.

[*Payable Invariably in Advance.*]

DAILY EDITION.

One year	$12 00 cents.
Six months	6 00 "
Three months	3 00 "
One month	1 00 "
One copy	5 "

Rates of Advertising—All Transient Advertisements, first insertion, per square, $1 50; each subsequent insertion, 75 cents.

Advertisements inserted at intervals to be charged as new each insertion.

Arrangements, advantageous to advertisers, will be made for all advertisements.

WEEKLY EDITION.

One year	$2 25 cents.
Six months	1 20 "
One copy	5 "

The following gentlemen are authorized to act as our Agents:

At Baton Rouge, Mr. Louis François, for East and West Baton Rouge.

At Hermitage Landing, West Baton Rouge, Mr. J. Landraud.

At Opelousas, Mr. Gustave Donato, for that locality and the Parish of St. Landry.

At St. Martinsville, Mr. Charles Muller, for that locality and the whole Attakapas.

At Markaville, Mr. J. J. Guérineau, for the parish of Avoyelles.

Official Organ of the Republican Party of Louisiana.

To Every Citizen His Rights:
UNIVERSAL SUFFRAGE.
EQUALITY BEFORE THE LAW.

To Every Laborer His Due:
AN EQUITABLE SALARY.
Eight Hours a Legal Day's Work.

Our issues of yesterday and day before have been exhausted, notwithstanding the large number of copies that had been struck off. Most of the matter relative to the massacre will be found in our weekly edition, which will appear on Saturday morning. Thousands of TRIBUNES have been taken by our Unionists to be sent at the North.

The Rebels Ashamed and Put Out of Countenance.

We continue to copy W. H. C. King's dispatches to the N. O. Times. Mr. King, as we stated yesterday, is—morally and politically—a fair specimen of the Johnson men of New Orleans.

We will first give the telegram, and then make some remarks:

"WASHINGTON, August 1, 1866.—The Radicals are making a great outcry against the President, charging him with being the cause of the riots. On the other hand developments will soon appear fully establishing the fact that plans for inciting the riot were concocted in this city.

"It is reported that Mr. Hahn went to New Orleans fully prepared to inaugurate measures which would lead to the commission of violence.

Major-General Baird is loudly censured, and his course does not meet with the approval of the Administration. With a full knowledge of what was likely to transpire, it is charged that after the mass meeting and procession of negroes he took no preventive steps until too late, and his every act unmistakably proved him in full sympathy with the Convention people.

"His failure to immediately recognize the order sent to Attorney General Herron, has been met with a repeated and very decided demand.

"Gov. Wells is denounced by everybody—Radicals and Conservatives.

"None so poor to do him reverence."

"It is quite likely his functions will be suspended until impeachment takes place. He can only save himself by resigning. This is positive.

"Gov. Wells and Gen. Baird are regarded as the authors, aiders, and abettors of the rioters.

"The President fully comprehends the situation, and highly colored dispatches, no matter from what source, are understood and regarded at their proper value.

"The officers and people of New Orleans must, in every respect, deport themselves in such a way that the stain of recent occurrences may, as much as possible, be wiped out. The President demands this.

"Quite a number of prominent Louisianans are here."

We see first that the impression made on the mind of the Northern people has not abated. It will be deep and lasting. Such a wholesale massacre of Union men, in the great rebel metropolis will not be without effect. The last paragraph of King's dispatch is pretty clear. You have to keep very quiet and very orderly, or you are politically dead. Should a single assassination take place, at the present moment, should a single name, however obscure it may be, be added to the list of victims, your power would be irretrievably lost—lost forever.

We understand the ire of the rebels against Gen. Baird. Would God that he be as much hated as Butler. Gen Baird, however, is now under the immediate control of his superior in command, Gen. Sheridan, and he has no longer the responsibility for maintaining martial law. But, whatever may be telegraphed from Washington to the rebel sneets of this city, with a candor worthy of the proverbial good faith of "reconstructed" Confederates, it is clear enough that the action of Gen. Baird has been sustained at Washington, and the Heron government set aside. How is it clear? Simply because martial law has been maintained, and the military authority remained in power. Had the President telegraphed to our Generals to relinquish the control of affairs, would not our Generals have obeyed? Who will be made to believe that Gen. Sheridan and Gen. Baird are now acting contrary to the positive instructions, orders or "demands" of President Johnson? Who will be made to believe that they are now in a state of disobedience to the orders of the Executive, and in the position of rebels to their Government? This is, indeed, too obviously absurd to be credited, and was even too coarse an invention to be published in any respectable or in any sensible paper.

We know what tremendous pressure the rebels tried to bear on President Johnson to do away not only with the military power, but before all with the Investigation. But the very dispatch of King shows that the facts were so bad and that the indignation in the North ran so high that the President shrunk from the responsibility of a second massacre, and had—although, perhaps, unwillingly—to set aside, at least for a while, the Heron's scheme of Goverment.

There is another point very curious. The rebels at Washington say that Gov. Hahn concocted there the plan of the riot. Every body knows what Gov. Hahn "concocted." It was the reassembling of the Convention of 1864. This was no mystery indeed. It was not done through any underground means. It was advocated in public meetings, discussed in the press of the city and State. The Convention was called by proclamations of the Governor and of Judge Howell, Chief Justice of Louisiana. Whether the call was legal, it was a question for the judiciary to decide. The meeting of a Convention is not an act of violence, it is not a riot. The Convention, when dispersed by the assassins, had done nothing, not even a bare quorum was present; therefore no act whatever could be charged against them, besides the mere fact of having met pursuant to the call of the Governor.

"High colored dispatches" cannot controvert this simple assumption of facts.

Now it is said that Ex-Governor Hahn wished violence and blood shed. If so, the rebels of New Orleans have been terribly "green"—to use a somewhat vulgar but expressive word—since they played in his hand like unsophisticated school boys. If Gov. Hahn wished for violence, the rebels gave him more perhaps than he had desired. If, on the contrary, as the evidence shows, he wished to bring about the readmission of the State into the Union, and at least to test the legality of the reconvening of the Convention, then the rebels in becoming aggressors, have committed a horrid crime.

If the rebels have permitted themselves to be enticed into a snare, they are fools, and they must abide by the consequences. Fools are not the kind of men to rule a community. If they have acted spontaneously, they are criminals of the deepest hue, and they add hypocrisy to their other crimes by attempting to throw the responsibility of the atrocious deeds upon their innocent victims.

Loyal Militia.

Though the measures taken by Gen. Baird to insure the peace of the city have been approved by Lieut. Gen. Grant and the administration at Washington, still we must foresee the time when military rule will be relinquished, and the civil government reinstated. What will then be the condition of the unfortunate Union men of this city? They will not dare to hold a meeting. And although under free institutions, this liberty will only be a sham and a by-word. Freedom of speech will exist but for one party only, as it was during the slave regime.

The Union men should petition our Commanding General to organize, while it is time yet, a loyal militia. The militia law of the State should be enforced, with this exception, that loyalty should be made a condition to enter the companies and receive arms.

We have the satisfaction to apprise our readers that, according to a private dispatch to the Times, the Bullitt delegation has no chance of admission to the Philadelphia Johnson Convention, and the rebel delegation, composed almost exclusively of out and out rebels, will be accepted. Let the Northern men see what kind of "patriots" want to reconstruct the Union, after fighting against its flag, and showing all possible contempt for it.

TO THE N. O. TIMES.—The Times asks why we call the rioters and their abettors *rebels*. Because, after Dr. Dostie had been shot and was considered dead, said rioters gathered around him, and hurrahed three times for Jeff. Davis. Will the Times call this the utterance of a loyal sentiment, by good reconstructed friends of the Union? Witnesses to the above mentioned fact are now before the Investigation Board.

V. LACROIX.—We deny *in toto* the narrative of the N. O. Times in relation to that gallant young man. All is imaginary in that narrative, from beginning to end, as evidence will prove.

NEWS FROM THE WOUNDED.

At the Marine Hospital there are now about one hundred and fifty wounded, most colored. Rev. J. W. Horton is still alive, but no hope is entertained of his recovery.

At the Hotel Dieu, Dr. Dostie seems to be more cheerful, but his condition remains very critical. S. S. Fish is improving. Also Dr. Hire. Rev. R. H. Jackson is improving slowly, but his recovery remains doubtful.

Central Executive Committee.

SESSION OF AUGUST 2.

At the usual hour, the Committee met, pursuant to adjournment. At roll call there being no quorum present, a motion to adjourn was put and carried.

PAGES FOR A NARRATIVE OF THE NEW ORLEANS MASSACRE.

II.

While the rebel papers were highly clamoring for their rights and the admission of their representatives to Congress, we, the union men, were attacked by them in our most sacred right—the right to hold a public meeting. When freedom of speech is gone, the liberties of citizens are in danger.

An infuriated mob rushed into the Mechanics' Institute. The New York riots, in July 1863, were disgraceful and atrocious in the extreme. But the number of their killed was not so large as the number of our dead. At New York they were set on in various wards of the city; here the massacre was done by the wholesale. Inoffensive citizens, boys, women, were indiscriminately shot or beaten to death. Some black men on Baronne street, were so cruelly hit with clubs and stones, that their heads were reduced to a kind of jelley.

As fast as the work of assassination took place, robbery was going on. Some of the dead bodies were decently left untouched, but others were robbed of everything valuable they had about them. Many of the wounded men, picked up in the Hall after the arrival of the Federals, had lost their watches, chains, port monnaies, coats, hats, shoes, and some even their shirts and undershirts. Prisoners were searched for arms, and were at the same time robbed of their money. We have witnesses to testify of these facts before the Investigation Board.

The attack, as our readers know, began in the street, not far from the entrance of the building where the Convention was sitting, and was directed at the inoffensive crowd that stood in front of the Mechanics' Institute. Very few among that crowd of spectators had arms, and therefore, very few were able to return the fire. But, seeing themselves fired at by volleys, and in so wanton and unprovoked a manner, they threw stones and brickbats at the assailants. For a while they succeeded to keep at bay the "thugs" and the police. But they had soon to fall back into the hall.

It is at that precise moment that the doors were closed. But no organization existed among the four or five hundred persons now shut up in the building. There was none to command, and nobody willing to obey.

Mr. King Cutler signaled himself by his coolness and his efforts to control this large assemblage, made up of so diversified elements. There were there members of the Convention, reporters from the press, politicians, ex-officers and soldiers of the Federal army, laborers, colored men, black men, grown persons and boys.

The police made three successive onslaughts in the hall, retreating at each time to load their revolvers. Our friend and brother of race, Victor Lacroix, fell three times, and three times in succession rose up to defend his life with unsurpassed courage. His body was horribly mangled. Gov. Hahn, reclining on his crutch, gallantly emptied two revolvers on the assassins before he fell and was overpowered.

The slaughter then began in the neighboring houses and streets, where some of the attendance had taken refuge. The Federal troops did not come on the spot till about half-past three o'clock. Rumor says that Lieut. Gov. Voorhees had deceived Gen. Baird as to the time of the meeting of the Convention, and had told him that it would not take place until six o'clock in the afternoon. Every one sees the advantage that the plotters had to obtain by this misstatement; they gained time, to have the city to themselves, and perpetrate their bloody deeds. For the honor of the second magistrate of the State, we hope that rumor will prove untrue.

Be it as it may, three hours of assassination and carnage was not enough for our enemies. Two policemen were heard to say—as will be testified before the Investigation Board—"Where was X....(meaning one of our most respected Union men)? Where was he? I could not find him. *But I'll find him elsewhere.*"

The intense excitement of the disloyal population has not yet entirely passed away. On Wednesday several affrays, of little consequence, it is true, were reported in various parts of the city. We are informed that in the evening a black man was set on by some ruffians on Camp street, near Thalia.

THE CASE OF JEFF. DAVIS.

REPORT OF THE JUDICIARY COMMITTEE.

Washington, July 28.—The committee submit a mass of testimony, showing that the rebel authorities, under the direction of Davis, decided not to give negro soldiers and their officers the treatment due to prisoners of war. It is shown that Gen. Kirby Smith objected to the capture of negroes in arms, and letters from him to Dick Taylor accompany the report, in which he says: "I have been unofficially informed that some of your troops have captured negroes in arms. I hope that it is not so, and that your subordinates in command of capturing parties may have recognized the propriety of giving no quarter to negroes and their officers."

Considerable space is devoted to the machinations of Clement C. Clay, George N. Sanders, Beverly Tucker, and others in Canada, during the war, and it is shown that a portion of the rebel secret service money was paid to one Hirams, who rendered service in conveying boxes of small-pox clothing to be sold in Washington. In connection with those matters a large number of documents are submitted. In all of these schemes it is known that Davis was concerned, and the committee argued that the fact is a bar to the plea that he and his associates are incapable of the crime of assassination.

In further confirmation of this view, copies are given of letters from a foreigner named DeKalb, who proposed to blow up the Capitol at Washington, when Abe, his myrmidons, and the Northern Congressmen were assembled there. One of these letters is indorsed by Walker, rebel Secretary of War. Another letter, from Paramer, stating that he had found a means of disposing of the leading characters at the North in an under-handed manner approved by Jefferson Davis. Another letter, from Dunham, directly pressing the assassination of Seward, Lincoln, Greeley, Prentice, etc., written to Davis and referred by him to the rebel Secretary of War, is produced. The Committee think from these letters that Davis and his Cabinet knew that the plot of assassination was going on.

Copious extracts from the testimony given at the trial of Payne, Mrs. Surrat and other accomplices, are submitted, all tending to confirm the opinion. It is also stated that affidavits have been taken by the Judge Advocate from several persons, who swore that they were present at an interview between Surrat, Davis and Benjamin, further establishing the guilt of Davis but being brought before the committee those parties retracted, but without giving any satisfactory reason for so doing. The report closes with resolutions declaring there is nothing to prevent the trial of Davis for treason, and that it is the duty of the Executive to investigate the facts connected with the assassination.

MEMPHIS RIOTS.

The Argus of yesterday contains a letter from "Anti-Negro Worshiper" upon what he is pleased to call "Major Galbreath's hell-registered report of our riots." He is down especially upon the report of the surgeon who examined the wounds of officer John Stephens and declared that he accidentally shot himself, and adds:

"I presume that his opinion was non-professional; it was either partially, or reluctantly given to please those negro worshipers who came to report on the riots, as also to combine with theirs in falsehood and Radical corruption."

We are informed by a gentleman who heard the testimony, that the unfortunate surgeon whom this classic writer thus demolishes, is Dr. Creighton, a well-known member of the Board of Aldermen. We advise that Board to expel him immediately. Just think, this high-toned body allowing a member to tell the truth when crime is being charged by white men upon negroes.
[Memphis Post.

PHILOSOPHY OF "MY POLICY."

The order of President Johnson of the 7th of April, directing that the men who had fought for the Union should have the preference in all future appointments, if they were otherwise qualified, is having some amusing definitions. The first difficulty in the way is the great number of heretofore doubtful patriots who have been suddenly converted from pure copper into Andrew Johnson brass, and who demand payment for their pains. As this gentry never fired a gun on the Union side, they have a natural horror of all who have; but as the "boys in blue" are too often radicals, the new men have things pretty much their own way. A correspondent puts the case very strongly in a recent letter, when he says, speaking of the removal of his friend, "a soldier, competent and worthy, who had served four years against the common enemy, but who was removed to make way for a citizen, not more competent, who has never seen a grayback, simply because he has always been a good democrat himself, and is, of course, an ardent friend of the "President policy." Now, while nobody supposes that all the soldiers could have been taken care of, if Andrew Johnson had been true to the people and the principles that elected him, it is terribly hard to realize that hundreds of these deserving men are cut out of their chances for political promotion because his new policy has produced such a swarm of parasites, who never drew a breath that was not in sympathy with the rebellion, and who never drew a sword or fired a gun save on the side of the rebellion. [Washington Chronicle.

A SPLIT IN THE DEMOCRATIC PARTY.

We extract the following from a special correspondence from Washington to the N. O. Commercial:

Vallandigham, the most consistent, the most truly conservative and independent Democrat, and conspicuous exponent of constitutional principles, has been denied admittance to the meeting of the Andrew Johnson National Union Club. A fear of the Radicals it seems possessed its officers, and this gentleman has consequently been rudely and egregiously insulted. The result is that he last night called a meeting of his friends and followers in order to cast themselves adrift from the would-be Radical Johnson Conservatives. Vallandigham and his party are nevertheless the only ones to be relied on. Congress adjourned on Saturday at meridian, and the happy family at last take pity on the poor people and leave their friends to pine and die at their absence, after having nearly doubled their pay and tickled the Generals, Major Generals and Brigadiers by confirming their promotions, the mutual admiration society dispersed.

It is thought here that the Philadelphia Convention will prove a failure, as some of the States, and Indiana particularly, have instructed their delegates to withdraw if any but "consistent loyal men" from *the South* are admitted.

Throckmorton's majority for Governor of Texas over the Radical candidate, Pease, foots up nearly 12,000.

METEOROLOGICAL TABLE REPORTED BY C. DUHAMEL, OPTICIAN.

August 2, 1866.

	Farenheit.
6 o'clock A. M.	81 degrees
Noon	87 "
3 o'clock P. M.	90 "
6 o'clock P. M.	77 "

Strayed.

A brown-bay MULE, right hind foot swelled, left Ursuline street, between Miro and Tonti. Any person that will take said mule to No. 45 Royal street, between Customhouse and Bienville streets, will receive a liberal reward. aug3 3t

CENTRAL EXECUTIVE COMMITTEE.

REPUBLICAN PARTY OF LOUISIANA.

The Central Executive Committee of the Republican Party of Louisiana will meet on EVERY THURSDAY EVENING, at 7½ o'clock precisely, at No. 114 Carondelet street, First District.

W. R. CRANE, President.
J. L. MONTIEU, Secretary. oct3

Freedmen's Aid Association of New Orleans.

This Association meets, at 114 Carondelet street on the FIRST AND THIRD TUESDAYS of each month, at 7 o'clock P. M.

W. R. CRANE, President.
J. L. MONTIEU, Secretary. m18

YOUNG REPUBLIC COFFEE-HOUSE.

MR. F. AUGUSTE respectfully informs his friends and the public generally that he has taken charge once more of his former establishment, at the corner of St. Ann and Marais streets, where they will find, as formerly, the best and most complete stock of liquors. Close to the Coffee-House is a splendid Grocery. jy 26 1m

The People's Bakery.

LOUISIANA ASSOCIATION OF WORKINGMEN.

Persons who wish to become Shareholders or to buy Tickets of Bread may apply at the Bakery, No. 299 Maine street, between Derbigny and Roman.

By order of O. J. DUNN, President.
R. ANDERSON, Secretary. jy6 1m

The Treme Market STORE,

Corner of Robertson and Orleans.

The undersigned, being on the point of receiving large assortments of GOODS, both from Europe and the North, will offer for sale his present stock at the lowest market prices, beginning on July 2, such as:

5000 yards JACONET at 25, 30, 35 and 40 cents per yard.
2000 yards BAREGE at 30 and 35c. per yard.
4000 yards MOZAMBIQUE at 40 and 50c. "

Also a large assortment of COTTON, Bleached and Unbleached.

Also a splendid assortment of French, English and American CALICOES.

DRILLING for Pantaloons, and TOILE DU NORD do., at 60c per yard.

HALF PARASOLS; GLOVES; FILET MITTS; FANS; RIBBONS for Bonnet; TRIMMINGS, and many other articles too numerous to mention.

All for sale at the lowest rates.

☞ Country merchants will find it profitable to call at our store before going elsewhere.

jy1 ERNEST PRAGST.

cède jamais aux passions du jour"; "Satan sur d'autres règne en despote d'enfer"), among them specifically "that man-jackal beast / [...] clad in municipal uniform" who spurs law enforcement to perform a "deadly duty" by crying, "Attack them! Club them! Kill" ("ce chacal fait homme / [...] portant l'habit municipal"; "ordre fatal"; "Attaque, tue, assomme"). The poem condemns also, as responsible for the massacre or too craven to denounce it, "the vicious journalist, [...] cowardly apologist / Of terrorism, crime, and such atrocities," and "the judge, rebellious, ignorant, / Who rides roughshod o'er laws to his desire contrary" ("ce vil journaliste, [...] ce lâche apologiste / De l'attentat, du crime, et de l'atrocité"; "ce juge ignorant et rebelle / Qui foule aux pieds la loi contraire à son désir").

The publication of Camille Naudin's "Ode aux martyrs" ("Ode to the Martyrs") coincided with the one-year anniversary of 30 July 1866. For that occasion, *La Tribune* organized a solemn commemoration at the Mechanics' Institute. Mass was celebrated by the renegade abolitionist priest Paschal Maistre — then in open schism with the Catholic hierarchy — followed by a speech by the attorney Rufus Waples, wounded during the attack. The erstwhile Spiritualist medium Cora L. V. Daniels read a poem in English, "In Memoriam — July 30," and a concluding address was delivered by the Rev. J. B. Smith.[52] Like the commemorative editorials, Naudin's impassioned ode shares tropes and references used by the orators. On 5 August 1866, the paper had rebutted conservatives' characterizations of the convention itself as a "riot" by remarking in an English-language editorial that the arguments of "[p]roslavery men, accustomed to despotism in their very homes, and debased by the traffic of human flesh" could only play well "with the New Orleans slavedrivers and their New Orleans sycophants." The first stanza of "Ode aux martyrs" casts blame on "Un peuple d'assassins — anciens esclavagistes, / [...] Gentilshommes du fouet, armés de leurs poignards, / Cohortes de bourreaux" ("A clan of killers — former owners of slaves, / [...] Gentlemen of the whip, with daggers armed, / Hordes of hangmen"). Like the paper's editorialist in 1866 and Maistre in his homily, the poet draws a parallel with the St. Bartholomew's Day Massacre. The enumeration of prominent victims cast as martyrs for a greater cause is the main organizing principle of the "Ode" and is likewise a feature of Waples's speech and Daniels's poem.

Though Naudin's poem does uphold francophone cultural specificity, namely through the structuring of the conclusion around *liberté, égalité, fraternité*, the text of "Ode aux martyrs," like so many others, uses shared language in a quest to make sense of violence and to cast loss in terms of historical progress.

The following year brought victory for the Radical Republican cause but defeat for *La Tribune*. Triumph for supporters of racial

equality, though brief, came in the form of the constitution ratified by the convention held in 1867–68, "probably the most radical of any of the [state] constitutions which resulted from the Reconstruction Acts" (fig. 17).[53] Concise and readable, it opened with a Bill of Rights declaring all men "created free and equal" (Art. 1) and outlawing racial discrimination in public places (Art. 13); it further provided for integrated public schools (Art. 135). The constitution disenfranchised any former Confederate who had not signed "a certificate setting forth that he acknowledges the late

FIG. 17. Portraits of delegates to the Louisiana Constitutional Convention of 1868. *Extract from the Reconstructed Constitution of the State of Louisiana with Portraits of the Distinguished Members of the Convention and Assembly*; lithograph; 1868; The Historic New Orleans Collection, 1979.183.

rebellion to have been morally and politically wrong" (Art. 99).[54] In truth, many of its provisions remained dead letter to some extent. Nonetheless, it enshrined civil rights in law and thereby established a framework to continue working for their realization.

The Louisiana state elections under way at the same time flushed out partisan rivalries that fractured the coalition centered around *La Tribune*. The intricacies of the conflict boiled down to divergent support for the governorship. Against the advice of Houzeau, Roudanez and others first backed Major Francis E. Dumas, a wealthy Afro-Creole who freed those enslaved to him in order to enlist them in the federal army. When Dumas failed to win the nomination, which went instead to the moderate "carpetbagger" Henry Clay Warmoth, they sought an alternative ticket to oppose Warmoth, eventually settling on James Taliaferro, with Dumas as candidate for lieutenant governor. The Taliaferro-Dumas ticket's loss discredited the newspaper; Houzeau left, and *La Tribune*'s contract with the Republican Party was reassigned to the New Orleans *Republican*, "the latter representing the more conservative views of Louisiana carpetbaggers and white Unionists" (Tunnell 117). In April 1868, *La Tribune* suspended publication for seven months, and its return in December was halting and short-lived.

Even though each faction had supporters of both races, the division was cast in racial terms. Houzeau criticized "the spirit of caste" (153). Warmoth, portraying the matter quite differently in his autobiography, blamed the "Dominican and Haytian predilections" of "San Domingo refugees" eager to achieve "the Africanization of the State" (57). To a limited degree, *La Tribune* did blame prejudices about "the inferiority of the Franco-African race" (26 Jan. 1868). The schism of 1868 is not explicitly addressed in the poems of *La Tribune*, but the underlying issues are ever present, most obviously as a claim of black identity, a move connected to an equally fundamental search for national community.

It is on these two issues, racial identity and the search for community, that the analysis of the poems as poetry will focus.

"Ces Fils de Race Noire": Crafting a Racial Poetics

The anthropologist Sidney Mintz remarks, "North American ideas about what 'color' someone is are far more hindrance than help in understanding Haiti" (qtd. in Trouillot 112). For many reasons — not the least of which being cultural carryover from Saint Domingue — the same observation can be applied to Creole Louisiana. Francophone Afro-Creoles self-identified as *Créoles*, were considered *gens de couleur* by state law, and were marked either "black" or "mulatto" on the federal census. In some contexts, they could be called "*nègre*" or "negro," but in Louisiana Creole society, family background and skin tone could translate to any of several racializing labels such as "*quarteron*" (quadroon) or "*octavon*" (octaroon).[55] Perceived skin color was often meaningless as an indicator of racial category.

During Reconstruction, this phenotypical diversity would collide head on with the role of skin color in the rest of America's racial divide. The lawsuit brought by Victor Eugène Macarty against the Opera House in 1869 (mentioned above) underscores the sheer incoherence of many acts of discrimination: Macarty had purchased his ticket to the parterre reserved for whites without the employee's ever realizing he was "colored."[56] At the same time that most of the country was, for good or for ill, lumping all people of color together, the black community in Louisiana was defined by considerable internal diversity. The experiences of the free Afro-Creole community — their long and rich cultural history and attachments, their language, religion, education, societal status, and economic accomplishments as *libres de couleur* — stood in stark contrast to the experience of the vast majority of freedmen in the state, many of whom were English-speaking and Protestant and lacked the urban Afro-Creoles' educational and economic advantages.

For Houzeau, this cultural divide represented a political obstacle, one that had to be overcome at all costs. In his memoir, he speaks frankly about "the alienation of the black slave from the free man of color," arising in part from some Creoles' sense of superiority. Closing this breach required aligning Afro-Creole interests with those of the rest of the black population and resisting the temptation to ensure only their own gains through alliance with white conservatives. One measure, the so-called Quadroon Bill proposed in 1864, would have granted suffrage to men with less than one-fourth African heritage. Houzeau, in full agreement with his bosses and colleagues at *La Tribune*, believed that such enticements were a trap: "A strange error in a society in which prejudice weighed equally against all those who had African blood in their veins, no matter how small the amount!" (19–20).

Through racial solidarity, the Afro-Creole elite — educated, prosperous, and possessing leadership experience — could and felt they should guide their fellow black citizens after emancipation.[57] Afro-Creole activists adopted a number of strategies aimed at coalition building. *La Tribune*'s outreach to anglophone black people was not limited to mere bilingualism; beginning in 1865, the paper's "Religious Department" was managed by two ministers of the African Methodist Episcopal Church. The Freedmen's Aid Association, formed with the support of *La Tribune*, brought together French- and English-speaking black people to organize charity events, with one major goal being to help with the purchase of land confiscated from planters and intended for redistribution to freedmen. As Mary Niall Mitchell argues, the francophone Afro-Creole tone could at times be "patronizing, [but] it was also politically keen and seems to have been genuine, given that they supported the creation of offices to field complaints from freedpeople" (207).

The poetry of both newspapers demonstrates the day-to-day challenges of uniting the communities and the importance of awareness of Atlantic history in imagining a new racial solidarity, centered on blackness and adapted for the American context.

Editorials by Afro-Creole leaders, especially in the early days of *L'Union*, provide a window onto their conception of the intersection of race and culture. The term *population de couleur* predominates, as in Trévigne's editorial of 1 October 1862, "Un mot sur la population de couleur" ("A Word on the Population of Color"). In that piece, he unambiguously refers to racial duality when judging that the "préjugés [. . .] trop enracinés de la population blanche aux États-Unis, élèveront pour longtemps encore une barrière infranchissable entre les deux races" ("deeply rooted prejudices of the white population of the United States will erect, for a long time to come, an insurmountable barrier between the two races"). In regard to freedmen, an essay by François Boisdoré, "La liberté" (18 Oct. 1862), squarely blames the conditions of slavery for any seeming inferiority:

> Le nègre ou le mulâtre peut-il vous développer ses facultés intellectuelles, alors que du berceau, courbé sous le joug d'un maître inexorable, il travaille sans relâche et sans fruit [. . .] et que, dans ses rares moments de loisir, loin de pouvoir cultiver son intelligence, accablé qu'il est sous le joug qu'il supporte, il gémit en silence[?]
>
> Can the negro or the mulatto hope to demonstrate his intellectual faculties if, from the cradle, bent under the yoke of an unyielding master, he works without respite or reward [. . .] and, in his rare moments of leisure, instead of cultivating his intelligence, weighed down by the yoke he must bear [. . .], he whimpers in silence?

Boisdoré further admonishes fellow Creoles: "expulsons sans scrupule de nos cœurs toute haine de caste" ("Let us expel without qualms all caste hatred from our hearts"). A few issues later, in his essay "Considérations" (15 Nov. 1862), he envisions the social integration of freedmen as requiring civic and moral education by the former *libres de couleur*.

Two years later (8 Aug. 1864), an editorial in *La Tribune* (published before Houzeau's arrival) conceded a shared racial identity even as the author insisted on merit-based distinctions:

> [B]ien que nous soyons de la même race que les infortunés fils de l'Afrique qui ont gémi jusqu'ici sous le joug d'un cruel et abrutissant esclavage, on ne saurait, sans se rendre injuste, confondre avec les nouveaux affranchis notre population intelligente qui, par son industrie et son éducation, s'est rendue aussi utile à la société et au pays que n'importe quelle autre classe de citoyens.

> Although we are of the same race as the unfortunate sons of Africa who until now have moaned beneath the yoke of cruel and stultifying slavery, one cannot, without being unfair, confuse the new freedmen with our intelligent population who, by its industry and education, has rendered itself as useful to society and to the country as any other class of citizens.

Opinions such as these have led some historians to conclude that *L'Union* — and their assessment would extend to *La Tribune* without Houzeau — remained "a caste journal which accepted many of the social and economic distinctions between the free-born men of color and the former slaves" (Connor 162).

Rather than reduce the paper's ideological endeavor to one position, it seems more fruitful to recognize the variety of positionings the new context flushed out as Reconstruction challenged the old order. The aforenoted ambivalence presents a marked contrast with the poetry of Duhart, Questy, the poet signing Camille Naudin, and their literary comrades. Though a single conclusion cannot be drawn about all the writers in this collection, the will to invest in blackness, and to fill it with political content, runs throughout the corpus. The strongest identification of a poet's voice with marginalized blackness occurs in a poem by the anonymous "Pierre (l'Hermite)" (Peter the Hermit), "Au Père Chocarne," ("To Father Chocarne"; 16 Apr. 1867), addressed to a visiting priest from France. The opening lines tell of the moving effect of Father Chocarne's sermon upon one of the parishioners, "Un nègre obscur et méprisé" ("A negro, unknown and shunned"). Just as he is about to recommit to Christianity, the listener recalls that the church itself is segregated — that the local Catholic clergy are sanctioning injustice. The "negro's" identity — he is the author of the poem — is revealed when Father Chocarne is asked to remember the "poète obscur et méprisé" and to deliver this message: "any white man who refuses a negro as brother / Forfeits the right to refer to God as his Father" ("un blanc, qui ne veut pas qu'un nègre soit son frère, / N'a plus le droit sacré d'appeler Dieu son père").

The poets, where they identify, do so as black, in a unified sense — a choice Caroline Senter explains as follows:

> *Tribune* writers, acknowledging their past near-white privilege under French colonialism and making clear their political purpose in throwing their resources behind the newly freed blacks, were symbolically stating that race *is* a construct that had been used against them, and they were now going to use it to make the most of Reconstruction's promises. (283)

Blackness as a political identity has a powerful precedent in the history of Haiti. In the wake of the civil wars between mulatto and black leaders during the later years of the Haitian Revolution, Jean-Jacques Dessalines, independent Haiti's first head of state, enshrined in the Imperial Constitution of 1805 the following article: "Toute acception de couleur parmi les enfants d'une seule et même famille [...] devant nécessairement cesser, les Haïtiens ne seront désormais connus que sous la denomination génériques des noirs" ("All significations of color among children of one and the same family [...] needing to cease, Haitians shall henceforth be known solely by the generic category of blacks"; Janvier 32). Famously, the provision encompasses not only *mulâtres* (mulattoes) but also naturalized white citizens. This common identity was intended to fuse the various elements of the nation (under Dessalines's paternal authority).

In the US context, progressives called upon blackness not to define nationhood but to unite all who fell on the "other side" of the color line so that they could win the struggle for equality. Questy's "Aux conservateurs" ("To the Conservatives") best encapsulates this aspiration:

> Pensez-y: le Progrès dans son rapide élan,
> Sous un niveau de fer égalisant deux races,
> Veut que le nègre soit concitoyen du blanc
> Et qu'ils aient tous les deux des droits aux mêmes places.

> Just think: Progress, advancing at rapid pace,
> Is leveling the field for blacks and whites,
> And will make fellow citizens out of each race,
> In order that both may climb to equal heights.

The poem's choice to rhyme "deux races" and "mêmes places" — an effect rendered in translation as "blacks and whites" and, more metaphorically than the original, "equal heights" — can be read as emphasizing the fundamental equality of races and the soundness of their occupying the same place in society.[58] But that poetic *égalité* does not erase discontinuities: the claim to blackness implies acceptance of the black-white dichotomy.

Conceiving of racial difference in terms of black-white falls within a long-established tradition of oppositional or complementary dichotomies rooted in Western philosophical thought (e.g., good and evil, masculine and feminine, light and darkness). Rhetoric, or the art of crafting and presenting an argument, draws heavily on binary oppositions — blame and praise, or a thesis and its antithesis, for example; in turn, much of classical poetics has been grounded in rhetoric.

Straightaway, a semantic challenge beset the appropriation of blackness by Creole poets: the centuries-long sedimentation of negative connotations attached to *noir* ("black" or "dark" in English) in the European imagination. In this collection, the verse of Duhart in particular is replete with expressions like "le chagrin noir" ("black chagrin"), "noir cercueil" ("dark coffin"), and "Pourquoi tant de pleurs au noir gouffre" ("Wherefore such tears in this black abyss"). In "Poésie! Vox Dei!" he even states hopefully, "L'avenir apparaît moins noir" ("The future seems less dark" — or "black"), thanks to poetry.

The twentieth-century French philosopher Jacques Derrida famously observed the "violent hierarchy" involved in the classical philosophical tradition's binary thinking. "[W]e are not dealing with the peaceful coexistence of a vis-à-vis," Derrida asserts: instead, "One of the two terms governs the other [. . .], or has the upper hand" (41). It is easy to recognize, as one critic has put it, that "[w]ithin the white/black binary opposition in the West, the African American is defined as devalued Other" (W. Hogue 45). In identifying politically and poetically as "noir," Louisiana Creoles did not enter a level playing field, and the poets addressed this unbalanced dichotomy in various ways.

Honoré's "Le capitaine André Caillou et ses compagnons d'armes" ("Captain André Caillou and His Comrades-in-Arms") features both a celebration of blackness and an egalitarian argument. The opening stanza first declares that, in his martyrdom, Cailloux "abattit un indigne soupçon" ("laid to rest a vile suspicion") that black men could not fight as soldiers. Now, a black officer had become a hero and model for all defenders of freedom:

> Consolons-nous, nous, hommes de sa race,
> Devant Dieu seul il courbait le genou.
> Que Blancs et Noirs suivent la noble trace.
>   Du brave André Caillou. (*Bis.*)

> Let us take heart, we men of his race;
> Before God alone did he deign to bow.
> May whites and blacks follow the noble ways
>   Of courageous André Caillou. (*Bis.*)

In these lines the racial dichotomy seemingly allows for interracial solidarity: the poet first states his own belonging to the "men of his race" before enjoining "whites and blacks" to come together to follow Cailloux's example.

It is Cailloux, the black officer, who stands as a leader to all. The inequality inherent in the *blanc-noir* binary gives rise to an exaltation of blackness in the next stanza, as Honoré recalls how "ce héros, au front noir et si fier" ("this hero, of countenance black and proud") led into battle "[s]es frères noirs, braves comme le fer!" ("his black brothers, stalwart as iron!"). These verses echo contemporary observations regarding Cailloux's physical qualities: a *New York Times* correspondent who witnessed the battle described Cailloux as "a man so black that he actually prided himself on his blackness."[59] In the poem, the "white" counterpart has been set aside in favor of black self-fulfillment, realized through both physical beauty and manly virtue — virtue not merely visible in but fundamentally constituted by Cailloux's pride, his physical (black) appearance, and his pride in that appearance ("au front noir et si fier"). Thanks to these qualities, the *fers* or "irons" of enslavement have been recast into the (black) metal of courage. Honoré's deployment of the *blanc-noir* dichotomy reveals the slippage inherent in a structure whose poetic equilibrium struggles with what Derrida calls "the phase of overturning." Because of "the conflictual and subordinating structure of opposition," it is necessary "to overturn the hierarchy at a given moment" (41). Clearly, this operation is at work in the poem. However, the aim is not to reverse the racial order, but to destroy it. Though an officer in an all-black regiment, Cailloux, in his death, proves himself worthy of leading both "whites and blacks" (contrary, of course, to actual military policy). Traced and retraced on the shifting sands of Reconstruction, this "interminable analysis" (Derrida 42) of blackness against and with whiteness — simultaneously — entails denying white supremacy while envisioning interracial unity.

Like Honoré's tribute to André Cailloux, Naudin's "Ode aux martyrs" ("Ode to the Martyrs") calls on "Noirs et Blancs" to honor a deceased martyr for equality, in this instance a victim of the 1866 massacre: Victor Lacroix, son of the internationally renowned tailor François Lacroix, who was one of the main supporters of the Institution catholique and many other philanthropic initiatives. Victor Lacroix is one of several dead whose memory is evoked; not all are Creoles or people of color, but the assault on black people at the convention receives emphasis: "Ils tombaient! ils tombaient!

ces fils de race noire / Comme tombent au froid les feuilles." ("How they fell! How they fell, these sons of the black race, / Like leaves do fall in the cold.") Lacroix's death, however, elicits the most pathos, heightened by the Christ allusion in his surname (*la croix*, "the cross"). The poem's final couplet raises the irony of Lacroix's death and the former Confederate president Jefferson Davis's continued existence: "Mais je dirai toujours mulâtres, noirs, blancs, / Victor Lacroix est mort, Jeff Davis est vivant" ("But, mulattoes, blacks, whites, this fact I must tell: / Victor Lacroix is dead; Jeff Davis lives still.") Racial duality, here recognized as not entirely commensurate with social reality, has been transferred onto a rhetorical duality, an antithetical climax organized not (solely) on race but on the failure of justice: all defenders of equality, whatever their "race," fall victim to the injustices of reactionary forces, a tragic irony encapsulated in the relative impunity enjoyed by Jefferson Davis. (In the spring of 1867, the former president of the Confederacy, captured in 1865, had just been released on bail; he would never face trial.)

In February 1869 Victor Lacroix's spirit would "visit" — at least, according to the beliefs of the Creole Spiritualists — Henry Louis Rey's Cercle harmonique.[60] His communication celebrates the sacrifices of "blacks, sons of the Republic" who had fought to end "domination over a portion of the Republic's citizens, whose only crime is to be black" ("Les noirs, fils de la République"; "la domination sur une partie des citoyens de la grande République [...] dont le seul crime est d'être noir"; Rey 194).

Neither the poem nor the spirit message refers explicitly to the complexities of Lacroix's familial circumstances, though the poem touches on them obliquely when calling for *blanc-noir* unity in honoring him:

> VICTOR LACROIX est mort! C'était une belle âme,
> Depuis trois mois à peine il avait pris sa femme
>   Qui versa plus d'un pleur.
> Il est mort! pardonnant, mais demandant justice!
> Honorons, Noirs et Blancs, ce vaillant sacrifice
>   D'un mort au champ d'honneur!

> VICTOR LACROIX is dead! His soul was simply splendid;
> Just barely three months before, he'd taken a bride
>   Who's poured out many a tear!
> He's dead and gone! Forgiving, but asking for justice!
> Let's honor, both blacks and whites, his valiant sacrifice
>   Upon the field of honor!

The likenesses between Lacroix and Cailloux are obvious, but the comparison is perhaps not as clear-cut as it might appear at first glance. In her book *American Routes: Racial Palimpsests and the*

Transformation of Race, the sociologist Angel Adams Parham argues that two racial orders operated concurrently in nineteenth-century Creole Louisiana, though the binary Anglo-American system would eventually win out over the colonial system of the Caribbean and Latin America. To explain this uneven transformation, she deploys the notion of a palimpsest, a manuscript document on which a new text has been written over an older one whose traces remain visible nonetheless. The "*racial palimpsest* occurs when a preexisting racial system is almost fully eclipsed by a new racial system," a process that, in the nineteenth century, "disrupted earlier, taken-for-granted understandings of race in Louisiana and imposed new social and political challenges and opportunities for those living under its influence" (2). "Ode aux martyrs" draws from and speaks to these complex dynamics. To the reader comparing the martyred Lacroix with the martyred Cailloux, whose blackness was clearly visible and a point of personal pride, does it matter that Lacroix's own identity as one of "ces fils de race noire" ("these sons of the black race") was far less fixed? That Lacroix's mourning wife, Sarah Brown, was not legally married to Lacroix because she was white and therefore could not marry him? Does it matter that a few years later, Brown would claim that she believed her husband to be white as well (Thompson 142–44)?

On one level, it does not matter, of course. However, racial ambiguity and the politics of "passing" did impair the attempt to construct a cohesive political community, most especially after Radical Reconstruction succumbed in 1877 to so-called Redemption (a political movement designed to restore white supremacy), ultimately leading to Jim Crow segregation. As late as 2008, a descendant of Louis Charles Roudanez, Mark Charles Roudané, wrote powerfully about discovering his *Créole de couleur* background after having been raised white in the latter half of the twentieth century and considering himself as such well into adulthood. Even the poet Adolphe Duhart chose to distance himself from black identity. After 1880, he presented himself as and was accepted as white, even while a number of former activists from *La Tribune*, strengthened by the younger generation, were preparing to launch legal challenges against post-Reconstruction segregation. Though the Supreme Court's verdict in the 1896 case of *Plessy v. Ferguson* remains well-known in US history, the role of francophone Creole activists therein has been somewhat eclipsed. The lawsuit brought by the French-speaking Louisiana Creole Homer Plessy, challenging discrimination in access to public facilities, was the culmination of an antisegregation campaign mounted by New Orleans's Comité des citoyens. Despite a defeat validating segregation under the "separate but equal" doctrine, the effort laid groundwork for future civil rights activism that continues to the present day.

"Je Suis la Fraternité": Articulations of Community

The issues about the poetry raised in this essay point to a central challenge of Afro-Creole political action: imagining — and enacting — an inclusive political community as the basis for reconstructed nationhood. In terms of the triad of French revolutionary values, *fraternité* stands as the keystone. As later shown by Jim Crow segregation, *liberté* and *égalité* are impossible without *fraternité* to promote social cohesion, productive political debate, respect of religious and cultural differences, and fair access to economic resources — in short, full participation as citizens of a nation. "Separate but equal," Reconstruction's eventual negation, represents *fraternité*'s perverse and oppressive opposite.

Concretely, Afro-Creoles developed within their ethnolinguistic community a solid tradition of *fraternité* as a system of overlapping and mutually reinforcing social bonds. Family ties were extremely important, as was the acquisition, consolidation, and transmission of property. Equally crucial, however, was the dense web of organizational life composed of professional associations, charitable groups, benevolent societies, mutual aid associations, religious fraternities and sororities, and Masonic lodges.[61] Extremely visible in the newspapers' articles and announcements, these networks undergirded the social relationships present in the poems; sometimes they appear explicitly, as in Adolphe Duhart's "Deux novembre" ("The Second of November"), dedicated to the Francs-Amis, a Creole fraternal society whose hall is considered one of the birthplaces of jazz. While such configurations contributed to the *gens de couleur*'s supposedly insular character, they also widened social relations. In particular, the interracial practices of transnational Freemasonry, which held itself to be a "fraternité universelle," clashed with pre–Civil War segregation (Bell, *Revolution*, ch. 5).

The politics of Reconstruction required expanding the bounds of practiced *fraternité* to imagine and then create a political community around universalist ideals. The poetry of *L'Union* and *La Tribune* supports this project in two ways.

The poetry's extensive thematic treatment of *fraternité* as a universal ideal — expounded, for example, in "La Marseillaise noire" — constitutes one part of the effort. This universalist conception casts nationhood and citizenship in terms reflective of the broader transformations of the francophone Atlantic world after the French and Haitian revolutions.

The other manifests itself through the constitution of a poetic community, the "brotherhood" of writers whose discursive practices mirror and build on actual social relations and personal relationships. These practices include dedications, overt direct address (e.g.,

Duhart's "Le poète"), poetic dialogs (such as between "Antony" and Armand Lanusse), allusions to one another's personal lives, and mentions of shared literary and cultural references. Such practices establish and regulate a model community, or *confrérie*; at the same time, the tensions running throughout the Afro-Creole relations with Reconstruction, a national project based on collective experience that was both local and transnational, are visible in the poetry. This productive tension bears exploration.

The emergence of the poet "Yacoub," or Joseph Mansion, illustrates neatly the functioning and textual performance of poetic community. Aptly titled "La poésie" (14 Oct. 1866), Yacoub's first piece enumerates the positive effects of poetry on human spirit. Its dedication, "À mon ami Lélia D...t," acknowledges the intellectual mentorship of Adolphe Duhart (who wrote poetry pseudonymously under the name of his sister Lélia). It also implicitly invites a response from Duhart himself, which came two weeks later as the poem "Poésie! Vox Dei!" (28 Oct. 1866). After encouraging Yacoub to "[l]et your fingers dance across your exalted lyre" ("Laisse courir tes doigts sur ta lyre inspirée"), the elder writer offers direction: given the recent destruction of slavery, the young poet must take up the prophetic responsibility of his art, thus heralding "the sure and sacred time / Of purest Fraternity" ("l'heure sainte et certaine / De la pure Fraternité").

Yacoub's poetic initiation continued later that year with the poem "Méditations" (16 Dec. 1866), addressed to Armand Lanusse, a close friend of Joseph Mansion's father. In a letter to *La Tribune*, Lanusse praised Yacoub's verse in these terms: "This piece, like all of yours that I have read, is to be commended for the exactitude of its versification, the nobility of feeling, and the evidence you've given us that your fervent study of the great masters has proven very fruitful" ("Cette pièce, comme toutes celles que j'ai lues de vous, se recommande par l'exactitude de la versification, la noblesse des sentiments et la preuve que vous nous donnez que l'étude que vous avez ardemment faite de nos grands maîtres vous a été fructueuse").[62] The young Joseph Mansion has met all standards for full participation in the poetic community: mastery of form, ideas worthy of expression, and an understanding of French literary tradition sufficient to enable him to build on it in Creole Louisiana.

As part of their discursive strategy for overcoming racial strictures while simultaneously affirming identity, the Afro-Creole poets' linguistic practices are deeply embedded in universalist aspirations. Even before the French Revolution's proclamation of *liberté, égalité, fraternité*, French had come to be regarded as "a universal language that belonged to all people and so rose above national interests" (Casanova 72). The language's claim to humanistic universalism invited these Afro-Creole writers to develop a poetic practice in their native French, even as English was becoming the dominant language of New Orleans and Louisiana. Lanusse's emphasis on "fervent study of the great masters" and "exactitude of [...] versification" underscores the letter's underlying message: mastering French style and poetic conventions demonstrated intellectual worth, an ability to join the concert of universal thought.

As political philosophers have pointed out, universalism — despite its most ambitious claims to speak for all humanity — is itself situated in and from a particular context. From that position it is projected outward. In this case, we will want to consider two facets of Afro-Creole universalism as inflected through *fraternité*: gender and empathy for suffering.

All the poets in this volume (with one exception) are almost certainly men, even when a female poetic voice is assumed (e.g., Duhart's choice to use his sister's name as his pseudonym), and the discursive space of the newspapers is by and large male. The lone inclusion known to be written by a woman is one of the aforementioned plagiarized poems: "L'existence de Dieu," written in 1832 by the French writer Hortense de Céré-Barbé, published in *La Tribune* in 1866 with the title "Il est" and attributed to the masculine pseudonym Antony.[63] On one level, the masculine bias appears inherent to the political project of *Liberté, égalité, fraternité* — a fact suggested by the very term and notion of "brotherhood." The conflation of universal rights with masculine identity comes to the fore in an English-language editorial from late 1868, when *La Tribune* was attempting to recover from the election crisis:

> The one word which condenses into the smallest compass the great aim of this journal, is the word *Manhood*. We place ourselves on the broad platform of universal manhood, and upon that we design to urge the particular claims of the colored man. ("Our Aim," 12 Dec. 1868)

This emphasis on manhood in public discourse does not mean that the role of *femmes de couleur* was limited to the private sphere in practice. The very public roles of women poets and speakers visible throughout this essay are but the tip of the iceberg of women's community-organizing activities and civic engagement as educators, fundraisers, artists, orators, members of religious orders (such as the Sisters of the Holy Family, founded in 1837 by Henriette DeLille, a Creole *femme de couleur*), and more. It does mean that male subjectivity, and even the possibility of *fraternité*, is premised upon asserting normative patriarchy, an issue already foundational in *Les Cenelles*. For the most part, the Creole radicals failed to link their antiracist cause to the burgeoning struggle for women's rights. Their activism differed in this respect from Northern abolitionism, for which the link was a defining, if not uniform, feature.

Lucien Mansion's "Hommage au sexe" ("Homage to the Fairer Sex"), the longest poem in this corpus, provides an extended statement on acceptable roles and behaviors for women. Here, as throughout the poems, women are *spoken to* and *spoken about* as objects of discourse, normally to position them in relation to the male subject. In praising women's roles as mothers and partners, while deploring the suffering they often endure at the hands of men and institutions, the poet focuses on the moral necessity of "vos belles vertus / Qui rayonnent encore quand la beauté n'est plus" ("your lovely virtues / That shine forth still when beauty's faded from use"). A lighter tone is used in Questy's "Une dépêche télégraphique" ("A Telegraphic Dispatch," 24 Jan. 1869), which seeks to goad a friend into choosing a husband. Pronouncements like these would be utterly unremarkable for the period, perhaps, were it not for the backdrop of the particular familial structures of the Afro-Creole community (and Creoles overall).

Questy's and Lucien Mansion's familial structures are cases in point. Both men were sons of European fathers and *femmes de couleur libres*: because interracial marriage was illegal, both were born out of wedlock, as were many other Afro-Creoles. Many of those same children then grew up to regard as normal the practice of having children with one's wife and with another woman. As an adult, Lucien Mansion had two families concurrently, eventually leaving one longtime partner, Elizabeth Francis of New York (the mother of the poet Joseph Mansion), to live with the other, Marie Aline Palao, an illiterate woman of color.[64] Lucien Mansion, Questy, and other poets in this volume often ignore or seek to smooth over such complex social dynamics — here, "Hommage au sexe" and "Une dépêche télégraphique" bring them into the purview of "universal manhood." As Kristi Richard Melançon has persuasively argued, the discourse of *La Tribune*, including but certainly not limited to this corpus of poetry, sought to perform patriarchal gender normativity in the public sphere — whatever private relations may have been like in the Creole community. This performance involved not only projecting images of chaste domesticity but even walking back, in editorials published in 1865, from an endorsement of women's suffrage to a more conservative position (Melançon 142–43). (It would appear that Houzeau's prosuffragist stance lost out to his Creole colleagues' investment in more traditional gender roles.) This hypocritical attitude, albeit coherent by the norms of the day, must be acknowledged and accounted for when studying literature of the era and the gaps in the written records. A history of francophone Creole women's tremendous role in the civil rights struggles of Reconstruction remains to be written.

In dynamic counterpoint to abstract universality, the radical discourse of *L'Union* and *La Tribune* displays overt solidarity with Haiti. However, while featured prominently and favorably in news reports in both papers, the black Caribbean nation is evoked in only one poem: Duhart's "Pour les incendiés de Saint-Domingue" ("For the Victims of the Saint Domingue Fire," 6 May 1866), written to elicit support for aid to Haiti after a fire ravaged the capital city of Port-au-Prince in 1866.[65] In an attentive analysis of this text, Anna Brickhouse shows how Duhart's poem participates in the genre of the classical Greek ode, which had been repopularized in French by Lamartine. The first movement of the ode, or the strophe, paints Port-au-Prince on the morning of the fire. The description of the waking dawn is interrupted when the poet recalls how "un cri de suprême terreur / [...] A traversé l'espace... Au feu!... Malheur!..." ("A cry of [...] baleful horror, took flight / Through the air ... 'Fire! ... Misery! ...'"). The poem shifts into its second movement, the antistrophe, as the flames die down and the passing sun "[é]claire d'Haïti les toits abandonnés" ("[i]lluminates the forlorn homes of Haiti"). Duhart shows victims' suffering and grief: orphaned children, the elderly lacking shelter, mothers praying over their children's bodies. The epode, or final section effecting a synthesis, beseeches the reader: "Donnez, vous tous aussi qui connaissez les pleurs" ("Give, all ye who also have known tears").

In Brickhouse's reading, not only does the call for charity reactivate "the affective bonds connecting readers — and fostering human agency — across national lines," but, through the toponymic anachronism "Saint-Domingue" — the name of the former French colony, not the nation that it became in 1804 — it recalls a shared past in order to tug on nostalgic heartstrings. Given the Creole community's ties with the Caribbean, the poem, as Brickhouse insists, reactivates "the mourning transamerican community" of readers in Louisiana and victims in Haiti (1121–22).

Duhart's poem is but one of myriad illustrations of Thompson's argument, inspired by a concept from the Martinican philosopher Édouard Glissant, for considering "mid-nineteenth-century New Orleans as a 'point of entanglement' where overlapping national, diasporic, and intensely local understandings of belonging alternately challenged, displaced, and reinforced one another" (116). In that light, Brickhouse's transnational reading can be further enriched by setting it against an elegy that lamented a national tragedy one year earlier: Duhart's "Le 13 avril" ("The 13th of April"), composed a few days after the assassination of Abraham Lincoln.

Though its six-line stanzas differ somewhat from the successive rhyming couplets of "Pour les incendiés de Saint-Domingue," the rhetorical structure of "Le 13 avril" is strikingly similar. The poem opens with the familiar Romantic trope of sunset. The day having faded, a cry of alarm rings out: "Au meurtre!... à l'assassin!... ô crime épouvantable!..." ("'It's murder! . . .' 'Assassin! . . .' 'Oh horrendous crime! . . .'"). The antistrophe, covering the fourth and fifth stanzas, names that crime — "Abraham Lincoln est perdu!" — and its immediate effect: "Un deuil universel entoura l'Amérique" ("America sank into universal grief"). Shared grief cements national unity. Finally, the three-stanza epode reassures readers that Lincoln's legacy will live on through the regeneration of the nation — i.e., Reconstruction. This message is addressed to all, black and white, Northerners and Southerners, but the third-to-last stanza addresses itself first to former Native Guards, then directly to the recently emancipated freedmen:

> Pleurez incessamment... pleurez celui qui tombe,
> Votre Libérateur descendu dans la tombe.
>   Natifs, vous tous, cœurs pleins de foi!...
> Oh! pleurez sur celui dont la mort vous sépare,
> Sur celui qui s'en vint, comme Christ à Lazare,
>   Vous dire: Esclave, lève-toi!

> Unceasingly weep . . . weep for him who falls,
> Your Liberator laid into his grave,
>   Ye natives, hearts of worth.
> Oh! Weep for him whom death has stolen away,
> For him who came, like Christ to Lazarus,
>   To tell you, "Slave, come forth!"

The Biblical allusion to Christ's resurrection of Lazarus displaces Lincoln's messianic impact from his death to the act of giving life or at least freedom to millions.

But importantly, Duhart is actually recasting a section of a work by Alexandre Dumas *père*, a five-act verse drama from 1839, cowritten with Gérard de Nerval and entitled *L'Alchimiste*. The plot is set in sixteenth-century Italy, but Duhart's poem recasts a moment in which Dumas's protagonist sings of his country in lyrics that seem to refer to the nineteenth-century struggle to unify the fragmented Italian peninsula into one nation, a struggle that riveted the attention of the world, including Creoles in Louisiana:

> Priez incessamment, priez pour l'Italie,
> Qu'ont ses propres enfants, vivante, ensevelie...
>   Priez, cœurs pleins de foi!
> Afin qu'au jour caché, que l'avenir prépare,
> Vienne la liberté, comme Christ à Lazare...
>   Lui dire: Lève-toi! (90)

> Unceasingly pray; pray for Italy,
> By her own children buried, though alive ...
> Yes, pray, ye hearts of worth!
> So that at some hidden, future hour,
> Freedom may come, like Christ to Lazarus,
> To tell us, "Now come forth!"

Duhart's intertextual borrowing is likely a wink to his poetic *confrères* who knew Dumas's play, but its transatlantic significance comes into view when we recall that Dumas was himself of African descent. His father, Thomas-Alexandre Davy de la Pailleterie (1762–1806), a mulatto born in Saint Domingue, was the French army's first black general; despite this background, Dumas occasionally suffered racist swipes and caricatures from detractors over the course of his literary career. In this respect, the famous writer shared a common heritage with many New Orleanian Afro-Creoles, and his successes were touted by *La Tribune* as a source of pride.[66]

Duhart's choice to rewrite a passage about a struggle for national unity written by a mixed-race French author of Caribbean heritage suggests that liberation struggles — like suffering — are both specific and universal. It will be for other scholars to situate in greater depth this body of poetry in relation to other black literatures of the Americas and the francophone world. In undertaking that work, it will be best to approach Louisiana Afro-Creole textuality as a site of multiple articulations of belonging, a dense interweaving of perhaps unexpected "entanglements."

Presenting the Corpus

The texts in this collection were selected and organized to give fullest access to the radical Afro-Creole poetry published in *L'Union* and *La Tribune de la Nouvelle-Orléans*. The book does not contain every poem printed in the newspapers. Only French-language poems have been included. (Both periodicals feature literary pieces in English, though fewer and farther between, and occasionally in Spanish.) A few poems in French were excluded because their composition had no direct connection to Louisiana. For example, though Adolphe Pécatier's song "La liberté et l'esclavage" (13 Aug. 1865) appears in Cowan's collection *La Marseillaise noire* and some others, it is omitted here because its lyrics were composed in the 1840s in France. No racial criterion was applied to authors: most of the poets in this collection are *hommes de couleur*, but not all, and some we cannot say for certain.

Archival research has also brought to this book several poems that were previously unknown, lost, or simply not mentioned in other work on this subject. Among those that have escaped attention until their appearance in this volume are Duhart's "Sonnet," dedicated to Louise de Mortie (9 Apr. 1865), and his poem "Rêve" (8 Oct. 1865). "La fleur indiscrète" (22 July 1866), signed "Antony," attributed by earlier scholars to Macarty though in fact copied from the French writer Henri Blaze, can be found among the formerly missing issues of *La Tribune* at the American Antiquarian Society. Similarly, three poems are reproduced from rarely consulted issues from 1868 in the holdings of the Boston Athenaeum: Duhart's tongue-in-cheek "Idéalisme — Matérialisme" (19 Jan. 1868), his homage to the just deceased Armand Lanusse, "!" (18 Mar. 1868), and the witty "Pot-pourri" (21 Apr. 1868) by the well-known French immigrant journalist Jean-Sylvain Gentil of St. James Parish.

To preserve the dialogues among the poets and to make visible the crucial social interconnections among members of the Afro-Creole community, the poems in this volume are organized thematically instead of being grouped by author. The reader is encouraged to read through them in order, to see poets writing explicitly back and forth to each other and to witness an intellectual community discussing philosophy, politics, identity, and art, as well as coming together to mourn the tragedy of the Mechanics' Institute massacre.

These seventy-nine poems have been divided into five categories and are arranged chronologically within each grouping. Texts openly affirming the political vocation of poetry in heralding a new social order have been grouped in the section entitled Poetry as Prophecy, which opens the collection. (As mentioned earlier, prophecy is understood here in the biblical sense: namely, texts that warn of divine judgment on humanity, foretell change, or both.) Topical pieces on events of the period are featured in The War and Reconstruction, while poems dealing with human and civil rights, though not necessarily referring to major events of the day, are found in the following section, Liberty, Racial Equality, and Fraternity. Philosophical poetry composes The World of Ideas. Finally, poems of love and friendship are placed under the heading Matters of the Heart, a title that encompasses the treatment of issues around a variety of social and interpersonal relationships, from love to friendship and family, in addition to more abstract reflections; this is the largest category, with twenty-eight poems.

This classification scheme aims to draw out the overarching coherence of the corpus. With very few exceptions, poems fell neatly into one category or another, and poetic exchanges (such as "Il est" ["He Is"] and "Il n'est pas" ["He Is Not"]), even implied, are grouped together. This choice of arrangement foregrounds the ideological and political thrust of the poetry while allowing for maximal inclusion of sentimental poems, which do not overwhelm the rest if kept together. One must also keep in mind that, even if substantial in number, the poems were originally scattered over nearly eight years; by March 1870, near the very end of its life, *La Tribune*'s run exceeded thirteen hundred issues. The dispersal of the original poems, generally published as stand-alone pieces but not always, obliges the modern editor to determine what organization will make the works most accessible to a contemporary audience.

Let there be no mistake: these poems retain much of their relevance, firmly rooted though they are in their particular moment in time and in the culture from which they emerged.

More than 150 years after the Louisiana state constitution of 1868, the legacy of slavery and the Civil War are still hotly debated. While prominent monuments to the "Lost Cause" of the Confederacy were taken down (amid controversy) in New Orleans in 2017, others remain, there and elsewhere across the South. While plaques have been added at *La Tribune*'s Conti Street address and other New Orleans locations important in African American history — including several acknowledging the city's central role in the slave trade — no significant monument marks the spot of the 1866 massacre or other sites of pivotal events of Reconstruction. Racially motivated violence against African Americans continues to erupt, a continual, heartbreaking reminder of the structural racism that still defines the American social fabric.

The radical Afro-Creole poetry of nineteenth-century Louisiana has as much to say today as it did then. Its struggles have never been confined to one moment or nation. Its language has much in common, for example, with that of Frantz Fanon, the anticolonialist freedom fighter from Martinique who, a century later, sought both to acknowledge and liberate himself from history in the effort to overcome the deep damage of racism:

> La densité de l'Histoire ne détermine aucun de mes actes.
> Je suis mon propre fondement.
> Et c'est en dépassant la donnée historique, instrumentale,
>   que j'introduis le cycle de ma liberté. (187)

> The density of History determines none of my actions.
> I am my own foundation.
> And it is by stepping beyond the historical, instrumental fact
>   that I initiate the cycle of my freedom.

In Fanon's lines, the Reconstruction-era faith in a fraternal forgive-and-forget approach has receded, and reliance on the individual has taken its place, in keeping with the Martinican thinker's existentialist outlook. But their prophetic tone and preoccupation with shedding the bonds of the past suggest that Fanon, himself the descendant of enslaved Africans, could have felt some kinship with these poets. Even if unable to share the idealism of an exhortation such as Lanusse's in "L'astre s'est levé!," he likely would have found it poignant and compelling, as will many readers today:

> Et puisque parmi nous les maux de l'esclavage
> Vont cesser, oublions nos souffrances d'hier;
> Honorons nos martyrs et pardonnons l'outrage,
> C'est ainsi que se venge un peuple libre et fier!

> And since, in our midst, the ills of slavery
> Will cease, let's turn the page on yesterday's misery;
> Let's honor our martyrs and pardon all injury,
> For that is how vengeance is wrought by a people proud and free!

FIG. 18. The poem "Les tyrans au tribunal de l'histoire," by an unknown author, as it originally appeared in the 20 Dec. 1862 issue of *L'Union*.

LES TYRANS AU TRIBUNAL DE L'HISTOIRE.

—Quand l'histoire fait voir le mérite opprimé,
Et la vertu proscrite, et le crime honoré,
On rougit de savoir tant de maux, tant de crimes ;
On voudrait que l'oubli pût rouvrir ses abîmes.
Vœux imprudents ! du mal le souvenir affreux
Au souvenir du bien donne un prix plus heureux ;
L'âme, sur les vertus qu'aux forfaits elle oppose,
Avec plus d'intérêt s'arrête et se repose......
Non, le crime ne peut, même après le remord,
S'absoudre et se cacher dans la nuit de la mort ;
Il existe un vengeur, dont la main implacable
De sa tombe ébranlée arrache le coupable,
Et le traîne, honteux de sa triste clarté,
Devant le tribunal du lecteur irrité :
Notre voix lui reproche et sa vie et ses crimes ;
Nous aimons sur sa cendre à venger ses victimes,
Nous pardonnons aux cieux, puisque leur équité,
Créa pour les pervers une immortalité ;
Et de ce châtiment terrible, inévitable,
Lui montre en ses succès l'image épouvantable
Qui, tourmentant ses nuits, empoisonnant ses jours,
Comme un fer suspendu, le menace toujours ;
O ! que les opprimés embrassent cette idée !

Note on the Text

The textual treatment of the original French poems reflects two priorities. This edition strives both to respect the nineteenth-century French texts' value as historical documents and to affirm their relevance for a contemporary francophone audience, in Louisiana and throughout the French-speaking world. For these reasons, choices regarding standardization, modernization, and emendation generally resemble those commonly adopted for editions of classic French-language texts.

Nineteenth-century newspapers in general present challenges, and *L'Union* and *La Tribune* add some particular challenges of their own (fig. 18). Owing to the scarcity of issues of the papers, which are scattered in various holdings throughout the United States, it was in most cases possible to consult only one version of the original text. Print copies were used where possible, but often the only version available is microform; a page damaged or incompletely reproduced may mean that a missing word or line remains missing forever. Furthermore, the fast-paced nature of journalistic printing, compounded with the fierce urgency of Reconstruction-era life, made for more errors and inconsistencies than would likely have occurred had these poems been published in book form. Publishing in two languages entailed two sets of punctuation conventions: the original French poems could be set with French-style punctuation, English-style, or a mix. In a few cases, an editorial change or guess is marked with brackets. On the whole, however, because this volume is designed not as a critical edition for textual scholars but as a readable edition for a general audience, punctuation has to some degree been silently regularized and spelling errors corrected silently.

In that light, the following guidelines have been adopted for the original French versions of the poems.

Spelling and Vocabulary

Since the French Revolution, spelling in French has undergone two major reforms. The first, introduced in 1835, set modern orthographic norms; *L'Union* and *La Tribune* followed that standard, and thus the poems *in situ* look very modern, even today. The second, commonly called *la nouvelle orthographe*, was proposed in 1990 to rectify irregularities in certain types of words, simplify some spellings, and reduce extraneous usage of diacritics; to date, it has not been fully implemented. With few exceptions, this edition of the French versions of these poems does not avail itself of the *nouvelle orthographe.* This choice respects the nineteenth-century provenance of the texts without compromising twenty-first-century readability, since the *ancienne orthographe* is unlikely to seem noticeably outdated for some time to come.

Obvious spelling errors have been corrected throughout. Capitalization of nouns has been standardized, except those used for poetic or rhetorical effect. Small capitals used decoratively have been regularized. Small capitals used for emphasis have generally been rendered as italics, though in the few instances where removing or changing the capitals threatened to skew the meaning or emphasis of the poem, they have been retained. The occasional word or line missing from or illegible in the original has been noted in brackets.

Punctuation, Diacritics, and Line Arrangements

Lines of poetry frequently exceed the narrow columns of the newspaper page. Fortunately, poetic line breaks in these texts are very easy to identify, either because of the structure of the poem itself, including rhyme, or, more explicitly, brackets that sometimes mark a line's continuation. In all cases, the entire line has been restored in this edition, and the bracket marking a wrapped line has been omitted.

The use of punctuation indicating pauses, stops, separation of clauses, and delimitation of appositives (i.e., commas, colons, semicolons, dashes, periods, etc.) can be somewhat erratic in the originals. Though the preference has been for the least intervention possible, ambiguous usage has occasionally required some interpretation in the English rendering; in such case, my choices seek to respect the overall spirit of the poems. Question marks have been appended to questions, usually rhetorical, that lack them. Ellipses, which often run wild in nineteenth-century texts, have been standardized as suspension points. This mark is a single typeset character not to be simply equated with an English ellipsis: suspension points constitute a pause sometimes better represented in the translation by a comma or a period. The mark consists of three closely spaced dots, with a small space after: "Vous tressaillez... Pourquoi?" (In contrast, an ellipsis is rendered with three periods separated by standard character spaces: "You quiver . . . Why?") In almost all cases, multiple exclamation points have been reduced to a single one. "Le capitaine André Caillou" retains the three exclamation points at its end because they render the ending especially emphatic and thus carry meaning in a way they might not in another position.

Nineteenth-century typesetters omitted accents on capitalized vowels not for reasons having to do with meaning but because most of the time there was not sufficient space between lines; new technology now allows us to include the marks. In this volume, accents have been placed on capitalized vowels where they would normally occur; in addition to following current North American usage in French, the retention of diacritics on capitals can assist readers not completely familiar with the language.

Punctuation has in general been regularized according to the guidelines of the French Imprimerie nationale, which largely resemble the typographical norms employed by the publishers of *L'Union* and *La Tribune*. A small nonbreaking space precedes colons, semicolons, question marks, and exclamation marks, and text inside guillemets is preceded and followed by a space. When text within guillemets is a complete sentence, punctuation is usually inside; otherwise, punctuation follows the closing guillemet. When dashes mark emphasis or set off parenthetical elements, their use in this volume, in both French and English, follows the European style: namely, a space is placed on either side, which allows the translations to retain some ambiguities present in the originals.

The original newspapers generally used English quotation marks for attributed speech. In keeping with standard practice for modern editions of older North American French texts, guillemets have been used instead for the French poems in this volume. Their use has been standardized and very sparingly modernized (e.g., to facilitate reading, guillemets have occasionally been added where a twenty-first-century reader would expect them).

Note on the Translation

> La rime est une esclave, et ne doit qu'obéir.
>
> Rhyme is a slave and merely must obey.
>
> — Nicolas Boileau-Despréaux,
> *L'Art poétique* (1674)

"Translation is an art of analogy, the art of finding correspondences," claimed the twentieth-century Mexican poet and essayist Octavio Paz, himself a translator. Paz's assertion reminds us that there can be no "exact" translation of a literary work, because different languages offer diverse poetic resources, for which there is rarely a one-to-one equivalent. Instead, by crafting "with different means, analogous effects," the translator strives to create "with a different text, a poem similar to the original."[1]

In undertaking to translate this particular body of nineteenth-century poetry in French, it was necessary to question the basis of potential similarities. In addition to the linguistic divide, there is a temporal distance to be crossed. Not only have historical circumstances changed, but the nature and conventions of poetry have also evolved considerably. It bears consideration that aesthetic transformations both reflect and affect ideological and societal ones. Concretely, the translator is always having to ask what constitutes an "analogous effect." He or she may operate between two poles: that of seeking language and poetic forms analogous with those of the time period — for example, by mirroring selected conventions of nineteenth-century poetry in English — or that of modernizing in hopes of producing an analogous effect in today's reader, since there is a case to be made that newer poetic forms stand a better chance of generating the surprise, anger, pleasure, or other response elicited by the original in its nineteenth-century audience. The approach taken will guide choices regarding structure, tropes, rhythm, meter, diction, and sound repetitions, including rhyme — the very stuff that characterizes poetry as such.

My translations in this anthology attempt to create for readers of English a sense of distance analogous to that which a Francophone today would experience when reading the originals. Many of these poems are protest poetry: such poems were created to communicate a specific message, and their authors' sense of urgency often emerges in their choice of a relatively straightforward tone. The texts' lexicon and syntax, while sophisticated, do not sound particularly archaic to the twenty-first-century ear. No attempt has been made to create English versions that pass for English-language poetry of the nineteenth century — say, works by Tennyson or Longfellow, or popular poetry that would have appeared in newspapers.[2] If any of these translations read as such, that is a secondary effect.

That said, the poets of *L'Union* and *La Tribune* do adhere to the forms, norms, and constraints of poetry as practiced up to the second half of the nineteenth century. To ignore their engagement with these conventions would be to efface their efforts to showcase their mastery and appropriation of respected literary norms. The poets of *L'Union* and *La Tribune* were not alone in their efforts or their reasoning: commenting on the poetry of the earlier Creole anthology *Les Cenelles* (1845), which included pieces by poets who would later write for *La Tribune*, Henry Louis Gates, Jr., attributes an antiracist impulse to the choice to compose "poems which share as silent second texts the poetry written by Frenchmen three thousand miles away." Gates's description of the *Cenelles* poets (quoted above, in this volume's introduction) describes most of the poets in this volume and bears repeating: in "imitat[ing] the styles and themes of the French Romantics," these poets produce work that sends the message, "We are just like the French — so, treat us like Frenchmen, not like blacks" (25). The literary historian Pascale Casanova has argued that Paris, through the intellectual and aesthetic standards associated with a city sometimes called "the capital of the nineteenth century," long held a special status as "the universal place of universal thought" ("capitale du XIXe siècle"; "le lieu universel de la pensée universelle"; 43; 50). To be able to write like a French writer was to show one's equal standing with the best thinkers and artists of the world — and, by implication, to negate ideas of white writers' literary supremacy.

Particularly relevant for this group of Civil War–era poems is the fact that one of the most influential treatises on French poetics describes the challenge of versification in terms of mastery and slavedom. In *L'Art poétique* (1674), the poet and critic Nicolas Boileau-Despréaux (1636–1711) denounced the all-too-common choice to sacrifice quality of expression to the exigencies of rhyme, a complaint to be repeated by other critics in French and in English for as long as rhyme would remain a central feature of poetry. Discouraging fellow writers from "mistaking for genius the love of rhyming" ("prendre pour génie un amour de rimer"), Boileau insists that "rhyme is a slave and merely must obey" ("La rime est une esclave, et ne doit qu'obéir").[3] Specifically, rhyme, argues Boileau, must be placed in the service of "reason" ("la raison") — that is, the ordered, logical thoughts of the poet — and of "good sense" ("le bon sens"), or common understanding intelligible to others.

Boileau's image is a provocative one: unmastered rhyme grows "rebellious" ("elle devient rebelle"), forcing meaning to chase after it rather than direct it ("le sens court après elle"). This alignment of the poet with the master of a recalcitrant or fugitive enslaved person confronts us with a central issue regarding the sociopolitical identification of the Creole poets of color, some of whom, as we know, came from slaveholding families. Rhyme, along with the rest of nineteenth-century literary convention, becomes an important site of struggle for poets coping with the challenges and contradictions of Civil War–era Louisiana Creole society's changing relation to the institution of slavery.

These Louisiana Creole poets were quite literally writing against slavery; were they to show themselves mere slaves to convention, their rhetorical endeavor would be compromised. Imperfection of form or, even worse, imitative doggerel would demonstrate inability to wield the tools of literary convention — and thus imply subservience to them. Freedom through poetry required mastering language.

Having received a classical French education, the circle of activist writers affiliated with *L'Union* and *La Tribune* were familiar with Boileau's admonition, which they invoked in a variety of contexts. An editorial from November 1862 ("Les Journaux" ["The Newspapers"]) used Boileau's language to assert the supremacy of historical fact over pro-Confederacy European newspapers' propaganda (i.e., their misreportage of the progress of the war), asserting, in italics for emphasis, "*La presse est une esclave et ne doit qu'obéir*" ("The press is a slave and merely must obey"). Interestingly, this particular reformulation of Boileau originally came from a statement by the defense lawyer of the French poet-songwriter Pierre-Jean de Béranger (1780–1857), tried and imprisoned in 1828 for his politically charged compositions; its quotation in *L'Union* demonstrates strong awareness of the role of free speech in challenging oppressive political structures (Béranger 193). A few years later, in 1867, Joanni Questy recast Boileau's verse in the preface to his novella *Monsieur Paul*: bemoaning the primacy of money in Louisiana society, he states, "Le chiffre est un esclave et ne doit qu'obéir" ("A number is a slave and merely must obey"; 25 Oct. 1867). Though the language of enslavement may seem problematic, Boileau's original and the sly recastings all present slavery as a relationship exclusively between a nonhuman entity (rhyme, history, numbers [i.e., money]) and humans as a group, undifferentiated by race. Either everybody is a slave, or nobody is.

A translation approach sensitive to the aspirations, literary and ideological, of these Afro-Creole Francophones requires understanding and conveying a sense of their relation to French poetic tradition. To that end, a few remarks on nineteenth-century French poetic conventions are in order, along with the English conventions used in translating them.

Nearly all the poems in the anthology are composed in rhymed metrical verse. Nineteenth-century French verse is syllabic, meaning that the basic units for creating regular patterns are syllables, with variation occurring in the number of stress accents. The most common verse type used in traditional French poetry is the alexandrine, a twelve-syllable line, as found in the anonymous "Les tyrans au tribunal de l'histoire" ("Tyrants before the Judgment of History"):

> 1   2   3   4   5   6   7   8   9   10   11   12
> On | rou|git | de | sa|voir | tant | de | maux, | tant | de | crimes;

Other types of verse exist, of course, and the reader will find a variety of forms in this anthology. Still, the basic principles of metrics remain the same.

English poetic meter is based not on syllables but on stress accent. The most common type of verse in English, iambic pentameter, contains five "feet," each two syllables long, one syllable marked by a stress accent, like a beat. However, because English poetic tradition is organized around stressed beats in a line, pentameter that is not strictly iambic (i.e., the verse has five feet per line, but not every foot in the line has exactly two syllables) is also common. Both types of pentameter appear in the following couplet, taken from my translation of the aforementioned "Les tyrans au tribunal de l'histoire":

> x   /   x   /   x   /   x   /   x   /
> At such | misdeeds, | such crimes, | we take | offense;

> x   x   /   x x   /   x   x x   /   x   /   x   /
> We'd prefer | to be buried | in a chasm | of ig | norance.

The first line is iambic: it consists of five two-syllable feet (unstressed [x]–stressed [/]). The second line of pentameter includes alternative rhythmic patterns such as anapest (unstressed [x]–unstressed [x]–stressed [/]), in feet sometimes three syllables long. Though the first line has ten syllables and the second line has fourteen syllables, both lines contain five stressed syllables. The ability to vary the number of syllables in an English poetic foot increases the translator's flexibility.

Additional classical conventions fixed in the seventeenth century shaped the work of many nineteenth-century poets writing in French. A line of French poetry was subject to strict rules concerning its organization: each line was supposed to form a complete and coherent syntactic unit (such as the example from "Tyrants"). Furthermore, a pause after the sixth syllable, called the *césure* (caesura), typically divided the line into two equal halves, or *hémistiches* (hemistich). Symmetry, then, defined a "perfect" line of French verse.

In the 1820s and 1830s, innovative Romantic poets, Victor Hugo chief among them, had cast off classical rigidity by experimenting with forms that broke down the strict organization of traditional verse. For example, syntactic units were made to stretch across line boundaries, a technique called enjambment. In representing a questioning of order, tradition, and hierarchy, this poetic modernization was strongly associated with political freedom and societal liberalization. The Creole poets of the Civil War era, who had come of age after the advent of Romanticism, needed the respect accorded the old forms more than some poets did — yet were more ideologically aligned with the new. They needed both to have mastered classical forms and to know how to deviate from them; they needed to know the rules and how to break them.

In the light of these historical conditions, I use traditional poetic forms in English, but only to the extent that they open up "analogous effects." Most obviously, each English-language version features a metrical framework, to give the reader an experience corresponding to reading metered rhyme in French. However, I have not reproduced the rhyme schemes mechanistically. Alexandrines have often been translated as iambic pentameter, but not always; sometimes English alexandrines (six-foot verse) work better, as in my translation of Questy's "Aux conservateurs" ("To the Conservatives"). More generally, the English meters are not intended to be worn as a straitjacket; in striving for "the much-sought equilibrium between dominance of sound and undercurrent of meaning" (Lefevere 26), I have, for the sake of the latter, permitted rhythmic irregularity more frequently than occurs in the French texts, which in turn creates new effects in the English translations. In a few instances, the translated poem may shift rhythms where the source text does not, depending on the needs of the English version. These adaptations may reflect requirements of content or the search to produce "analogous effects" on another level, such as mood or alliteration.

Today's reader does not need end rhymes (or even regular metrical forms, for that matter) to experience poetry as poetry. As Donald Wesling notes in *The Chances of Rhyme*, "rhyme has lost its centrality, is no longer the very name of poetry," either in English or French (xi). For this very reason, the use of rhyme can be used to capture historicity.

Nevertheless, rhyme should not be used simply to signal poeticity and historicity. The aesthetic functions of judiciously applied rhyme — namely, "supplying a harmony of sound which is itself beautiful, and of articulating poetic structure by marking off lines and other segments and otherwise acting as the auxiliary of rhythm" (Wesling 5) — have effects the translator often hopes to capture.

Since strict adherence to consistent rhyming would yield unfortunate results in English, I consider rhyme within the larger category of sound repetition. Some translations have rhyme structures that closely resemble the French originals, while others displace the original strict end-rhyme effects onto other harmonic elements and techniques, such as internal rhymes. The translations also feature more occurrences of consonance and assonance than the French-language originals.

As in much of the French-language verse that served as models for these Creole writers, rhyme in this corpus often sets off not only semantic but also thematic parallelism, which sometimes implies kinship and other times heightens contrasts. Universalist terms like *humanité*, *égalité*, and *liberté* frequently reinforce each other through rhyme; the translator's task is eased by equivalent rhyming words in English, ending in *-ity*. Another typical example is the pairing of *crimes* with *victimes*, which occurs in Henry Louis Rey's "L'Ignorance" (the 1865 version), the anonymous "Les tyrans au tribunal de l'histoire," and Camille Naudin's "La Marseillaise noire." To recover the equilibrium of sound and meaning, the slant-rhyming English pair "crimes"-"victims" suffices.

Many other considerations influence choices and strategies for individual poems. The subject matter of Adolphe Duhart's "Pour les incendiés de Saint-Domingue" dissuaded me from leaning too heavily on consistent rhyme. The poem offers a lengthy elegy on a fire that ravaged Port-au-Prince, Haiti, in 1866; its violent imagery and jarring shifts in tone called for some deviation in English so as to unsettle expectation. Since "La Marseillaise noire" is written for the tune of the French "La Marseillaise," the English lines, while not corresponding to the French anthem, do use repetitions, rhythms, rhymes, simple syntax, and line breaks that suggest a sung piece rather than the more formal iambic pentameter and syntax used throughout much of the corpus. (Yes, this involved singing while translating!) Émile Honoré's "Le droit de suffrage des noirs," composed in a French imitation of Robert Burns's Scots-dialect poetry, presented a peculiar challenge, which I attempted to resolve by pseudo-retrotranslating into Burnsian English. Though my recourse to Scots may at first glance appear extreme, the translation is intended to match the level of oralized vernacular found in Honoré's poem, which is a pastiche of Burns's hymn to political egalitarianism, "Is There for Honest Poverty," better known as "A Man's a Man for A' That." Honoré's original verse does not reflect any particular regional dialect of French; it is a peculiar creation that uses abbreviated forms associated with vernacular speech in general. Honoré's francophone American readers encountered unfamiliar words and a language both foreign and not, much as Burns's anglophone readers did. The translation strives to present Honoré's anglophone readers an analogous experience of unfamiliarity.

The translation of "Le 13 avril" uses a combination of these strategies. Duhart's elegy to Abraham Lincoln consists of sextains that follow the a-a-b-c-c-b rhyme scheme. This type of stanza is called a *sizain hétérométrique* because of the shorter third and sixth lines (octosyllabic in the original; trimeter in my version), which generally offer points of climax. To preserve the points of climax in the third and sixth lines, I retained the end rhymes, even after judging that consistent end rhyme risked damaging the somber tone of the piece. (Natural rhymes appear frequently in Romance languages — especially Italian and Spanish — and do not especially draw attention to themselves, whereas in English they can have a distracting singsong quality if not handled carefully.) The final stanza reads:

> Il n'est plus! mais le peuple en pleurs qui l'examine
> Dira dans l'avenir quels honneurs il destine
>   À celui qui vient de partir.
> Et ce n'est pas à nous, faible et petit atome
> Jeté par le Destin, à juger ce grand homme,
>   Régénérateur et martyr!

> He is no more! But the people, after their tears,
> Will proclaim in the future for him who has just gone
>   A fitting tribute of honor.
> And it is not for us — trifling atoms
> Flung forth by Fate — to judge a man so great,
>   Regenerator and martyr!

In place of the pair "partir"-"martyr" (which emphasizes the martyr's having departed — "partir"), I offer a new semantic parallel that highlights Duhart's prediction for Lincoln's legacy: "honor"-"martyr," relocating and highlighting the notion of "honneurs" that appears in the preceding line in the French. In the English, the relation between funeral honors and Lincoln's assassination, a martyrdom for the cause, comes to the fore. The French text builds momentum toward the last line's appositional exaltation by repeating the voiced fricative [ʒ] (*jeté, juger, régénérateur*): the translation builds that momentum through increasing occurrences of the unvoiced [f], coupled with the internal rhyme of the penultimate line ("fate"-"great"). The "fate"-"great" rhyme seeks also to compensate for the weakness of the approximate rhyme of "honor" and "martyr."

Poetic concerns have at times conflicted with my goal of recreating historicity without undue archaisms. I have drawn from English poetic idiom of the period to create corresponding images, lexical items, and prosodic effects. In certain instances of direct address or the imperative, the French plural *vous* calls for the

English "ye." To my ear, "you" or "you all" would violate the poem's overall character: "you" loses the specificity of number, often essential to meaning, whereas "you all" bears an undeniable clunkiness. "Ye" is of course archaic, as are "o'er" and "e'er," literary forms that can nonetheless lend themselves to rhythm. Regarding the poetry's gendered universalism, I have chosen to retain and even make visible implicit masculinist assumptions. Grammatically, French and English do not express gender in the same ways, and sometimes gender is obvious in French but disappears in English. Conversely, my translations often make gender explicit in English, as inferred through interpretation, where it might be only implied in French. Whereas a modernizing translation might try to neutralize implied gender, applying meaning to all whenever possible, this divide, though perhaps problematic, seems to me inherent in confronting the limits of these poets' radical vision.

On many levels, the endeavor of translation involves grappling with the otherness of a text or collection of texts. Burton Raffel points out that "translation assumes that we have chosen to move the poem rather than the reader" (35). True as this may be, the choice to "move the poem" does not mean that the reader is not also asked to "move" as well. For example, though it is tempting to project African Americanness, as a preconstituted reality, onto this French-language corpus, the poetry of these Creole writers shows us instead their coming to blackness as a political identity. A twenty-first-century audience will better understand the import of certain poems if we can "move" ourselves toward the idea of African American identity as a process, one that unfolds in the lines of "La Marseillaise noire" and "Ode aux martyrs."

Much debate among translation theorists has centered on the degree to which a target text should highlight the "foreignness" of a source. Lawrence Venuti has written forcefully about the "domestication" of foreign works through their selection according to certain criteria and the dangers of "the development of discursive strategies to translate them" (180). Domestication — its temptation and its risks — has been a constant concern as I worked. For example, in seeking turns of phrase that carried a certain historical distance, I found myself referring to "comparable" nineteenth-century sources — topical poetry or religious hymns — simply out of curiosity as to whether a particular expression had been used at the time. If it had, that fact sometimes affected my choice. Historical equivalence goes a long way toward the goal of simultaneously preserving temporal difference and giving the reader a rich experience of the text. However, Creole culture existed in rivalry with Protestant English-speaking America, white and black: such a technique of semantic verification thus risked forcing onto Afro-Creole texts elements with an ambivalent relationship to them. At the same time, the radical Afro-Creoles were invested in forging alliances, and their culture and community incorporated many influences and thinkers of different backgrounds. A turn of phrase was not to be ruled out simply because it was used in English texts of the era.

Much recent translation theory continues to assume that cultures are clearly bounded entities and that languages map neatly onto national identities, thus discounting linguistic diversity within a country. Such is not the case with the poems of *L'Union* and *La Tribune*: they are fully francophone and fully American, both Creole and African American. Never abandoning their specificity, they belong to all nonetheless. It is my hope that the English translations in this anthology will lead us to question further our notions of how national identity is constituted.

AFRO-CREOLE POETRY *in* **FRENCH**
from **LOUISIANA'S RADICAL**
CIVIL WAR–ERA NEWSPAPERS

POETRY AS PROPHECY

Les tyrans au tribunal de l'histoire

[anonyme]

— Quand l'histoire fait voir le mérite opprimé,
Et la vertu proscrite, et le crime honoré,
On rougit de savoir tant de maux, tant de crimes ;
On voudrait que l'oubli pût rouvrir ses abîmes.
Vœux imprudents ! du mal le souvenir affreux
Au souvenir du bien donne un prix plus heureux ;
L'âme, sur les vertus qu'aux forfaits elle oppose,
Avec plus d'intérêt s'arrête et se repose...
Non, le crime ne peut, même après le remord,
S'absoudre et se cacher dans la nuit de la mort ;
Il existe un vengeur, dont la main implacable
De sa tombe ébranlée arrache le coupable,
Et le traîne, honteux de sa triste clarté,
Devant le tribunal du lecteur irrité :
Notre voix lui reproche et sa vie et ses crimes ;
Nous aimons sur sa cendre à venger ses victimes,
Nous pardonnons aux cieux, puisque leur équité,
Créa pour les pervers une immortalité ;
Et de ce châtiment terrible, inévitable,
Lui montre en ses succès l'image épouvantable
Qui, tourmentant ses nuits, empoisonnant ses jours,
Comme un fer suspendu, le menace toujours ;
Ô ! que les opprimés embrassent cette idée !

[publié le samedi 20 décembre 1862]

Stanza

À M. A. P...

LÉLIA D... T [Adolphe Duhart]

Ami, vous ressentez dans le fond de votre âme
    Une étrange sensation.
C'est un vague murmure, une céleste flamme,
    Une indicible émotion.

Une voix dit en vous des notes inconnues,
    Un chant d'amour et de bonheur...
Et ces notes — peut-être enfin des cieux venues —
    Vous rendent soucieux, rêveur.

Tyrants before the Judgment of History

[anonymous]

— When history shows that merit is oppressed,
While crime is honored, and virtue is suppressed,
At such misdeeds, such crimes, we take offense;
We'd prefer to be buried in a chasm of ignorance.
A foolish wish! For memories of vice
Give memories of good a higher price;
The soul, on virtues weighed against sin's pains
With greater interest pauses, then remains ...
No, evil cannot by remorse be set right,
Nor be absolved and hid in death's dark night.
There is an avenger whose unrelenting hand
Shatters the tomb and makes the guilty stand,
Saddened by the shame of truth's harsh light,
Before the judgment of the reader's spite:
Our voice denounces both his life and his crimes;
We curse his ashes on behalf of his many victims;
We forgive heaven, whose knowing justice gave
Unto the wicked life beyond the grave,
And, forging punishment from former delights,
Shows him, in worldly triumphs, hellish sights
Which, torturing his nights, poisoning his days,
Like a sword o'erhanging, threaten him always.
May all the oppressed take heart in this idea!

[published Saturday, 20 December 1862]

Stanza

For Mr. A. P——

LÉLIA D——T [Adolphe Duhart]

My friend, deep down within your soul you feel
    A truly strange sensation —
A muted murmuring, a flame celestial,
    An indescribable emotion.

A voice within you speaks in notes unknown
    A song of love ringing merry ...
These notes — perhaps from heaven handed down —
    Imbue you with worry and reverie.

Vous tressaillez... Pourquoi ? Relevez votre tête ;
        Suivez, suivez votre destin ;
L'Espérance apparaît, brillante en la tempête
        Comme l'étoile du matin.

Qu'importe que la foule en son hideux délire
        Vous jette en passant un affront...
Laissez courir vos doigts : les accords de la lyre
        Doucement vous consoleront.

Chantez : Tout ici-bas est mystérieux et sombre,
        Le sourire cache des pleurs ;
Sous nos pas chancelants il est des maux sans nombre ;
        Le poison est dans toutes fleurs.

Oh ! Chantez ! À chaque heure en cette triste vie
        Le cœur exhale des sanglots,
Et la frêle nacelle au port lointain ravie
        Disparaît bientôt dans les flots.

Chantez donc pour qu'au ciel nous apparaisse encore
        Comme l'écharpe aux sept couleurs,
Comme une vision échappée à l'aurore,
        Le Christ penché sur nos douleurs.

Chantez donc comme aux jours de nos plus saintes fêtes
        Un doux cantique à l'Éternel.
Sous vos doigts peut vibrer la harpe des prophètes
        Et dire un chant au Mont-Carmel.

        [publié le dimanche 19 février 1865]

Le poète

   À mon ami, Armand Lanusse

Lélia D... t [Adolphe Duhart]

        Dans ces instants de molle rêverie
Où mon luth, faible encor, prélude sous mes doigts,
Comme un son fugitif d'une note chérie,
Accueille doucement un accent de ma voix.

Je n'ai point oublié la suave espérance
Ami, que me donna ta douce tolérance ;
Je me souviens toujours que par toi soutenu,
Sur des bords plus riants je suis enfin venu.

You quiver ... Why? Lift up your head from your breast;
        Pursue your destiny, however far.
For Hope appears, shining through the tempest
        Just like the glow of the morning star.

It matters not that the crowd flings insults towards
        You, in its ugly agitation ...
Allow your fingers to fly; the lyre's chords
        Will offer gentle consolation.

Sing: all is dark and mysterious here below,
        And even a smile disguises tears.
Beneath our shaky steps lie countless sorrows;
        And poison resides even in flowers.

Oh! Sing! Throughout this dismal life, the heart
        Does sob and moan and wail and weep,
And the fragile vessel snatched from a distant port
        Will vanish soon into the deep.

Sing so that the sky will show us again,
        Just like the seven-colored cloak
Or a vision woven by the hand of dawn,
        The Christ comforting our heartache.

Sing, as if for the highest holy days,
        A sonorous psalm for the Lord Eternal.
By your fingers touched, the harp of the prophets plays
        A song that rings atop Mount Carmel.[1]

[published Sunday, 19 February 1865]

1. Located on the coast of northern Israel, this mountain range is referenced in the Hebrew scriptures as a symbol of beauty and spiritual harmony.

The Poet

To my friend, Armand Lanusse

Lélia D——t [Adolphe Duhart]

    In my moments of mellow musing,
When my lute, though feeble, a prelude does dispense,
And amidst the fleeting sounds of notes of my choosing,
With tenderness welcomes my voice's accents.

I've not forgotten, my friend, that sweet confidence
Afforded by your kindly tolerance.
To this day I remember that, by your strength revived,
On happier shores I have finally arrived.

Caresse encore, ami, ma jeune et frêle lyre ;
Songe au feu du printemps que m'a donné le sort,
Et combien il me faut de douleur, de délire
Pour arriver tremblant jusqu'au céleste port.

Oh ! tends ta main propice à celui qui chancelle ;
J'ai besoin, pauvre enfant, qu'on veille à mon berceau,
Et l'aigle sait toujours à l'ombre de son aile
        Protéger le timide oiseau.

❖

Malheur à l'enfant qui, dans son âme inquiète,
Porte un rayon brûlant de l'archange-poète ;
La foule avec dédain lui jette un sombre affront
Et l'envie infernale — affreuse ignominie —
Flétrit de son poison cet auguste génie
        Qui porte une auréole au front.

Comme on vit autrefois monter sur le Calvaire
L'Homme-Dieu poursuivi par le peuple en colère,
Sans fléchir le poète, en ce monde banni,
Porte aussi son fardeau, ses sanglantes injures.
Oh ! ne pourrait-il pas à ces lâches parjures,
        Crier ! *Lamma à Sabactani.*

Mais la foule égoïste en son hideux délire
Passerait furieuse et briserait sa lyre
Comme on voit l'ouragan au sein des flots amers
Engloutir l'Alcyon, ce noble oiseau-prophète,
Qui vient par ses longs cris annoncer la tempête
        Aux pêcheurs perdus sur les mers.

    Pourtant de sa harpe divine
    Sortent des sons mélodieux ;
    Elle pressent, elle devine
    Du malheur le sort odieux,
    Oh ? C'est que par un bon génie,
    Elle est inspirée et bénie,
    C'est que le poète en son cœur
    Ressent un amour sans mélange,
    C'est qu'il est ici-bas un ange
    Exilé du céleste chœur.

Caress once more my lyre, young and frail;
Remember the fire of spring that's been my lot,
And how much grief and folly pressed my sails
Before I reached, still trembling, that celestial port.

Oh! To him who stumbles, stretch out your helping hand;
A poor child, I need someone to wrap their arms
Around my crib, as the eagle does its wings extend,
       To protect the timid bird from harms.

❖

Woe to the child who, within his troubled soul,
Bears a burning ray of the poet-archangel;
Upon him the crowd heaps insults and dark disdain,
And his genius, august as the halo lighting his face,
By infernal envy's poison — that dreadful disgrace —
       Is withered and brought to ruin.

As long ago our God-made-Flesh was cast
Onto Calvary's hill, by the angry mob harassed,
The poet, unflinching, though into this world exiled,
Must bear his burden — their offensive villainy.
Could he not exclaim to the cowards who've defiled
       The truth, "*Lamma à Sabactani!*"?[2]

But the selfish crowd, by hysteria set afire,
Would run amok and surely smash his lyre,
As, amidst the bitter waves, the hurricane
Engulfs the Halcyon, this noble prophet-bird
That heralds the storm, when its lengthy cries are heard,
       For fishermen lost on the ocean.

    And yet with melodious sounds
    His sacred harp resounds;
    It foresees and it perceives
    The woe that fate receives.
    How so? It's inspired and blessed
    By a spirit who wishes the best,
    And the poet feels in his breast
    A love unspoiled, of endless worth,
    For he is an angel here on earth,
    From heaven's choir banished.

---

2. This biblical phrase is taken from Jesus's cry on the cross as reported in Gospel of Matthew (27.46): "Eli, Eli, lamma sabachthani!" ("My God, my God, why have You forsaken me?"). This translation reproduces the phrase as it appeared in *La Tribune*: whether the idiosyncratic spelling and inclusion of *à* are deliberate choices or simple mistakes is not clear.

N'est-ce pas lui qui toujours chante
Pour calmer nos vives douleurs,
Et qui par sa voix si touchante
Fait sourire au milieu des pleurs ?
À chaque pas sa tête penche
Et son cœur généreux épanche
Tout ce qu'il renferme de miel ;
Mais la foule impie et brutale,
Dans son ignorance fatale,
Lui verse à grands flots tout son fiel.

N'est-ce pas lui qui sur la terre
Caresse l'enfant au berceau,
Qui le berce, qui le fait taire
D'un baiser lui donnant le sceau ?
C'est que sa voix douce plaintive
Pourrait de sa mère craintive,
Attirer la pieuse foi ;
Mais toujours il est là qui veille ;
La pauvre mère qui sommeille
Peut fermer les yeux sans effroi.

Il a des chants pour la patrie,
Des chants qui réveillent les cœurs,
Et le tyran, l'âme flétrie,
Tremble enfin à ses cris vainqueurs.
Et l'esclave qui dans les chaînes
Gémit sur les rives lointaines,
Entend ces chants avec fierté,
C'est qu'il lui donne l'espérance
De voir terminer sa souffrance ;
Il espère la liberté !

Qui dit au pauvre : confiance,
Il est un meilleur avenir ;
Au riche pervers : méfiance,
L'ange de la mort peut venir.
Oh ! dis, n'est-ce pas le poète
Dont la lyre à chaque heure est prête
À vibrer sous sa noble main.
Un souffle céleste l'anime.
D'un noir destin chaque victime
Est consolée en son chemin.

Is it not he who always sings
To ease whatever pain we feel,
Whose voice, so touching, always brings
Amidst our stinging tears a smile?
At every step his head does tilt,
His heart pours forth, with largesse filled,
Its honey, as wrung from a honeycomb;
But the crowd, immoral and cruel,
Under ignorance's deadly rule,
Upon him spills and spews its venom.

Is it not he who cradles the child
Beside his crib? Who rocks the infant
And then, with a kiss on the forehead sealed,
Makes all things calm and silent?
For his voice's tones, plaintive and soft,
Will stir, when through the air they waft,
The pious faith of his fearful mother;
But always he keeps watch nearby:
The poor mother, when she grows sleepy,
May close her eyes, without a care.

He has songs to sing for his country:
They're songs that cause the heart to stir,
And, before these cries of victory,
The trembling tyrant's soul to wither.
The slave who, languishing in chains,
On some far shore bemoans his pains,
Will hear these songs with proud delight;
They give him hope that soon, indeed,
From suffering he will be freed:
For he can now see liberty's light!

He tells the poor, "Have faith:
The future holds a better path";
To the rich and wicked, "Beware:
The angel of death will soon be here."
Oh, say, is it not the poet
Whose lyre waits, ready and set
To reverberate in his noble hands?
A breath divine inhabits him.
Against fate's dark ways, each victim
Is comforted where'er he stands.

C'est que sa mission est sainte,
Il sait qu'il faut souffrir encor
En passant loin de cette enceinte
Pour arriver jusqu'au Thabor
Qu'il meure en une triste agonie,
Et la phalange d'harmonie,
Et les Séraphins gracieux,
À l'éclat de leurs blanches ailes
Ouvrant les portes éternelles
Lui montreront enfin les cieux.

[publié le dimanche 4 juin 1865]

Hommage au poète

À mon ami le Dr. J. Chaumette

HENRY [Henry Louis Rey]

Quand un barde inspiré par une cause sainte
Fait parler la raison dans un chant solennel ;
Quand au nom du progrès son éloquente plainte
En appelle de l'homme aux lois de l'Éternel,
L'opprimé se rassure et vibre d'espérance ;
Dans ces chantres il voit des messagers divins ;
Le pouvoir, les tyrans en ressentent l'offense,
      Mais l'humanité bat des mains.

Ainsi dans tous les temps, les bienfaiteurs du monde
Quand du « Millénium », sublimes précurseurs,
Ils jettent leurs saints vœux dans une ère inféconde,
Ils ameutent contre eux les ventrus-oppresseurs ;
Mais la raison finit par vaincre l'ignorance,
La liberté par faire un pas plus ferme encor,
Le Droit l'emporte enfin sur l'injuste Puissance
      Et prophétise l'âge d'or.

Mais, toi, chantre immortel des droits sacrés de l'homme !
Tandis que, comme toi, de vrais réformateurs
Étaient mis à l'index par le pouvoir de Rome,
Pour avoir fait briller de sublimes lueurs ;
Ou que bravant les rois, les grands et les empires,
Ils subissaient la mort dans des tourments cruels,
Et laissaient à l'histoire à venger leurs martyres
      En leur élevant des autels ;

His mission is of the sacred kind;
He knows that one must ever suffer
When leaving these bounds far behind
To reach, at road's end, Mount Tabor.[3]
Though he die in doleful agony,
Both the phalanx of harmony
And the graceful seraphim,
With wings glimmering white,
Will open eternity's gates
To offer the skies unto him.

[published Sunday, 4 June 1865]

3. Site in Israel where, according to Christian belief, Jesus became radiant in the company of the ancient Hebrew prophets Moses and Elijah, an episode known as the Transfiguration.

Homage to the Poet

For my friend Dr. J. Chaumette[4]

HENRY [Henry Louis Rey]

When a bard, for a sacred cause demanding redress,
Gives voice to reason by way of solemn song;
When his eloquent complaint, for the sake of progress,
Recalls God's laws and accuses mankind of wrong.
The oppressed take heart and grow in confidence:
They see these defenders as divine messengers;
The powers-that-be, the tyrants take offense,
      But the whole of humanity cheers.

As in all times, when the saviors of the world
Acting as the Millennium's[5] sublime precursors,
Onto this sterile era their vows have hurled,
Against themselves they array pot-bellied oppressors.
In the end, however, reason beats ignorance,
And Liberty boldly moves to its next stage;
The Right will vanquish unjust Dominance,
      And prophecy a golden age.

But you, immortal champion of the sacred rights
Of man! Whereas real reformers and dissidents,
Like you, were once proscribed by Rome's mandates
If they merely let shine their sublime radiance;
Or, defying the might of kings and powers and empires,
They suffered death, to terrible tortures subjected,
But left history to avenge them as martyrs,
      With a shrine to them someday erected;

4. A white Creole physician, Joseph Chaumette had recently written a lengthy poem entitled "Les droits de l'homme" ("The Rights of Man") denouncing slavery and praising universal suffrage. The work was published by *La Tribune*'s press (Roussève 194). Like most newspapers of the era, *La Tribune* had a press, which published convention proceedings, pamphlets, and a range of other (usually political) works.

5. According to Christian eschatology as interpreted from the Book of Revelations, the thousand-year reign of Christ that will precede God's final judgment of humanity.

Toi ! tu n'as rien à craindre en ce siècle où nous sommes.
Il a déjà proscrit tout sacrifice humain,
Le principe absolu contrôlant les royaumes
S'effacera bientôt comme un fantôme vain ;
Sur son trépied sacré, que ta lyre immortelle
Retentisse toujours de Dieu, de liberté,
D'égalité des droits, d'entente fraternelle.
   Et d'amour de l'humanité !

Interprète éloquent d'une race proscrite,
Ne suspends point l'essor de ton luth d'harmonie !
Les méprises ont droit à ton verbe d'élite,
Il leur faut s'abriter sous l'aile du génie ;
Que jamais rien n'arrête, en son cours généreux,
La sainte mission de ta muse si sage,
Jusqu'au moment où Dieu comblera tous nos vœux
   Par l'égalité du suffrage !

Qui donc pourrait douter de notre ère future
De fraternel amour, d'abondance et de paix ?
Dieu ne peut s'endormir au sein de la nature,
Et les temps sont venus de semer ces bienfaits ;
Ce que sa providence a promis de sublime
Se réalisera dans notre nation,
La vertu, le devoir, succéderont au crime,
   La concorde à l'oppression.

Mon nom, par trop obscur, qu'a prononcé ta lyre,
Ne saurait plus périr, désormais, oublié ;
Ton poème immortel que l'indulgence inspire,
Dans ses alexandrins s'en est fait un allié.
Si je ne puis combattre avec toi dans l'arène,
Je pourrai t'applaudir du geste et de la voix
Antée, annihilant tout obstacle qui gêne
   Le divin progrès dans nos lois !

   [publié le dimanche 18 juin 1865]

But you — you have nothing to fear in these times of ours.
Our age has abolished all human sacrifice;
The notion of government by absolute powers
Will vanish soon, leaving but a ghostly trace;
May your immortal lyre's sacred chords,
Forever sing of God, of liberty,
Of equality of rights, of fraternal accord,
      And true love of humanity!

Outspoken defender of a downtrodden race,
Halt not your lute, soaring and harmonious!
Your lofty word must aid erroneous ways,
For the lost need shelter beneath the wing of genius;
Let nothing stop its course on the generous path
Of its holy mission, set out by your muse, a sage,
Until that day when God shall reward our faith
      With the coming of equal suffrage!

Who then can doubt the promise of the future —
The blessings of brotherly love, abundance, and peace?
For God cannot slumber within the bosom of nature,
And the time has come to sow all things that please;
All that Providence shows us to be sublime
Will be bestowed ere long upon our nation.
Virtue and duty will take the place of crime,
      And concord that of oppression.

My name, quite unknown till pronounced by your lyre,
Will never perish nor slip from common remembrance.
Your immortal poem that indulgence did inspire
By force of alexandrines forged an alliance.
Although I cannot join you in the fray,
I shall applaud you and lift my voice, fused to the cause,
As you demolish all obstacles that delay
      Divine progress in our laws!

      [published Sunday, 18 June 1865]

La poésie

À mon ami Lélia D...t

Yacoub [Joseph Mansion]

La poésie, ami, c'est le reflet de l'âme,
Le sublime miroir de la Divinité,
C'est le baiser brûlant que dépose une femme
Sur le front d'un époux quelquefois attristé.
Aux pieds de l'Éternel c'est le rêve de l'ange,
Le murmure du vent dans nos sombres forêts,
Les doux propos d'amour que parfois on échange
      Avec les sylphes égarés.

C'est la voix de l'enfant qui doucement répète
Une sainte prière adressée au Seigneur ;
C'est le frêle roseau qui s'incline et s'apprête
      Au coup du moissonneur.

Au milieu du désert c'est l'ouragan qui passe,
C'est le rire infernal des ombres de la nuit ;
C'est l'aigle vigoureux qui vole dans l'espace
      Comme une ombre qui fuit.

Et puis c'est une enfant, une vierge divine,
C'est un ange envoyé par le Maître Éternel,
Qui vient nous consoler de sa voix enfantine,
Puis s'échappe en riant pour remonter au Ciel.

C'est le hardi marin qui s'élance sur l'onde
Sans craindre le torrent qui peut l'anéantir ;
Habile nautonier, c'est ta nef vagabonde
Que l'océan balance avant de l'engloutir.

Ô douce illusion ! Ô vision étrange !
Ô charme séducteur de mon cœur attristé,
Concert mélodieux qui parfois se mélange
Avec les chants perdus dans cette immensité.

Octobre 1866

                [publié le dimanche 14 octobre 1866]

Poetry[6]

For my friend Lélia D——t

YACOUB [Joseph Mansion]

Poetry, my friend, is the soul's reflection,
The Divinity's mirror casting an image sublime,
The burning kiss that a woman lays upon
Her husband's saddened brow from time to time.
Before the Eternal it is an Angel's dream,
The forest's somber rustling when the winds come to play,
The words of love exchanged from time to time
      With sylphs who've lost their way.

It is a child's voice softly repeating
A holy prayer into the Lord's ear prayed;
It is the fragile reed that bends, conceding
      Beneath the reaper's blade.

It's the hurricane in the midst of the wilderness,
The hellish laughter of shadows in the night,
The powerful eagle soaring o'erhead through space
      Just like a shadow's flight.

And then it's a child, a virgin from Paradise,
An angel sent by our Eternal Master
Who brings solace to us with her childlike voice.
Then escapes to Heaven, letting fall her laughter.

It's the hardy sailor embarking upon the swell,
Not fearing the torrent's annihilating power;
Oh skillful seafarer, it is your wandering vessel
By the ocean tossed and tumbled ere being devoured.

Oh sweet illusion! Extraordinary vision!
Seductive charm of my heart in sadness immersed,
Melodious concert that blends now and then
With songs that have vanished into the universe.

October 1866

      [published Sunday, 14 October 1866]

---

[6]. This poem by "Yacoub" (the pen name chosen by Joseph Mansion, son of Lucien Mansion and soon-to-be member of the Louisiana House of Representatives [1868–72]) generated a number of responses, including the poem that follows ("Poésie! Vox Dei!" by Adolphe Duhart) and an encouraging note sent to *La Tribune* by Armand Lanusse. On this exchange and the intellectual and creative mentoring that characterized the tight-knit Afro-Creole community, see pp. 53–54.

Poésie ! Vox Dei !

À mon ami Yacoub

LÉLIA D... T [Adolphe Duhart]

Pour la première fois ta lyre frémissante
Fait entendre ses sons, sa note ravissante
        Au milieu de nos longs sanglots.
Pour la première fois la douce Poésie
A couronné ton front d'une étoile choisie
        En versant l'harmonie à flots !
Laisse courir tes doigts sur ta lyre inspirée ;
Enivre-toi d'amour — parfums de l'Empyrée —
        Ô fils des harpes d'or du ciel !
Chante encor quand la brume inonde la ravine,
Quand monte la prière à la voûte divine
        Sur les blanches ailes d'Ariel.

N'entends-tu pas sonner à l'horloge lointaine
L'heure de tant d'espoirs, l'heure sainte et certaine
        De la pure Fraternité ?
N'entends-tu pas vibrer ces voix mystérieuses
Qui passent en courbant ces têtes sérieuses,
        Ces voix fortes de Liberté ?

C'est l'heure ! — Lève-toi ! — L'aube qu'on voit éclore
Nous annonce le jour au zénith qu'elle dore.
        Lève-toi ! — C'est l'instant d'agir...
Oh ! regarde ! regarde à l'horizon immense.
Quels feux ! quelles splendeurs ! quel hymne qui commence !
        Lève-toi ! — L'Astre va surgir !

Quel tumulte joyeux vient frapper notre oreille ?
C'est un peuple avili qui maintenant s'éveille.
        Ô poète ! reprends ton luth !
Les carcans sont brisés ! — Plus de honteux servage !
De notre sol enfin disparaît l'esclavage !
        Liberté ! — Liberté — Salut !

Chante donc pour calmer les âmes inquiètes.
Redis[-]nous tous les chants de nos lyres muettes :
        L'avenir apparaît moins noir.
Chante sur un ton pur, prophétique, sonore,
Le soleil ardent qui, bientôt, va luire encore
        Sur nos fronts radieux d'espoir !

Poetry! Vox Dei![7]

For my friend Yacoub

Lélia D——t [Adolphe Duhart]

[7] The title plays on the Latin expression *Vox populi, vox dei* ("The voice of the people is the voice of God").

For the very first time, your lyre, still trembling,
Produced its sounds, its luscious notes assembling
      Amidst our endless tears.
For the very first time, delectable Poetry
Set a star on your brow to guide your artistry
      Through harmony's waters!
Let your fingers dance across your exalted lyre;
Grow drunk on love: let Empyrean's perfumes inspire
      You, of heavenly harps the offspring!
Sing once more when the fog comes to fill the ravine,
When a prayer ascends to the vaults where dwells the Divine,
      Atop Ariel's white wing.

Do you not hear, distantly ringing, the chime
Of the hour of hopes, the sure and sacred time
      Of purest Fraternity?
Do you not hear these enigmatic voices
That speak to heads weighed down with serious choices,
      The forceful voices of Liberty?

It is time! Arise! The dawn that we see breaking
Proclaims on high the golden day that's waking.
      Arise! The time to act is here!
Oh, look yonder! Behold the horizon's expanse . . .
What fires! What wonders! What a psalm they do commence!
      Arise! — The Star will soon appear!

What joyous uproar is it that strikes our ears?
A people, disgraced, awakens from its fears.
      Oh poet! Reclaim your lute!
All fetters are smashed! Servitude's shame shall end!
And slavery will finally vanish from our land!
      Freedom! Freedom we salute!

So sing to soothe those souls filled with disquiet.
Revive the songs of our lyres, fallen quiet:
      The future seems less dark.
In tones prophetic, profound, and pure, now sing
Of the blazing sun which ere long will be shining
      Upon us with hope's spark!

Chante. Tout prête au luth et tout prête au poème,
Depuis le petit grain que la Nature essème [1]
    Sur le sol humide et brumeux,
Jusques au chêne au faîte orgueilleux et superbe,
Jusques au Léviathan se broyant comme l'herbe
    Sous les coups des flots écumeux !

Le poète, en ses chants, est un reflet de l'ange
Que le ciel nous envoie en cette vie étrange
    Pour calmer nos vives douleurs.
Écho triste ou riant, il tient bien haut la lyre,
Et dispense de Dieu le pardon ou son ire,
    La vie ou la mort... et les pleurs !...

14 octobre 1866

    [publié le dimanche 28 octobre 1866]

1. A variant spelling of *essaimer* ("to swarm") — here, "to scatter."

Fiat Lux !

  À Armand Lanusse

Lélia D... t [Adolphe Duhart]

Pour vous les flots amers n'ont point eu de tempête.
L'inflexible destin, jaloux, capricieux,
Rapide passe au loin sans courber votre tête,
Et sans ternir l'éclat de votre étoile aux cieux.

Votre existence, inscrite au livre d'or de fête,
Ne contient pas la page aux chagrins soucieux,
Et chaque heure qui fuit et jamais ne s'arrête
Sonne pour vous un chant toujours délicieux.

Et vous avez pleuré... C'était un jour de rage,
De sinistres moissons, de meurtre et de carnage,
Où des frères le sang rougissait le pavé...

Le ciel s'était voilé sous des ombres funèbres ;
Mais regardez là-bas, au-dessus des ténèbres... ;
Reprenez votre luth, l'astre enfin s'est levé !...

18 novembre 1866

    [publié le dimanche 25 novembre 1866]

All serves the lute, all serves the poem: so sing.
From the tiny grain that Nature's hands fling
    To the damp and foggy ground,
To the oak tree, spreading into a prideful mass,
To Leviathan, shredding itself like grass
    As the waves churn all around!

Through his songs, the poet casts an angel's reflection,
Dispatched by heaven's will in our direction
    To calm our direst woes.
In echoes sad or merry, he holds up his lyre,
Dispensing either God's mercy or his ire,
    Either life or death...and sorrows!...

14 October 1866

    [published Sunday, 28 October 1866]

Fiat Lux! [8]

8. "Let there be light."

For Armand Lanusse

LÉLIA D——T [Adolphe Duhart]

For you the bitter waves have known no storm.
Intractable fate pursues its distant course,
Capricious and jealous, while you've remained firm
And never let fade the star in heaven that's yours.

Your existence, inscribed in the registry of feasts
Does not contain the page of fretful sorrows,
And every hour that passes, never to cease,
For you proclaims a song of lovely tomorrows.

And you've wept as well...It was a day of rage,[9]
Of sinister harvests, of murder and of carnage,
When brothers' blood upon the pavement splashed.

9. Likely a reference to the July 1866 Mechanics' Institute massacre in New Orleans: see pp. 35–42.

The sky concealed itself in solemn shadows;
But look over there, beyond where darkness goes...
And take up your lute, for the star has risen at last!

18 November 1866

    [published Sunday, 25 November 1866]

L'astre s'est levé !

À Lélia D...t

ARMAND LANUSSE

L'astre enfin s'est levé, dites-vous ; mais quel astre
Est-il, ami, venu luire à votre regard ?
Réparateur de maux, de plainte, de désastre,
Doit-il chasser la nuit de notre ciel blafard ?
En vain du firmament j'interroge l'espace,
Rien de nouveau pour moi n'y paraît jusqu'ici ;
À ma vue affaiblie, ô Lélia, de grâce,
Veuillez le désigner, je vous dirai merci...

Est-ce un lumineux signe, un flambant météore
Qui vient dire à Sumner, à Kelley : — Vous vaincrez ?
Est-ce le précurseur de la nouvelle aurore
Des jours d'égalité qu'on nous dit : — Vous aurez ?
De Constantin alors suivons l'antique exemple :
Gravons ce saint objet sur notre labarum :
De ses feux bienfaisants illuminons le temple
De ceux à qui l'on doit un vibrant Te Deum.

Mais n'est-ce pas un point fatal à plus d'un traître ?
Une prédiction pour quelque homme puissant
Qui d'un vaste pays se croyait bien le maître,
Et dont la vanité va rentrer au néant ?
Peut-être est-ce un éclair qui précède la foudre ;
La foudre qui dira bien fort aux spadassins :
« Je descends, je descends pour vous réduire en poudre,
« Vous fûtes sans pitié, malheur aux assassins !... »

Non, dans ce cas perplexe, il est bien mieux de croire,
Lélia, que votre astre est un brillant soleil,
L'emblème glorieux de la page d'histoire
Que produira bientôt un illustre Conseil.
Et puisque parmi nous les maux de l'esclavage
Vont cesser, oublions nos souffrances d'hier ;
Honorons nos martyrs et pardonnons l'outrage,
C'est ainsi que se venge un peuple libre et fier !

Le 30 novembre 1866

[publié le dimanche 2 décembre 1866]

The Star Has Risen!

For Lélia D——t

ARMAND LANUSSE

The star has risen at last, you say[10]; but which star
Has come, my friend, to shine upon your face?
Must it act as a mender of ills, of grief, of disaster,
By chasing the night from our heaven's pallid space?
Although in vain I question the firmament's sphere,
There's nothing new to me that does appear.
To my waning sight, I beg, please make it clear,
Oh Lélia; then my deepest thanks you'll hear …

Is it a luminous sign, a fiery meteor,
To say to Sumner and Kelley[11]: "You will be conquerors"?
Is it the coming dawn's golden precursor
To the days of equality promised: "They'll be yours"?
Let us follow ancient Constantine's example
And engrave this holy object upon our labarum[12]:
With its auspicious fires let's illumine the temple
Of those to whom we owe a lively *Te Deum*.

But does it not prove fatal to many a traitor?
A prediction about some man of power and clout
Who o'er a vast country fancied himself master,
And whose vanity will be reduced to nought?
Perhaps it's the lightning that strikes before the thunder:
That thunder that sternly warns any hired swordsmen:
"I now descend in order to crush you to powder,
For you showed no pity — misfortune on every assassin!"

No, in this puzzling case, it's better by far
To believe that your star is really a shining sun
— A glorious symbol, Lélia, of history's chapter
That's soon to produce a Council of great renown.
And since, in our midst, the ills of slavery
Will cease, let's turn the page on yesterday's misery;
Let's honor our martyrs and pardon all injury,
For that is how vengeance is wrought by a people proud and free!

30 November 1866

[published Sunday, 2 December 1866]

---

10. Lanusse seems to be referring to the star of hope mentioned by Duhart in the previous poem, though we cannot say with certainty that the reference does not allude to other exchanges, in other settings, between the two.

11. Charles Sumner (1811–74), senator from Massachusetts, was a staunch abolitionist and, during Reconstruction, an advocate for the rights of freedmen. In 1856, he was famously assaulted by Representative Preston Brooks of South Carolina after giving a speech denouncing the spread of slavery to Kansas. Benjamin Franklin Kelley (1807–91) raised troops for the federal army in soon-to-be West Virginia before being promoted to the rank of major general.

12. A military standard featuring letters from the Greek name for Christ, first used by the Roman emperor Constantine I (272–337 CE).

Espérance

Lélia D... t [Adolphe Duhart]

> Poète, vous *rêvez, et vous voyez sans doute,*
> Dans vos rêves charmants,
> L'avenir inconnu qu'en secret on redoute
> Dans ce val de tourments.
> — L. M.

Non ! je n'ai pas rêvé ! Non ! ce n'est pas un songe,
    Enfant du paisible sommeil,
Qui révèle à ma lyre, en un charmant mensonge,
    L'aurore à l'Orient vermeil.

La tempête est passée,... et dans la nuit qui tombe,
    En laissant le ciel entrouvert,
Mon regard a suivi dans son vol la colombe,
    Tenant enfin le rameau vert.

Et j'ai souri, joyeux, dans le fond de mon âme
    — Mes pleurs étaient évanouis —
À ce doux messager qui portait le dictame
    Pour calmer nos maux inouïs.

Et, puis, au cœur meurtri si belle est l'espérance,
    Qu'il ne faut pas désespérer.
L'homme serait-il né dans un jour de souffrance
    Pour blasphémer et pour pleurer ?

Le seul but, il est vrai, que le sort lui propose
    Porte l'empreinte du malheur,
Et qu'il ne peut monter sans que son pied ne pose
    Sur l'échelon de la douleur.

La vie est pour nous tous une chose imparfaite :
    Nul n'est heureux, nul triomphant.
Les pleurs brûlent nos yeux même au sein d'une fête
    Et troublent les jeux de l'enfant.

Mais au milieu de l'ombre, au travers de la brume
    Le clair-midi surgit aux cieux,
Et l'oiseau captif jette au dôme qui s'allume
    Ses accords plus harmonieux,

Hope

Lélia D——t [Adolphe Duhart]

> You dream, oh poet, and surely do behold
> In all your dreams' delights,
> The future's secrets, feared though unforetold
> In the valley of our plights.
> — L. M.[13]

No, I didn't dream! No! It's no fantasy,
    Oh child of sleepful rest
Who reveals to my lyre, telling a charming lie,
    The dawn of ruby-colored East.

The storm has passed … and as the night fell o'er
    The sky, still lying half open,
My eye pursued the flight of a dove that bore
    A branch, tender and green.

My tears had dissipated, and I smiled,
    Joyous throughout my soul's expanse,
At this soft messenger bringing a balm to calm
    Our indescribable torments.

And though one's heart be wounded, how alluring
    Is the hope that it must keep.
Might man be born on a day of suffering
    Merely to blaspheme and weep?

It's true: the mark of grief has been engraved
    Upon the goal set out by fate.
To climb at all, onto the rungs of pain
    It's forced to set its feet.

None is happy, none triumphant; for all of us,
    Life's but an imperfect thing:
Our tears disturb our childhood games, and even
    At parties our eyes will sting.

But amidst the shadows, through the fog and the mist,
    The day-bright noon attacks the skies,
And the captive bird throws toward the burning dome
    Its best-tuned harmonies.

---

13. The epigraph comes from Lucien Mansion's poem "L'avenir" (see p. 218 in this vol.), composed in December 1868 and published 1 Jan. 1869 — i.e., a full year after the date Duhart supposedly wrote this poem (3 Jan. 1868, according to the date of composition printed in the original publication). It is possible that Duhart wrote his poem in early 1868 and appended Mansion's brand-new lines as an epigraph just before publishing "Espérance," in January 1869. A more likely sequence of events, however, is that Duhart wrote "Espérance" on 3 Jan. 1869, with Mansion's poem of 1 Jan. fresh in his mind, and then he or the typesetter mistakenly printed "1868" instead of "1869," an error common in January.

Seul, n'ouvrirez-vous pas votre oreille endormie
    À ces profonds ébranlements ?
Et votre luth, écho du sombre Jérémie,
    N'a-t-il que des gémissements ?

Espérez et croyez : Lincoln, nouvelle hostie
    Choisie entre tous les élus,
En ce val d'exil eut son œuvre convertie :
    Il libéra comme Jésus !

Oui, l'Éternel voyant la faiblesse des hommes
    Leur légua ses lois ici-bas.
Le feu du Sinaï dans le gouffre où nous sommes,
    Éclaire chacun de nos pas.

Croyez donc, ô poète ! en ce divin symbole
    Gravé dans tout cœur désolé,
À cet espoir caché dans une parabole :
    « Qui pleure sera consolé ! »

Nouvelle-Orléans, 3 janvier 1868

        [publié le dimanche 17 janvier 1869]

À toi

ASTER [pseudonyme d'un auteur inconnu]

À l'œil droit de Philippe. Ô fils de l'opulence !
Tu veux glorifier le malheur en démence
Lorsque ton coffre est plein, que debout sur ton or,
Tu viens nous faire ouïr ton poétique cor !

Oh ! garde donc pour toi ton marc de poésie !
Car nous avons marqué ta lâche apostasie
Sur l'arène sanglante où nous tombâmes tous,
Où l'avenir verra le sceau de nos genoux !

Ne viens point profaner le seuil du sanctuaire ;
D'autres Dieux ont reçu ta flatteuse prière :
Loin de les renier garde tes dons pour eux ;
Courtise leur puissance, adulateur fiévreux !

Alone, shall you not open your sleeping ear
      To these shocks that cause the ground to shudder?
And has your lute, echoing Jeremy's gloom,
      Only moans left to utter?

Hope and believe: Lincoln, a Host renewed,
      Among the elected, elevated,
In exile's vale, did have his work transformed:
      Like Jesus, he liberated!

Yes, the Eternal One, when seeing men's failings,
      His laws for us decreed.
In the pit where we stand, the fire of Sinai
      Will light the path we tread.

Believe, oh poet, in this symbol divine,
      That's carved in every ravaged heart,
In this hope kept hidden within a parable:
      "Whoever weeps shall be given comfort!"

New Orleans, 3 January 1868

      [published Sunday, 17 January 1869]

To You

ASTER[14] [pseudonym of unknown author]

To Philip's right eye. Oh scion of wealth!
You try to praise misfortune's rotten health,
Whenever, atop your gold-filled coffer borne,
You come to us to sound your poetical horn.

You can keep for yourself those dregs of poetry!
For we have marked your craven treachery
Upon the blood-soaked arena that heard our pleas,
Where the future will find the imprint left by our knees!

Dare not to come profane this sanctuary.
Other gods have received your prayers of flattery:
Your offerings should go to them instead;
Before their power bow your groveling head!

14. The text of the poem and the pen name of its anonymous author are drawn from the story of Aster, a skilled archer of ancient Greece. Tradition holds that, his services having been refused by King Philip II of Macedon, Aster took revenge during the siege of Methone by piercing the king's eye with an arrow, upon which were carved the words, "To Philip's right eye" (Swift Riginos). The poem appears to be targeting a onetime political ally whose support has proved itself merely lip service during Reconstruction.

Quand l'heure était venue où les vaillants courages
Anxieux, te cherchaient au milieu des orages,
Voulant se revêtir au moins de ton appui,
Grand fut leur désespoir, car... Thersite avait fui.

Quand, vaincus dans la lice, après mille batailles,
Nous entendions chanter nos tristes funérailles,
Quand nous buvions à flots l'absinthe de l'affront,
Qu'on nous descendait tous dans un oubli profond,

Toi, qui pouvais sauver notre jeune mémoire,
Toi, tu comptais ton or, renégat de la gloire !
Tu voyais froidement préparer les tombeaux
De ces lutteurs tombés que leur sort rend si beaux !

Enfin, à ce moment de nos adieux suprêmes
Où du monde sur nous, tombaient les anathèmes,
Tu trahis ton devoir : nous t'invoquions encor...
Ton luth resta muet, et ton cœur, sans remord.

Maintenant que, gisant sur nos couches funèbres,
Du noir oubli sur nous s'étendent les ténèbres,
Ah ! laisse-nous dormir dans notre long repos,
Et ne reviens jamais insulter à nos os !

Va brûler ton encens aux autels de l'usure !
Toujours avide, bois le fiel de ton parjure !
Plutôt que de marcher dans tes cendres encor,
Remonte sur ton faîte, adule le veau d'or !

Oui, transfuge, apostat, sur ton faîte remonte !
Remonte avec ton or, remonte avec ta honte !
Efface, si tu peux, de ton piètre blason
La tache de l'opprobre et de la trahison.

Persifle, à mon insu, mon grossier laconisme ;
Affiche impunément un fourbe stoïcisme ;
Comme un piège vivant je suis sur ton sentier ;
Tu trahis, moi, je venge : à chacun son métier.

    [publié le dimanche 28 février 1869]

When came the hour when valor's best and finest,
Attempted to seek you out amidst the tempest,
Though nervous, hoping to cloak themselves in your aid,
How they despaired ... for Thersites[15] had fled.

When, after countless clashes, in battle laid low,
We heard our funeral dirge, mournful and slow,
When the absinthe of disgrace, in gulps, we drank,
When into oblivion, to the last, we sank,

Although you could have saved our memory,
You counted your gold, a renegade from glory!
You stood and callously watched as tombs were prepared
For these fallen warriors whose grandeur fate has declared!

When the time arrived to give our final farewell,
And the world's condemnation upon us fell,
You betrayed your duty: still, we implored your recourse ...
Your lute sat mute, and your heart felt no remorse.

At present, recumbent upon our funeral beds,
The darkness drapes oblivion over our heads.
Grant us eternal respite from our pains,
And never again return to insult our remains!

Let your incense perfume the altars of usury!
Let your greed imbibe the bile of perjury!
Instead of trudging once more through the dust of your ashes,
Go worship that calf whose gold alluringly flashes!

Yes, defector, return to the heights whence you came!
Apostate, go back with your gold, go back with your shame!
If you can, from your paltry coat of arms, erase
The enduring stain of betrayal and public disgrace.

Go ahead: display a deceitfully stoic demeanor;
Deride behind my back my curtness of manner.
Like a living trap, on your path I wait for the kill.
You betray, I avenge: to each his own skill.

[published Sunday, 28 February 1869]

15. In Homer's *Iliad*, Thersites, a commoner, argues against continuing the Trojan War; according to tradition, he was later killed by Achilles.

THE WAR AND RECONSTRUCTION

La guerre et l'avenir

Dialogue entre un Américain et un Étranger

L. DE P. [auteur inconnu]

L'ETRANGER

Après vingt ans passés sur la terre africaine,
Je revois donc encor la rive américaine.
Mais que s'est-il passé ? Pourquoi, de tous côtés,
Tant de fronts soucieux, de regards attristés !
Ce ciel paraît chargé d'éclairs et de tonnerre.
Pourquoi voit-on partout ces appareils de guerre !
Pourquoi tous ces fossés, ces mortiers, ces canons,
Et ces bruits de tambours, de cornets, de clairons ?
Pourquoi ces officiers à la mine guerrière ?
Pourquoi tous ces soldats sur une libre terre ;
Tous ces vaisseaux aux flancs de canons hérissés,
Et ces fauves bateaux de fer tout cuirassés ?
Et toi, Reine du Sud, si gaie et si brillante,
Quand dansait dans ton port une forêt flottante,
Où sont-ils ces vaisseaux par qui tous ces trésors,
Des arts et du commerce arrivaient sur tes bords ?
Et ces Léviathans à la gueule enflammée
Mugissants et jetant des torrens de fumée
Par leurs naseaux dressés ; sur les plantations,
Pourquoi ne vont-ils plus se gorger de cotons ?

L'AMÉRICAIN

C'est que, sur un théâtre où s'agite la foule,
Un grand drame depuis plus d'un an se déroule.
Et ce vaste théâtre a pour voûte le ciel,
Pour acteurs des soldats, pour lustre le soleil,
Il a les champs de dix ou douze États pour scène,
D'hommes un million dans cette immense arène
Sont descendus déjà ; de nouveaux combattants
Viennent pourtant toujours grossir encor leurs rangs.
Quel effroyable choc, quand de rage enflammées
Viennent à se heurter ces terribles armées.

L'ETRANGER

Mon Dieu ! c'est ce pays qui goûta de la paix
Et de la liberté si longtemps les bienfaits,
Lui que j'avais laissé si grand et si prospère,
Que désole aujourd'hui cette effroyable guerre.
Faut-il, hélas ! les voir se déchirer le sein,
Ceux que semblait unir un si puissant lien.

The War and the Future

Dialogue between an American and a Foreigner

L. DE P. [unknown author]

THE FOREIGNER

Having spent twenty years in the African land,
Again I lay my eyes on America's strand.
But what's happening here? Why, in all places,
So many worried brows and saddened faces?
The skies seem heavy with lightning and thunder's roar.
Why are there everywhere machines of war?
Why all these trenches, these mortars, these cannonballs,
And these noises of drums, and bugles' and trumpets' calls?
Why these officers with war in their eyes?
Why all these soldiers where the flag of freedom flies?
These boats with guns that bristle along their flanks
And these fearsome vessels armored with iron planks?
And you, Southern Queen, once dazzling and light of heart
When a forest of masts danced blithely in your port,
Where now are the ships that brought the stores
Of art and commerce unto the river's shores?
And these Leviathans with mouths aflame
That bellow and belch their smoke by the column
Through their flared nostrils: why do they not call on
The plantation in order to feast on cotton?

THE AMERICAN

You see, upon the stage where bustles this crowd,
For more than a year, a drama has played out.
The sky plays the role of ceiling in this theater,
The actors are soldiers, and the sun its chandelier.
It has the fields of a dozen states as a stage,
Where a million men have already begun to engage
In this giant arena; new combatants still
Arrive in steady stream, their ranks to fill.
What a frightening shock when, in a raging crash,
These terrible armies come together to clash.

THE FOREIGNER

My God! This is the country that once grew strong
In peace and enjoyed freedom's fruits for so long,
Which I left behind, prosperous and great,
And which this war threatens to desolate.
Must we, alas, watch against each other fight
Those whom a powerful bond did once unite:

Eux, les fils des soldats qui, chers à la Victoire,
Ensemble ont combattu pour se couvrir de gloire
À Trenton, Bunker's Hill, Germantown, Lexington,
À Princeton, Yorktown, guidés par Washington.
J'aime à me rappeler cette époque critique.
Alors on vit, bravant le lion britannique,
Ce pays se dresser soudain, et ses enfants,
Soldats improvisés, abandonner leurs champs,
Et s'armer pour chasser leur oppresseur inique.
Puis, ces nobles lutteurs au courage héroïque
Firent trembler bientôt cet ennemi puissant.
Le vieux monde observait ce spectacle imposant,
S'étonnant de l'audace, à ses yeux téméraire,
De ce peuple bravant l'arrogance insulaire.
La vieille Gaule alors vit ses fils valeureux
Offrir aux opprimés leur appui généreux.
Jeté dans le plateau, le sabre de la France
En faveur des colons fit pencher la balance.
Le superbe lion par la lutte épuisé,
En dépit de sa force, enfin fut terrassé,
Se laissa museler et rentra dans sa cage
Tout en grinçant les dents et rugissant de rage
Ce peuple libre enfin dès lors put concevoir,
Du plus riche avenir le légitime espoir.
Ah ! depuis qu'il reçut, dans sa virile enfance,
Ce baptême de sang, de gloire et de souffrance,
Quel degré de puissance et de prospérité,
À l'ombre de la paix et de la liberté,
N'avait-il pas atteint ? Oh ! dans les temps antiques
Quel empire ou royaume ou quelles républiques,
Vit-on prendre jamais un si rapide essor !
Et pourtant ce pays devait grandir encor ;
C'est qu'on s'y reposait sous l'arbre au doux ombrage,
À la tête superbe, au frais et vert feuillage,
Sous cet arbre depuis quatre-vingts ans planté,
Et qui, dans sa splendeur et dans sa majesté,
Devant rois et tyrans se dressait comme un spectre,
Prêt à leur arracher leur couronne et leur sceptre.
Qu'il était beau de voir des rivages lointains
Sous son ombre accourir tous ces fiers plébéiens
Fatigués de porter d'humiliantes chaînes,
Ou d'avoir à courber sous des lois inhumaines ;
Car à ces opprimés au cœur endolori
Cette terre toujours offrait un doux abri,
Mais le deuil suit souvent les plus joyeuses fêtes.
Voilà votre ciel pur troublé par les tempêtes.

They, soldiers' sons who, dear to Victory,
Together fought to cover themselves in glory
At Trenton, Bunker Hill, Germantown, Lexington,
At Princeton, Yorktown, guided by Washington.
I like to remember those crucial times bygone.
We saw then, ready to brave the British lion,
This country revolt, and her children, of one mind,
Impromptu soldiers, leave their fields behind
And take up arms to rid of tyrants their land.
These noble fighters, with heroes' valor in hand,
Soon caused to tremble that powerful foe.
The Old World observed this impressive show,
Surprised by the boldness, brash in a sense,
Of this people defying the islanders' arrogance.
Ancient Gaul did see its stalwart sons
Offer the oppressed the generous aid of its guns.
Thrown onto the scale, the saber of France,
In the colonists' favor finally tipped the balance.
The haughty lion, exhausted by the fight,
Was at last laid low despite its might,
Then muzzled and thrust behind the bars of its cage
All while gnashing its teeth and roaring in rage.
This free people could finally embrace
Legitimate hope for a future full of promise.
Ah! Baptized, in its manly infancy,
In a bath of blood, glory, and adversity,
What degree of power and prosperity
At ease in the shelter of peace and liberty,
Did it not reach? Oh! In times of yore,
What republics, what kingdom, or what empire
Were ever known to have ascended higher?
Nevertheless this country would grow yet more;
We used to rest beneath the shade of a tree,
Its head upraised, its foliage green and balmy,
— A tree planted eighty years prior,
And which, in all its majesty and splendor,
O'er kings and tyrants towered like a specter
Ready to rip away their crown and scepter.
How pleased we were to see beneath its shade
Common folk from distant shores seek aid,
Weary of wearing humiliation's chains
Or enduring laws that humanity disdains;
To these oppressed afflicted with wounded hearts
This land gave welcome shelter behind its ramparts,
But grief often follows joyful feasts:
Indeed, the sunny sky soon filled with tempests.

Avez-vous attiré le céleste courroux ?
Quoi ! de si grands maux ont-ils fondu sur vous ?
Pourquoi le ciel, pour lui faire expier quelques crimes,
L'aurait-il donc plongé dans ces profonds abîmes,
Ce peuple dont partout les autres nations
Ne pouvaient qu'admirer les institutions ?

L'AMÉRICAIN

Ah ! ce pays serait république modèle,
S'il avait en tous points voulu rester fidèle
À ces droits proclamés avec solennité,
Et si, tout en vantant si fort la liberté.
Il n'eût pas malgré tout voulu la voir restreinte.

L'ETRANGER

Et comment a-t-il donc pu lui porter atteinte ?

L'AMÉRICAIN

Quoi ! vous le demandez, pourtant vous savez bien
Quelle hideuse plaie il nourrit dans son sein.

L'ETRANGER

Ah ! vous voulez parler de la race africaine
Qui gémit sous le poids de sa cruelle chaîne,
Et que les châtiments, le fouet des commandeurs
Contraignent sans relâche aux plus rudes labeurs.
De ces êtres privés de tous les droits de l'homme,
Qui, placés au niveau de nos bêtes de somme,
Ne boivent qu'à la coupe amère des douleurs,
Qui, labourant ces champs qu'arrosent leurs sueurs
Ne peuvent cependant rien posséder au monde.
Pas même un coin du sol que leur travail féconde.

L'AMÉRICAIN

Ah ! je commence à voir que nous nous rencontrons
Par les élans du cœur, les aspirations ;
Votre raison vous crie aussi que l'esclavage
Et la liberté font un choquant assemblage.
Mais vous pouvez ouvrir votre âme au doux espoir
De voir bientôt briser les fers cruels du noir ;
Car la destruction de toute servitude
Doit être au moins le prix d'une lutte aussi rude.
Dieu ne laissera pas la grande iniquité
Étouffer le progrès, l'esprit de liberté
Qui vont anéantir enfin le despotisme,
Les préjugés de race, et le lâche égoïsme.

What! Have you provoked heaven's wrath?
Have great misfortunes fallen upon your path?
Why would providence, merely annoyed
By minor offenses, thrust into the void
This people whose judicious institutions
Attracted the admiration of all the nations?

THE AMERICAN

Ah! This country a model republic would be
If only it had upheld faithfully
The rights proclaimed with such solemnity,
And if, all while applauding liberty,
It hadn't sought to render it powerless.

THE FOREIGNER

And what did it do to infringe upon it thus?

THE AMERICAN

What! You ask, yet you know it turned a blind eye
To the hideous wound that grew upon its body.

THE FOREIGNER

Ah! You wish to speak of the African race
That groans beneath the weight of its chains' disgrace,
And whom abuse and the whip of the overseer,
Unceasingly compel to the hardest of labor —
Of these beings deprived of all the rights of man,
Who, set at the level of our beasts of burden,
Can only drink from the bitter cup of sorrows,
Whose sweat, as they plow, waters the field's furrows,
Who possess in this world nothing to call their own,
Not even the parcel of land whose soil they've sown.

THE AMERICAN

Ah! I'm starting to see that we share one goal
By our aspirations and stirrings of the soul;
Your reason exclaims to you that slavery
And freedom make for shocking company.
But now you can open your mind to the hope unspoken
Of soon seeing the black man's fetters broken;
Indeed, by destruction of all servitude
Must such a vicious struggle as this conclude.
God won't permit a great iniquity
To smother progress and the spirit of liberty
That will at last demolish despotism,
Racial prejudice, and gutless egotism.

Ne fixons pas des yeux troublés sur l'avenir :
Notre sombre horizon doit bientôt s'éclaircir.
Si dans ces temps d'épreuve il faut que ma patrie
Se torde et se débatte, et saignante et meurtrie,
Nous verrons se calmer ces agitations,
Tous ces déchirements et ces convulsions ;
Nous verrons revenir la paix et l'harmonie :
La grande nation doit être encore unie.
Et lorsque de ses plis nous aurons effacé
La tache qui blessait les yeux dans son passé,
Notre noble bannière, exempte de souillure,
Flottera dans les airs et glorieuse et pure.

[publié le mercredi 5 novembre 1862]

Le capitaine André Caillou et ses compagnons d'armes

Air : Un Haïtien n'agit pas de la sorte

E. H. [Émile Honoré]

Quoi ! vous pleurez le brave capitaine,
Dont la valeur étonnera Port Hudson !
Mais en tombant sans abri dans la plaine
Il abattit un indigne soupçon.
Consolons-nous, nous, hommes de sa race,
Devant Dieu seul il courbait le genou.
Que Blancs et Noirs suivent la noble trace
      Du brave André Caillou. (*Bis.*)

Oui, c'est parmi les boulets, la mitraille
Que ce héros, au front noir et si fier,
Guide ses pas, conduit dans la bataille,
Ses frères noirs, braves comme le fer !
C'est au milieu des balles ennemies,
Sifflant la mort, et la portant partout,
Que ses soldats, possédant mille vies,
      Suivent André Caillou ! (*Bis.*)

Dieu, quelle ardeur ! quel sublime courage !
Sans nul appui, dans ce sanglant combat,
Ils font trembler l'ennemi dans sa rage ;
Banks reconnaît les sauveurs de l'État !

Let's not look to the future with troubled eyes:
Soon o'er our dark horizon the sun will rise.
Even if, through these trials, my country, abused,
Must writhe and wriggle, bloody and battered and bruised,
In the end we'll live to see this turmoil abate,
As well as all these rifts that agitate;
We'll see the return of peace and harmony:
When this great nation restores its unity.
And when from its folds we shall have erased
The stain that wounded the eyes within its past,
Our noble banner, from all blemish secure,
Will wave on high, glorious and pure.

[published Wednesday, 5 November 1862]

Captain André Caillou and His Comrades-in-Arms [16]

To the tune of "Un Haïtien n'agit pas de la sorte" [17]

E. H. [Émile Honoré]

What's this? You weep for the brave captain
Whose worth will astonish Port Hudson!
But when he fell on that naked plain,
He laid to rest a vile suspicion.
Let us take heart, we men of his race;
Before God alone did he deign to bow.
May whites and blacks follow the noble ways
      Of courageous André Caillou. (*Bis.*)

Yes, there, amidst bombs and bullets' spray,
This hero, of countenance black and proud,
Guided the way, through the battle's fray,
For his black brothers, with iron courage endowed!
There, facing the fire of the enemy's lines,
As death whistled by, in fullest view,
His soldiers, reborn a thousand times,
      All followed André Caillou! (*Bis.*)

My God, what ardor! What lofty courage!
Without any aid in this bloody combat,
They cause the foe to quiver in rage;
Then Banks salutes the saviors of our state!

---

16. The body of the Civil War hero André Cailloux, slain during the Union's 27 May 1863 assault on the Confederate stronghold of Port Hudson (see pp. 27–28 and 49–50), was still rotting on the battlefield when this poem was written (Confederate sharpshooters would not allow anyone to approach the dead). Cailloux's body would not be recovered until August, at which time a public funeral would be conducted by the schismatic abolitionist priest Paschal Maistre. The irony of the poem's being published on US Independence Day would not have been lost on its audience.

17. The song title translates as "A Haitian Does Not Act This Way." Whether or not the song has a specific relation to Cailloux or to the poet is not clear. However, the poet's choice to invoke its melody and meter suggests that the audience could be expected to be familiar with the song and attests to Haiti's perennial presence in Creole social circles.

Six fois, ce jour, ils tentent la victoire :
Mille canons les écrasent partout...
Ces nobles morts, au séjour de la gloire !
  Suivent toujours Caillou ! (*Bis.*)

Ô Liberté ! notre mère, contemple
Ce que pourront désormais tes enfants !
Le doute a fui ; pour eux s'ouvre ton temple,
Et l'Union peut compter sur les temps.
Vaincus bientôt les indignes rebelles,
Hommes de sang de ta grandeur jaloux,
Disparaîtront, ou te seront fidèles
  Par cent mille Cailloux ! ! ! (*Bis.*)

    [publié le samedi 4 juillet 1863]

Votre temps est passé !

Ode lyrique
Dédiée à M. le major-général N. P. Banks
Commandant le département du Golfe
À son départ pour l'expédition de Port-Hudson

[anonyme]

 I
Union sainte ! Une nouvelle aurore
De l'avenir va féconder tes champs !
La liberté que l'univers adore,
Grandit notre âme et réveille nos chants ;
Aux aquilons le ciel vous abandonne,
Honteux soutien d'un système insensé ;
Contre vos lois l'univers entier tonne.
La foudre a lui... Votre temps est passé !

 II
La liberté, cette vierge immortelle,
Du Sud enfin va calmer les douleurs ;
Cet ange pur, à ses martyrs fidèle,
Sur leurs tombeaux vient effeuiller des fleurs.
Vous qui du pauvre éternisiez les peines,
Devant le crime avez-vous balancé ?
Pour le Lion vos mains forgeaient des chaînes :
Il a rugi... Votre temps est passé !

Six times they charged for victory;
A thousand cannons shot them through . . .
These hallowed dead in the house of glory
    Still follow André Caillou! (*Bis.*)

Oh Liberty, our mother, behold
All that your children can henceforth do!
You open to them your sacred fold,
For the Union's doubts have proven undue.
Soon vanquished, these unworthy rebels —
Thirsty for blood, of your greatness jealous —
Will vanish, or will become loyal,
    By a hundred thousand Caillous! (*Bis.*)

[published Saturday, 4 July 1863]

Your Time Has Passed! [18]

A lyric ode
Dedicated to Major N. P. Banks
Commanding the Department of the Gulf
Upon his departure for the expedition at Port Hudson

[anonymous]

I

Oh holy Union! A brand new dawn
Will fertilize the future's fields!
Our songs awake, our soul is drawn
To liberty, to whose love the cosmos yields.
To the wind the sky abandons your cause
In shameful support of a system unjust;
The universe rebukes your laws.
The thunder has flashed . . . Your time has passed!

II

Liberty, that Virgin immortal,
Will finally soothe the South's wounds.
This pure angel, ever faithful,
Will scatter blooms on her martyr's tombs.
Though oft you stretched the sentences of poor men,
Is there no crime you've not amassed?
Your hands forged fetters for the Lion,
But now he roars . . . Your time has passed!

18. The dedication and the date of composition suggest that this poem was written before the Siege of Port Hudson, which lasted from 22 May to 9 July 1863. However, the poem was published more than two months later, suggesting that the outcome of the battle, a crucial engagement in the Union's Red River campaign, might have influenced the final version submitted to *La Tribune*.

III

Nos vétérans, revoyant leur bannière,
Ont répandu des larmes de bonheur :
Nos citoyens ont franchi la barrière
Pour s'assembler sous son blason d'honneur.
Hommes vendus à l'esclavage impie,
Son astre faux soudain s'est éclipsé.
La trahison par l'opprobre s'expie :
Dieu vous punit... Votre temps est passé !

IV

Mortels déchus que le néant demande,
Que vos beaux jours ont d'horribles revers !
Infortunés, votre douleur est grande :
N'emportez pas nos reproches amers.
La liberté vous offrait son égide.
Mais votre orgueil se sentit offensé :
Vous grandissiez en la prenant pour guide.
Allez en paix... Votre temps est passé !

V

Hélas ! du Sud la jeunesse éperdue
Quitte en pleurant le doux sein maternel.
Noirs conseillers, vous qui l'avez perdue,
Soyez rongés d'un remords éternel !
En vain courbés sous la botte étrangère
De vos fronts vils l'orgueil s'est abaissé,
Hommes sans cœur qui vendez votre mère,
Honte sur vous !... Votre temps est passé !

VI

Entendez-vous l'Europe bâillonnée
Dire bien bas : « Enfin, voilà leur jour » ?
Voyez les grands dans leur sphère agitée,
S'ils sont puissants, les pauvres ont leur tour.
Fuyez, tyrans !... L'Union rajeunie
Dit à Mammon, par son glaive percé :
« Place aux vertus à la gloire, au génie !
« Place à l'honneur !... Votre temps est passé ! »

VII

Pour tous ces fils, dont l'avare folie,
Malgré l'honneur de leur lointain guéret,
Les fit pencher pour l'Aristocratie
Qui veut fonder la Noblesse du fouet,

III

Our veterans, seeing their banner again,
In joy were shedding tear upon tear;
The blockade has been crossed by our citizens
As they gather beneath its shield of honor.
Those men enthralled to unholy slavery,
Whose phony star has been eclipsed,
Will pay with disgrace for their treachery:
You're punished by God ... Your time has passed!

IV

Ye fallen mortals claimed by the void,
What dreadful defeats have despoiled your days!
Unfortunate souls whom pain has destroyed,
Don't carry with you my reproachful phrase.
The aegis of Freedom was offered to you,
But your pride felt an insult had been cast:
With her as your guide, to adulthood you grew.
Go ye in peace ... Your time has passed!

V

Alas! The South's tormented youth
In tears desert their mother's sweet breast.
Ye dark advisers who've debased the truth,
Be gnawed by remorse in your eternal rest!
In vain bent under the heel of another,
Down from your brow has your pride been cast;
Ye heartless men who sell your mothers,
May shame be upon you ... Your time has passed!

VI

Do you hear now Europe, by gag repressed,
As she whispers, "At last their day's begun"?
Behold the lords, in castles distressed:
Despite their might, the poor will rise up soon.
Take flight, ye tyrants! The Union made new
Proclaims to Mammon, by its blade pierced:
"Make way for glory, talent, and virtue!
Make way for honor! Your time has passed!"

VII

To all those sons whose greedy folly,
Renouncing the soil's stewardship,
Inclined them toward Aristocracy,
Enthroning the Majesty of the whip,

Sois indulgente ô patrie et pardonne...
Sur eux la honte, et que ce soit assez...
À leurs enfants comme autrefois redonne,
Pour l'avenir, les leçons du passé !

    VIII

D'un flot jaloux qui se dépêche et roule
Vers les emplois, les places, les faveurs,
Que le pouvoir sache arrêter la foule
Et distinguer les loyaux des jongleurs.
Oui, d'Israël viendrait la fin dernière
Si le Lion au vil intéressé
Ne dit bientôt, lui montrant sa crinière ;
« Allez en bas... Votre temps est passé ! »

    IX

Vous étrangers, vous citoyens de France,
Dont les destins aux nôtres sont liés,
À raffermir cette sainte alliance
Par l'Éternel vous êtes conviés,
Quatre-vingt-neuf, pour ranimer tes fibres !
De Rome il faut que les fils soient cassés.
Enfants du Christ, comme lui soyez libres !
Or c'en est fait... Vos destins sont passés !

    X

Grands généraux de notre République,
Et citoyens quels que soient vos partis,
Le monde ancien convoite l'Amérique :
Oubliez tout, redevenez amis !
Sinon, aidé du pouvoir janissaire
Qui doit sous lui vous livrer terrassés,
Double vampire, en son bec et sa serre
S'il vous étreint, vos destins sont passés !

    XI

Sous les traits de César l'esprit du Mal s'avance,
Délégué d'Escobar et des Rois du Festin,
Pour changer l'Union en un vaste butin...
Mais l'Aigle américain, a mis dans la balance
La bannière étoilée et le fer de Yorktown,
        De victoire et de résistance
        Ces gages donneront le ton !

Be clement, oh Country, and do forgive . . .
May they know shame . . . That's all that's asked.
To their children you will surely give,
For our future, lessons drawn from the past!

VIII

May the powers that be restrain the deluge
Of the crowd that hurries madly toward
Employment, offices, patronage —
And distinguish the loyal from the wayward.
For Israel would soon no longer remain
If, to the jealous, drunk with self-interest,
The Lion did not shake its mane,
And say, "Go down . . . Your time has passed!"

IX

Ye foreigners, citizens of France,
Whose fate is bound unto our own:
To fortify our holy alliance,
You're called by the Eternal One.
Awaken 'eighty-nine[19] in memory:
From Rome we must sunder all ties, to the last.
Ye children of Christ, like him be free!
For it is done . . . Your fates have passed!

19. The year 1789 is a reference to the French Revolution and its legacy.

X

Great generals of this Republic of ours
And citizens, rather than partisans,
The Old World covets America's powers:
Forget everything and learn to be friends!
Or else, with the help of Janissaries[20]
Obeying orders to cut you down,
In beak and claw, a vampire twice,
He'll seize you up; your fate will be done!

20. In the Ottoman Empire, elite guards recruited among Christians converted to Islam.

XI

Disguised as Caesar, the spirit of Evil does advance,
Dispatched by Escobar and the Kings of the Feast[21]
To transform the Union into a treasure chest . . .
But America's Eagle has set on the balance
The star-spangled banner and the steel of Yorktown:
    For victory and for resistance,
      These symbols shall surely set the tone!

21. Antonio Escobar y Mendoza (1589–1669) was a Spanish Jesuit whose theological positions on matters of morality earned him a reputation of laxism. Several French writers used Escobar's name to mean someone who makes up rules for his or her own advantage.

XII
Gages sacrés ! Sur nous veille l'Archange
Qui fut jadis l'auteur de vos exploits ;
Et les esprits des chefs de la phalange
De Colombie et des braves Gaulois
Sont avec lui !... Washington, Lafayette
Le grand Kosciusk, Rochambeau le sensé,
Du sein brillant de leur belle planète
Disent des rois : « Que leur temps soit passé ! »

XIII
Et par nos chants ils prédisent : Victoire !...
Comme jadis aux populations
Qui sous nos aigles chercheront la gloire
Dieu bénira leurs générations,
Les comblera de bonheur, de génie,
Et de son bras le méchant terrassé,
De l'Union redoutant l'harmonie,
Dira : « Malheur ! Notre temps est passé ! »

Nouvelle-Orléans, le 2[2?] avril 1863

[publié le samedi 19 septembre 1863]

Le 13 avril

LÉLIA D... T [Adolphe Duhart]

Le jour pâlit, expire. Et la lune sanglante
Éclaire à peine encor de sa lueur tremblante
      Un ciel entouré de brouillards.
Tout se tait. C'est la nuit avec ses ailes sombres,
Couvrant comme un linceul la ville de ses ombres.
      Tout disparaît à nos regards...

Tout à coup, au milieu de ce triste silence,
Un bruit confus s'élève, une clameur s'élance,
      Parcourt les airs épouvantés.
Quel tumulte effrayant !... quelle voix lamentable !...
Au meurtre !... à l'assassin !... ô crime épouvantable !...
      Dit la foule de tous côtés.

XII

Oh sacred wages! The archangel, once
The doer of our deeds, keeps watch o'er us,
And the ghosts of the chiefs of the legions
Of Columbia[22] and the Gauls, still fearless,
Are with him! Washington, Lafayette,
The great Kościuszko, Rochambeau[23] steadfast,
From the radiant heart of their beautiful planet
Do say of kings, "May their time be passed!"

XIII

And our songs will foretell, "Victory!"
As long ago, to the earth's populations
Beneath our eagles seeking glory.
Our God will bless their generations
And grant them talent and contentment.
Then the wicked slain by him at last,
Alarmed by the Union's reconcilement,
Will cry out, "Woe! Our time has passed!"

New Orleans, 2[2?] April 1863

[published Saturday, 19 September 1863]

22. The United States.

23. Tadeusz Kościuszko (1746–1817), a Polish-Lithuanian military officer, and Jean-Baptiste Donatien de Vimeur, count Rochambeau (1725–1807), a French general, both took part in the American Revolution.

The 13th of April

LÉLIA D——T [Adolphe Duhart]

The day grows pale, then dies. And the moon, bloodwashed,
Now barely casts its trembling glow upon
      A fog-enveloped sky.
Now all is hushed. There are but night's dark wings,
A shroud of shadows covering the town.
      All vanishes from the eye …

Then suddenly, amidst this saddened stillness,
A commotion erupts, a clamor starts and spreads,
      Streaks, frightened, through the air.
What an awful din! … What a melancholy voice!
"It's murder! …" "Assassin! …" "Oh horrendous crime! …"
      The crowd cries everywhere.

Que s'était-il passé dans cette nuit profonde ?
Qui frappe ainsi de crainte et d'effroi tout ce monde,
      Tremblant de rage et de terreur ?
Dans tous les yeux l'on voit couler d'amères larmes.
Qui peut causer ces cris, ces plaintes, ces alarmes
      Et ces frémissements d'horreur ?...

❖

Le jour vint dissiper cette nuit de ténèbres...
Partout le canon gronde, et les cloches funèbres
      Révèlent au peuple éperdu,
Brisé de désespoir et demandant vengeance,
Un horrible attentat, un crime affreux, immense.
      Abraham Lincoln est perdu !...

Assassiné, frappé par un traître... — Le lâche
Ne sentit pas l'horreur de cette infâme tâche.
      Oh ! ce fut un triste réveil !...
Un deuil universel entoura l'Amérique ;
La Liberté pleura ce crime atroce, inique ;
      Au ciel se cacha le soleil...

Il n'est plus ! mais son nom appartient à l'histoire.
Son nom environné de respects et de gloire,
      Son nom à jamais vénéré
Ira, du Nord au Sud, apporter l'espérance
À celui qui, tombant de douleur, de souffrance,
      Avait longtemps désespéré...

Pleurez incessamment... pleurez celui qui tombe,
Votre Libérateur descendu dans la tombe.
      Natifs, vous tous, cœurs pleins de foi !...
Oh ! pleurez sur celui dont la mort vous sépare,
Sur celui qui s'en vint, comme Christ à Lazare,
      Vous dire : Esclave, lève-toi !

Il n'est plus. Mais sa chute a fait trembler la terre...
Il est tombé, cet homme à l'esprit juste, austère,
      Cet illustre Législateur.
Il n'est plus... Pleurons tous ce sublime génie
Qui, comme Washington, eut son heure bénie...
      Pleurons le grand Libérateur.

Just what had happened in the depth of night?
What strikes the people with such fright and fear,
      With rage and trembling terror?
In their eyes we see the swell of bitter tears.
What causes these shouts, these moanings, these alarms,
      And these shudderings of horror?

❖

The day now comes to dispel the darkness of night ...
While cannons roar all 'round, the funeral bells
      Announce the people's dread.
Broken by sorrow, they cry out for revenge
Against an odious deed, a crime immense:
      Abraham Lincoln is dead!

Struck down by an assassin's hand ... — The coward
Feels not the horror of his heinous act.
      Oh, 'twas sad to wake that day!
America sank into universal grief;
Liberty mourned that wicked, horrid crime.
      In the sky the sun hid away ...

He is no more! But history owns his name.
His name, all wrapped in respect and in renown,
      His name, forever revered,
Will go, from North to South, to carry hope
To him who, burdened by suffering and pain,
      Has for too long despaired ...

Unceasingly weep ... weep for him who falls,
Your Liberator laid into his grave,
      Ye natives, hearts of worth.
Oh! Weep for him whom death has stolen away,
For him who came, like Christ to Lazarus,
      To tell you, "Slave, come forth!"

He is no more. But his fall has shaken the earth ...
He has fallen, this man of just and austere soul,
      This brilliant Legislator.
He is no more ... Let us mourn this genius sublime,
Who, like Washington, had his blessed hour ...
      Let us mourn the Liberator.

Il n'est plus ! mais le peuple en pleurs qui l'examine
Dira dans l'avenir quels honneurs il destine
  À celui qui vient de partir.
Et ce n'est pas à nous, faible et petit atome
Jeté par le Destin, à juger ce grand homme,
  Régénérateur et martyr !

    [publié le mardi 25 avril 1865]

Washington et Lincoln

HENRY TRAIN

Washington et Lincoln ! Le burin de l'histoire
De ces noms immortels sera le protecteur.
Illustres héritiers d'une commune gloire,
L'un fit un grand pays, l'autre en fut le sauveur.

Dans tous les libres cœurs de l'un à l'autre pôle,
Vous vivrez, noms chéris, grands et sacrés pour tous,
Rayonnant tous les deux dans la même auréole,
La liberté, pleurant sur votre urne, à genoux.

Le courage de l'un fonda la république,
Du progrès sa sagesse assura les bienfaits ;
L'autre assassiné meurt du coup d'un fanatique,
Fécondant par son sang le sol libre à jamais !

    [publié le mercredi 17 mai 1865]

La rébellion du Sud en permanence

Réponse à un ami qui me demandait si ma muse était muette

HENRY [Henry Louis Rey]

Oui, ma muse est muette en ces jours d'épouvantes ;
Lorsque l'esclavagisme épanche en vain son fiel,
Lorsque du Roi Coton les dignes sycophantes,
De leurs immondes vœux, importunent le ciel,
Que pourrait-elle faire et que doit-elle dire ?
Sa mission d'amour, de paix, de vérité,
Lui permet-elle, ami, d'exécrer, de maudire
Ces lâches oppresseurs de toute humanité ?

He is no more! But the people, after their tears,
Will proclaim in the future for him who has just gone
    A fitting tribute of honor.
And it is not for us — trifling atoms
Flung forth by Fate — to judge a man so great,
    Regenerator and martyr!

        [published Tuesday, 25 April 1865]

Washington and Lincoln

HENRY TRAIN

Washington and Lincoln! The chisel of history
Of these immortal names will serve as protector.
Illustrious heirs of a jointly held glory,
One founded a country, the other was its savior.

In all free hearts, on shores both far and near,
Your sacred names, belov'd by all, will dwell,
Shining from the same celestial sphere
While, to weep o'er your urn, Liberty comes to kneel.

The courage of one of them founded the Republic;
His wisdom ensured that our progress will not spoil.
The other was slain by the hand of a fanatic,
His blood forever watering freedom's soil!

        [published Wednesday, 17 May 1865]

The South's Unending Rebellion

In reply to a friend who asked me if my muse had fallen silent

HENRY [Henry Louis Rey]

Yes, my muse is mute in these days of fright,
When slavery pours out in vain its spite,
When the Cotton King's honorable slanderers
Contaminate the heavens with impure prayers,
What could she do? What could she even say?
Does her mission of love, of truth, of harmony,
Allow her, my friend, to curse and to decry
These craven oppressors of humanity?

Quand la presse est vendue à l'or de l'esclavage,
Quand le spectre du Sud, sans vergogne et sans peur,
Ajoute à ses forfaits l'universel outrage
D'armer la barbarie au profit de l'erreur,
Pour combattre le Nord, dont, à ses yeux, le crime
Est d'être à tout jamais l'asile respecté
De tous les libres cœurs que l'arbitraire opprime,
Et ton sacré refuge, ô sainte liberté !

Quand ce Sud réfractaire où l'horrible domine,
Condamné par le ciel, la raison, le devoir,
Vaincu, déshonoré, dans sa lutte intestine
Pour son indépendance et le cruel pouvoir
D'étendre l'esclavage et de river les chaînes
De frères, comme tous, fils d'un Père éternel.
Doués, comme les blancs, de facultés humaines,
Et comme eux animés du rayon immortel ;

Quand ce Sud, qui portait sur sa cotte de maille :
« Esclavage des noirs et licence pour nous »,
N'est pas plutôt vaincu sur le champ de bataille,
Qu'il essaie au scrutin, de son pouvoir jaloux,
D'annuler, par le dol, ce que la Providence,
Par arrêt du canon, a déjà décrété :
« Rivons les fers, dit-il, par rebelle ordonnance,
Et torturons les noirs suspects de loyauté. »

Voilà pourquoi ma muse est muette et voilée,
Car elle pressent bien plus d'un nouveau combat,
Et l'espérance, ami, de son sein envolée,
La laisse morne et triste et son destin l'abat.
Quoiqu'on fasse, mon luth ne peut vibrer de rage,
Il prêche la concorde et la fraternité ;
Aux opprimés, il dit : « Frères, debout, courage,
L'heure est près de sonner, sauvez la liberté ! »

[publié le dimanche 24 septembre 1865]

When the press is sold wholesale to slavery's gold,
When the Southern specter, lacking shame or fear,
Compounds its wicked ways with an outrage as bold
As arming barbarity to fight for error,
To combat the North, whose only crime, we've guessed,
Is always offering open sanctuary
To all free hearts by inequity oppressed
And your sacred refuge, oh holy liberty!

When this South of ours, defiant, controlled by horror,
Condemned by heaven, by reason, and by duty,
Conquered, dishonored in internecine war
For sovereignty and the brutal capacity
To spread enslavement and set in chains their brethren —
The Eternal Father's sons, like all below,
And blessed, like whites, with faculties most human,
Possessing, just like them, an immortal glow.

When the South, who bore upon its plates of mail,
"Slavery for blacks, for us reprieve,"
No sooner on the battlefield did fail,
It tried by vote its power to retrieve,
To cancel, through willful misrepresentation,
What God by cannon's judgment did decree:
"Let's fasten their chains, by rebel proclamation,
And torture blacks suspected of treachery."

And that is why my muse does silent stay:
For she foresees much more than war renewed,
And hope, my friend, from her now flown away
Has left her in despair, by fate subdued.
Do what we will, my lute can know no rage;
It preaches goodwill and sings fraternity;
To the oppressed, it says, "Brothers, stand in courage,
The hour soon will toll: we must save liberty!"

[published Sunday, 24 September 1865]

Extrait de *Jeanne d'Arc : trilogie nationale* (1846), par Alexandre Soumet, recopié, modifié, et publié dans *La Tribune* sous le titre :

Combat de l'Aigle Républicain et du Copperhead

Pour la *Tribune de la Nouvelle-Orléans*

[attribué dans *La Tribune* à « A. », probablement Victor Eugène Macarty]

Un grand aigle, englouti dans l'orbe d'un reptile,[2]
Traînant le poids sanglant de son aile inutile,
Frémit de voir descendre au niveau du serpent
Les périls sinueux de son combat rampant,
Sillonne les rochers, sent dans sa forte serre,
Comme une onde qui fuit, glisser son adversaire,
Et, nuage poudreux, le sable des déserts
De son œil en colère aveugle les éclairs.
Il roule, il ne voit plus l'ennemi qui l'assaille ;
Sa plume se déchire aux dards de la broussaille ;
Et déjà le reptile, aux triples nœuds d'airain,
Lui cède la moitié de son nid souterrain :
Mais l'aigle, en imprimant une plus large entaille,
Dans son empire à lui lance enfin la bataille ;[3]
Soudain, loin de la terre aux périls décevants,
Il appuie à plein vol sa force sur les vents...[4]
Malheur à son rival dans l'azur diaphane !
L'aigle rampait. Il faut que le reptile plane !
Il faut que l'ennemi, convulsif et sifflant,
Expire sans combattre ou combatte en volant.
Il faut, tout éperdu, qu'il prolonge la guerre,
Sans gonfler ses poisons des fanges de la terre.
Un bec infatigable arrache, plis à plis,
Du dragon écaillé les orbes assouplis,
Et s'élevant toujours sur la route inconnue,
Le monstre est expirant lorsqu'il touche la nue.
Loin de son antre obscur enfin il se débat ;
Le soleil à son tour vient juger le combat ;
La victoire attend l'aigle au berceau du tonnerre ;
Sa lutte est un festin qu'il destine à son aire ;
Et du pic élevé de la roche on peut voir
Des débris de serpent sur ses aiglons pleuvoir !

[publié le dimanche 23 septembre 1866]

2. This text is an excerpt from part 2, *chant premier*, of Soumet's verse drama (137–38). The first two lines have been modified so as to give the impression of a coherent poem. The passage in Soumet's *Jeanne d'Arc* reads, "Tel un aigle englouti dans l'orbe d'un reptile, / Traine le poids sanglant de son aile inutile [...]."

3. "A." has changed this couplet's syntax slightly to form a complete sentence. Soumet's text reads, "Mais si l'aigle, imprimant une plus large entaille, / Dans son empire à lui peut lancer la bataille."

4. In Soumet's original text: "S'il peut, loin de la terre aux périls décevants, / Appuyer à plein vol sa force sur les vents [...]."

Excerpt from *Joan of Arc: National Trilogy* (1846), by Alexandre Soumet, copied, modified, and republished in *La Tribune* as:

The Clash of the Republican Eagle and the Copperhead [24]

For the *New Orleans Tribune*

[attributed in *La Tribune* to "A.," probably Victor Eugène Macarty]

A great eagle, entangled in a reptile's ring
And dragging the bloody weight of its useless wing,
Shudders to see descend to the serpent's level
The sinuous perils besetting his crippled struggle,
Traverses the rocks, and feels in his talons' clasp,
Like a passing wave, his enemy slip from his grasp;
The desert sands, climbing in a dusty cloud,
Soon blind his eyes, filled with anger unbowed.
He fitfully rolls and reels in the thorny brush
Which shreds his feathers, and sees not the enemy's rush.
Already, the reptile, in iron knots all dressed,
Has yielded to him half of his underground nest,
But the eagle, cutting an even deeper gash,
Sets on his own terrain the terms of their clash;
Abruptly, far from the earth's disheartening threats,
With the fullest force of his will to fly, he greets
The winds ... Woe to his foe in the crystalline azure:
The eagle once crawled; the reptile in turn must soar!
The enemy must perish without a fight,
Hissing and writhing, or else combat mid-flight.
Though frantic and frenzied, he must prolong the fray,
Resigned to run out of poison to finish his prey.
An untiring beak detaches, one by one,
The supple scales of the soon-to-be-skinned dragon,
And, rising still along this highway unknown,
He'll soon face death in the sky's upper zone.
His struggle will end far away from his lair,
As the sun now comes to judge how each will fare.
The eagle's triumph awaits where the thunder is released;
For his home this battle's outcome will yield a feast,
And there rains down from the rocky heights
Bits of serpent flesh upon his eaglets!

[published Sunday, 23 September 1866]

24. On the literary hoax involving the poet "Antony," see pp. 31–35. The copperhead is a venomous North American snake that in the 1860s was the namesake of a faction of Northern US Democrats who opposed the Civil War and were suspected by some of treasonous aims. By changing the text's generic serpent into a copperhead, the new title presents the excerpted 1840s patriotic French drama as a Civil War–era US text. Adding "For the *New Orleans Tribune*" in the next line furthers the deception, telling the reader that the poem was written for express publication in the paper. On the small modifications made to allow the excerpt to stand alone as a poem, see notes on the facing page.

Aux conservateurs

JOANNI QUESTI [5]

Mes chers Conservateurs, que le ciel vous conserve !
Moi, qui vous aime en frère et que vous n'aimez pas,
Je voudrais vous sauver du sort qu'il vous réserve
Si vous continuez d'inutiles combats.

Pensez-y : le Progrès dans son rapide élan,
Sous un niveau de fer égalisant deux races,
Veut que le nègre soit concitoyen du blanc
Et qu'ils aient tous les deux des droits aux mêmes places.

Vous avez vu tomber vos rêves orgueilleux,
Vos sinistres projets contre la République ;
Dans l'exil, en prison vos chefs ambitieux
Ne se nourrissent plus d'un espoir chimérique.

Ils savent que leur cause est à jamais perdue
Et que, pour châtiment de leur témérité,
Tout chargés du remords de l'avoir défendue,
Ils descendront honnis dans la postérité.

Et c'étaient des géants ces chefs esclavagistes !
Ils avaient le génie et la puissance et l'or ;
Et vous qui n'avez rien, Reconstructionnistes,
Vous voulez au Progrès vous opposer encor !

Vous voulez, ravivant l'hydre liberticide,
Quand nous prenons l'essor, nous tenir en arrêt !
Pouvons-nous oublier quelle main homicide
Tenait le revolver le Trente de Juillet ?

Tandis que nous pleurons nos martyrs, vos victimes,
Vous, si fiers autrefois, vous ne rougissez pas,
Désireux de monter aux lucratives cimes,
De venir courtiser notre appui, chapeau bas ?

Cessez de mendier aujourd'hui nos suffrages ;
Laissez le temps nous faire oublier tous vos torts,
Le forfait de Monroe et sa police à gages,
Enfin la lâcheté d'un trop indigne corps.

---

5. Joanni Questy's name was rendered in a variety of ways in his byline. Bylines in this volume are reproduced as they originally appeared in the paper.

To the Conservatives

JOANNI QUESTY

My dear Conservatives, may heaven conserve you!
I love you as brothers, though you do not love me,
And wish to save you from the fate that awaits you
Should you continue to fight so uselessly.

Just think: Progress, advancing at rapid pace,
Is leveling the field for blacks and whites,
And will make fellow citizens out of each race,
In order that both may climb to equal heights.

You've seen your arrogant dreams crumble to dust,
Your sinister plots against the Republic, foiled;
Your leaders, into exile and prison thrust,
No longer feed on hopes so badly spoiled.

They know their cause to be forever doomed
And that, to punish such temerity,
They'll live their days henceforth by remorse consumed,
Their names despised for all posterity.

And they were titans, these lords of slavery!
Talent and power and gold did they possess;
And you have nothing, Reconstructionists,
Yet still oppose the steady march of Progress!

You wish to summon the freedom-killing hydra
To hold us down as we begin to fly!
Can we forget the face of the murderer
Who held the gun on the thirtieth of July?[25]

We mourn our martyrs, your victims without redress,
While you, once proud, without a blush of shame,
Eager to climb to the lucrative heights of success,
Now court us, hat in hand, to advance your aim.

Stop begging, today, stop pandering for our votes;
Your wrongs require time to run its course
To forget Monroe's[26] malfeasance, his police cutthroats,
In short, the unworthiness of so craven a force.

25. A reference to the 30 July 1866 Mechanics' Institute massacre in New Orleans, during which forty-four black people were killed when marchers supporting black suffrage at the reconvened Louisiana Constitutional Convention were attacked by a crowd of white opponents that included police.

26. Mayor John T. Monroe (1822–71), whom many suspected of complicity in the massacre.

Vous pourriez bien trouver parmi vous quelques Pierres,
Quelques Judas nourris du pain confédéré ;
Mais, au jour solennel, croyez-moi, ces faux frères
Craindront de se couvrir d'un opprobre assuré !

[publié le dimanche 12 mai 1867]

Ode aux martyrs

CAMILLE NAUDIN [pseudonyme d'un auteur inconnu]

Le *Soleil de Juillet !* dorait encor la ville,
Qu'agitait le brandon de la guerre civile,
Par une infâme main le tocsin agité
Sonnait pour la terreur, non pour la liberté.
Un peuple d'assassins — anciens esclavagistes,
Dont l'avenir un jour vous donnera les listes,
Gentilshommes du fouet, armés de leurs poignards,
Cohortes de bourreaux — sortit de toutes parts.

Liberté ! liberté ! toi fille de Phrygie !
Par tous les peuples, Sainte, en tous lieux si chérie,
     Ne régneras-tu pas ?
Si ! bientôt, espérons ! Qu'au nom du grand prophète
Sous le talon maudit, levant ta fière tête,
     Sainte ! tu régneras !

Écoutez ! le tocsin redouble sa romance
De fer, de feu, de sang ; le massacre commence !
     Sommes-nous revenus
Au temps où Charles IX, de son palais du Louvre,
Pâle, défait, de la fenêtre qui s'entrouvre,
     Tuait les *bienvenus ?*

Barthélémy des Noirs ! le grand mot est trouvé !
Venez voir *un enfant* sur le sol achevé.
DOSTIE, un noble cœur, digne de me comprendre,
Sur un pavé sali, sans prêtre, vient de rendre,
Non son dernier soupir, mais son dernier élan.
Est-il noir, celui-ci ? — Non, messieurs, il est blanc.
Au capitaine LOUP, un vaillant, sergent d'armes,
Sur ce papier de deuil, donnons aussi des larmes.

You surely can find among you a few Peters,
Some Judases fed full on Confederate bread;
But, in the hour of truth, these false brothers
Will shrink from the scorn heaped upon their heads!

[published Sunday, 12 May 1867]

Ode to the Martyrs

CAMILLE NAUDIN [pseudonym of unknown author]

The city still basked in the golden *Sun of July*,[27]
That warmed the torch of civil war, held high;
The tocsin, stirred by a foul and villainous hand,
Was ringing for terror, rather than liberty's land.
A clan of killers — former owners of slaves,
A list of whose names posterity carefully saves,
Gentlemen of the whip, with daggers armed,
Hordes of hangmen — from all directions swarmed.

Liberty! Liberty! Phrygia's [28] daughter, you!
Beloved by all peoples, Holy One, in all lands, too,
      Will you not reign over all?
Indeed! And soon — let's hope! — a prophet's name
Will lift your proud head from under the heel of shame,
      And Holy One, reign you shall!

Listen! 'Tis the ballad sung by the tocsins,
Of iron and fire and blood; the massacre begins!
      Have we now reverted
To the days when Charles the Ninth,[29] inside his château,
The Louvre, pale and defeated, perched in his window,
      The killing of innocents concerted?

The blacks' Bartholomew's Day! The word has been found!
Come see *a mere child* laid low upon the ground.
DOSTIE,[30] noble and knowing that I speak what's right,
On a filthy street has drawn, with no priest in sight,
No, not his last sigh, but his final ounce of fight.
Is he black, you ask? — No, *Messieurs*, he is white.
For another brave man, a sergeant-in-arms, Captain LOUP,[31]
On this page of mourning, some tears we must shed, too.

---

27. "Sun of July" refers to the French Revolution of 27–29 July 1830. Known as the July Revolution, the popular uprising established a liberal monarchy after the fifteen-year reactionary Restoration.

28. Phrygia, an area of ancient Anatolia (modern-day Turkey), became associated with the Phrygian cap, a bonnet worn by manumitted slaves in Rome; the cap later came to symbolize republican government (as opposed to monarchic rule).

29. The French king Charles IX permitted the 1572 St. Bartholomew's Day massacre, in which thousands of Protestants were killed by Catholics.

30. The radical activist Anthony Paul Dostie (1821–66), a dentist of French descent from New York State, had given a speech at the Mechanics' Institute rally on 27 July exhorting the freedmen to armed self defense if attacked by opponents of the reconvened constitutional convention.

31. Constance Loup was fired upon while helping others escape and subsequently died of a stab wound.

VICTOR LACROIX ! ce nom qui fait frémir ma lèvre,
Chez tout homme de cœur amènera la fièvre,
   Il s'appelait Lacroix.
Souvenez-vous aussi de ce fils du martyre
Que depuis dix-huit cent ans l'univers admire,
   Christ mourant sur la croix.

VICTOR LACROIX est mort ! C'était une belle âme,
Depuis trois mois à peine il avait pris sa femme
   Qui versa plus d'un pleur.
Il est mort ! pardonnant, mais demandant justice !
Honorons, Noirs et Blancs, ce vaillant sacrifice
   D'un mort au champ d'honneur !

Ils tombaient ! ils tombaient ! ces fils de race noire,
Comme tombent au froid les feuilles. — Oui, l'histoire
Racontera ceci : dans un sanglant ruisseau
M*** trempa son mouchoir pour en faire un drapeau.
Et les paletoquets[6] qu'on a vus dans la cave
Quand le canon tonnait, faisant jaillir leur bave,
En lâches finiront comme finissent tous
Les lâches animaux, chacals, corbeaux et loups.

Le drapeau blanc paraît ! Assassins, c'est un prêtre ;
Pour un instant, au moins, laissez-le apparaître :
   HORTON, le bienveillant.
Non pas ! il faut des morts à cette horrible fête !
Femmes, vieillards, enfants, apportez votre tête
   À leur couteau sanglant.

Viennent policemen et pompiers ! c'est le calme
Non ! des horreurs du jour ils emportent la palme.
   T*** n'est-il pas là !
« Tuez ! tuez ! dit-il. Vive la boucherie.
En répandant ce sang nous sauvons la patrie ! »
   Et, ma foi, l'on tua !

Mechanics' Institute ! HENDERSON, tu voulus
De la *Convention* être l'un des élus ;
Cela te coûta cher ! tu tombas ; une balle,
Pâle et chaud, sans pitié, te jeta sur la dalle.
La dalle était jalouse, elle te soulevait.
Tu crias bien longtemps, ton bras dans l'air mouvait.
Je crois te voir encor, sur ton lit d'agonie,
Dans un dernier effort disant : Ô ma Patrie !

6. This more etymological spelling of *paltoquets* was likely chosen to fit the meter of the line.

VICTOR LACROIX![32] As it makes my lips to quiver,
To any man of heart, his name will bring fever:
    Lacroix he was called.
Remember also that son of sacrifice
Universally loved for eighteen centuries —
    The dying Christ, on the cross nailed.

VICTOR LACROIX is dead! His soul was simply splendid;
Just barely three months before, he'd taken a bride
    Who's poured out many a tear!
He's dead and gone! Forgiving, but asking for justice!
Let's honor, both blacks and whites, his valiant sacrifice
    Upon the field of honor!

How they fell! How they fell, these sons of the black race,
Like leaves do fall in the cold. — History, yes,
Will tell of this: in a stream with blood all reddened,
M***[33] dipped his handkerchief to make a pennant;
And the curs who down in the basement cowered
And choked on their drool, whenever the cannon roared,
Like cowards will end as do all animals
Of cowardice — crows and wolves and jackals.

The white flag is raised! Assassins, it's a priest;
Allow him to show himself, for a moment, at least:
    It's HORTON,[34] of kindness made.
But no! Your banquet requires more of the dead!
Each of ye — elderly, women, and children — bring your head
    Before their blood-stained blade.

Policemen and firemen, come! Does calm arise?
No! For atrocities they win the prize.
    Is not T*** right there?
"Kill! Kill! And long live butchery,"
Says he, "By spilling this blood, we'll save our country!"
    And, by God, they killed their share!

Mechanics' Institute! HENDERSON,[35] 'twas your ambition
To serve as delegate during the Convention.
How dearly it cost you! You fell; pale and warm,
A merciless bullet threw you to the floor.
Jealous, the floor tried to lift you up once more.
For some time you cried out, beating the air with your arm.
On that bed of woes, I still see you again and again,
In one final charge, saying: "Oh Country of mine!"

---

32. Son of the wealthy Creole tailor and philanthropist François Lacroix, Victor Lacroix (1839–66) had served in the Native Guards. At the memorial service held one year after the massacre, the Reverend Rufus Waples evoked his brutal murder in these terms: "Here fell the brave young Victor Lacroix, cut from head to foot, butchered and mutilated in the most shocking and barbarous manner. He had served with honor and distinction upon the field fighting for liberty and law, but his bright career of glory was thus suddenly arrested" (qtd. in Reed 338).

33. The identities of "M***" and "T***" (below) are not clear.

34. The Reverend Jotham W. Horton (1826[?]–66), black pastor of the Union Church, offered the opening prayer both at the original 1864 convention and in 1866.

35. The white lawyer John Henderson, an ardent Unionist and supporter of black suffrage, had also given a speech at the 27 July rally.

Les martyrs ! les voici ! les principaux sans doute !
Moi, de tous les *grands morts* ne puis suivre la route,
      Puisque, bien loin étant,
Je n'ai pu voir le crime à chaque coin de rue,
Fusillant, poignardant, la première venue,
      Portât-elle un enfant !

Allons ! finissons-en ! Qu'à jamais la concorde
Vous apporte demain de JOHN BROWN la corde
      Faite *d'Égalité*.
Vous êtes frères ! tous. Cherchez donc dans vos âmes
Un mot : pardon ! Au nom des enfants et des femmes
      Je dis : *Fraternité.*

Encore quelques vers ! Ne parlez plus de guerre ;
Parlez de *Liberté !* Blancs et Noirs, si naguère
Vous vous êtes battus, oubliez ! oubliez !
Soyez justes et bons, vous serez pardonnés.
À vous martyrisés cette dernière feuille
Que votre âme là-haut au pied de Dieu l'accueille.
Mais je dirai toujours mulâtres, noirs, blancs,
VICTOR LACROIX est mort, Jeff Davis est vivant.

Nouvelle-Orléans, 29 juillet 1867

        [publié le mardi 30 juillet 1867]

Pot-pourri

J. G., LOUISIANAIS DE ST-JACQUES [Jean-Sylvain Gentil]

Miss *Abeille* voltige aux fleurs de rhétorique,
      Pour faire son miel d'or :
La *Picayune* attend que l'argent métallique
      Chez nous résonne encor.

Le vieux *Propagateur* propage et repropage
      Sans tort ni sans travers,
Les sermons de Veuillot qu'on trouve à chaque page
      De l'immense *Univers.*

L'enfant du renouveau, la tendre *Renaissance*
      Porte fort bien son nom.
Renaître n'est-ce point revenir à l'enfance ?
      Le franc dira-t-il non ?

Behold these martyrs — the most important, indeed!
I could not follow the path of these *glorious dead*,
    Because, not being present,
I witnessed not the crimes on every street,
As they shot and stabbed each passerby they'd meet,
    Were she with child expectant!

Let's go! Get on with it! May harmony, our hope,
Come tomorrow to offer you JOHN BROWN's rope,
    Woven from *Equality*.
Brothers are ye! All! Let your souls' only aim
Be one word: forgiveness! In the women and children's name,
    I say: *Fraternity*.

Just a few lines to go! Of war speak no more;
But speak of *Liberty*! Whites and blacks, if heretofore
You fought against one another, forget and move on!
Be good and be fair, and you will receive pardon.
For ye fallen martyrs, this final page I write;
May your soul collect it up yonder, at God's feet.
But, mulattoes, blacks, whites, this fact I must tell:
VICTOR LACROIX is dead; Jeff Davis lives still.

New Orleans, 29 July 1867

    [published Tuesday, 30 July 1867]

Potpourri

J. G., A LOUISIANIAN FROM ST. JAMES [Jean-Sylvain Gentil]³⁶

Miss *Bee*³⁷ flutters toward flowers of rhetoric
    To make her golden honey;
The *Picayune*³⁸ hopes to hear once more the metallic
    Music of jingling money.

The old *Propagator* goes on repropagating
    With no effects adverse,
And Veuillot's sermons continue populating
    The immense *Universe*.³⁹

Renewal's child, the little *Renaissance*,⁴⁰
    Carries its name quite well.
Is not rebirth a return to the state of infants?
    What else is there to tell?

36. Gentil, a prolific journalist who contributed to a variety of newspapers and other publications throughout his career, had immigrated to the US from France in the 1850s; the adjective "Louisianian" is a reference to the newspaper he edited in St. James Parish, *Le Louisianais*.

37. *L'Abeille de la Nouvelle-Orléans*, New Orleans's longest running French-language newspaper (1827–1923).

38. Founded in 1837, the *Picayune* later merged with the *Times-Democrat*. As the *Times-Picayune* / the *New Orleans Advocate*, the organization remains one of New Orleans's main sources of local news.

Au siècle où nous vivons couçi couça, l'*Époque*
      Passe tambours battants ;
Et personne ne dit qu'elle bat la breloque,
      Marchant avec le *Temps*

Le *Croissant* amincit sa corne musulmane
      En souple Yagatan ;
Le *Salut,* nouveau-né de couleur diaphane,
      Au ciel s'en va montant.

La *Tribune* bronzée a l'ardente parole ;
      Mais le *Républicain*
Radical à tous poils, à tête moins que folle,
      Rime avec Publicain.

          [publié le mardi 21 avril 1868]

In this so-so century of ours, the *Epoch*[41]
    Is beating its marching drums,
And no one would say it's following the clock
    That ticks and tocks with the *Times*.

The *Daily Crescent* has sharpened its Muslim horn
    Into a yatagan;[42]
The *Salut*,[43] translucent like the skin of a newborn,
    Is ascending up to heaven.

The tanned *Tribune* possesses words of flame;
    But the *Republican*,
Radical lacking any reasonable claim,
    Rhymes with Publican.[44]

[published Tuesday, 21 April 1868]

---

39. *Le Propagateur catholique* (1842–88) was the French-language newspaper of the Catholic Church in Louisiana. *L'Univers*, a pro-Catholic French newspaper founded in 1833, was managed at this time by the conservative polemicist Louis Veuillot (1813–83).

40. Though it did publish texts by people of color, *La Renaissance louisianaise* (1861–71) defended slavery and the Confederate cause.

41. A French-language weekly edited by Louis-Placide Canonge, a white Creole writer, journalist, politician, and language activist.

42. These two lines provide a playful take on the conservative stance of the *New Orleans Crescent*. Though the paper's name refers to the bend of the Mississippi River from which New Orleans derives the nickname "Crescent City," Gentil links it to the yatagan, a curved sword that serves as the symbol of the Ottoman Empire. The analogy implies that the *Crescent* acts not as a mere mouthpiece but as a weapon in service of its political views.

43. Bilingual weekly founded in 1867; the paper's name means "salvation."

44. Founded in 1867, the English-language *New Orleans Republican*, a rival paper to *La Tribune*, had just replaced the latter as the official organ of the Republican Party during the political feud of 1867–68. Under the Roman Empire, publicans were government contractors whose duties often included tax collection. Gentil's comparison suggests that *La Tribune*'s rival, beholden to state authorities, will lack objective independence.

LIBERTY, RACIAL EQUALITY, AND FRATERNITY

Étrange coïncidence

[probablement Armand Lanusse]

    Le colonel Ferrier (prononcez en anglais *keurnel*) et l'abbé Châlons
ont chacun fait la nuit dernière le rêve suivant qu'ils racontent,
ce qui est non moins étrange, à peu près de la même manière.
Ce rêve nous rappelle celui de Patrice. Le voici :

RÊVE DE L'ABBÉ

Cette nuit je songeais que de mal consumé,
Côte à côte d'un noir, on m'avait inhumé.
Ne pouvant supporter cet affreux voisinage,
En mort de qualité, je lui tins ce langage :
Retire-toi coquin ! va pourrir loin d'ici,
Il ne t'appartient pas de m'approcher ainsi.
Coquin ! ce me dit-il, d'une arrogance extrême ;
Va chercher les coquins ailleurs, coquin toi-même ;
Ici, tous sont égaux, je ne te dois plus rien,
Je suis sur mon fumier comme toi sur le tien.
Et pourtant sans songer au ver qui nous dévore
Comme à l'église ici tu m'insultes encore.

    Le songe du colonel est le même à l'exception des deux
derniers vers conçus comme suit :

Un simple nègre ici vaut bien, ne t'en déplaise,
Un brillant colonel de brigade française.

                    [publié le mardi 19 mai 1863]

Le triomphe des opprimés

  Pour La Tribune

[anonyme]

Pourquoi vouloir troubler notre terre bénie ?
Pourquoi tant d'intérêt à la race avilie
Du nègre qui, pour nous, fertilise nos champs ?
Lui seul doit travailler pour nous, pour nos enfants ;
« Tandis qu'à l'animal on donne sa pâture,
N'a-t-on pas satisfait à la loi de nature ? »
        Nous disent les méchants.

A Strange Coincidence

[probably Armand Lanusse]

Last night, colonel Ferrier[45] (pronounced *keurnel* in English) and Abbott Châlons[46] each experienced the following dream, which they recalled, no less strangely enough, in more or less the same way. The dream resembles that of Patrice. Here it is:

THE ABBOT'S DREAM

Last night I dreamed that, at illness's behest,
Beside a black man I'd been laid to rest.
Unable to bear his wretched proximity,
I spoke to him thus, as a corpse of quality:
"Be gone, you scoundrel! Go somewhere else to rot,
For you have no business near my burial plot."
"A scoundrel?" with utter arrogance he replied,
"You're a scoundrel yourself; this cannot be denied,
For all are equal here, I'm pleased to say:
We both decay in precisely the same way.
Ignoring the worms devouring our skin,
As you did in church, you insult me once again."

The colonel's dream is identical with the exception of the final two lines, which are as follows:

Down here, a simple negro is worth, I'm afraid,
A brilliant colonel commanding a French brigade.

[published Tuesday, 19 May 1863]

45. Alphonse Ferrier, a French citizen of New Orleans and an officer of the Brigade française (a former Confederate militia composed of French nationals), expressed displeasure at his troops having been placed side-by-side with the black soldiers and *gens de couleur* of the original (i.e., Confederate) Native Guards. "A Strange Coincidence" was published together with a letter from Armand Lanusse, who denounces Ferrier's hypocritical attitude; the scathing irony and otherwise similar tone of both the poem and the letter suggest that Lanusse wrote both texts.

46. During his Civil War–era tenure at St. Mary's Church in New Orleans, the French priest Gabriel Chalon (the spelling found in most nineteenth-century documents) reinstated segregation at mass.

The Triumph of the Oppressed

For The Tribune

[anonymous]

Why do they come to trouble our blessed land?
Wherefore this concern for the Negro, a race condemned
Who merely serves to fertilize our fields?
To us, to our children belong his labor's yields;
"As long as an animal receives its feed,
Has not the law of nature been satisfied?"
      Such are their wicked appeals.

Mais à ces oppresseurs une voix plus humaine,
Une voix qui flétrit et le fouet et la chaîne
Dit : « Ces noirs Africains qu'ici vous maudissez,
Ces esclaves soumis que vous avilissez,
Ne sont-ils pas aussi de Dieu l'œuvre sublime,
Des hommes, vos égaux, qu'un noble cœur anime ?
        Tous frères vous naissez. »

Et quand sonna l'appel de cette voix sacrée,
Les enfants courageux de la race outragée
Se levèrent gaiement pour voler aux combats,
Vaincre leurs oppresseurs ou mourir en soldats :
Leurs bataillons nombreux et ardents à la gloire
Devant eux et toujours portèrent la victoire
        Sans craindre le trépas.

La sainte liberté, ce droit si cher à l'homme,
Ce droit qu'avec envie en tous lieux on renomme
Sera le prix sacré que vos travaux auront,
Le bien que vos enfants de vous hériteront :
Si vous tombez frappés au chemin de la gloire
Et si vous succombez en cherchant la victoire,
        Tous ils vous béniront.

Pour prix du sang versé, pour ces larmes amères
À la mémoire aimée et d'époux et de frères,
Oui, vous aurez conquis des droits à l'équité ;
Vous aurez votre rang parmi l'humanité.
La chaîne ni l'encan, broyés par vos batailles,
Ne viendront plus, hideux, déchirer vos entrailles,
        Fils de la liberté.

        [publié le mardi 8 novembre 1864]

Le chien et le chat

Imitation

LÉLIA D... T [Adolphe Duhart]

Connaissez-vous Pataud ? C'est un petit chien noir ;
Il a pour compagnon Raton, un chat de race,
 — Un bel angora blanc ; — mais entre eux point de trace
De mauvais procédés, que c'est plaisir à voir !

But a more humane voice by the oppressors is heard,
Crippling both the whip and the chain with this word:
"These black Africans whom you have cursed,
These slaves subdued and condemned by you to the worst,
Are they not also God's wondrous works of art
And men — your equals — endowed with noble heart?
      Brothers were ye at first!"

And when they finally heard that sacred voice,
The sons of the downtrodden race did make the choice
To answer the call as cheerful volunteers
To vanquish their oppressors or die as soldiers:
Their battalions, numerous and eager for glory
That lay ahead, rushed toward victory,
      Discarding all mortal fears.

Holy liberty, that right so dear
To man, that right whose name rings bright and clear,
Shall be the sacred prize secured by your deeds,
The bequest that forever will meet your children's needs.
Should you be struck down on the road to glory,
Should you sell your life to purchase the victory,
      Their blessings will be the proceeds.

Having paid the price of blood, of bitter tears
Over the cherished remembrance of husbands and brothers,
Indeed, you'll have won the right to equity
And your proper rank among humanity.
Neither chain nor auction, shattered by your swords,
Shall ever return to attempt to crush your innards,
      Ye sons of liberty.

      [published Tuesday, 8 November 1864]

The Dog and the Cat

Imitation

LÉLIA D———T [Adolphe Duhart]

Do you know Clumsy? A little black pup is he;
His companion is Ratty, a cat of pedigree,
A lovely white Angora. Between them you'll find
No trace of ill-treatment; it's truly one of a kind!

   Pataud folâtre avec Raton en frère,
Sans mordre, sans gronder, comme font les moutons ;
   Mais Raton fait tout le contraire,
— Les chats, nous a-t-on dit, sont traîtres et félons —
Raton, — et ce n'est pas friction de la lyre, —
   Raton, bien qu'il jurât toujours
   De faire patte de velours,
Le griffait bel et bien ! — « C'est histoire de rire »,
Disait-il à Pataud prêt à se lâcher :
   « Ne sais-tu pas quand on badine,
   « On ne doit point faire la mine ?
« D'ailleurs n'avons-nous pas — pourquoi donc le cacher —
« Les mêmes intérêts et la même existence ?
   « Ne suis-je pas ton frère et ton ami ? »
   — Tout beau. Raton ! un peu moins de jactance !
« Prends le nom qui convient, ne sois rien à demi ;
« Crois-moi, j'aime bien mieux un loyal ennemi
« Qu'un frère qui trahit dans l'ombre et le silence. »

    [publié le dimanche 26 mars 1865]

Stanza

À M. Th. J. Durant

LÉLIA D...T [Adolphe Duhart]

Enfin, l'heure a sonné ! Chaque jour dans l'arène,
Quelle que soit la main qui vers nous vous entraîne,
   Ou le frein qu'impose un César,
Vous arrivez sans peur, vous brisez la barrière,
Et le préjugé tombe, et sa lutte éphémère
   Ne peut enrayer votre char.

Courage jusqu'au bout ! et marchez d'un pied ferme ;
Évitez le chemin dont la honte est le terme.
   Brisez la coupe de l'erreur.
Et dans ces sombres temps de délire et de fièvre,
Ne reculez jamais ! — faites de votre lèvre
   L'interprète de votre cœur.

Anathème ! anathème ! à qui cache en son âme
De la Fraternité la douce et pure flamme,
   Qui sur nous tous enfin a lui !

    Clumsy frolics with Ratty just like a brother would,
No biting, no growling — as gentle as a lamb.
    But Ratty's behavior is not as good,
For cats are traitorous, or so they claim.
But Ratty, however — and this is no poet's fancy —
    Despite repeated vows
    Never to use his claws,
Would scratch for real! "It's only for play, you see,"
He'd say when his buddy Clumsy prepared to react.
    "Don't you know that we're just joking?
    There's no reason at all for sulking.
Besides, don't we share — why bother to hide the fact? —
The same interests and the very same lifestyle?
    Am I not your friend and your brother?"
    "So be it. Ratty! Enough of that arrogant smile!
Let's call things by their proper name, and know
That I truly do prefer a loyal foe
To a brother who strikes from the shadows with silent guile."

    [published Sunday, 26 March 1865]

Stanza

For Mr. Th. J. Durant [47]

LÉLIA D——T [Adolphe Duhart]

At last, the hour has rung! To the arena's floor —
Whatever hand might pull you toward our door,
    Whatever hurdle some Caesar may place —
Each day you come without fear; you smash the gate,
And prejudice falls, for its paltry attempts at combat
    Cannot slow your chariot's pace.

Have courage till the end! And march toward your aim.
Avoid that path whose final stop is shame;
    Shatter the goblet filled with error.
In these gloomy times which a fever of madness grips,
Don't ever back down! Instead, allow your lips
    To be your heart's interpreter.

Anathema! A curse on those who'd dare
To seal away fraternity's sweet, pure fire,
    That finally shines upon us all!

47. A Pennsylvania native who settled in New Orleans as a teenager, Thomas Jefferson Durant (1817–82) was an attorney, a politician, an activist with the Democratic Party, and, during the war, an antislavery supporter of the Union. A disciple of the French social theoretician Charles Fourier, he believed in utopian socialist reform. Durant left New Orleans for good in the wake of the Mechanics' Institute massacre.

À qui renie un fils à cette heure bénie
Et le traîne devant la haine et l'ironie,
    Anathème ! à jamais sur lui !

Honte à lui ! honte au siècle ! il veut laisser encore
Boire au calice amer ce peuple qui l'implore,
    Et lui ravir la liberté...
Il ne sera pas dit que né dans la tempête
Notre âge ne pourra voir briller sur sa tête
    Les rayons de l'Égalité.

Oh ! non ! marchez toujours ! À cette foule immense
Faites comprendre enfin sa honteuse démence
    Et son projet plus criminel...
Dites-lui bien : « L'éclair s'éteint devant le Maître,
Et le vent de demain va déchirer peut-être
    Le nuage où dort l'arc-en-ciel. »

        [publié le dimanche 22 octobre 1865]

Communication d'outre-tombe

Cantate à mes amis
Air : À la grâce de Dieu

J. B.

Enfants chéris de la victoire,
Vrais amis de la Liberté,
Francs admirateurs de la gloire,
Apôtres de l'Humanité,
Ô disciples du spiritisme,
Suivez le chemin des croyants ;
Bientôt la ruine et le mutisme
Abattront les sots, les méchants.
    Écoutez Béranger,
    Votre cher chansonnier. *Bis.*

Votre sublime république,
Que l'on appelle États-Unis,
Sera bientôt la terre unique
Des hommes d'honneur réunis.
Bientôt votre illustre contrée,

Upon whomever denies a son in these hours
Of triumph, exposing him to hatred and jeers,
      May anathema ever fall!

Shame on him! And upon our time! It wishes still
To force the people to swallow a bitter pill
      By cheating them of their liberty ...
It shall not be said that, born of the storm, our age
Will never be able to feel upon its visage
      The sunlight of Equality.

Oh, no! March onward! Make this monstrous crowd
Realize the shame of the lunacy it's avowed
      And its even more criminal schemes.
Tell them, "Before the Master, the lightning wears a shroud;
And perchance tomorrow's wind will shred that cloud
      Where the sleeping rainbow dreams."

      [published Sunday, 22 October 1865]

Message from beyond the Grave

Cantata to my friends
To the tune of "À la grâce de Dieu"[48]

J. B.[49]

Dear children of the victory
And truest friends of Liberty,
Admirers of glory,
Apostles of Humanity,
Disciples of spiritualism,
Go follow the believer's way;
Ere long ruin and mutism
Will strike the wicked and the stray.
      Now listen to Béranger,
      Your beloved songwriter. *Bis.*

That Republic sublime and grand
Which you call the United States,
Ere long will stand as the only land
Where men of honor congregate.
For soon your country, proud and dear,

48. A song by French lyric composer Gustave Lemoine (1802–85), set to music by Loïsa Puget (1810–89).

49. This poem is presented as an otherworldly Spiritualist communication from a deceased French author to New Orleans progressives. As the refrain indicates, the initials "J. B." refer to (Pierre-)Jean de Béranger (1780–1857), the most popular French songwriter of the nineteenth century. An ardent republican (in the French sense), Béranger was idolized by radicals for having been imprisoned as punishment for his politically charged lyrics. Though it is not known who submitted this poem for publication, Henry Louis Rey is certainly a possibility.

Par l'organe de son Congrès,
Dictera la loi vénérée...
La « loi du monde, du progrès ! »
  Écoutez Béranger,
  Votre bon chansonnier. *Bis.*

Le jour arrive, il est bien proche...
Où le suffrage universel,
Des fous le remords, le reproche,
Régnera pour tous, immortel !
Alors, ô bonheur indicible,
La Liberté, l'Égalité,
Ces mots divins de l'Invisible,
Voudront dire : Fraternité !
  Écoutez Béranger,
  Votre vieux chansonnier. *Bis.*

   [publié le dimanche 17 décembre 1865]

Pour les incendiés de Saint-Domingue

 Pour La Tribune

Lélia D... t [Adolphe Duhart]

L'horizon dissipait ses vapeurs abondantes ;
Déjà l'Astre du jour de ses flammes ardentes
Ranimait doucement la ville à son réveil ;
La mer réfléchissait le ciel pur et vermeil ;
Des roses du printemps la terre était parée ;
Les oiseaux gazouillaient, à la brise enivrée
Des parfums du matin, leurs plus douces chansons,
La cloche y répondait par de plus joyeux sons.
Jamais l'œil n'avait vu, comme en ce jour, éclore
Sous le dôme azuré l'étincelante Aurore.

❖

Mais tout à coup un cri de suprême terreur,
Un cri de désespoir et de sinistre horreur
A traversé l'espace... Au feu !... Malheur !... La foule,
Roulant ses flots troubles comme la mer sa houle,
Accourt, morne, hagard... Tout reste suspendu...

❖

By authority of its Congress
Will declare the law that we revere,
The "law of the world and of progress!"
>> Now listen to Béranger,
>> Your beloved songwriter. *Bis.*

The day shall come; it has drawn nigh . . .
When suffrage, universal,
Which only fools do dare deny,
Shall reign for all, immortal!
Then — oh happiness sublime —
Freedom and Equality,
The Invisible One's words divine,
Will signify "Fraternity!"
>> Now listen to Béranger,
>> Your beloved songwriter. *Bis.*

[published Sunday, 17 December 1865]

For the Victims of the Saint Domingue Fire [50]

For The Tribune

LÉLIA D——T [Adolphe Duhart]

The horizon was slowly dissolving its heavy haze;
Already the daytime star, with its flames ablaze,
Was bringing to life, ever so gently, the city.
A pure sky of ruby lay mirrored in the sea;
The earth was fully bedecked with the roses of spring,
And into the breeze, grown drunk on the perfumes of morning,
The birds were chirping their softest, sweetest strains.
By way of reply, the bells rang joyous refrains.
No eye had seen, beneath the azure dome,
In quite this way, the sparkling Dawn come home.

❖

But all of a sudden, a cry of utter fright,
A cry of despair and baleful horror, took flight
Through the air . . . "Fire! . . . Misery! . . ." Rolling
In troubled waves like the sea's swelling,
The crowd hurried, haggard, disheartened . . . Everything halts.

❖

50. On 19 Mar. 1866, a fire destroyed nearly half of the buildings in Port-au-Prince, Haiti, leaving some nine thousand people homeless and killing scores of others.

Déjà de toutes parts, du ciel fermé, tendu,
Triste comme la nuit à l'aile ténébreuse,
L'éclat a disparu sous sa voûte cendreuse.
Des nuages de feu, par masses dans les airs,
Roulant rapidement ainsi que des éclairs,
Au souffle du mistral, qui par trois fois domine,
Portent encore au loin l'épouvante et la ruine...
Bientôt tout disparaît... De moment en moment
Une maison chancelle et tombe lourdement...
Toujours le feu dévore et la cloche soupire...
Toujours de cet airain le triste appel transpire
Et la foule y répond par de sombres rumeurs...
Et par le désespoir aux sinistres clameurs...

Enfin le feu s'éteint, et le soleil qui passe
Sous le dôme infini, dans l'azur, dans l'espace,
Éclaire d'Haïti les toits abandonnés.
Les enfants demi nus, les vieillards consternés
Pleurant le vieux foyer, respecté des tourmentes,
Des hommes isolés sur des ruines fumantes,
Une mère éplorée, abattue, à genoux,
Conjurant le Seigneur de calmer son courroux...

Dans ce fracas de cris, dans l'ouragan de flammes,
Que de purs dévouements. Ici de saintes femmes,
À genoux au milieu des débris empilés,
Veillent en gémissant leurs sauveurs mutilés ;
Une mère plus loin enlève, délirante,
De ce gouffre fatal une fille expirante ;
Là-bas, c'est un jeune homme emportant un berceau
Qui fléchit et qui tombe en sauvant son fardeau.

Cependant à travers les cendres, la fumée,
Au milieu de la ville à demi consumée,
Au souffle violent du terrible aquilon
Ranimant du fléau le triste tourbillon,
Par dessus les clameurs, les plaintes des victimes,
Et plus haut que la voix des profondes abîmes,[7]
Entendez-vous vibrer sous le ciel irrité
Un long cri de douleur... C'est l'humble Charité...
Dites, resterez-vous aussi froid que la pierre
Où vient s'agenouiller la modeste prière.

Donnez, vous qui toujours avez cueilli des fleurs.
Donnez, vous tous aussi qui connaissez les pleurs.
Oh ! donnez au vieillard qui chancelle et qui tombe,
Pour qu'il puisse bénir et sourire à la tombe ;

7. The noun *abîme* was treated as feminine before the eighteenth century, though since then it has been masculine. Here, Duhart uses the feminine to ensure six syllables in the second half of his alexandrine. The choice also enables him to use the feminine adjective *profondes* which adds gravity to the phrase by lengthening it prosodically.

From every which way, from the sky, tense, closed off,
And sad like the night with shadowy wing, the flash
Has faded beneath the firmament's vault of ash.
Clouds of fire, filling the air with their mass,
Rolling through like lightning bolts that quickly pass,
When the mistral blows, thrice a conqueror,
Continue to spread afar the ruin and terror.
Ere long, all disappears . . . Periodically
A house totters, then collapses heavily . . .
Still the fire devours, the bell does sigh . . .
Still its bronze exudes a saddened cry,
And the crowd replies with mournful murmurs . . .
And, with despair, answers the ill-boding clamors.

The fire dies down at last, and the sun, in its race
Across the infinite dome of azure and space,
Illuminates the forlorn homes of Haiti.
Half-naked children, the dispirited elderly
Who weep for their homes untouched by hurricanes,
Men off on their own, standing on smoking ruins,
A grieving mother, despondent, on bended knee,
Beseeching the Lord to soothe his seething fury.

In this uproar of screams, in the hurricane of flames,
Such acts of devotion! Attending the mangled frames
Of their saviors, here we see virtuous women, bowed down
Amidst the mountains of rubble, whimper and moan;
Farther afield, a bewildered mother lifts
Her dying daughter out of this fatal abyss.
And yonder, transporting a cradle, a young man we see:
He struggles to save his load before falling helplessly.

But through it all, through the ash and the smoke, in the midst
Of the city, halfway consumed, and the violent blast
Of the dreadful northern wind, reviving the tempest
Of this sad scourge, over and above the unrest,
Above and beyond the woeful laments of the victims,
And higher still than the voice that calls from the chasm,
Can you hear resonate, beneath the angry sky,
A long howl of pain? 'Tis humble Charity.
Do tell, will you remain as cold as the stone
Before which lowly prayers do come to bow down?

Give, all ye who always have picked flowers.
Give, all ye who also have known tears.
Oh! Give to the old man who stumbles and falls,
So that he may smile before the graveyard's walls.

Donnez pour que l'enfant qui pleure en son berceau,
Joyeux, reçoive encor, d'un baiser, le doux sceau ;
Oh ! donnez à sa mère, une angélique femme,
Pour qu'elle puisse aimer et prier en son âme.
Donnez à tous enfin !... en tout temps, en tout lieu :
L'aumône est un bon ange, elle est fille de Dieu ;
Oh ! donnez pour avoir, à votre heure dernière,
Contre tous vos péchés sa puissante prière.

[publié le dimanche 6 mai 1866]

Le droit de suffrage des noirs

Imitation en français du style de Burns

E. H. [Émile Honoré]

> Fais tête au malheur qui t'opprime :
> Qu'une espérance légitime
> Te munisse contre le sort.
> — J. B. Rousseau

Bien qu' parc'que noirs on nous refuse
Le droit d'suffrage, — rien qu' pour ça ;
Espérons, car l'préjugé s'use,
Le temps triomphe et l'on rit d'ça.
Et blanc sensé, qui connait ça,
Revient déjà d'ces bêtiss's-là ;
Et tout honteux lui-mêm' s'accuse
D'avoir été si sot que ça.

Car il sait bien que tous les hommes,
Blancs, noirs et roug's, et cœtera,
Sont tous les mêm's, et que nous sommes
Les fils d'Adam, pas moins que ça.
Si l'esclavag', le fouet, tout ça
Nous dégradaient, malgré cela
Au champ de Mars, en gentilshommes
Nous le vainquîmes — il sait bien ça.

Depuis ce temps la calomnie,
La hain', la rage et puis tout ça,
À notr' couleur font qu'on dénie
Un droit qu'on donne à moins que ça.

Give so that the child who cries in his bed,
Will feel, with joy, the seal of a kiss on his head;
Oh! Give to his mother, a woman resembling an angel,
So that she may love and pray within her soul.
Give to all, that is! All the time, everywhere:
Almsgiving is an angel — God's true daughter.
Oh! Give in order to have, at your final hour,
Against all your sins, his powerful prayer.

[published Sunday, 6 May 1866]

Blacks' Right to Vote

Imitation in French of the style of Burns [51]

E. H. [Émile Honoré]

> Resist misfortune that does oppress:
> May hope's legitimate redress
> Protect you against the slings of fate.
> — J. B. Rousseau [52]

Though 'cause we're black they dare deny
Our right ta vote — for naething but that,
Let us hope, for prejudice does steady die;
Time will conquess an' we laugh a' that.
The complowsible white wha knows a' that,
Hae already forsook such daffery
An' accuses himsel' full shamefully
For having once been as gawkie as that.

For he ken full well that a' men,
Whuther white, black, red, et cetera,
Are a' tha same, an' also he ken
That we're Adam's lad-bairns each an' a'.
Though slavery, the whip, an' a' that
Did cruelly nither an' bemean,
Upo' Mars' Field, as gentlemen
We conquess'd 'im — an' he knows that.

That day syne the mongers o' slander,
Hatred, anger, an' a' that,
Towart our colour hae refused to render
A right wha's gien for less tha' that.

51. Considered Scotland's national poet, Robert Burns (1759–96) gained fame for his composition and adaptation of songs in the Scots language. His support for the French Revolution earned him the admiration of liberals and radicals of the nineteenth century. Honoré's poem is a pastiche of the Burns poem commonly known as "A Man's a Man for A' That." On the approach to translating the vernacular dialect used in the original, see p. 74.

52. Jean-Baptiste Rousseau (1671–1741), a French playwright and poet remembered for his pithy verse; of humble birth, he died in exile after falling out of favor at court.

Mais attendons, on verra ça
Un jour justice se fera ;
Alors dans notr' chère patrie
Tous seront frèr's en dépit d'ça.

Ô Liberté, Liberté sainte !
Quatre-vingts ans, et plus que ça,
Tu pleuras et tu fus contrainte
À ne point voir ce bonheur-là.
Mais les méchants, traîtr's et tout ça
Aujourd'hui sont punis pour ça ;
Et ton âme de joie empreinte
S'épanouit après tout ça.

[publié le dimanche 10 juin 1866]

Un cri de l'alcyon

Lélia D... t [Adolphe Duhart]

Le spectacle que nous donne depuis quelques semaines la classe qui s'intitule « supérieure », n'est pas fait pour la rehausser à nos yeux. Cette classe si fière, qui ne nous a jamais couverts que de sa haine et de ses dédains, vient aujourd'hui à nos pieds, avec des flatteries, pour suborner notre vote, et reconquérir au prix de nos fautes son pouvoir renversé.

L'astre du jour, montant la voûte orientale,
Laisse brillante encor la zone occidentale ;
Et pendant la tempête, au milieu de l'éclair,
Le nautonier perdu croit voir un ciel plus clair ;
Mais le soleil, plongeant aux flots amers son disque,
Imprime à l'occident la nocturne astérisque ;
Mais la tempête, trompant l'attente du pêcheur,
Efface au fond du ciel la dernière blancheur :
Telle est des factieux la fragile espérance.

Debout ! frères, debout ! — Chassez l'indifférence !
Ne vous endormez pas : l'ennemi veille la nuit,
Et déjà sous vos pieds tend son piège sans bruit.
Veillez ! — Ne vous fiez pas à l'étreinte hypocrite
De ceux qui vous ont fait la vie aigre et proscrite ;
De ceux qui dédaignant le plus divin devoir,
Ont vendu froidement par un lâche pouvoir
La vertu révérée en toutes les familles :
Le respect de leurs fils et l'honneur de leurs filles !

Take heart, we've but to wait an' see:
One day justice'll trowth prevail;
A'where across our country
Everyone'll be brothers, of equal avail.

Oh Freedom, sacred Freedom! We're told
That eighty years syne, an' more tha' that,
Ye've wept frae fear ye'd ne'er behold
This happiness wha's made ye wait;
But the fiends, the traitors, an' a' that
A' last hae been punished for that,
An' thy soul, wi' joy abundantly filled,
Shall finally flower after a' that.

[published Sunday, 10 June 1866]

The Halcyon's Cry [53]

LÉLIA D——T [Adolphe Duhart]

For several weeks the class calling itself "upper" has provided a spectacle that can hardly enhance its standing in our eyes. This class, so proud, having never given us anything other than its hatred and its disdain, now comes to us with words of flattery, in order to corrupt our vote and thus win back, through our error, the power it no longer holds.

The daytime star, showing the Eastern dome,
Brightens a little longer the Western realm;
And through the storm, amidst the lightning's play,
A pilot, lost, holds hope for a clearer sky;
But the sun drops into the bitter deep its disk
And marks the West with nighttime's asterisk;
But the storm deceives the fisherman's expectations,
Erasing from the sky its milky glow:
Such are the fragile hopes offered by traitors.

Arise, my brothers! — Cast off indifference!
Sleep not: at night the enemy prepares,
And under your feet lays silently his snares.
Be vigilant! — Beware the false embrace
Of those who've sought to poison your existence,
Who dare defy those duties most divine,
Who've coldly sold, with coward's authority,
The virtues that any family reveres:
Their sons' respect and the honor of their daughters!

53. The title refers to a bird of Greek mythology, associated with the kingfisher, which came into being when the gods transformed two lovers, Alcyone and Ceyx, into halcyon birds. Its symbolism as an auspicious omen is linked to the political developments of the early months of 1867, which saw the passage of the first Reconstruction Acts establishing Congressional or Radical Reconstruction. As Duhart's subsequent note indicates, these changes caused some conservatives to woo Radicals of color, and these realignments ultimately led to the 1868 split in Louisiana's Republican Party. Duhart's exhortation, in the seventh stanza, to "[r]aise up tribunes everywhere," hints at the importance of the newspaper itself in defending the cause of political equality and social justice.

Ne vous endormez pas aux frivoles serments
De tous ceux qui, mentant aux nobles sentiments,
Et de leur amitié, déguisant l'imposture,
Vous cachent de leur cœur et l'affront et l'injure.
Non ! de leurs préjugés ils n'ont pu triompher !
S'ils vous ouvrent les bras, c'est pour vous étouffer !

Rien encor n'est certain ; travaillez sans relâche.
Que chacun soit à l'œuvre et chacun à sa tâche.
L'avenir est à vous. — Ne désespérez pas,
Le passé disparaît ! S'effaçant pas à pas
Dans le gouffre profond aura sa propre lave,
Il vous laisse debout sur sa dernière épave,
Le présent fléchissant aux coups des factieux.

Ne vous endormez pas aux présages des cieux :
Derrière le soleil la foudre qui se lève
Peut engloutir la barque attachée à la grève.
À la manœuvre tous ! — Déjà vient l'ouragan !
Craignez l'azur trompeur du perfide océan !

Debout donc ! que partout se dresse une tribune
Pour défendre vos droits et la cause commune !
En ce moment sacré nul ne doit rester froid
À la grande action qui surgit et qui croît.
Veillez et soyez prêts [!] Nul cœur ne peut se taire,
Quand du bonheur de tous chacun est solidaire !
Toi, si tu n'as qu'un sou, donne-le sans regret,
Il pourra te sauver de qui te le prendrait.
Et toi, pauvre opprimé, si tu n'as qu'une pierre,
Écrase des tyrans la tête impie, altière !

Oui, réveillez-vous donc ! voici l'aube du jour
Attendue ardemment par tous avec amour.
Oh ! oui, donnez encore à l'œuvre commencée
Tout votre dévouement, toute votre pensée,
Et confondez vos cœurs dans la même fierté,
Dans ce cri solennel : Vive la Liberté !

Nouvelle-Orléans, 4 avril 1867

[publié le dimanche 14 avril 1867]

Do not be lulled to trust by the faithless dealings
Of those who, making a sham of noble feelings,
Concealing well their friendship's fraudulence,
Disguise the slights and insults in their heart.
No! They have not conquered their prejudice!
They open their arms only to suffocate!

Since nothing is certain, work without relent.
May each and all on their task remain intent.
The future is yours. — There's no need to despair,
For, bit by bit, the past does disappear:
Into a lava-washed abyss, it sinks
And leaves you standing on its final wreckage,
The present yielding to the traitors' blows.

Be wary of the heavens' premonitions:
The lightning bolt that breaks beyond the sun
May swallow up the boat tied to the shore.
All hands on deck! — The hurricane draws nigh!
The faithless ocean's azure tells a lie!

Arise, then! Raise up tribunes everywhere
To defend your rights and the cause that we all share!
In this sacred moment none must close his eyes
To the mighty act that grows and gains in force.
Be ready! No heart can suffer its own silence
When each supports the happiness of all!
Have you but a penny, give it away,
And thus avoid to the robber falling prey.
And you, oppressed one, have you but a stone,
Go crush the wicked, haughty tyrants' head!

Awaken now and see the day that dawns,
So long awaited, ardently, by all.
Go forth to give your fullest dedication,
Your finest thought to the work that has begun,
And unite your hearts in a single, solemn cry,
Proclaiming proudly: Long live Liberty!

New Orleans, 4 April 1867

[published Sunday, 14 April 1867]

Au Père Chocarne

Pierre (l'Hermite) [pseudonyme d'un auteur inconnu]

Mon Très Révérend Père,
Un nègre obscur et méprisé,
Écoutait enivré, la semaine dernière,
Votre verbe irisé.

Il sentait dans son être,
Entrer comme un éclair de foi :
Il allait rejeter son consolant « Peut-être »
Et rembrasser la croix ;

Mais cet homme, ce nègre, ô Révérend Père,
Tandis qu'il se laissait emporter, éperdu,
Au tumulte pompeux de votre accent austère,
Détacha ses regards et son cœur de la chaire ;
Et le suprême appel qu'il avait entendu,
Comme un soupir divin, adresser à son âme,
Ne fut bientôt qu'une mourante flamme,
Qu'un fugitif souvenir
Que la réalité fit vite évanouir ;
Car il se rappela que, même en cette église,
Les apôtres du Christ souffrent que l'on méprise
Que l'on relègue, en certains bancs,
Non pas de grands pécheurs, non pas d'impurs tyrans,
Mais bien de pauvres gens
Dont le seul tort, dont le seul crime,
Aux yeux du blanc qui les opprime,
Est d'avoir
Le teint noir.

Vous allez donc tonner contre cette injustice :
Du temple Jésus-Christ sut chasser les marchands,
À votre tour, chassez-en les méchants,
Et ne paraissez pas en être complice.
En pensant au poète obscur et méprisé
Que captiva votre verbe irisé,
Vous leur direz, ô très Révérend Père,
Qu'un blanc, qui ne veut pas qu'un nègre soit son frère,
N'a plus le droit sacré d'appeler Dieu son père.

[publié le mardi 16 avril 1867]

To Father Chocarne [54]

PETER (THE HERMIT)[55] [pseudonym of unknown author]

>   My Reverend Father most dear,
>   A negro, unknown and shunned,
>   Last week did happen to hear
> Your rainbow-colored words, which left him stunned.
>
>   Asudden he did feel
>   Faith's lightning strike his being's core;
>   He was just about to repeal
> His complacent "maybe" and take up the cross once more ...

But this man, this negro, oh Reverend Father,
Having let himself be carried away by delight
At the pompous noise of your language most austere,
From the pulpit then detached his heart and his sight,
And that sovereign call that he had happened to hear,
As though a divine whisper pronouncing his name,
        Became nothing more than a dying flame,
            A fleeting memory,
Dissolved by reality,
For he recalled that within this very church
The apostles of Christ permit that some besmirch
        His name by assigning to certain pews,
Not hardened sinners or fiends with tyrannical views,
            But ordinary folks
        Whose only crime, whose only sin,
        In the eyes of oppressive white men,
                Is to dwell in
                Black skin.

It falls to you to denounce this grave injustice:
From the temple Jesus drove the moneychangers;
    Expel in turn these wicked strangers
To truth, and avoid appearing to be their accomplice.
Remembering the poet, unknown and shunned,
    Whom your rainbow-colored words so stunned,
    You must tell them, dearest Reverend Father,
That any white man who refuses a negro as brother
Forfeits the right to refer to God as his Father.

            [published Tuesday, 16 April 1867]

---

54. Bernard Chocarne (1826–95), a French priest of the Dominican order, came from France to the United States in 1866, visiting New Orleans before undertaking work in Canada.

55. This pseudonym of an unknown author pays homage to Peter of Amiens (1050–1115), a medieval priest who participated in the First Crusade and died in Jerusalem.

La Marseillaise noire (*) : chant de paix

Air : La Marseillaise

CAMILLE NAUDIN [pseudonyme d'un auteur inconnu]

      Fils d'Africains ! Tristes victimes,
      Qu'un joug absurde abrutissait.
      De monstres oubliant les crimes,
      Pensons à Jésus qui disait : (*bis*)
      « Peuples, plus de sang, plus de guerre
      « Qui font rougir l'humanité,
      « Moi je suis la *Fraternité*,
      « Embrassez-vous, vous êtes frères. »
Debout ! l'heure est venue, à chaque travailleur
Le pain (*bis*) qu'il a gagné, qu'importe sa couleur.

      Assez longtemps ! le fouet infâme
      De ses sillons nous a brisés,
      Sans nom, sans patrie et sans âme ;
      Assez de fers ! de honte, assez ! (*bis*)
      Que dans une sainte alliance
      Les noirs et les blancs confondus
      À la mort des anciens abus,
      Marchent tous pleins de confiance,
Debout ! etc.

      Debout ! c'est l'heure solennelle !
      Où sur le vieux monde écroulé
      Le despotisme qui chancelle
      Vient couronner la *Liberté* ;
      La discorde reprend sa pomme,
      La raison humaine grandit ;
      C'est l'intelligence et l'esprit
      Et non plus la peau qui fait l'homme.
Debout ! etc.

      Plus d'ombre ! partout la lumière,
      C'est l'Évangile qui paraît ;
      Le Blanc dit au Noir : mon frère,
      À jamais Caïn disparaît[.]
      Plus de sang ! l'impie ignorance,
      Arme terrible du tyran,
      Aux peuples s'entredéchirant
      Ne dit plus : mort, sang et vengeance.
Debout ! etc.

The Black Marseillaise (*): Song of Peace

To the tune of "La Marseillaise"

CAMILLE NAUDIN [pseudonym of unknown author]

      Sons of Africans! Sad victims,
      Crippled by a yoke absurd,
      Let us forget those heinous crimes
      And think instead on Jesus's words: (*bis*)
      "Ye peoples, let war no more
      "Shed blood on humanity,
      "For I am *Fraternity*;
      "Embrace each other, for brothers are ye."
Arise! The hour is come: to every laborer,
The bread (*bis*) that he has earned, whatever his color.

      For long enough, the lash's infamy
      Has carved its cruel mark on our frame,
      Without name, nor soul, nor country;
      Enough of chains! Enough of our shame! (*bis*)
      In a most holy alliance
      May blacks and whites all unite,
      Once wrongs of old have turned to right,
      And walk together in confidence.
Arise! etc.

      Arise! It is the solemn hour!
      As the old world tumbles down,
      Despotism's faltering power
      Upon *Liberty* sets a crown;
      Discord unsows its own seeds;
      Human reason does advance;
      Character and intelligence
      — Not color — will secure man's needs.
Arise! etc.

      No more darkness! Light will shine,
      And the Gospel now appears;
      White says to black: Brother mine,
      Cain's curse forever disappears.
      No more bloodshed! Vile ignorance,
      The deadly arm of tyrants,
      To nations locked in war,
      Says no more: death, blood, and vengeance.
Arise! etc.

>   Allons ! malgré votre race,
>   Hommes de cœur, unissez-vous ;
>   Ici-bas chacun à sa place,
>   Car le soleil luit pour tous.
>   Que chaque peuple heureux, prospère,
>   Au fronton de l'humanité,
>   Grave ces mots : en toi j'espère,
>   Tu régneras, *Égalité*.

Nouvelle-Orléans, 17 juin 1867

(*) M. de Lamartine, dans son drame, intitulé *Toussaint Louverture*, a fait une Marseillaise Noire. Bien entendu qu'il n'y a que le titre qui ressemble à mon poème.

[publié le dimanche 21 juillet 1867]

!

Lélia D...t [Adolphe Duhart]

Encore un qui fuit cette vie,
Encore un que fauche le Temps,
Encore une âme ici ravie,
Encor l'hiver sur nos printemps !
La mort, sous les lourds plis funèbres
Du manteau de plomb des ténèbres,
Au ciel a voilé les rayons.
Entendez-vous sous son vol sombre
Ces longs gémissements sans nombre ?...
Seules plaintes que nous ayons...

Tant qu'en notre sphère on existe,
Le jour le plus pur est flétri ;
On s'abreuve, morose et triste,
À la coupe de miel aigri.
Les pleurs en notre amère extase,
Comme l'eau débordant d'un vase,
Dans nos yeux ne tarissent pas...
Chaque heure la glaneuse avide
Laisse au foyer un siège vide,
Et creuse un tombeau sur nos pas.

Forward! In spite of your race,
Men of heart, now all unite;
Here below, each has a place,
For one and all the sun shines bright.
May each people on the pediment
Of a prosperous humanity
Engrave these words: In you I hope,
Ever shall you reign, *Equality*.

New Orleans, 17 June 1867

(*) Mr. de Lamartine included a "Black Marseillaise" in his drama *Toussaint Louverture*. It goes without saying that only the title bears any resemblance to my poem.[56]

56. The French poet Alphonse de Lamartine's *Toussaint Louverture*, an antislavery verse drama set during the Haitian Revolution, was first performed and published in Paris in 1850.

[published Sunday, 21 July 1867]

![57]

LÉLIA D——T [Adolphe Duhart]

Another one has left this life,
Another harvested by Time,
Another soul snatched by a thief,
Another winter falls on springtime!
Beneath the heavy burial shrouds
Of the leaden cloak of the darkest clouds,
Death has concealed the rays of the sun.
Do you hear the long and endless groanings
Beneath the gloomy flight of its wings?
These are our dirges — these alone ...

As long as we inhabit this sphere,
The boldest day can only cower;
We're forced to drink, morose and somber,
At the cup of honey all gone sour.
Through tears of bitter ecstasy,
Like a vase that one cannot empty,
Our crying eyes continue to plead ...
At every hour the gleaner's greed
Leaves behind an empty seat
And digs a grave beneath our feet.

57. Composed soon after Duhart learned of the death of Armand Lanusse (who died unexpectedly on 16 Mar. 1868), this elegy, found in rarely consulted 1868 issues of *La Tribune* at the Boston Athenaeum, has been until this publication unknown to scholars.
  Lanusse's sudden passing would have sent shock waves through the Creole community. Duhart's poem about his friend, mentor, and fellow educator offers a uniquely personal window onto an important public figure and likely voices the feelings of many of Lanusse's contemporaries.
  If the specified date of composition is accurate, the poem was published the very day it was written. Intentional or not, the matching dates give the appearance of Duhart's penning "!" in a fit of inspiration and publishing it immediately, possibly to coincide with his mentor's funeral.

Ainsi l'existence est remplie
De noirs chagrins sur nous penchés,
Et le destin fatal délie
Tous ceux qu'il avait attachés...
Et dans l'immense fourmilière,
Dans nos sillons pleins de lumière,
Dans nos nuits aux rêves troublés,
La mort, que rien ne peut distraire,
Fait sa récolte funéraire,
Comme le faneur sur les blés !

Il ne sera pas dit, poète,
Que ma lyre longtemps en deuil,
Oublieuse, froide et muette
N'aura rien dit sur ton cercueil ;
Qu'une larme de ma paupière
N'aura pas mouillé l'humble pierre
Qui maintenant scelle à jamais
Au fond de l'humide ossuaire
Le morne et sinistre suaire
Où tu dormiras désormais...

Toi, dont la vie est effacée
De nos tristes sentiers perdus,
Sens-tu sur ta tête glacée
Les fleurs de nos seins éperdus ?
Toi qui partis l'âme sereine,
Courbé sous la main souveraine,
Entends-tu, Armand, les sanglots,
Les prières interrompues
De ces existences rompues
Que tu délaisses dans nos flots ?

Oh ! si ta voix noble, sonore,
Pleine d'équité, de raison,
Pouvait se faire entendre encore
Au milieu de notre horizon,
Tu dirais aux partis : — Arrière !
Vos promesses sont que poussière !
Tu dirais à l'orgueil superbe
Qu'il n'est qu'une seule Genèse,
Et que dans la même fournaise
Dieu fit sortir la fleur et l'herbe.

Our earthly life will know no peace
From darkness where sorrows around us abound
And destiny's hands will soon release
Everyone whom it had bound ...
Amidst the immense and bustling hive,
Throughout our nights where nightmares thrive,
Along our furrows filled with light,
Death, whom nothing can deceive,
When harvesting of souls grants no reprieve,
Just like the gleaner reaping wheat!

Never shall it be said, oh poet,
That my lyre, long in mourning interred,
Forgetful, cold, and fallen quiet,
Upon your coffin spoke not a word —
That nary a tear from my eyelid sown
Did ever wet the humble stone
That now and hereafter does enclose
In the dark depths of the ossuary
The burial shroud, dank and dreary,
Where you sleep in eternal repose.

You whose life will no more tread
Our sad and lonely road,
Do you feel upon your freezing head
The flowers our frantic bosoms unload?
You who left with tranquil goal
Directed by a sovereign will,
Do you hear, Armand, the sob-filled pleas,
The interrupted prayers
Of disrupted lives whose cares
You've abandoned to our rolling seas?

Oh! If your noble voice, resounding
With fairness, justice, and reason,
Could once again be heard sounding
Across the length of our horizon,
You'd tell all parties with disgust,
"Your promises are nothing but dust!"
You'd surely say to the prideful powers
That only one Genesis ever occurred
And into one crucible speaking his Word
Did God create the grass and flowers.

Tu dirais : — Tiens-toi sur tes gardes !
Peuple, l'ennemi ne dort pas.
Sur la route où tu te hasardes,
Il est des pièges sous tes pas.
Tu nous dirais à tous : — Courage !
Au firmament s'éteint l'orage ;
Et la douce Fraternité,
À l'Orient bleu qui s'allume,
Brise chaque jour sur l'enclume
Les chaînes de la Liberté !

Et chacun à ta voix austère,
Attentif et pieux se tairait,
Comme Sparte savait se taire
Devant ceux qu'elle vénérait.
Et dans ce siècle plein de doute,
L'on voudrait suivre alors la route
Indiquée ainsi par ta main ;
Et tous, vers le fraternel pôle,
Marcheraient sans autre boussole
Pour les guider dans le chemin.

Mais dans l'enceinte glaciale
Tu dors du sommeil du tombeau...
Ta vie ici-bas fut loyale,
Tu peux en souffler le flambeau.
Dors ! Laisse pour nous le présage
D'un futur que nous croyons sage.
Dors tranquille loin de nos yeux,
Toi qui finis le drame auguste
Couché dans le linceul du juste,
Et souviens-toi de nous aux cieux...

Nouvelle-Orléans, 18 mars 1868

[publié le mercredi 18 mars 1868]

You'd say as well, "Remain on guard!
For, people, the enemy never sleeps,
And whether the road be easy or hard,
Beware the traps beneath your steps."
To all of us you'd say, "Courage!
The storm exits the heaven's stage,
And each day sweet Fraternity,
Illumining the Orient's blue,
Upon its anvil cuts in two
The chains of Liberty!"

The sound of your voice on each and all,
At silent attention, wrought its effect,
Just as in Sparta silence did fall
For those who commanded the city's respect.
And in this era plagued by doubt,
It's better that we follow the route
Delineated by your hand;
Toward fraternity's pole the masses
Would march, forgoing other compasses
To guide their path across the land.

Inside the casket's cold enclosure
You've sunk into the sleep of the tomb . . .
Your life was loyal, its good faith pure;
The time has come to snuff out its flame.
Sleep! But leave for us a sign
To believe in the future's sound design.
Sleep in peace, far from our eyes;
Through a glorious drama having progressed
And lying draped in the shroud of the just,
Remember us from the heights of the skies . . .

New Orleans, 18 March 1868

[published Wednesday, 18 March 1868]

THE WORLD OF IDEAS

L'Ignorance

Henry [Henry Louis Rey]

C'est le mal de l'Humanité.
C'est le ver rongeur qui l'épuise,
Ce qui de tout temps la maîtrise,
Et muselle la Liberté.

C'est par ses lois que Galilée,
En instruisant, est accusé ;
Que la science est ravalée
Et l'absurde divinisé.

C'est par arrêt de l'Ignorance
Que Jésus, l'apôtre divin,
Subit une ignoble sentence,
En voulant le progrès humain ;

Que Jeanne d'Arc, Socrate et d'autres,
Christophe Colomb, Swedenborg,
De la vérité les apôtres,
Sont ou raillés ou mis à mort !

Oui, dans le monde politique,
Social ou religieux,
Comme dans le monde artistique,
L'Ignorance trône en tous lieux.

C'est l'éteignoir de la science,
La cause de tous nos revers ;
C'est l'enfer vrai de l'existence,
Le seul Satan de l'univers.

Mais ce siècle de lumière,
À sa barre veut juger tout ;
Et notre raison, libre et fière,
Pénètre maintenant partout.

De ses assises solennelles
Sort l'arrêt de la vérité :
Liberté, paix universelles,
Bonheur humain, fraternité !

Ignorance [58]

HENRY [Henry Louis Rey]

It is the bane of Humanity.
It is the gnawing worm that feeds,
That which in all times impedes
And seeks to muzzle Liberty.

Galileo stood accused
Because its laws were applied,
As is science still refused
And utter nonsense deified.

It was by decree of Ignorance
That Jesus, our divine witness,
Received a wrongful sentence
For wanting human progress;

That Joan of Arc, Socrates,
And other apostles of truth —
Swedenborg, Columbus —
Were either mocked or put to death!

Yes, in political affairs,
In religious and social domains,
As well as in artistic matters,
Unchallenged, Ignorance reigns.

'Tis the hand that snuffs out science;
'Tis the cause of each and every loss,
The true hell of human existence,
The sole Satan in the cosmos.

But judgment will come, clear and loud,
From this enlightened age of ours,
For reason, rising free and proud,
Increasingly extends its powers.

Its solemn courts will soon release
The terms of truth's decree:
Freedom, universal peace,
Happiness, and harmony!

58. This poem appeared in the inaugural issue of *L'Union*. Later, in 1865, Rey published a slightly modified version in *La Tribune* (see pp. 180–83).

Qu'importe si le canon gronde,
Si partout s'entrouvre un tombeau :
C'est le départ d'un mauvais monde,
L'aurore d'un autre plus beau !

Nouvelle-Orléans, 22 septembre 1862

[publié le samedi 27 septembre 1862]

Maris Stella

À Mme P. D.

LÉLIA D... T [Adolphe Duhart]

Étoile, pure étoile,
Oh ! sur les flots amers
Guide ma blanche voile,
Douce étoile des mers.

Hélas ! qui va, sans toi, de ma frêle nacelle
Écarter l'aquilon qui souffle l'ouragan ;
Que ta prière au moins, mon étoile fidèle,
La conduise toujours sur l'immense Océan.

Vois, déjà sur les flots mollement balancée,
Ma nacelle dérive, et bientôt sans effort
Par le vent qui fraîchit vivement élancée,
Elle sillonne l'onde et fuit enfin le port.

Oh ! l'orage, mon Dieu ! le ciel rougit, s'allume ;
Comme un lion blessé la mer roule et bondit ;
Ma nacelle se tord sur les flots blancs d'écume,
Et semble s'engloutir dans l'Océan maudit...

❖

Voici qu'à l'horizon s'éteint l'ardente flamme ;
Le hardi matelot reprend son chant joyeux.
L'ouragan est passé... Maintenant chaque lame
Doucement s'aplanit et réfléchit les cieux !

Étoile ! douce étoile,
Oh ! sur les flots amers
Guide ma blanche voile,
Douce étoile des mers.

[publié le dimanche 15 janvier 1865]

What matters it that cannons roar,
That all around an open tomb yawns:
For 'tis the end of one bad world
As another, much more beautiful, dawns!

New Orleans, 22 September 1862

[published Saturday, 27 September 1862]

Maris Stella [59]

For Madame P. D. [60]

LÉLIA D——T [Adolphe Duhart]

Star, oh purest star,
Across the waves, will you please
Guide my white sails far,
Sweet, sweet star of the seas.

Alas! Without you, who is going to steer
Away from me the winds that drive the hurricane?
Please let your prayer, at least, my faithful star,
Escort me always o'er the endless Ocean.

Behold, upon the waves that gently sway,
My fragile craft does drift, and soon with ease
Propelled by the breeze that blows a refreshing spray,
She'll flee the port and finally roam the seas.

A storm, my God! The sky grows red with gloom;
Like a wounded lion the sea does leap and roll.
My boat now writhes upon the whitened spume
And starts to sink into the cursèd swell . . .

❖

Upon the horizon the flame that blazed now dims;
The stalwart sailor sings to his heart's content.
The hurricane has passed . . . Each wave, it seems,
Returns to calm and reflects the firmament!

Star, oh purest star,
Across the waves, will you please
Guide my white sails far,
Sweet, sweet star of the seas.

[published Sunday, 15 January 1865]

59. Latin for "Star of the Sea," *Maris Stella* refers both to Polaris (or the polestar), an important point in traditional navigation, and to the Virgin Mary.

60. These initials likely refer to the poet's spouse, Odilia Boyer — namely, Madame Pierre-Adolphe Duhart.

Le moqueur

À Mme L. S...

LÉLIA D...T [Adolphe Duhart]

C'était au mois de mai : le jour s'était voilé ;
Un silence profond régnait sur la nature ;
À l'Orient montait sous le dôme étoilé,
      Diane radieuse et pure.

Dans ce calme soudain d'un magique moqueur
Le poétique chant vibra large et sonore,
Et sa voix arrivant jusqu'au fond de mon cœur
      Le faisait tressaillir encore.

L'écho dormait aussi, le zéphyr l'imitait,
Les parfums s'échappaient des serres embaumées
Et du feuillage vert qu'au loin il agitait,
      Nul bruit de Péris alarmées.

Rien que ce chant si beau qui glissait à l'entour,
Descendait, remontait en gammes modulées,
Puis expirait encor, renaissait tour à tour,
      Et vibrait en phrases perlées.

Et ce sublime chant, toujours harmonieux,
Doucement réveillait, en mon âme éperdue,
De mon premier amour l'accent mélodieux,
      La suave note perdue...

        [publié le dimanche 5 mars 1865]

L'Ignorance

HENRY [Henry Louis Rey]

C'est le mal de l'humanité,
C'est le ver rongeur qui l'épuise,
Ce qui de tout temps la maîtrise,
Et muselle la Liberté.

C'est par ses lois que Galilée
En instruisant est accusé,
Que la science est ravalée
Et l'absurde divinisé.

The Mockingbird

For Mrs. L. S.

LÉLIA D——T [Adolphe Duhart]

'Twas in the month of May; the day was veiled;
A silence profound prevailed o'er all of nature;
To the East, beneath the starry dome, hailed
      Diana — radiant, pure.

Amidst the calm, a poetic song did start
From the magical mockingbird, resounding full,
And its voice, reaching the very depths of my heart,
      Its quivering strings did pull.

The echo then slept, and Zephyr followed suit;
From scented hothouses fragrances worked their charm,
And, from the green foliage that, afar, it shook about,
      No Peri[61] cried out in alarm.

Only this song, so lovely, starting to soar,
Descended and rose in modulated scales,
Then once again expired, to be born once more,
      And sounded phrases like pearls.

And this song sublime and ever harmonious
Did gently within my raptured soul awaken
Of my very first love the accent melodious —
      The sweet note, now long gone . . .

      [published Sunday, 5 March 1865]

61. A female fairy in Persian folklore.

Ignorance [62]

HENRY [Henry Louis Rey]

It is the bane of humanity.
It is the gnawing worm that feeds,
That which in all times impedes
And seeks to muzzle Liberty.

Galileo stood accused
Because its laws were applied,
As is science still refused
And utter nonsense deified.

62. This revised version of Rey's 1862 Spiritualist-themed poem (see pp. 176–79) includes minor adjustments and adds a stanza specifically condemning reactionary neo-Confederate ideology (stanza 6).

C'est par arrêt de l'ignorance
Que Jésus, l'apôtre divin,
Subit une ignoble sentence,
En voulant le progrès humain ;

Que Paul, Jeanne, Socrate et d'autres,
Colomb, Fourier et Swedenborg,
De la vérité les apôtres,
Sont ou raillés ou mis à mort.

Oui, dans le monde politique,
Ou social, ou religieux,
Comme dans le scientifique,
L'ignorance trône en tous lieux.

Elle fait naître tous les crimes,
Le Sud, l'Esclavage et leurs *droits*.
Le sang de leurs mille victimes
Baigne le sol en mille endroits.

C'est l'éteignoir de la science,
La cause de tous nos revers,
C'est l'enfer vrai de l'existence,
Le seul Satan de l'univers.

Mais ce grand siècle de lumière,
À sa barre, veut juger tout,
Et notre raison libre et fière
Pénètre maintenant partout.

De ses assises solennelles
Sort l'arrêt de la vérité,
Liberté, paix universelles,
Bonheur humain, fraternité !

Qu'importe si le canon gronde,
Si partout s'entrouvre un tombeau,
C'est la chute d'un mauvais monde
Préparant un autre plus beau !

[publié le dimanche 28 mai 1865]

It was by decree of ignorance
That Jesus, our divine witness,
Received a wrongful sentence
For wanting human progress;

That Paul, Joan, Socrates,
And other apostles of truth —
Fourier, Swedenborg, and Columbus —
Were either mocked or put to death!

Indeed, in political affairs,
In religious and social domains,
As in scientific matters,
Unchallenged, ignorance reigns.

'Tis the thing that spawns all crimes:
The South, Slavery, and their "rights."
The blood of thousands of victims
Soaks the soil at thousands of sites.

'Tis the hand that snuffs out science;
'Tis the cause of each and every loss,
The true hell of human existence,
The sole Satan in the cosmos.

But judgment will come, clear and loud,
From this enlightened age of ours,
For reason, rising free and proud,
Increasingly extends its powers.

Its solemn courts will soon release
The terms of truth's decree:
Freedom, universal peace,
Happiness, and harmony!

What matters it that cannons roar,
That all around the tomb lies open:
For 'tis the fall of one bad world
Preparing another more beautiful one!

[published Sunday, 28 May 1865]

Résignation

Henry [Henry Louis Rey]

Loin de la cité populeuse,
Loin de la foule et loin du bruit,
Que de fois mon âme rêveuse,
Sur l'œil du désir s'enfuit !
Vers la forêt la plus prochaine,
Où Dieu parle par mille voix,
Elle prend son essor sans peine
Et se dilate dans les bois.

Dans ce concert de la nature,
Parmi les fleurs, au sein des champs,
L'hymne saint de la créature,
À Dieu, s'élève en purs accents !
Ici, de paisibles ruisseaux
Serpentent gaîment dans la plaine ;
Là, le chant joyeux des oiseaux
Ravit les sens et les enchaîne.

Dans le lointain est le bocage,
Auprès duquel paît le troupeau ;
D'heureux groupes sous le feuillage
Dansent aux sons du chalumeau.
Tout nous séduit et nous enchante
Dans ce séjour délicieux ;
La foi dans l'âme est plus ardente,
L'homme s'est rapproché des cieux.

De cet asile favorable
À mes penchants, à mes souhaits,
L'arrêt d'un destin implacable
M'éloigne, hélas ! à tout jamais.
Plaignez mon sort, j'y voudrais vivre,
— Entouré de soins et d'amour —
Chimères dont le cœur s'enivre
Et que le temps dissipe un jour !

[publié le dimanche 11 juin 1865]

Resignation

Henry [Henry Louis Rey]

Far away from the populous city,
Far from the crowd and its noisy cries,
How often does my soul, grown dreamy,
Fly away on desire's eye!
Fleeing to a forest's nearby trees
Where a thousand voices speak, all God's,
It soon takes wing with utter ease
And swells with joy among the woods.

In this concert performed by nature
Amidst the flowers, upon the fields,
In sacred hymns each creature
To God its purest accents yields!
Here do peaceful streams wind by
Merrily across the plains;
There the birds sing joyfully,
Wrapping our senses in their chains.

Farther still awaits the bocage
Next to which a flock is grazing;
Happy groups gathered under the foliage
Dance to the chalumeau's musings.
All things seduce, all things enchant
In this delightful country;
The soul's faith becomes more ardent,
For man's drawn closer to the sky.

But from this refuge which supplies
My wishes and my fantasies,
The cruel decree of destiny
Forever — alas! — tears me away.
Surrounded by love and free of care
I wish to dwell; oh pity my fate,
For time will dispel, sooner or later,
These illusions that intoxicate!

[published Sunday, 11 June 1865]

Épître familière

*À ma muse qui m'engageait à adresser
une pièce de vers à une institutrice*

HENRY [Henry Louis Rey]

Puisque tu veux que je m'engage
À te charger d'un mot flatteur,
D'un vœu sous forme de message,
Pour ta savante et digne sœur ;

Dis-lui que le monde des causes
Pour instrument doit la choisir.
Dis-lui les merveilleuses choses
Qu'elle est sur le point d'accomplir ;

Que cette indigène jeunesse
Qu'elle retire de l'erreur
Fera sa gloire et son ivresse,
Et lui devra le vrai bonheur.

Dis-lui qu'il faut dans cette voie
Si rude de la vérité,
Subir le martyre avec joie,
Pour le bien de l'humanité.

Mais ton éloquente parole,
Qu'inspire le souffle divin,
Bien mieux que mon verbe frivole,
Saura lui tracer son chemin.

Dis-lui, dans ton style angélique,
Que surtout les grandes douleurs,
Et les luttes et les malheurs,
Ont enfanté l'âme héroïque.

Rappelle-lui mais, après tout,
À cette sœur, à quoi bon dire,
Ce que sa science, surtout,
À son esprit sans cesse inspire !

Implorons donc l'ordre Divin,
Pour ce pontife de la cause :
Sur elle aussi l'on se repose
Pour réformer le genre humain.

A Familiar Epistle

*To my muse who made me promise to compose
a work of verse for a schoolteacher*

Henry [Henry Louis Rey]

Because you want me to propose,
For you to use, a word of flattery,
A vow as a message composed
For your sister, learnèd and worthy.

You can tell her that the world of causes
Must choose her as its agent,
And tell her of the wondrous successes
Prepared for her attainment.

That the native youth of our country
Whom daily she rescues from blindness
Will be her joy and glory,
Owing to her their happiness.

You can tell her that along this
Arduous road of truth she'll find
A martyrdom replete with bliss
For the good of humankind.

But your eloquence, once heard,
Inspired by God's transcendent breath,
More surely than my empty words
Will guide her down her path.

Do say, in your angelic style,
That great unhappiness
And struggles and distress
Give birth to a heroic soul.

Remind her — but then what sense
Is there in telling your sister
The things that her intelligence
Inspires in her character?

So let us beseech divine grace
For this pontiff of the cause:
On her do we rely likewise
To reform the human race.

Que son auréole rayonne
D'un éclat bienfaisant et pur,
Que son ciel soit toujours d'azur,
Et la vérité sa couronne !

Dieu protège notre apôtre,
D'amour, de foi, de charité,
Et que son succès soit le nôtre
Pour le progrès, la liberté !

Que cette sœur que chacun aime
Sitôt qu'on a connu ses traits
Soit à jamais pour nous l'emblème
De la sagesse et des bienfaits !

L'heure du triomphe s'avance,
Que sa foi redouble d'ardeur,
Peines, sacrifices, labeur,
Tout recevra sa récompense !

[publié le dimanche 2 juin 1865]

Le saule pleureur

À Mlle N…e F…to

Lélia D…t [Adolphe Duhart]

> *Venite ad me omnes qui laboratis*
> *et onerati [estis] et ego reficiam vos.*
> — Math. [11]

Venez, vous qui souffrez… oh ! venez sous mon ombre ;
Je cache saintement sous mon feuillage sombre
Un génie, une femme au front pur et rêveur ;
Ses longs cheveux dorés voilent son œil humide
Et tombent mollement jusqu'à son pied timide :
    C'est la muse de la douleur.

Venez : autour de moi s'étend la verte mousse,
Et la brise qui passe est plus fraîche et plus douce.
Venez, vous dont le cœur se plaît à s'isoler,
Vous trouverez enfin — comme un divin dictame —
Celle que vous rêvez, et que cherche votre âme,
    Celle qui doit vous consoler.

Forever may her halo gleam
With a radiance kind and pure;
May her sky be of the truest azure
And truth her diadem!

May God protect this prophetess
Of love and faith and charity;
And may we share in her success
For progress and for liberty!

May this sister loved by each and all
Who come to make her acquaintance
Forever be to us a symbol
Of wisdom and benevolence.

The hour of triumph now moves forward;
May her faith increase in fervor,
For sorrows, sacrifice, and labor
Will all receive their just reward!

[published Sunday, 2 June 1865]

The Weeping Willow

For Miss N——e F——to [63]

Lélia D——t [Adolphe Duhart]

> *Venite ad me omnes qui laboratis*
> *et onerati [estis] et ego reficiam vos.*
> — Math. [11] [64]

All ye who suffer, come ... oh! come into my shade;
Beneath my somber foliage, devotedly I hide
A genie, a woman crowned with pure and dreamy brow.
Her long and golden hair keeps cloaked a tear-filled eye
And, all the way down to her timid feet, falls lazily:
    She is the muse of sorrow.

Come where all around me lies a greenish, mossy sheet,
And the breeze that passes through feels fresher and more sweet.
Come, all ye whose hearts desire isolation,
At last you'll find — just like a sacramental balm —
Her of whom you dream, from whom your soul seeks calm,
    To give you consolation.

63. The schoolteacher Nathalie Formento (1834–1926), later Populus after her marriage in 1870, was a friend and muse of several of the poets of *La Tribune*. The daughter of a well-known Italian surgeon and a woman of color, Félicia Mélot, she was a teacher at the Institution catholique. In the 1890s, she became involved in anti-segregation activism through publications in the civil rights newspaper the *Crusader*.

64. Matthew 11.28: "Come to me, all you who toil and are burdened, and I will give you rest." The original 1865 publication of the poem misidentified the source as Matthew, ch. 14.

Venez : amante et vierge elle écoute la plainte ;
Elle sèche les pleurs, éloigne toute crainte
Et vous fait espérer un meilleur avenir,
Vous promettant ainsi des heures moins amères,
Elle fait reparaître à vos yeux les chimères
        De votre lointain avenir.

D'un baiser qui désarme une main homicide,
Elle console ceux qui rêvent de suicide...
Sur leurs pas chancelants elle sème des fleurs.
Aimer et soupirer, c'est souffrir, leur dit-elle ;
Mais à cette douleur on est toujours fidèle,
        Tant elle plaît aux pauvres cœurs.

C'est ainsi qu'elle endort leur cruelle souffrance
En leur donnant toujours une douce espérance.
Quelle est donc cette femme ? — C'est votre ange gardien,
C'est votre chaste sœur, la plus fidèle amie
Qui veille encor sur vous quand votre âme endormie
        Vous laisse esseulé, sans soutien.

— Comment la nomme-t-on ? — Son nom ? Mélancolie.
Elle a sa douce sœur, la molle Rêverie
Qui demeure bien loin dans la sombre forêt.
Comme la frêle fleur que saisit la tempête,
Elle vient tous les jours pencher sa blonde tête
        Sur son sein aimant et discret.

Venez, vous qui souffrez... oh ! venez sous mon ombre ;
Vous trouverez toujours sous mon feuillage sombre
Les deux sœurs écoutant les doux chants des oiseaux,
Le souffle des zéphyrs dans mes feuilles plaintives,
Et des anges aimés les notes fugitives
        Rasant le bord des blanches eaux.

        [publié le dimanche 16 juillet 1865]

Come: let this virgin lover dry your tears;
She'll listen to your troubles and drive away your fears.
She'll give you cause to hope for a future more secure;
With promises of days less embittered by frustrations,
Before your eyes she'll make appear hallucinations
        That show your distant future.

With a kiss that can disarm the hand of homicide,
She comforts those who fantasize of suicide . . .
Behind their stumbling steps, she sows the seeds of flowers.
"To love and to long, that is to suffer," to them she says;
But to this pain we do remain faithful always,
        For it pleases these poor hearts of ours.

And thus she sets to sleep their cruelest sufferings
By always giving to them hope's sweet offerings.
Who can this woman be? — She is your guardian angel,
Your sister ever chaste, your ever loyal friend,
Who watches over you whene'er your soul, benumbed,
        Forsaking you, bids farewell.

By what name is she called? — Her name? Melancholy.
She has a sister, soft and sweet, known as Reverie,
Who dwells far away in the dark depths of the forest,
Just like the frail flower by the tempest carried away,
She comes here every day her blond-haired head to lay
        Upon the other's loving breast.

All ye who suffer, come . . . Oh! come into my shade;
You'll always find beneath my foliage's spread
Two sisters enjoying the sounds of the birds' gentle warblings,
The zephyr's breath that through my leaves sighs wistfully,
And fleeting notes from angels dearly loved who fly
        Near the water's edge which they graze with their wings.

    [published Sunday, 16 July 1865]

Une page de Hebel

Imitation
À Madame C... S...

LÉLIA D... T [Adolphe Duhart]

Il est temps d'en finir avec ces causeries
      Et ces serments vains et trompeurs ;
Il est temps d'enterrer toutes ces rêveries,
      Légères comme des vapeurs.

Allez donc me chercher — silencieux, dans l'ombre —
      Un immense et profond cercueil :
Qu'il soit de noir tendu, qu'il soit enfin bien sombre,
      Car j'y veux cacher un grand deuil...

Puis apportez ensuite une longue civière
      Faite de chêne épais et dur.
Elle doit être ainsi d'une force première,
      Que le bois soit bien sain, bien pur.

Enfin, faites venir de leurs lieux de supplice
      Ces géants maudits — les titans —
Ces damnés au front hâve et que la douleur plisse
      Sous ses aiguillons irritants.

Ce sont eux qui devront par un effort sublime,
      Calmant leurs cris et leurs sanglots,
Porter ce lourd cercueil au bord du sombre abîme,
      Et l'ensevelir dans ses flots.

Mais pourquoi ce cercueil sera si lourd, madame,
      Dites, le voulez-vous savoir ?
C'est que j'y placerai le secret de mon âme :
      Mon amour et mon désespoir !...

          [publié le dimanche 5 novembre 1865]

A Page from Hebel [65]

Imitation
For Madame C——S——

LÉLIA D——T [Adolphe Duhart]

[65]. Johann Peter Hebel (1760–1826), a German writer and theologian whose writings in the Alemannic dialect evinced innovative possibilities for vernacular expression in literature.

The time has come to end these long discussions
      And these frivolous, deceitful vows;
The time has come to bury these illusions
      That evaporate like misty dews.

Go find for me — as silently as a shadow —
      A coffin, immense and deep,
And drape it in black, so nothing will show,
      For a great sorrow there I wish to keep . . .

Then bring to me next a gurney of some length,
      Constructed of naught but purest oak.
Ensure that it possesses utmost strength
      And that the wood is hardy and thick.

And, last but not least, from their dungeons of torment, release
      Those accursèd giants — each a titan —
Such haggard souls, condemned to ceaseless distress
      Under the stabbing stings of pain.

It is they who must, in an effort sublime,
      First calming their sobs and hushing their howls,
Transport the heavy coffin to the chasm's brim
      And bury it in the ocean's bowels.

But why, Madame, will this coffin bear such weight?
      Do say: to know do you truly care?
'Tis because within it I'll place my soul's dark secret —
      My love and my despair!

      [published Sunday, 5 November 1865]

« L'existence de Dieu » (1832), par Hortense de Céré-Barbé,
recopié et publié dans *La Tribune* sous le titre :

Il est

   À M. Armand Lanusse

[attribué dans *La Tribune* à « Antony » (Victor Eugène Macarty)]

L'homme a reconnu Dieu sans jamais le comprendre :
Dans ce vaste besoin qu'on ne peut définir,
Son idée est venue avant qu'on pût apprendre ;
À l'esprit jeune encore il semble un souvenir.

Attrait de la raison, perspective de l'âme,
Il habite en effet dans notre humanité,
Traverse notre cœur comme une ardente flamme
Et fixe le remords sur notre iniquité.

Mais le génie en vain dans sa course orgueilleuse
Veut sonder le nuage où Dieu s'est arrêté,
De ce haut examen la chute est périlleuse,
Le blasphème est le fruit de la témérité.

Qui saurait pénétrer l'indivisible essence
De Dieu, qui contient seul sa triple infinité ;
Qui de l'éternité complique sa puissance
Et dont le grand secret est dans sa majesté.

Être, c'est l'attribut de son pouvoir extrême ;
Il est, partout sa force empreint sa vérité.
Lui-même a dit : *je suis* ; et dans ce mot *suprême*
S'explique sa présence et sa divinité.

Quel homme a bien compris cette existence entière,
Qui sans cesse accomplit son immortalité,
Enfante les esprits, compose la matière,
Dont la seule existence a toujours existé.

Quel œil a mesuré ces ténèbres profondes,
De l'abîme du vide empire illimité
Où Dieu par un regard, allumant tous les mondes,
Fit jaillir le néant en pompeuse clarté.

Lorsqu'il eut envahi le gouffre inabordable,
Qu'au bord du firmament son esprit fut porté,
Qui peut imaginer sans quel poids formidable
Dieu fit subitement mouvoir l'immensité.

"The Existence of God" (1832), by Hortense de Céré-Barbé, copied and republished in *La Tribune* as:

He Is [66]

For Mr. Armand Lanusse

[attributed in *La Tribune* to "Antony" (Victor Eugène Macarty)]

Mankind knew God, though understood Him not:
In our endless need that scarce can be defined,
His idea came before we formed the thought;
To the young he seems a memory in the mind.

An appeal to reason, an insight of the soul,
He dwells, in fact, in our very humanity;
He sears through our heart as though an ardent coal,
And casts remorse on our iniquity.

But, in its prideful course, the intellect
Seeks vainly in the clouds God's residence.
From a fall from such inquiry, nothing can protect:
For blasphemy is the fruit of arrogance.

For who can grasp the indivisible core
Of God, who contains his triple infinity,
Who complicates eternity with his power,
And whose secret resides within his majesty?

To be is the attribute of his sovereign might.
He is; his force inscribes its truth everywhere.
He said, *I am*, and this *supreme* insight
Explains his presence and his divine nature.

What man has understood this whole existence
Which ceaselessly makes its immortality,
Gives birth to souls, creates the elements —
Whose existence alone has existed eternally?

What eye has measured the depths of this dark expanse,
The boundless realm of the chasm of nothingness
Where God, lighting up worlds with only a glance,
Brought forth from the void a grand, resplendent brightness?

Once he'd overtaken the impassable abyss,
And once his spirit to the firmament's edge had gone,
Without the great weight necessary for this,
God suddenly set the immensity into motion.

66. On the literary hoax involving the poet "Antony," see pp. 31–35. The version in *La Tribune* titles the poem after one of the phrases emphasized in Céré-Barbé's original, dedicates the poem to Lanusse, and adds a fictitious date of composition. The poem and its new title generated a variety of responses, including Lanusse's "Il n'est pas," which follows.

Et quand la première heure, en silence attendue,
Sonna, qui nous dira le secret du passé,
Et comme chaque étoile, au sein de l'étendue,
Marcha, lorsque Dieu dit : le temps a commencé !

Ô soleils voyageurs ! lumières de sa gloire !
Courriers de l'Éternel, ombres de sa beauté,
Montrez, en déployant sa magnifique histoire,
Que si Dieu *n'était pas*, vous n'eussiez pas *été*.

Couronnez de vos feux son éclatant mystère,
Auprès du Créateur que plus loin je poursuis ;
Et passez dans le ciel pour avertir la terre
Que dans ses œuvres Dieu répète encor : *je suis*.[8]

25 août 1866

[publié le dimanche 2 septembre 1866]

8. The original text by Céré-Barbé ends with an exclamation point.

Il n'est pas

À Antony

ARMAND LANUSSE

Il est. Vous dites vrai, tout ici nous l'atteste,
La preuve abonde autant que le sable en la mer ;
Mais à beaucoup d'esprits, si Dieu se manifeste,
Satan sur d'autres règne en despote d'enfer.

Dieu n'est pas, Antony, pour cet enfant barbare
Qui s'assied chaque jour à de riches repas,
Lorsque chez ses parents la nourriture est rare,
Qu'ils ont besoin de tout : Il n'est pas, Il n'est pas.

Il n'est pas pour la mère indigne et criminelle
Qui jette au vent du soir le fruit de ses amours ;
Quand par nature, instinct et crainte maternelle,
L'hyène porte au sien un incessant secours.

Il n'est pas pour celui qui, fuyant l'arbitraire,
Est venu sur nos bords chercher des jours meilleurs ;
Au même affront auquel il a pu se soustraire
Il soumet maintenant même ses bienfaiteurs.

And once the first hour, anticipated in silence,
And which will tell the past's secrets, did chime;
And when each star, amidst the vast expanse,
Began to move, God said, "Now commences time!"

Oh traveling suns! Oh radiance of his glory!
Eternal messengers, shadows of his beauty,
Show us, by telling his regal history,
That if God *were not*, of you no trace would *there be*.

Crown with your fires the dazzling mystery
Whose Creator I follow as nearly as I can.
Traverse the sky to warn the earth and decree
That through his works our God proclaims, *I am*.

25 August 1866

[published Sunday, 2 September 1866]

He Is Not

To Antony

ARMAND LANUSSE

He is. You speak the truth, as all things do attest,
The proof abounds like, on the ocean's floor, the sand;
But though, to many people, God be manifest,
Satan reigns o'er others with despotic hand.

There is no God, Antony, for the child who feels
No pity for his parents by poverty distraught;
Each day the brute sits down before the finest meals
While they go hungry: He is not; no, He is not.

Nor is He for the mother, unfit and criminal,
Who throws the offspring of her pleasures to the wind;
When, by nature's law and all instincts maternal,
Hyenas even tend the young of their own kind.

Nor is He for the persecuted refugee
Who came to seek a better life upon our shores;
The very same offense that first caused him to flee,
He now commits against his kindest benefactors.

Non, il n'existe pas pour ce ministre oblique
Qui prétend le servir, et méprise sa loi ;
Ni pour ce faux chrétien, ce prêtre catholique
Qui veut qu'un préjugé soit article de foi.

Il n'est pas, Il n'est pas pour ce vil journaliste,
Ce cruel ennemi de toute vérité,
Ce fauteur de méfaits, ce lâche apologiste
De l'attentat, du crime, et de l'atrocité.

Il n'est pas pour ce juge ignorant et rebelle
Qui foule aux pieds la loi contraire à son désir ;
Il n'est pas pour ce « thug » qu'au prétoire on n'appelle
Qu'afin d'y consacrer celle du bon plaisir.

Il n'a jamais été pour ce chacal fait homme,
Pour ses suppôts portant l'habit municipal ;
Quand le premier s'écrie : « Attaque, tue, assomme »,
Chacun d'eux à l'envi remplit l'ordre fatal.

Il n'est pas même, hélas ! pour ce nouveau Moïse
Qui devait protéger un peuple humilié ;
Dans de honteux excès, aide longtemps promise,
Sympathie au malheur, tout s'est vite oublié.

Dieu n'est donc, Antony, que pour un petit nombre
Qui ne cède jamais aux passions du jour,
Quand les autres humains ne connaissent que l'ombre
De Celui qui pourtant les traite avec amour.

[publié le dimanche 9 septembre 1866]

No, for the phony preacher, He does not exist,
When he feigns to serve Him, yet mocks His law in deed;
Nor in the false religion taught by the Catholic priest
Who tries to consecrate his prejudice as creed.

He is not at all in the eyes of the vicious journalist,
That cruelest enemy of factuality,
That troublemaker, cowardly apologist
Of terrorism, crime, and such atrocities.

He is not for the judge, rebellious, ignorant,
Who rides roughshod o'er laws to his desire contrary;
He is not for the thug arrested on a warrant
Whose prosecution exalts the rule of the arbitrary.

Nor has he ever been for that man-jackal beast [67]
Or for his henchmen clad in municipal uniform;
"Attack them! Club them! Kill!" cries hatefully the first,
The rest all rush, their deadly duty to perform.

He is not even — alas! — for our modern-day Moses, [68]
Called on to protect a people humiliated;
In shameful excesses, the now-broken promise
Of aid and sympathy is all but repudiated.

There is no God, Antony, save for the very few
Whom passing passions never do obsess,
While other humans only recognize the shadow
Of Him who ever loves them nonetheless.

[published Sunday, 9 September 1866]

67. Lucien Adams, special sergeant of the New Orleans police and a notorious opponent of Reconstruction, commanded a secret squad whose members perpetrated some of the worst acts of violence during the July 1866 Mechanics' Institute massacre.

68. In a speech given in Nashville in October 1864, President Andrew Johnson compared himself to Moses leading the Israelites out of affliction in Egypt; his promises contrasted with his Reconstruction policies demonstrating leniency toward former Confederate leaders.

La fleur et le papillon

ERNEST DE LA VALETTE

Un papillon voltigeait au soleil
Et se posait tour à tour sur les fleurs,
        Blanches ou rouges ou vermeilles,
        Qui de l'aube buvaient les pleurs.
        Il adorait de l'aubépine
        La trop pénétrante senteur,
        Et lui contait comme à Justine
        Fleurette en lui donnant son cœur.
La pauvre fleur disait au papillon céleste
        Ne fuis pas !
Vois comme nos destins sont différents ! Je reste,
        Tu t'en vas.
Pourtant nous nous aimons, nous vivons sous les hommes,
        [Si] loin d'eux !
Car nous nous ressemblons, et on dit que nous sommes
        Fleurs tous deux.
Mais hélas ! l'air t'emporte et la terre m'enchaîne ;
        Sort cruel !
Je voudrais embaumer ton vol de mon haleine
        Dans le ciel.
Mais non !... tu vas trop loin, parmi des fleurs sans nombre,
        M'oublier ;
Et moi je reste seule à voir tourner mon ombre
        À mes pieds.
Enfin toi tu reviens, puis tu t'en vas encore
        Luire ailleurs ;
Aussi me trouves-tu toujours à chaque aurore,
        Tout en pleurs.
Ah ! pour que votre amour coule des jours fidèles
        Oh mon roi !
Prends comme moi racine, ou donne-moi des ailes,
        Comme toi.

        [publié le dimanche 23 décembre 1866]

The Flower and the Butterfly

Ernest de la Valette[69]

Toward the sun a butterfly flew,
Alighting on flower after flower
    Of white or red or vermilion hue,
      All drinking the tears of the morning hour.
    He loved the fragrance worn
    By the biting hawthorn,
    And, as if with Justine,[70] did flirt,
    Conceding to her his heart.
The poor flower said to the butterfly,
    Don't go away!
See how our fates differ! You can flee,
    And I will stay.
We love each other, and far beneath men we dwell,
    They know not where!
They say we're flowers both and cannot tell
    One from another.
Alas! While I lie in chains, you reach new heights —
    So cruel is fate!
How I'd like with my breath to perfume the path of your flight
    Toward heaven's gate.
But no! ... You go too far, amidst the flowers,
    And I'm forsaken;
Alone with my shadow I while away the hours,
    My spirit shaken.
At length you return, but then you leave anon
    Elsewhere to shine;
Every day, at the coming of each new dawn,
    In tears I pine.
Ah! So that our love might grow, my king,
    Faithful and true,
Like me, put down roots — or give me wings
    Like you.

[published Sunday, 23 December 1866]

---

69. St. Louis Cathedral baptismal records (Woods and Nolan 10: 431) list an Etienne Dufroisin Valet (1809–83; also spelled Vallette or Valette), but nothing definitive is known about this author. The name may be a pseudonym.

70. Perhaps an allusion to the protagonist of *Justine ou les malheurs de la vertu* (the Marquis de Sade's famous 1791 work of erotic and philosophical fiction), a young woman repeatedly punished for her virtue.

« Le cygne — À M. Sainte-Beuve » (1841), par Henri Blaze, recopié et publié dans *La Tribune* sous le titre :

À Théodule Delassize

[attribué dans *La Tribune* à « Antony » (Victor Eugène Macarty)]

    I [9]
Quand le cygne indolent a tout un jour nagé
Sur l'humide niveau du beau lac solitaire ;
Quand sur le frais cristal doucement ombragé
Le bel oiseau royal a longtemps voyagé,
Épuisant lentement, en sa molle carrière,
Toutes les voluptés des eaux, de la lumière.

    II
Quand il s'est égaré dans les joncs à loisir,
Quand il a promené sa superbe indolence
Autour des nymphéas que le cristal balance,
Tendu sa plume à l'onde, au soleil, au zéphyr,[10]
Et vu sous ses beaux flancs le ciel se réfléchir
Dans la mélancolique et vive transparence,

    III
Il plonge et disparaît dans l'abîme profond ;[11]
L'onde s'émeut d'abord et s'élargit en rond
Puis se ferme, et soudain toute ride s'efface,
Toute ombre disparaît,[12] et l'hôte vagabond
S'engloutit aussitôt sans qu'il reste une trace
De sa migration sur la claire surface.

    IIII
Heureux qui peut, semblable au cygne en ses ébats
Sur le lac de la vie errer à l'aventure,
Effleurant toute chose harmonieuse et pure,
Toucher sans les flétrir aux plus beaux nymphéas[13]
Et dans le sein vivant de la belle nature
S'effacer, sans que nul le remarque ici-bas !

6 décembre 1866

    [publié le dimanche 30 décembre 1866]

9. The roman numerals were added to the *Tribune* version; they do not appear in Blaze's poem.

10. Spelled "zéphir" in Blaze's text.

11. In Blaze's text, "sous l'abime profond."

12. "Toute ombre se retire" in Blaze's text.

13. In Blaze's text, "aux plus doux nymphéas."

"The Swan — For Mr. Sainte-Beuve" (1841), by Henri Blaze, copied and republished in *La Tribune* as:

For Théodule Delassize [71]

[attributed in *La Tribune* to "Antony" (Victor Eugène Macarty)]

I

When the ever-indolent swan has swum throughout the day
Upon the lovely, lonely lake's liquescent surface;
When across the crystal coolness where shadows softly play,
The splendid, stately bird has made its lengthy journey,
Exhausting at leisure over the course of its carefree race
All of the pleasures that the light and the waters embrace;

II

When he's wandered amidst the reeds, enjoying his ease,
When he's gone for a stroll, escorting his splendid laziness
Among the lilies swayed by the water's gentleness,
And stretched his feathers out to the waves, the sun and the breeze,
And seen beneath his handsome flanks just how the skies'
Reflection shines, so crisp and full of wistfulness.

III

He dives, and down into the depths of the abyss he sinks;
At first, the water stirs and widens into rings,
Then closes up, so as every ripple to erase.
The shadows vanish, all, and the prince of wanderings
Is suddenly engulfed, not leaving upon the surface,
As clear as glass, of his migration the slightest trace.

IIII

Happy is he who can, just like the playful swan,
Upon the lake of life meander through every detour,
Lightly caressing things harmonious and pure
Such as the loveliest waterlilies, which unwilted remain,
And in the living bosom of beautiful nature,
Unnoticed by anyone, vanish and be gone!

6 December 1866

[published Sunday, 30 December 1866]

---

71. On the literary hoax involving the poet "Antony," see pp. 31–35. The version in *La Tribune* retitles the poem and adds a fictitious date of composition. Born around 1818 to a French father and a woman of color from Louisiana, Louis Théodule Delassize made his name as an inventor beginning in the 1850s, filing a number of patents (see Houzeau 74n17). In 1865, he served as a delegate to the Republican Party's convention of the Friends of Universal Suffrage and in 1871 belonged to a state party committee that met with President Grant. Delassize's wife, Sophie *née* Wakes, had immigrated to the US from France; theirs was thus an example of an interracial marriage (USFCC, *Ninth Census of the United States* [1870], New Orleans, Ward 5).

« Les trois perles, élégie » (1832), par Amédée Pommier,
recopié et publié dans *La Tribune* sous le titre :

Les trois perles

[attribué dans *La Tribune* à « Antony » (Victor Eugène Macarty)]

Ibant obscuri sola sub nocte per umbras.

Je me suis dit souvent : Peut-être au fond des mers,
Dans quelque coin obscur de ces vastes déserts,
Sous cette masse d'eau qui murmure et qui roule,
Sous ces flots que le vent toujours foule et refoule,
Loin des regards de l'homme et des feux du soleil,
Repose un joyau rare, un trésor sans pareil,
Une perle brillante, une perle divine,
Richesse ensevelie et que nul devine,
Une perle admirable en éclat, en blancheur,
Mais pour toujours soustraite à la main du plongeur.
À l'univers entier le flot jaloux la cache,
Cette fille des eaux, merveilleuse et sans tache.
Si l'on pouvait descendre à son obscur séjour,
Si quelqu'un parvenait à la produire un jour [14]
Nous la verrions passer de sa couche d'arène
Sur le bandeau d'un roi, sur le sein d'une reine ;
Elle serait des cours l'orgueil et l'ornement :
Mais comment se douter qu'elle est là ? Vainement
La nature avec soin la travailla sous l'onde,
La fit blanche, la fit éblouissante et ronde.
Que lui sert sa beauté, son éclat, sa rondeur ?
Elle habite des mers la sombre profondeur ;
Elle y dort à jamais : destin injuste et triste !
Et personne ne sait seulement qu'elle existe ;
Car le grand Océan, invincible rempart,
Interpose ses flots entre elle et le regard.

Ainsi me fait songer cette perle inconnue,
Par un sort envieux dans l'ombre retenue.
Puis je poursuis mon rêve, et je me dis encor :
Peut-être un beau génie, autre riche trésor,
Un homme en qui le ciel mit une âme sublime,
Vit ainsi dans l'oubli comme au fond d'un abîme.
Connu, sur un autel nous l'eussions honoré :
Maintenant sous nos pieds il végète ignoré,
Et passe inaperçu sur la terre où nous sommes,
Profondément perdu dans un océan d'hommes,
N'ayant aucun moyen de sortir de sa nuit,

14. Pommier's original text reads, "Si quelqu'un arrivait à la produire au jour."

"The Three Pearls: Elegy" (1832), by Amédée Pommier, copied and republished in *La Tribune* as:

The Three Pearls [72]

[attributed in *La Tribune* to "Antony" (Victor Eugène Macarty)]

Ibant obscuri sola sub nocte per umbras.[73]

I've often thought: "Perhaps in the ocean's deep,
In some hidden corner down there, there does sleep,
Beneath the waters that endlessly murmur and roll,
Beneath the waves which the wind does push and pull,
Far from human eyes, from the fires of the sun,
In that vast wilderness, a jewel, a prize like none
Ever seen — a shining pearl, a pearl divine,
A buried treasure that no one could imagine,
A pearl exquisite in whiteness, in radiance,
But ever out of reach of the diver's hands.
She's concealed by the waves from the whole universe,
A marvel unblemished, this child of the waters.
If only we could reach her dark abode,
Or someone figured out just how she's made,
She'd soon be taken from her sandy bed
To the breast of a queen or upon a king's head.
O'er royal courts her beauty would surely reign:
But how would we even know she exists? In vain
Did nature finely fashion her down there
To be so round and white, to have such luster.
What good is her beauty, her shape, her radiance?
For she dwells at the murky bottom of the oceans;
She sleeps there forever — oh destiny's cruel twists! —
And no one even knows that she exists,
For the Ocean, as though an invincible barrier,
Interposes its waves between our glances and her.

So it is that I dream of this pearl unseen and unknown,
By jealousy's hand in shadows kept alone.
And then I dream on, imagining at leisure
That maybe some handsome genie, some living treasure,
A man whom heaven's endowed with a fine soul
Does live in this way at the bottom of some hole.
Were only he known, he'd be placed on a shrine and honored;
As it is, he remains beneath our feet, ignored,
Existing unnoticed on earth's inhabited surface,
Profoundly lost in the sea of the human race,
Deprived of any means of quitting the night,

72. On the literary hoax involving the poet "Antony," see pp. 31–35. The republished poem adds a dateline and purported site of composition: Grand Lac is located in southeast Louisiana, in the lower Atchafalaya Basin.

73. The epigraph comes from Virgil's *Aeneid*: "Under the lonely night, they went dimly through the shadows" (my trans.).

Et plus grand cependant que ceux qui font du bruit...
Les nobles sentiments que son esprit enferme,
Les fruits, dont la nature y déposa le germe,
Tout cela périra sans qu'on en ait joui,
Sans qu'on ait soupçonné le grand homme enfoui.

Cette pensée est triste, et bien souvent m'afflige.
Et puis je vais plus loin : Peut-être encor, me dis-je,
Quelque part, dans un coin d'une vaste cité,
Il existe une femme, un ange de bonté,
Pauvre perle qui dort tout au fond de la vie,
Ayant tout ce qu'on aime et tout ce qu'on envie,
Jeune, et vierge, et nubile, et pleine de douceur,
Qu'on serait fier d'avoir pour épouse ou pour sœur,
Mais qu'on ne connaît point, et que la destinée
A, sous un humble toit, pour toujours confinée.

Oh ! qui me donnera d'assez bons yeux pour voir
Tout ce que l'océan cache en son gouffre noir,
Pour trouver les talents,[15] les vertus que le monde
Retient ensevelis dans une nuit profonde ?
Quand pourrai-je arracher à leur obscurité
La perle dont le flot connaît seul la beauté,
Le grand homme qui vit sans gloire et sans couronne,
Et la vierge aux doux yeux, pauvre, naïve et bonne ?

Grand Lac, 9 mai 1867

[publié le dimanche 26 mai 1867]

15. Pommier's text features the older spelling "talens."

Tristesse

À Mlle Victoria K...y

Lélia D...t [Adolphe Duhart]

Pourquoi troublez-vous le silence,
      De la nuit
Où mon luth meurt sans espérance
      Et sans bruit ?

Comme une voix agonisante
      Qui gémit,
Sous ma main froide et languissante
      Il frémit.

Yet greater than those who make noise in open sight ...
The noble sentiments contained in his spirit
And the fruits whose seeds nature did deposit —
All this will perish to no one's benefit,
With none suspecting the great one beneath our feet.

Distressed by such an idea, into sadness I shrink
And then I go farther: perhaps there is, I think,
Somewhere, in the midst of some enormous city,
A woman, an angel of generosity,
The perfect sister or even an ideal wife,
A poor pearl, asleep at the bottom of life,
Possessing all that one needs to be safe and content,
A youthful virgin, nubile and utterly pleasant,
But whom we don't really know, and whom fate
Has kept behind a humble cottage's gate.

Will no one grant me sharp enough eyes to see
The treasures that hide in the dark abyss of the sea,
To discover the talents, the virtues that the world
Has wrapped in the shrouds of the night, so tightly furled?
How long will I wait to free from obscurity
This pearl who's shown to the waves alone her beauty —
The man without crown, of greatness unrefined,
And the doe-eyed virgin, poor, simple, and kind?

Grand Lac, 9 May 1867

[published Sunday, 26 May 1867]

Sadness

For Miss Victoria K——y

LÉLIA D——T [Adolphe Duhart]

Why do you dare disturb the still
      That covers the night,
As my lute lies dying with nary the will
      To put up a fight?

Like a voice in the throes of agony
      That whimpers and moans,
Beneath my hand's despondency,
      It shudders and groans.

Sa corde, qui maintenant sonne
        Comme un glas,
Ne réveillera plus personne
        Ici-bas.

Et pourtant comme la fauvette
        Du chemin,
J'ai chanté l'amour du poète
        Et l'hymen.

Mes sens ont béni la justice,
        L'amitié,
La vertu — nard de tout calice —
        La pitié.

J'ai salué la blonde aurore
        Au ciel pur,
La liberté brillante encore
        Dans l'azur.

À qui fléchissait sur la terre
        En secret,
J'ai révélé du juge austère
        Le décret.

Oui, mon luth, plaignant la souffrance,
        L'abandon,
Apportait à tous espérance
        Et pardon...

Et mes accords sont pour la tombe
        Aujourd'hui :
L'espoir, de mon cœur qui succombe,
        S'est enfui.

Les pleurs, qui montent de mon âme
        À mes yeux,
Ternissent l'éclat et la flamme
        De mes cieux.

Mon pauvre cœur à toute joie
        Est fermé...
Pour lui nulle fleur sur la voie
        N'a germé.

Its strings, which at present are ringing
        As a bell does toll,
Will never again, here below, with their singing
        Awaken a soul.

Like the warbler's song that falls from above,
        Nevertheless,
I've praised in turn the poet's love
        And nuptial bliss.

My senses have blessed the ways of justice,
        Of friendship's mirth,
Of virtue — the nard of any calyx —
        Of mercy's worth.

I've greeted the dawn that turns to gold
        The heavens so pure,
And freedom shining, bright and bold,
        Across the azure.

To those who on this earth have kneeled
        In secrecy,
Of our solemn judge I have revealed
        The stern decree.

Indeed, my lute, whom suffering
        Did stir to pity,
Extended to all its offering
        Of charity.

'Tis for the tomb I play these chords
        On this final day,
For hope from my heart's receding shores,
        Has flown away.

The tears which from my soul did rise
        Toward my eyes,
Extinguished the flame, the flash, and the blaze
        From all my skies.

My poor little heart is forever doomed
        To a joyless jail;
No flower, it seems, has ever bloomed
        Inside its cell.

Ne soulevez donc pas le voile
        De mon deuil ;
Laissez-moi le ciel sans étoile
        Du cercueil...

N'interrogez plus ma tristesse
        Ni mes pleurs,
Ils pardonnent à qui le blesse
        Ses douleurs.

Tout pour moi... tout fut sombre et rude
        En ce lieu...
Laissez-moi dans la solitude
        Prier Dieu !

Oh ! ne troublez plus le silence
        De la nuit
Où mon luth meurt sans espérance
        Et sans bruit.

        [publié le dimanche 2 juin 1867]

Sonnet

Réminiscences du « Monde Marche »

PIERRE (L'HERMITE) [pseudonyme d'un auteur inconnu]

Mon Dieu, vous connaissez toutes choses : pour vous
Sans ombre est le passé ; l'avenir, sans mystère,
Vous ignorez l'erreur qui, sur ce coin de terre,
Malgré notre science, existe encore pour nous.

À vos yeux la pensée est tangible ; aussi, tous
Nos secrets sont publiés ; rien ne peut vous les taire.
Vous seul vous remplissez l'univers solitaire
Et de l'humanité connaissez les deux bouts.

Puisqu'il en est ainsi, Souveraine Puissance,
Est-il vrai que la mort n'est qu'une renaissance ?
Est-il vrai que la vie est une heure d'exil ?

Ce papillon si beau, mon Dieu, se souvient-il,
De sa forme première ? — Envoyez donc un ange
Éclairer ma raison sur ce problème étrange.

        [publié le dimanche 16 juin 1867]

I ask that you not lift the veil
        That covers my grief,
For the calm of my coffin's starless vale
        Is my only relief.

Don't try to interrupt my sorrows
        Or to question my tears;
They forgive the brutal blows
        Of their aggressors.

For me all things were dark and coarse
        Wherever I trod ...
Now leave me alone; my only recourse
        Is to pray to God!

Oh, please! Dare not disturb the still
        That covers the night
Where my lute lies dying with nary the will
        To put up a fight.

        [published Sunday, 2 June 1867]

Sonnet

Recollections of "Monde Marche" [74]

PETER (THE HERMIT)[75] [pseudonym of unknown author]

My God, you know all things; for you the past
Is wrapped in no shadow, the future in no mystery.
You fathom not the ignorance, which, in this country,
Despite all our knowledge, continues to exist.

In your eyes, thought is tangible. Our secrets
Are all disclosed; nothing can keep them from you.
You alone fill the lonely universe through and through,
And understand humanity's ins and outs.

Since it is thus, Master of Heaven and Earth,
Is it true that death is nothing but rebirth?
Is it true that life is but an hour's exile?

My God, does a lovely butterfly recall
Its initial form? To enlighten my puzzled mind
Regarding this problem, an angel you must send.

        [published Sunday, 16 June 1867]

---

74. This note seems to refer to a collection of essays by the French writer and politician Eugène Pelletan (1813–84), *Lettres à Lamartine: le monde marche* (1857). A staunch republican, Pelletan opposed Napoléon III's authoritarian regime in the 1850s and 1860s.

75. On the pseudonym Peter the Hermit, see p. 165n55 ("To Father Chocarne").

Le souvenir des morts

À mon père

CAMILLE NAUDIN [pseudonyme d'un auteur inconnu]

Fronts, courbez-vous ! Le vent des froids automnes
A dévasté des tombeaux vénérés ;
Plus d'ornements, de fleurs ni de couronnes,
Mais un sol noir et des murs délabrés.
      Ah ! pour qu'un jour sans remords
      Nous y puissions tous descendre,
Prions pour qui n'est plus que poussière et que cendre ;
Ayons toujours, vivants, le souvenir des morts !

  I

Écoutons ! le bronze fidèle
À de saints devoirs nous appelle ;
En bons fils sachons les remplir.
Que nos doigts tressent l'immortelle,
Que dans sa puissance éternelle,
Hiver, été, Dieu fait fleurir.

  II

Ornons de couronnes bénies
Les croix de ces tombes chéries !
Que sur elles coulent nos pleurs.
Vous, saintes âmes, d'où vous êtes,
Jetez un regard sur nos têtes
Pour en écarter les douleurs.

  III

Écoutez aussi nos prières,
Esprits qui veillez sur ces pierres,
Anges gardiens des froids tombeaux !
Du vent du nord et de la neige
Que le Tout Puissant vous protège,
Ornements du dernier repos.

  IV

Ici-bas, puisque tout succombe,
Un jour, nous aussi, dans la tombe
À notre tour nous descendrons.
Alors nos fils, d'un cœur sincère,
Viendront aussi fleurir la terre
Où pour toujours nous dormirons.

Remembrance of the Dead

For my father

CAMILLE NAUDIN [pseudonym of unknown author]

All heads, bow down! The winds of chilly autumns
Have devastated these venerated tombs:
No more ornaments, nor wreaths, nor flowers' blooms —
Only the blackened ground and walls in ruins.
      Oh! If only someday, without regret,
      We might all go together down that path;
Let us pray for those who've turned to dust and ash;
Let us always, we who live, remember the dead.

I

Let's listen! The faithful bell
To sacred duties calls us all;
Like good sons, let us fulfill them.
May our fingers weave the immortelle
That God, possessing power eternal,
In winter or summer, causes to bloom.

II

With blessèd wreaths let us embellish
The crosses of these graves we cherish;
Upon them may our teardrops flow.
Ye holy souls, where e'er ye be,
Upon our heads, please cast your eye
To turn away our pain and woe.

III

Ye spirits keeping watch o'er these stones,
Ye guardian angels of these cold bones,
Please listen to our prayers as well!
From the northern wind and the snows that fall,
May Almighty God protect you all,
Adornments of sweet repose eternal.

IV

Since all things perish here below,
One day we, too, in turn must go
Into the grave that waits down there;
And then our sons, with hearts sincere,
Will come to deck with wreath and flower
The ground in which we'll sleep forever.

Et maintenant, le travail nous appelle !
Adieu ! chers morts, que nous ne verrons plus
Qu'à l'heure où Dieu, pour la vie éternelle,
Entre nous tous choisira ses élus.
    Ah ! pour qu'alors sans remords
    Aux pieds du Céleste Maître,
Calmes et le front haut, nous puissions comparaître,
Gardons toujours, vivants, le souvenir des morts.

Nouvelle-Orléans, 26 juillet

        [publié le dimanche 28 juillet 1867]

Deux novembre

Aux Francs-Amis

LÉLIA D… T [Adolphe Duhart]

Deux novembre là-haut, deux novembre ici-bas…
Triste date qui vient rappeler le trépas…
C'est le jour sans soleil, c'est la nuit froide et sombre,
Où quelques êtres chers ont augmenté le nombre
De ceux qui, de la vie éteignant le flambeau,
Gisent déjà longtemps dans l'oubli du tombeau.

C'est le jour des regrets, c'est la nuit de tristesse,
Où recueilli, chacun, voyant sa petitesse
Devant la souveraine et l'immuable loi,
Tombe à genoux enfin, prie et tremble pour soi ;
Car chacun, en ces lieux entraînant son suaire,
À sa fosse marquée en l'humide ossuaire.

C'est le jour de prière, et c'est la nuit des morts,
Où l'âme a des terreurs et de tardifs remords.
Jour et nuit que toujours la destinée humaine
Sur l'aile du malheur fatalement ramène ;
Heure sombre où chacun tristement songera
« Qu'ici, l'homme est poussière et poussière sera ».

Car, tant qu'au firmament luit l'étoile de flamme,
Nous croyons à la vie, au bonheur en notre âme ;
Nous ne prévoyons pas que le ciel si serein
Renferme en son azur la tempête et l'airain,
Et que, dans un instant, du dôme qui recule,
La foudre peut gronder dans un noir crépuscule…

And now the call of work to us does beckon!
Farewell, dear departed, with whom we'll reconnect
At the hour when God, for eternal life to reckon,
Will choose among us those of His elect!
      Ah! With spirit calm and uplifted head,
      May we be fully able, without regret,
To present ourselves at our Heavenly Master's feet.
Let us always keep, we living, remembrance of the dead.

New Orleans, 26 July

[published Sunday, 28 July 1867]

The Second of November

For the Francs-Amis [76]

LÉLIA D——T [Adolphe Duhart]

Both here and up there, the second of November ...
A gloomy date on which we're made to remember
Death ... A day of darkness, a night cold and somber,
When our dearly departed have gone to increase the number
Of those who, having extinguished their mortal flame,
Have long since lain in the oblivion of the tomb.

It's the day of remorse, the night of sadness's reign,
When each and all, recalling the sovereign
And changeless law from which there's no appeal,
To tremble and pray for their souls, bend down to kneel;
Advancing toward the grave, we all carry
Our burial shroud into a dank ossuary.

It's the day of prayer, and it's the night of the dead
When the soul, its regrets surveying, senses dread —
The day and the night that human destiny brings
Unfailingly, atop sorrow's wistful wings,
The solemn hour at which we face this concern:
That "man is dust, and to dust shall he return."

As long as heaven's torch remains alight,
We believe in life, in our soul's seeming delight;
We fail to foresee that the sky, appearing at rest,
Conceals behind its azure the roar of the tempest
And that, in but an instant, lightning can flash,
Disturbing the calm of the dusk in a mighty crash ...

76. The Francs-Amis was a Creole fraternal organization whose benevolent hall, located on Robertson Street just outside of the Tremé neighborhood in New Orleans, would later become a hotspot of early jazz.

À genoux donc !... Prions pour ceux qui sont passés,
Et dont, sur les chemins, les pas sont effacés.
Enfant, femme, vieillard, et toi, grand de la terre,
Dans l'enceinte sacrée et toujours solitaire,
Qui que tu sois enfin, à genoux ! à genoux !
Prie en ton cœur pour toi ! prie, implore pour nous !

Grand de la terre prie : au ciel seul est le maître
À qui, toi comme moi, nous devons nous soumettre...
Pour toi, comme pour moi, la fleur naît sous nos pas ;
Mais, comme elle, tout est éphémère ici-bas :
Chaumes, temples, lauriers, couronnes, tout s'écroule.
C'est le même destin qu'ont le grand et la foule.

Vieillard aux cheveux blancs qui pleures, qui n'as plus
Que de tes souvenirs les regrets superflus,
Qui chancelles et qui sous le poids des ans tombes,
Incline-toi, vieillard... déjà s'ouvre la tombe !
Songe à ce qu'il te reste encor d'instants ici
Pour implorer de Dieu la pitié, la merci !

Toi, femme, épouse et mère, ô trinité sacrée,
Toi, dont toute prière au ciel est révérée,
Demande avec ta foi grâce au juge éternel
Pour l'enfant qui sourit à ton sein maternel,
Pour le pécheur qui court vers un fugitif leurre,
Pour le maudit qui hurle, et pour celui qui pleure...

Et toi, petit enfant, qui ne sais pas tromper,
Élève aussi ta voix, laisse aussi s'échapper,
Comme un parfum suave, une douce prière
Pour ton frère et ta sœur, pour ton père et ta mère,
Pour tes autres parents, surtout pour l'orphelin,
Qu'il soit vêtu de soie, ou bien vêtu de lin.

Enfant, femme, vieillard, et toi, grand de la terre,
Qui que tu sois enfin, dans le champ solitaire,
À genoux donc ! prions pour ceux qui sont passés,
Et dont, sur les chemins, les pas sont effacés,
Afin que notre voix, qui pour eux prie, implore,
Les fasse tressaillir dans leur sépulcre encore.

Nouvelle-Orléans, 2 novembre 1867

[publié le dimanche 3 novembre 1867]

Get down on your knees! Pray for those who've passed
And whose footprints from the ground are now erased.
Child, woman, old man, and ruler o'er the earth,
In your hallowed hall and all alone since birth,
Whoever you may be: on your knees! On your knees!
Pray for your soul! And forget not our pleas!

You, earthly king: as you pray, admit
That only to one master must we submit . . .
For your eyes and mine do the flowers grow,
But, like them, all is fleeting here below:
Laurels and crowns, temples and homes most humble,
Whether for prince or pauper, all shall crumble.

White-haired old man with nought left but remorse
From memories that have run their useless course,
As you stumble and fall beneath the weight of years:
Down on all fours . . . the grave has opened its doors!
Consider what little remains of life's brevity
To implore God Almighty's mercy and pity!

Oh holy trinity of womanhood,
Wife, and mother, you whose prayer could
Appease the Eternal, speak to save the distressed,
For the infant smiling before his mother's breast,
For the sinner who falls into some worldly trap,
For the damned who cry out and for all who weep . . .

And you, young child, unaware of how to deceive,
Uplift your voice so that heaven may receive
Like a sweet perfume, the softness of a prayer
On behalf of your brother and sister, your father and mother,
For the rest of your kin and especially for the orphan,
Be he clothed in silk or humble garments of linen.

Child, woman, old man, and earthly ruler,
Whoever you may be, no matter where,
Get down on your knees! Let us pray for those who've passed
And whose footprints from the ground are now erased,
Such that, hearing our voices, whose prayers implore
On their behalf, they wake in their crypts once more.

New Orleans, 2 November 1867

[published Sunday, 3 November 1867]

L'avenir

À mon jeune ami Lélia D. [Adolphe Duhart]

L. M. [Lucien Mansion]

   Voyez-vous dans ce monde, ou plus tôt ou plus tard
   De douleurs, j'en suis sûr, chacun aura sa part.

Poète, vous rêvez, et vous voyez sans doute,
   Dans vos rêves charmants,
L'avenir inconnu qu'en secret on redoute
   Dans ce val de tourments.

Vous le voyez brillant, j'aime assez à le croire,
   Car vous avez souri ;
Vos regards pénétrants ont percé la nuit noire
   Pour trouver cet abri.

Contemplez à loisir, dans votre douce extase,
   Ce bonheur sans pareil ;
Car la réalité, ce faix qui nous écrase
   Vous attend au réveil,

Alors vous concevrez en voyant la misère
   Qui nous étreint ici
Que nous devons passer sur cette horrible terre
   De durs moments aussi.
Je sais que l'âge mûr garde encor l'espérance
   Malgré ses maux constants ;
Mais c'est l'âpre saison, — l'hiver de l'existence
   Sans le riant printemps.

Pourquoi donc le celer, c'est la règle certaine,
   Le malheur suit nos pas
En nous frappant de coups, jusqu'au jour où la peine
   Nous amène au trépas.

26 décembre 1868

     [publié le vendredi 1er janvier 1869]

The Future

To my young friend Lélia D. [Adolphe Duhart]

L. M. [Lucien Mansion]

    In this world, you see, whether today or tomorrow,
    It seems that all will have their share of sorrow.

You dream, oh poet, and surely do behold
    In all your dreams' delights,
The future's secrets, feared though unforetold
    In the valley of our plights.

For you all shines, I hope, splendid and bright,
    As your smile does suggest;
Your gaze has pierced the darkness of the night
    To find this place of rest.

Now contemplate, in your sweet ectasy
    This joy unparalleled;
For, each morning, crushed by reality,
    The illusion is dispelled.

And then you'll understand how poverty
    Constrains us here below,
And that this wretched earth holds misery
    Which we must someday know.
It's true that hope remains in later years,
    Although our pains increase;
But once the springtime's laughter disappears,
    Life's winter shall not cease.

Why hide the certain fact that no relief
    From the blows of unhappiness
Will come, until that final day when grief
    To death delivers us?

26 December 1868

    [published Friday, 1 January 1869]

Lettre à Nath

JOANNI [Joanni Questy]

Vous savez, Nath, ô mon amie,
Combien il m'est doux de vous voir
Marcher, toujours plus affermie,
Dans l'étroit sentier du devoir.
 Je voudrais, aujourd'hui
 Qu'un nouvel an commence,
 Vous parler de celui
  Qui donna l'existence
  À tant d'êtres divers,
  Et qui, par sa puissance,
Un jour créa tout l'univers ;
  Ne tremblez pas d'avance ;
Comptant sur votre tolérance,
Je n'aurai pas l'impertinence,
Abusant de ces droits que donne l'amitié,
D'oser impunément prêcher l'impiété.

 Je conçois bien que le vulgaire,
 Le chrétien superstitieux
 Croient en ces mensonges pieux ;
 Que, toujours, du haut de la chaire,
 Dans son zèle religieux,
 Un prédicateur téméraire
 Voudrait imposer à la terre ;
 Mais vous, que la raison conduit,
 Vous, Nath, que la science éclaire,
 Serez-vous, votre vie entière,
 Enveloppée en cette nuit
 Que l'imposture et l'ignorance,
 L'intérêt, la malignité
 Tout autour de la vérité,
 « Transformant un Dieu de bonté
 « En vrai monstre de cruauté ? »

 Ah, Nath ! Dieu, bon et tendre père,
 Ne peut avoir nos passions ;
 Comme l'astre qui nous éclaire,
 Il est sans haine, sans colère,
 Et toutes les corruptions
 De notre humaine fourmilière
 Ne sauraient, de ce tendre père,
 Épuiser les compassions.

Letter to Nath [77]

JOANNE [Joanni Questy]

>Do you know, dear Nath, oh friend of mine,
>How pleasing it is for me to see
>You walk, with ever stronger spine,
>The straight and narrow path of duty?
>>Since a new year has begun,
>>I wish upon this date
>>To talk about the One
>>>Who decided to create
>>>Forms of life so diverse
>>>And who, through his power,
>One day conceived the universe.
>>>You have no need to fear:
>Although friendship grants
>Goodwill and indulgence,
I shan't display the impropriety,
Of openly preaching brash impiety.

>I know that any white lie
>Appeals to the layman,
>The superstitious Christian,
>If it comes from on high,
>From the pulpit of priest or parson
>Whose religious zeal does try
>To delude society;
>But you, with reason unclouded,
>By science enlightened, Nath, *mon amie*,
>Will you, your whole life, be
>Within that night enshrouded,
>Allowing hypocrisy,
>Self-interest and enmity,
>To smother truthfulness,
>"Transforming God's goodness
>Into monstrous cruelty?"

>Oh, Nath! God, our father gentle and kind,
>Possesses not our emotion;
>No hatred impairs his mind,
>As clear as any star we find,
>And all the commotion
>That troubles humankind
>Will never be able to bind
>The arms of his compassion.

77. The French nickname Nath (pronounced "Nat") refers to Nathalie Formento: see p. 189n63 ("The Weeping Willow").

>   Il voit toutes nos actions,
>   Et charge notre conscience
>   Ou d'accorder la récompense,
>   Ou d'ordonner le châtiment.
>   N'écoutez qu'avec défiance
>   Ceux qui vous parlent autrement.
>   Dieu, vengeur ! Ils le calomnient !
>   Le bon sens, la raison le nient.
> Eh quoi, Nath ! Ce Dieu tout-puissant
> Se servirait de sa toute puissance
>   Contre des êtres sans défense ?
>   Soit dit entre nous, en passant,
>   De la divine Majesté
>   Ô ! quelle horrible lâcheté !
>   Il en résulterait, en somme,
>   Que Dieu vaudrait donc moins que l'homme,
>   N'est-il pas vrai, Nath ? Cette nuit,
>   Creusez un peu cette pensée ;
>   Retenez-la longtemps fixée
>   Sous les regards de votre esprit ;
>   Et si, de ce petit écrit,
>   Nath, vous n'êtes pas offensée,
>   Demain matin j'irai vous voir,
>   Car c'est bien assez pour ce soir.

Nouvelle-Orléans, 1ᵉʳ janvier 1869

              [publié le dimanche 10 janvier 1869]

La vie en rêve

À Mlle Pauline F.

AUGUSTE GIROD

> La vie est, dit-on, un sommeil
>   Dont la mort est le terme ;
> Pourtant, sans penser au réveil,
>   Dans un songe on s'enferme...
> Heureux celui qui, du bonheur,
>   Caressant le doux rêve,
> Le trouve lorsque, dans son cœur,
>   Nul remords ne s'élève.

        He sees our every action
        And calls upon our conscience
        To either give recompense
        Or enact a punishment.
        So listen with defiance
        To those with evil intent
        Towards our avenging Lord;
        They slander his genuine Word!
What's this, Nath? Omnipotent
God would abuse his power, losing patience
        With creatures bereft of defense?
        It would mean, in any event,
        That his divine Majesty
        Was acting cravenly!
        Would it not be a mess
        If God were worth even less
        Than man? Nath, tonight
        Examine this possibility —
        If needed, lengthily —
        Beneath your intellect's light.
        And if, by all I've dared to write,
        You're not offended, *mon amie*,
        Tomorrow morning, I'll call;
        As for tonight, that's all.

New Orleans, 1 January 1869

        [published Sunday, 10 January 1869]

The Dream of Life

For Miss Pauline F.

AUGUSTE GIROD

Life is but sleep, or so they say,
        And death, of course, is its end;
Without a thought for the waking day,
        Into a dream we descend ...
Happy is he who, entertaining
        A dream of delectable bliss,
Perceives no spot of remorse staining
        His heart's happiness.

Lorsque je vois des gens crier
        Après dame Fortune,
Et, pour elle, s'expatrier,
        Se riant de Neptune,
Ma pensée aussitôt les suit,
        Et je dis : c'est un rêve
Que leur ambition poursuit
        Et que l'enfer soulève !

Bien souvent de jeunes auteurs,
        Avides de la gloire,
Aux plaisirs préfèrent les pleurs,
        Pour vivre dans l'histoire...
Pauvres fous ! me dis-je, en riant,
        Puisqu'ici tout s'achève,
L'histoire s'appelle NÉANT :
        Brisez donc votre rêve !

Lorsqu'une indigente vertu
        Malheureusement penche,
Au milieu du sentier ardu,
        Si quelqu'un d'humeur franche,
Pour la sauver, lui tend la main,
        Pardonne et la relève !
Transporté ! je dis : c'est divin !
        Oh ! gardez ce beau rêve !

Mais aux faquins, hommes du jour,
        Qui brillent dans l'arène,
Et qui symbolisent l'amour
        Par une chose obscène,
Puissé-je à leur âme crier :
        Cessez ! car Dieu soulève
Le flot qui doit faire expier
        Votre cynique rêve... !

        [publié le dimanche 14 février 1869]

Whenever I see folks calling after
      Dame Fortune, and for her,
Preferring to go live elsewhere
      While casting Neptune naught but laughter
My thoughts follow them straightaway,
      And I say: it's a dream
That causes their ambition to stray
      Towards hell's depths agleam!

It happens oft that young authors,
      If overly eager for glory,
Deny pleasures in favor of tears
      For the sake of posterity ...
Pitiful fools! Under fate's regime
      All things will be destroyed;
I say: discard your silly dream!
      History's name is THE VOID!

When virtue, bearing poverty's load,
      Is bent by unhappiness
In the middle of some toilsome road,
      If someone, out of fairness,
To save her stretches out his hand
      With mercy that does redeem!
Delighted, I say: how truly grand!
      Cling to this lovely dream!

But to simple souls, men of the hour
      Who excel, for sure, in the ring
And fancy love's exquisite flower,
      As some obscene thing,
Would that I might exclaim to these knaves:
      Desist! For God supreme
Will unleash the force of a thousand waves
      To drown your cynical dream ...!

      [published Sunday, 14 February 1869]

MATTERS OF THE HEART

Hommage au sexe

L. M. [Lucien Mansion]

> Avec notre existence
> De la femme pour nous le dévoûment commence.
> — Legouvé

Quand Madeleine, un jour pleurant son déshonneur
      Se prosterna tremblante ;
Vous avez écouté sans la punir, Seigneur !
      Cette âme repentante.

Mesdames ! Veuillez bien permettre cette fois,
Qu'aujourd'hui bravement j'élève ici la voix,
Pour vous dire en ami dans un simple langage
Comment mon cœur se plaît à vous rendre un hommage
Justement mérité par vos belles vertus
Qui rayonnent encore quand la beauté n'est plus
Et dont le doux éclat illumine l'impasse
Où le destin toujours cache quelque disgrâce.
Si j'ai peu ménagé dans cette occasion
Le sexe le plus fort avec intention,
C'est que souvent aussi sa cruelle justice
Est le fruit corrompu d'un détestable vice ;
Mais quand son cœur est pur, on le voit à son tour
Docile à vos genoux implorant votre amour.
Chez vous, sexe indulgent, nous retrouvons nos mères,
Nos estimables sœurs, nos épouses si chères.
Trop sensible moitié du pauvre genre humain
C'est vous qui nous montrez du bonheur le chemin ;
Par vos sages avis vous nous mettrez à même
D'apprécier ici l'unique bien suprême,
Celui de la famille et son intimité
Qui fait vite oublier notre instabilité.
Passagers dans ce monde où l'horrible tourmente
Des passions nous traque et nous désoriente ;
Alors tout égarés nous voulons essayer
De regagner encore le paisible foyer,
Où nous ayons laissé dans l'humble solitude
Des êtres bien-aimés, dont la douce habitude
De leurs cœurs imprégnés de nobles sentiments
Est de prier pour nous dans nos débordements,
Qui de nous n'a connu la bonté maternelle ?
Douce sollicitude ! Active sentinelle
Qui veille nuit et jour, dont les soins assidus
Dans nos jours de malheur ne sont jamais perdus.
Plaignons celui qui fut privé de la présence

Homage to the Fairer Sex [78]

L. M. [Lucien Mansion]

> At the same time as our existence
> Devotion to woman for us does commence.
> — Legouvé

When Mary Magdalene, weeping her dishonor
    Bowed down one day, trembling,
You listened, Oh Lord, and, taking pity on her,
    Did not punish her soul's repenting.

Mesdames! I pray, please entertain my choice,
If just today, to bravely raise my voice
To tell you, as a friend, in simple language
Just how my heart delights to pay you homage
So rightly earned by all your lovely virtues,
That shine forth still when beauty's faded from use,
Whose radiance softly lights that hidden place
Where fate always conceals some disgrace.
If I've chosen not to spare on this occasion
The stronger sex, it is with this intention:
Too often do we see that his cruel justice
Is born of the fruit of some despicable vice.
But when his heart is pure, he seeks your love:
We see him then on bended knee, submissive.
In you, indulgent sex, we rediscover
Our mothers, our worthy sisters, our spouses dear.
Too sensitive half of our pitiful humankind,
It is you who must show us how and where to find
The road to happiness. Teach us, and we shall
Appreciate the truest good of all:
The private life enjoyed by family
That lets us forget our instability.
Passing through this world and its frightful torrent
Of relentless passions that disorient,
We wish to try, through gone astray, alone,
To return once more to the peaceful hearth we'd known,
Where we've left behind in humble solitude
Belovèd ones, whose gentle consuetude
Is to pray for us in our impenitence,
Their hearts filled full with noble sentiments.
Who among us has not known the goodness
Of a mother? An ever-vigilant guard whose kindness
Keeps watch both day and night, whose constant care
Is never in vain, despite our times of despair.
Let's pity those who've never known the ways

[78]. This long poem appeared in three installments, marked here by section breaks: lines 1–76 were published on 22 Sept., lines 77–138 on 26 Sept., and lines 139–98 on 1 Oct. 1863. (The third installment was accompanied by a list of corrections, which have been incorporated here.) The epigraph (by Ernest Legouvé [1807–1903], a French writer and literary critic known for his advocacy for woman's rights and progressive education) and the prefatory stanza were reproduced at the beginning of all three installments.

De l'amour d'une mère aux jours de son enfance ;
Car pour nous dans ce monde il n'est aucun lien
Qui puisse suppléer à ce souverain bien.
Voyez, ce frêle enfant que la fièvre torture,
Comment sa tendre mère à son chevet conjure
Avec humilité le Seigneur Tout-Puissant
De retrancher ses jours pour sauver l'innocent.
Elle sacrifierait dans sa vive tendresse
Ce trésor précieux — sa riante jeunesse,
Pour un sourire, un mot du petit malheureux,
L'objet de tant de soins qui languit sous ses yeux,
Ange ! toi qui parus un jour dans cette vie
Pour embellir le toit de ta mère chérie,
Écoute la prière et vois le dévoûment
Du plus constant amour de son esprit aimant,
Depuis la nuit affreuse où la fièvre rapace
Sous sa griffe te presse à cette même place,
Que de fois je l'ai vue, en pleurant déposer
Sur ta lèvre brûlante un caressant baiser ;
Les veilles ont éteint la brillante étincelle
Qui pétillait naguère au fond de sa prunelle ;
Ses membres amaigris, la pâleur de son front
Attestaient du chagrin le désordre profond.
Pourrais-tu la laisser seule ici dans la peine,
Toi qui fis les beaux jours de son âme sereine ?
Tu n'as donc pas compris ses sanglots, ses regrets,
Et ce noir désespoir répandu sur ses traits.
Vous ! Mères, qui suivez le cours de cette histoire,
À sa fidélité pouvez-vous ne pas croire
Quand vous avez déjà, c'est ma conviction,
Versé de pareils pleurs dans mainte occasion ?
Oui ! vous avez pleuré ; vous pleurerez encore
À ce triste récit que ma verve colore
Car votre cœur est bon, il sait trop compatir
Aux douleurs d'ici-bas pour ne point les sentir.
Mais, un jour, jour fatal, la mort impitoyable
Frappa le pauvre enfant d'un coup inévitable ;
Sur un cadavre alors la mère s'abattit,
Dans des convulsions elle se débattit
Sans proférer un son, une seule parole ;
Quand on la releva cette femme était folle.

❖

Et vous ! fidèle épouse, — esclave du devoir,
Victime, trop souvent d'un injuste pouvoir,
Femme de prolétaire, écoutez ma parole :

Of a mother's love in childhood's tender days,
For in our eyes there is no worldly tie
That ever could replace this good most high.
Behold this child whom fever racks, near dead,
And how his gentle mother, beside his bed,
Entreats with humility the Almighty One
To shorten her days to save her innocent son.
Through tenderness she'd sacrifice the treasures
Of merry youth, the dearest of life's pleasures,
If only the object of her cares, the poor child
Expiring before her, would speak or even smile,
Oh angel! You who did one day appear
To adorn the home of your dear, beloved mother,
Do listen to her prayer — do try to hear it —
And see the devotion of her loving spirit
Ever since that wretched night when fever
Did seize you with its savage claws, and leave her
Just where I've often seen her, lost in sobs
And leaning down to kiss your burning lips.
Her waking nights have left a heavy mark
And nearly robbed her eyes of their shining spark;
Her limbs grown thin, the pallor of her brow
Bear witness to the ravages of her sorrow.
How could you leave her here, alone in pain,
You who used to make her soul serene?
Did you not understand her sobs, her grief,
And the dark despair that gives her no relief,
You see! Mothers who've followed this story's course,
You know full well her constancy lacks force,
For all of you have — at least, it's my conviction —
Shed tears like these on many an occasion
Indeed! You have wept; and you will shed more tears
At this woeful tale made poignant by my verse
For your heart, too good, knows how to sympathize
With earthly pains and can but empathize.
One day, one fateful day did merciless death
Strike down the child upon its relentless path.
Upon the corpse the mother then collapsed,
Convulsing and thrashing; some time elapsed
Without her saying a word or making a sound.
And when they came for her, she'd lost her mind.

❖

And you, devoted husband — and duty's slave,
Too often a victim, whom unjust power gave
Over to some worker: now listen to my words;

C'est l'amicale voix d'un frère qui console,
Et qui veut relever par son modeste éclat
Votre front resté pur dans un si triste état.
J'aime à vous contempler dans votre humble ménage
Quand de l'adversité menace au loin l'orage,
Ou quand la foudre éclate, et que l'explosion
Laisse de tous côtés la désolation ;
C'est alors que l'on voit votre âme courageuse
Loin de se désoler se montrer généreuse,
En cachant sa douleur ainsi que son tourment
Aux regards d'un public qui juge méchamment
Et dont l'unique soin de sa triste manie
Est d'encenser toujours la noire calomnie.
Épouse, vous gardez purement le dépôt
Que vous fit un époux de son honneur sans tache ;
Vous avez dignement rempli la noble tâche
D'un cœur tout dévoué : de la femme en un mot.
Laissez-moi vous citer un exemple touchant
D'un saint et pur amour souillé par un méchant.
Nous avons vu naguère une enfant trop docile
Se laisser entraîner par un trompeur habile
Qui l'épousa sans doute avec le vil espoir
D'anéantir ses jours ainsi que son avoir,
Car la pauvre victime eut à payer de suite
Les imprudents écarts de sa folle conduite.
Le monstre à face humaine envoyé par l'enfer,
Pour briller en rampant comme un ignoble ver,
Mit en œuvre bientôt sa pensée infernale
En vivant largement comme un Sardanapale.
Un luxe raffiné dans ses moindres détails
Semblait se refléter sur sa face rougie ;
Et sur ses pas heureux s'ouvraient divers sérails
Où le vice étalait sa laideur dans l'orgie.
Notre nouveau Don Juan, alors tout radieux
Et fier, passait la nuit dans des tripots affreux
Choyé de tous côtés par une longue suite
D'amis officieux — la gente parasite.
Il voyait s'écouler bruyamment l'heureux temps
Où la vie apparaît comme un riant printemps.
Il s'amusait encore malgré sa dette immense
Qui grandissait toujours par sa folle dépense.
L'épouse résignée aperçut certain jour
Comment s'était trompé son confiant amour,
Mais il était trop tard, car l'horrible misère
Avait tout envahi dans la maison prospère
Où tout était bonheur et joie, où les plaisirs
Toujours renouvelés fatiguaient les désirs.

'Tis the friendly voice of a brother who comforts
And with his modest grandeur wishes to uplift
Your still-pure brow in sadness gone adrift.
How I like to see you in your humble home
When adversity's storms away in the distance loom,
Or when thunder bursts the sky, and the explosion
Leaves nothing in its wake but desolation.
It's then that we see your soul's tenacity,
Discarding despair, display its charity
By hiding its pain as well as its agony
From the eyes of others who'd circulate calumny
And whose sole concern, whose pathetic preoccupation
Consists in praising the darkest defamation.
Oh wife, your purity guards the sacred store
Entrusted to you by a husband's spotless honor.
With dignity, you completed the noble task
Of a caring heart — of woman, should anyone ask.
Allow me to provide a touching example
Of a pure and holy love by a villain trampled.
Not long ago a girl, too impressionable,
Was deceived by a hustler, far too capable,
Who married her just for the vicious scheme, it seems,
Of destroying her life as well as her worldly means.
Indeed, his victim was soon to pay in full
The price of having acted like a fool.
So as his wormlike slithering to disguise,
This hell-sent monster dressed in human guise
Soon put his fiendish plan to its wicked use
By living as lavishly as Sardanapalus.[79]
The refinement of meticulous luxuries
Appeared reflected in his ruddy face,
And before him countless harems opened with ease,
Where orgies exhibited vice in all its disgrace.
Our new Don Juan, all beaming with pride, would spend
The night in seedy dens, where friends did attend
To his every whim — an endless retinue
Of overeager parasites, through and through.
He watched the good times noisily roll by,
When, like springtime, life laughs merrily.
Enjoying himself despite the mounting debts
That grew and grew as he spent with no regrets.
One day his wife came finally to realize
Just how her love had been abused by lies,
But it was far too late, for poverty
Already had ravaged the home's prosperity,
Where all was joy and happiness, where pleasure
Went farther than desires could even measure.

79. One of the last kings of ancient Assyria, Sardanapalus supposedly avoided enemy capture by committing suicide, taking his numerous concubines with him in death. This scene is famously depicted in the French painter Eugène Delacroix's *La mort de Sardanapale* (1827).

Un matin la saisie avec son long cortège
De juges, d'avocats, d'usuriers et que sais-je,
Apparut au milieu de nos époux surpris
Pour s'emparer des biens jusqu'aux derniers débris.
Le mari depuis lors en proie à la tristesse
Dans des libations trouve une sale ivresse,
Pressé par la douleur il croyait entrevoir
Dans l'azur de son ciel un sinistre point noir.
C'était vrai ! le chagrin à l'humeur dévorante
Mordit un soir au cœur son épouse souffrante.
Le démon aviné fut sans doute étonné ;
Car l'ange en s'envolant avait tout pardonné.

❖

Jeunes filles, il faut faire aussi votre éloge :
À cette douce loi jamais je ne déroge.
Je me fais un devoir de payer un tribut
Toujours à l'innocence en parcourant mon but.
Colombes qui portez la joie et l'espérance,
Dans l'arche paternelle aux jours de votre enfance,
Écoutez, je vous prie, aujourd'hui les accents
De mon cœur ulcéré par des chagrins récents.
Vous qui nous attachez à cette vie amère,
Vous nous faites chérir le foyer solitaire,
Car vous l'embellissez en y semant des fleurs
Qui cachent bien souvent de poignantes douleurs.
Oui ! Mes chères enfants, votre gaîté naïve
Fait reverdir l'espoir dans notre âme craintive.
Que nous sommes heureux quand nous avons surpris
Dans vos tendres regards un caressant souris
Qui nous fait oublier par sa douce influence
Les nombreux accidents d'une triste existence ;
Puis, quand l'hiver de l'âge affaiblira nos sens,
Que nos bras engourdis resteront impuissants,
Nous trouverons au sein du foyer domestique
Pour étancher nos pleurs votre main sympathique.
Tendres sœurs, regardez dans ce sombre avenir ;
Vous verrez les devoirs que vous devez remplir :
Vous êtes de la Vierge aujourd'hui les servantes,
Vous célébrez en chœur ses grâces ravissantes,
Et puis à son autel dans le recueillement,
Pures, vous recevez un très saint sacrement.
Vous trouvez le bonheur dans la douce pratique
De ces pieux devoirs d'une âme catholique.
Ensuite, dans la nuit, vous retrouvez encor
Pendant votre sommeil vos brillants rêves d'or.

One morning, foreclosure, with its long escort
Of judges, lawyers, lenders, and their sort,
Showed up at the door, to our couple's surprise,
To confiscate every possession they did prize.
The husband, ever since beset by grief,
In libations sadly sought out drunken relief.
Besieged by pain, he thought he saw o'erhead
The heavens' blue besmirched by a baleful cloud.
And so it was! Then sorrow's hungry claws
One night sank into the heart of his suffering spouse.
No doubt the devilish drunkard knew not what to say,
For the angel forgave it all as she flew away.

❖

Young women, you surely deserve much applause,
And never do I disobey such laws.
I promise, as I continue to pursue
My goal, to render in full the tribute that's due
To innocence. Ye doves who, after your birth,
To your father's ark come carrying hope and mirth,
I pray that today you'll heed this declaration
From my heart, of late consumed by frustration.
Ye who allow us to love our bitter life on earth
And teach us to cherish the solitude of the hearth
Embellished by flowers with which you decorate
To hide the sorrows whose sharp pangs desolate!
Indeed! Dear children, your merriment grows
Like a garden of hope within our fearful souls.
How happy we feel when we happen to spy
A smile caressing us from your tender eye,
Permitting us, through its gentle influence,
To forget the misfortunes of our sad existence.
And then, when the senses are dulled by the winter of age
And our arms, benumbed, have reached their final stage,
Within the bosom of hearth and home we'll find,
To quench our tears, your hand, steadfastly kind.
Behold, sweet sisters, the future's somber will;
You'll see the obligations you're bound to fulfill
Today you serve as helpers to the Virgin;
You extol her lovely charms in unison,
And then, at her altar, steeped in reverence,
You receive the holiest of sacraments.
So pure, you rejoice in these quiet pieties
Like every Catholic soul true to its duties.
And next, in the night, you return again and again,
As you sleep, to glittering dreams all dressed in gold

Mais vienne l'hyménée avec son lourd bagage
De tourments, de soucis, attributs du ménage,
Adieu les beaux projets dans l'avenir lointain,
Quand l'horrible discorde apparaît un matin
Et s'installe au logis comme une souveraine
Qui prend possession de son vaste domaine,
Et vient mettre en vigueur dans son gouvernement
Ses despotiques lois sans nul ménagement.
Alors plus de gaîté dans la triste demeure ;
On entend très souvent une femme qui pleure
Ou la puissante voix de son maître et Seigneur
Qui résonne très haut dans sa mauvaise humeur.
La malheureuse épouse en butte à tant d'alarmes
S'étiole en versant d'intarissables larmes.
Vous frémissez, mes sœurs, et trouvez ce tableau
Trop chargé des traits noirs de mon sombre pinceau ;
C'est que mon cœur navré, peut-être, désespère
Et craint trop du destin l'inflexible colère.
Pauvres femmes ! ici, vous avez à souffrir
Dans votre court passage, et puis, il faut mourir.
Pour quelques pâles fleurs qui bordent votre route,
Qui charment vos regards, que vous cueillez sans doute,
Que de ronces aussi dans ces sentiers fleuris
Qui déchirent vos pieds et vos doigts amaigris ;
Mais auprès du Seigneur, dans sa sainte clémence
Un jour vous trouverez la douce récompense
Réservée à tous ceux qui savent endurer
Les peines, les tourments, d'ici, sans murmurer.

[publié le mardi 22 septembre ; le samedi
26 septembre ; et le mardi 1er octobre 1863]

Des baisers

Lélia D... t [Adolphe Duhart]

Comme il y a trois personnes en Dieu, trois points dans un triangle, trois Grâces, trois vertus théologales, etc., etc., il y a aussi trois baisers :
Le baiser négatif ;
Le baiser positif ;
Le baiser superlatif.
Le premier consiste à embrasser la main d'une femme, le second ses joues et le troisième ses lèvres.

But then comes matrimony, always laden
With turmoil and worries typical of the household.
Farewell to the distant future's promising plans
When one morning heinous discord abruptly lands
In the midst of the home just like a wicked queen
Who's come to take control of her domain,
And by the same occasion to decree
Despotic laws devoid of leniency.
From this wretched home all joy has disappeared —
A woman's sobbing is often to be heard,
As well as the mighty voice of her master and Lord
Resounding on high where his holy displeasure is stored.
The miserable wife, beset by so many woes,
Now withers away in a tearful torrent of sorrows.
You shudder, my sisters, and judge this course of events
Unduly painted with my palette's somber pigments;
The reason is that my heart despairs of late
And, feeling forlorn, now fears the fury of fate.
Unfortunate women! To suffer you're bound
Throughout your time on earth — and then, to die.
For the few fading flowers that you've found
And picked along the way as they caught your eye,
How many thorns as well upon these paths you meet
That rip your meager fingers and your feet;
But near the Lord, as his belovèd ward,
One day you will receive the sweet reward
Reserved for all who've learned how to endure
Ordeals and trials without so much as a murmur.

[published Tuesday, 22 September; Saturday,
26 September; and Thursday, 1 October 1863]

On Kisses

Lélia D——t [Adolphe Duhart]

Just as there are three persons in God, three vertices on a triangle, three Graces, three theological virtues, etc., etc., there are also three kisses:

The negative kiss;
The positive kiss;
The superlative kiss.

The first consists in kissing the hand of a woman; the second, her cheeks; and the third, her lips.

Le premier n'est souvent qu'une froide politesse, c'est un courtisan menteur plein de fatuité ; — le second est bourgeois et candide, c'est le provincial qui sent palpiter son cœur pour la première fois ; — le troisième est tout amour, c'est l'amant frémissant de volupté.

Le baiser négatif, c'est le pimpant abbé dans le boudoir d'une marquise ; — le baiser positif, c'est le gentillâtre campagnard caressant sa timide vassale ; — le baiser superlatif, c'est l'haleine parfumée d'une vierge tremblante, c'est Louis XIV et La Vallière sous les chênes de Fontainebleau.

Il y a aussi deux baisers auxiliaires :

Le baiser passif ;

Le baiser actif.

Le premier est infligé par une vieille fille, et se voit *par conséquent* refusé presque toujours, tandis que le second est sollicité — celui-ci se cache, il est mystérieux et clandestin ; celui-là aime le grand jour ; il est franc, pur et familier. L'un, c'est la jeune fille, modeste et virginale, qui va au-devant de son père ; l'autre, c'est la femme adultère qu'un rendez-vous retient dans un sombre bosquet.

Le premier est bénédiction, c'est Benjamin aux pieds de Jacob.

Le second est anathème, c'est Judas livrant le Christ.

Mais, indépendamment de ceux-là, il y en a encore qui sont pleins de suavité.

Le baiser de circonstance — froid et poli — c'est le baiser de rencontre et de visite.

Le petit larcin — c'est l'adolescent à ses premières amours.

Le baiser à la tourterelle — caresse enfantine d'un enfant plus frêle que les fleurs, dont l'âme est plus sereine que les cieux.

Le baiser muet — mystérieux soupir d'un cœur timide, songe idéal qu'on voudrait achever à genoux.

L'écho — c'est le lourd campagnard qui répand sa tendresse.

Le sucre d'orge — affection pure et divine, c'est l'enfant au berceau qui — ange au ciel, espérance sur la terre — essaie ses petits bras à vous enlacer.

Le baiser d'adieu — c'est le triste et plaintif murmure d'une âme froissée au bord d'un tombeau.

Et enfin celui qui contient à lui seul toutes les joies, toutes les caresses, toutes les prières ; celui qui est toute espérance et toute bénédiction ; celui qui guérit toutes les souffrances, et dont on garde un souvenir éternel ; celui enfin qu'on reçoit en ouvrant les yeux à la vie et qu'on apporte comme une perle précieuse à Dieu : c'est le baiser maternel.

[publié le dimanche 20 novembre 1864]

The first often results only from cold politeness; it comes from a lying sycophant, full of conceit; the second, bourgeois and sincere, comes from the small-town type who feels his heart throb for the very first time; the third is pure love, given by the paramour quivering with desire.

The negative kiss is the prim abbot in the boudoir of some marquise; the positive kiss is the country gentleman caressing his shy vassal; the superlative kiss is the perfumed breathing of a trembling virgin, or Louis XIV and La Vallière[80] beneath the oaks at Fontainebleau.

There are also two supplementary kisses:

The active kiss;

The passive kiss.

The first one is inflicted by an old maid, who finds herself *as a result* nearly always rejected, while the second one is requested. The latter hides; it is mysterious and clandestine. The former likes broad daylight; it is candid, pure, and intimate. One is the young girl, modest and virginal, going before her father; the other is the adulterous woman that a secret meeting draws to a dark grove.

The first is a blessing — Benjamin at Jacob's feet.

The second is blasphemy — Judas handing over Christ.

But, independently of those two, there are still more that are full of sweet delight.

The circumstantial kiss, cold and polite, belongs to meetings and visits.

There's petty theft, the teenager who first encounters love.

And the turtledove kiss, the childlike caress of a child frailer than the flowers, and whose soul is more serene than the skies.

The mute kiss — the mysterious sigh of a timid heart, the perfect daydream that one might like to finish on bended knee.

The echo: this one is the bulky country dweller spreading his tenderness.

The barley sugar, affection pure and divine: it's the infant in the cradle who — like an angel in heaven and hope here on earth — tries to embrace you with his little arms.

The farewell kiss, which is the sad and plaintive murmur of an offended soul on the edge of a tomb.

And finally there is one that contains alone all joys, all affections, all prayers; one that is every hope and every blessing; one that soothes all suffering and leaves an eternal memory; the one that we receive when we open our lives to life and that we carry to God like a precious pearl: it is the kiss of a mother.

[published Sunday, 20 November 1864]

80. Louise de La Vallière (1644–1710), who as a teenager became the official mistress of Louis XIV of France.

Pensée

À Mme ***

Lélia D...t [Adolphe Duhart]

Suave passagère,
Pensée, ô douce fleur,
Va, sois la messagère
De mon timide cœur.

Près de ma bien-aimée,
Va, fleur, passer tes jours ;
Va, tu seras charmée
Près d'elle mes amours.

Dis-lui, ma fleur chérie,
De mon amour discret
La molle rêverie,
L'ineffable secret...

Fidèle confidente,
Oh ! va lui dire encor
De mon âme constante
Les brillants rêves d'or.

Quand sa tête rêveuse
Se penchera sur toi,
Fais naître, ô fleur heureuse,
Un doux penser pour moi.

Oh ! sois frêle, légère
Et gracieuse fleur,
Sois alors messagère
Des aveux de son cœur.

[publié le dimanche 27 novembre 1864]

Pansy [81]

For Mrs. ──

LÉLIA D──T [Adolphe Duhart]

Delightful traveler,
Oh pansy, sweetest of flowers,
Go, my messenger: tell her
My timid heart's desires.

In my dear beloved's arms,
Go now to spend your days;
Go where you'll know the charms
Of love's alluring ways.

Tell her, my darling flower,
Of my love, however discreet—
The fantasy's gentle power:
The ineffable secret.

Devoted confidant,
Go to her once more to tell
Of the golden dreams that enchant
My ever steadfast soul.

When, leaning her head to admire,
Upon you she gazes, dreamy,
Oh happy flower, inspire
A tender thought of me.

Be delicate and frail —
Oh, most graceful of flowers! —
And, messenger, come tell
Of her heart's hidden desires.

[published Sunday, 27 November 1864]

81. The French *pensée* means both "pansy" and "thought." The English term derives from Middle French.

L'échelle de l'amour

Imitation

Lélia D... t [Adolphe Duhart]

À tous les attributs de l'enfant de Cythère,
Ailes, flambeau, carquois, dès longtemps consacrés,
Ajoutez son échelle ; elle enferme un mystère
      Admirable en tous ses degrés.

Cette échelle, tressée en nœuds d'or et de soie,
Fut faite pour l'Amour par les doigts du Désir.
Une main adorée à nos pieds la déploie :
      Chaque échelon est un plaisir.

Cette échelle en tous lieux se porte et se transporte ;
Et l'on peut la trouver dans le moindre pourpris,
Pendue à la fenêtre, attachée à la porte
      De l'objet dont on est épris.

Pourtant il ne faut pas que l'amant s'y mécompte !
Ce chef-d'œuvre est fragile autant qu'ingénieux ;
L'échelle porte en l'air, et jamais on n'y monte
      Qu'avec un bandeau sur les yeux.

          [publié le dimanche 11 décembre 1864]

Sonnet

À Mme Louise de Mortie

Lélia D... t [Adolphe Duhart]

Le cantique sacré qu'un ange dit aux cieux,
Les accords des oiseaux quand l'horizon s'irise,
Tous les bruissements que soulève la brise
Dans des bois en son vol léger, capricieux ;

Le rire d'un lutin folâtre et gracieux,
Le murmure des eaux que le vent ride et frise,
Et l'accent virginal d'une vierge surprise
À son premier aveu, tendre et délicieux ;

The Ladder of Love

Imitation

LÉLIA D——T [Adolphe Duhart]

To all the attributes of Cythera's child —
Her wings and torch, her quiver, known and renowned —
Let's add her ladder; a mystery lies veiled
      Within it, wondrous all around.

This ladder, braided in knots of silk and gold,
Was crafted for Love by the nimble hands of Desire.
Before our feet our beloved sets it to unfold:
      Each rung offers a different pleasure.

This ladder can be carried anywhere;
It can be found in the humblest secluded garden,
Hung onto the window, or tied to the door
      Of the object of our affection.

The suitor, however, must not misunderstand!
This masterpiece is both fragile and well-designed;
The ladder leads upward, and one can only ascend
      With his eyes covered to keep him blind.

      [published Sunday, 11 December 1864]

Sonnet

For Madame Louise de Mortie [82]

LÉLIA D——T [Adolphe Duhart]

The sacred hymn that an angel sighs to the sky,
The horizon's changing hues as the birds harmonize,
The rustlings that the wind does stir as it flies
Across the woods, lighthearted and full of whimsy;

The laughter of elves, elegant and spry,
The murmur of water when wrinkled by the breeze,
And the virginal voice of a virgin caught by surprise
At her very first avowal, tender and lovely;

---

82. The abolitionist and social activist Louise de Mortie (1833–67) has been considered "one of the most important black Americans of her time" (Smith 173). Based in Boston, she came to New Orleans during the war to found an orphanage for children of color. De Mortie was a well-known orator and public reader: Duhart's choice in this poem to characterize her voice as "soft" contrasts with other nineteenth-century texts, which describe her voice as "voluminous" and "richly-toned" (Majors 113; Williams 449). In May 1865

Les préludes naïfs d'un amoureux trouvère,
La prière du Christ tombant sur le Calvaire,
Et son cri de pardon exhalé sur la croix,

Et tout ce que le ciel promet quand on l'implore,
Madame, a moins de charme, est moins divin encore,
Pour nos cœurs captivés, que votre douce voix.

[publié le dimanche 9 avril 1865]

Guzla

À Marie C...se

Lélia D...t [Adolphe Duhart]

Est-ce un écho des lieux
Qu'un long voile nous cache ?
Ou le vol gracieux
De ses cygnes sans tache ?

Ou bien, ô vaste mer !
Serait-ce ta voix haute,
Qui de ton sein amer
Résonne sur la côte ?

Est-ce un accord du ciel
Qui vient dans ma pauvre âme
Apporter son doux miel,
Plus doux que le cinname ?

Non, le cygne me dit,
Ce n'est pas moi qui chante ;
Non, la mer répondit,
Ma voix est moins touchante.

Et le ciel à son tour,
Où jamais rien ne change,
Dit : cet accord d'amour
N'est pas l'accord de l'ange.

Cependant j'écoutais.
Sous la voûte infinie,
Je ne sais, j'entendais
Une molle harmonie.

The naive preludes sung by a love-struck minstrel,
The prayer of Christ as he stumbles on Calvary hill,
And his pardoning cry exhaled from the height of the cross,

And all that, for our pleas, is promised by heaven,
Madame, have less charm, are still less divine,
To our captivated hearts, than your soft voice.

        [published Sunday, 9 April 1865]

she held a "Patriotic and Literary Reading," organized with Paul Trévigne of *La Tribune* and others; the event featured performances by local musicians, including Victor Eugène Macarty (*La Tribune*, 9 May 1865). She died in 1867 of yellow fever, which she contracted while taking care of the sick.

Gusle [83]

   For Marie C——se

LÉLIA D——T [Adolphe Duhart]

Is it an echo from the sites
That behind a long veil vanish?
Or perhaps the graceful flight
Of a swan without blemish?

Or rather, oh sea so deep and vast,
Could it be your voice thus sounding,
Rising up from your bitter breast
And along the shore resounding?

Is it a chord struck by the sky
And unto my poor soul sent
To bring its sweetest honey,
Sweeter than cinnamon's scent?

"No," the swan said to me,
"It is not I who sing."
"No," replied the sea,
"My voice is not so touching."

And, speaking in turn, the heavens above,
Where no change has ever occurred,
Then said, "This chord of love
Is not the angel's chord."

I sat listening, however,
Beneath the vault's infinity
To I-know-not-what, and I did hear
A mellow harmony.

83. Single-stringed instrument common among various peoples of the Balkans and associated with recitations of epic poetry.

C'était ta main, enfant,
Sur le piano sonore,
Qui disait doucement
Le chant d'Éléonore.

Alors à mes frissons
Je compris le mystère :
C'étaient bien là les sons
D'un ange de la terre.

Et mon cœur étonné
Voudrait toujours entendre
Ce chant passionné
Si suave et si tendre !

[publié le dimanche 25 juin 1865]

Étoile du soir

À Mme C...na S...

Lélia D...t [Adolphe Duhart]

Pense à moi pour calmer en ton âme la peine,
Quand le soleil ardent qui s'est au loin enfui
Sous l'horizon de pourpre isolément entraîne,
Comme à triste regret, ses vapeurs après lui.

Sur le front azuré de la nuit bien sereine,
Quand la première étoile, ô mon bel ange, a lui
Comme un beau diamant de l'écrin d'une reine ;
Oh ! pense alors à moi pour chasser ton ennui.

Car c'est l'heure d'extase où tout bas l'on soupire,
Où l'absent soucieux, et vers qui l'on aspire,
Tient ses mornes regards au ciel d'azur fixés.

Il cherche avidement cette première étoile,
Et de larmes alors son œil brûlant se voile
Au souvenir si doux de ses beaux jours passés.

[publié le dimanche 6 août 1865]

It was your hand, dear child,
Upon the ringing piano
Whose clear voice spake the song
Of Eleanor, soft and slow.

The shivers along my spine
Did this mystery dispel,
For those were indeed the sounds
Of an earth-dwelling angel.

And unto this very day
My astonished heart does long
To hear this tender, gentle,
And so very sensual song.

[published Sunday, 25 June 1865]

Evening Star

For Madame C——na S——

LÉLIA D——T [Adolphe Duhart]

Do think of me to soothe your soul in pain,
When the fiery sun, having fled to parts remote,
Carries away, into the purple horizon
Its vaporous trail, as though with sorrow smote.

When the very first star, oh angel of mine, did shine
On the azure face of the night's serenity,
Like a diamond's beauty from the jewelry case of a queen;
Do think of me to oust your apathy.

For it is the hour of delight when we breathe a sigh,
Aspiring toward that absent one, laden with worry,
Who upon heavens' blue keeps his gaze held fast.

He's eagerly seeking that very first star of all,
And his burning eye now shrouds itself in a veil
Of tears, in remembrance so sweet of days that have passed.

[published Sunday, 6 August 1865]

Rêve

À Madame C... S...s

Lélia D...t [Adolphe Duhart]

> *Ahi, null'altro che pianto al mondo dura !*
> — Petrarca

Je voyais un bel ange,
Doux habitant des cieux ;
De la sainte phalange
Tendre élu radieux.

Sa voix enchanteresse
Me parlait de bonheur,
Et répandait l'ivresse
Dans mon malheureux cœur.

Comme une vive flamme
D'espérance et de foi,
Son regard en mon âme
Portait un doux émoi.

À sa voix consolante,
Suave souvenir —
Ma pauvre âme souffrante
Croyait en l'avenir.

Mais comme au ciel s'élève
Le parfum d'une fleur
S'évanouit mon rêve,
Hélas ! tout mon bonheur !

[publié le dimanche 8 octobre 1865]

Dream

For Mrs. C—— S——s

Lélia D——t [Adolphe Duhart]

> *Ahi, null'altro che pianto al mondo dura!*
> — Petrarca [84]

A lovely angel I beheld:
Among the hosts of heaven,
Gentle and radiant he dwelled,
Surely the chosen one.

His soft and captivating voice
Told me of happiness
And poured, by draughts, ecstatic joys
Onto my heart's distress.

Afire like a living coal
Of faith and expectation,
His gaze, piercing into my soul,
Induced a sweet commotion.

The sound of his voice does soothe and console;
Recalling its accents, pure,
My poor, sad, and suffering soul
Began to believe in the future.

Alas! Just as a flower's scent
Toward heaven does ascend,
My happiness was quickly spent:
My dream has reached its end!

[published Sunday, 8 October 1865]

[84]. "Alas, nothing but weeping will last in this world" (from Petrarca's *Rime sparse*, canzone 323, "Standomi un giorno solo a la fenestra"; my trans.).

À une enfant

Lélia D... t [Adolphe Duhart]

Tu me demandes, chère enfant,
Gracieuse et chaste créole,
Un accord de ma lyre, un chant —
Qu'emportera trop tôt Éole.
Mais si facile est ton bonheur,
Bonheur de joie et de lumière,
Et si doux est ton petit cœur :
Comment repousser ta prière ?

Ne te hâte point de jouir,
Enfant, la vie est bien amère
Et ne peut longtemps éblouir,
Tant le bonheur est éphémère.

Hélas ! sur les ailes du Temps
Trop vite viennent les alarmes.
Chante encore, jouis du printemps ;
Laisse pour nous les tristes larmes.

Oh ! laisse pour nous les regrets ;
Garde encor ton insouciance,
Les petits jeux, naïfs secrets
De ta douce et pure innocence.

Ah ! que toujours dans tes beaux yeux,
On lise la suave ivresse ;
Que ton âme, miroir des cieux,
Ne réfléchisse la tristesse.

Ma lyre, à ta prière, enfant,
Gracieuse et chaste créole,
Évoque du bonheur un chant
Que ne puisse emporter Éole.

[publié le dimanche 21 janvier 1866]

For a Child

Lélia D——t [Adolphe Duhart]

You request of me, child so dear,
Graceful and virtuous Creole,
A chord from my lyre, a song for your ear …
That Aeolus would simply steal.
But, in truth, your wish is easy to meet,
A simple wish for joy and light,
And your little heart so very sweet:
How could I deny you your delight?

Hurry not to consume your pleasure,
For bitter is life, my child,
And ephemeral is ever the measure
Upon which happiness has smiled.

Alas! The wings of time will bring
All too quickly frightful fears;
Sing once more, enjoy the spring;
Entrust to us your worried tears.

Oh! Entrust to us your regrets;
For a while, keep your insouciance —
The little games, the naïve secrets
Of your sweet and pure innocence.

Ah! May we always, in your eyes,
Behold an ecstatic gladness;
May your soul, mirror of the skies,
Never reflect any sadness.

My lyre, dear child, at your request,
Graceful and virtuous Creole,
Will strike up a song, by happiness blessed,
That even Aeolus cannot steal.

[published Sunday, 21 January 1866]

La fleur blessée

À Madame ... S...

LÉLIA D...T [Adolphe Duhart]

> *Fermossi al fin il cor che balzò tanto.*
> — Ippolito Pindemonte

    Les larmes de la blonde Aurore,
    Mes sœurs, au jour, m'ont fait éclore.
    Aux premiers rayons du soleil
    Je me suis doucement ouverte
    Sur ma tige flexible et verte :
    Les oiseaux chantaient mon réveil,
    Et maintenant je vais mourir...

    Ce matin une jeune fille,
    Rêveuse en sa blanche mantille,
S'arrête près de moi. — Je venais de fleurir. —
Elle me regarda ; je la trouvais si belle
Que ma tige pencha timidement vers elle,
Comme l'ange se penche aux pieds du Dieu martyr.

Sur mes feuilles sa main, distraitement errante,
Passait et les faisait frissonner de bonheur.
Tout à coup je sentis une vive douleur,
    Et je tombai sur ma tige expirante...

Cruelle enfant ! pourquoi ne me cueillis-tu pas,
    Pauvre et frêle fleur méprisée ?
    Indifférente à mon trépas,
    Tu me laissas ainsi brisée.

    De ma blessure lentement
    S'échappent ma sève et ma vie ;
Ma corolle pâlit ; ma tige jaunissant,
    Par l'aquilon maintenant poursuivie,
    Laisse tomber ses feuilles tristement.

Le soleil s'est caché sous l'horizon dans l'ombre ;
Le silence est profond, mystérieux et sombre ;
    Tout disparaît... tout fuit...
    Est-ce déjà la nuit ?

The Wounded Flower

To Madame ———— S————

LÉLIA D————T [Adolphe Duhart]

> *Fermossi al fin il cor che balzò tanto.*
> — Ippolito Pindemonte[85]

Dawn's blond tears, my sisters, when waking,
Enticed me to blossom as day was breaking.
As the sun's first rays caressed the earth
Slowly and softly did I open
Atop my stem, supple and green:
In song the birds announced my birth
And now, alas, I'll soon be doomed.

A maiden came to me this morning,
In whitest mantilla, dreamy and dreaming,
And stopped to speak. — I'd only just then bloomed.
She looked at me; she seemed so very lovely
That toward her frame my stem bent timidly,
As an angel kneels before the feet of God.

Upon my leaves her hand, which wandered free
To touch me, made them quiver happily.
A sudden pang of pain I then did feel;
Upon my dying stem I fell ...

Oh child so cruel! Why didn't you prize
This poor and fragile flower, disdained?
Indifferent to my sad demise
You left me thus, forlorn and pained.

Then slowly from my wound
My sap and my very life were drained;
My petals grew pale; my stem, drooping to the ground
And chased by the north wind,
Began to drop its yellowed leaves, chagrined.

The sun then hid itself, all shrouded in shade,
The silence is deep, in mystery arrayed;
Everything starts to disappear ...
Is night already here?

---

85. "It has finally stopped, this heart that beat so strongly" (my trans.). The epigraph is a misquotation of "Fermasi alfin quel cor, che balzò tanto," from "Clizia," a poem by the pre-Romantic Italian poet Ippolito Pindemonte (1753–1828), in which a nymph wastes away from a broken heart. Duhart's version may have its source in Germaine de Staël's misquotation in her 1807 novel *Corinne* or in Felicia Hemans's poem "Arabella Stuart," which reproduced Staël's error (Wolfson 339n5).

Oh ! non... non... c'est la mort ! — La moissonneuse austère
Qui glane les sanglots et les cris de la terre —
Je meurs !... Ce soir au ciel l'étoile brillera,
Et mon parfum si pur vers Dieu s'envolera,
        Vers Dieu qui bénit et console.

        Je n'ouvrirai plus ma corolle,
        — Calice fait pour retenir
        Les diamants de la rosée, —
Et ma fière dépouille, à la brise exposée,
N'aura pas de regrets ni de doux souvenir.

        Ô jeune fille ! à ton indifférence
        Mon spectre un jour apparaîtra ;
Mon spectre fugitif qui te reprochera
De mon amour naissant la cruelle souffrance,
        Et le remords me vengera.

Non... non... je te pardonne et ma douleur passée,
Et les regrets amers de mon âme oppressée ;
        Que jamais le destin un jour
        Ne vienne t'apprendre à ton tour
Tout ce que peut souffrir la pauvre fleur blessée.

        [publié le dimanche 29 avril 1866]

Guzla

À Mlle Blanche B...

LÉLIA D...T [Adolphe Duhart]

Que me demandes-tu gracieuse Créole ?
        La muse est rebelle à ma voix.
De ma lyre brisée, aucun chant ne s'envole ;
        Triste, elle vibre sous mes doigts,

Mais il me faut chanter... Ta prière me blesse ;
        Enfant, je n'ai plus que des pleurs ;
Je te les cacherai — pour toi, vois ma faiblesse —
        Pour ne te donner que des fleurs.

Jeune fille, à ton âge on commence à comprendre
        Un livre d'or au chiffre pur ;
Le cœur est plus ému, la voix suave et tendre,
        Et l'horizon toujours d'azur.

Ah! No ... no ... death has come! The grim harvester
Who gleans our sobs and screams the world over —
I'm dying! ... Tonight the star will shine in the sky,
And my fragrance, so pure, toward God in heaven will fly,
      Toward God who blesses and consoles.

      Not ever again shall I open my petals,
      Which spread like a chalice designed to collect
      The gleaming diamonds of the dew,
And my proud remains, o'er which the wind will blow,
Shall have no regrets nor sweet things to recollect.

      Oh maiden! One day my ghost
      Will confront your unconcern;
My fleeting ghost to scold you will return;
For the cruelty suffered by a love utmost,
      Remorse will avenge me in turn.

No! I forgive you my pain, now past its hour,
And my distressed soul's regret, biting and sour;
      May fate never come some day
      To make you bitterly pay
For the suffering that can be felt by a wounded flower.

      [published Sunday, 29 April 1866]

Gusle

For Miss Blanche B——

LÉLIA D——T [Adolphe Duhart]

My graceful Creole, what do you ask of me?
      The muse against my voice revolts.
Beneath my touch, my broken lyre sadly
      Shudders; from it no song unfolds.

But sing I must ... Your request brings me distress;
      A child am I, and have but tears;
I'll keep them hidden — for you, despite my weakness —
      And offer you naught but flowers.

At your age, young girl, one starts to understand
      A golden book with numbers pure;
One's heart grows tender, the voice more pleasant,
      The horizon ever bathed in azure.

C'est le rêve d'amour. À l'heure du silence,
      Ton sein s'agite doucement.
Tout te sourit : la vie et la molle espérance ;
      Tout est pour toi rayonnant.

Jouis de ton printemps : le bonheur a des ailes,
      S'il nous fait, il ne revient pas ;
Les larmes, les douleurs sont seules éternelles :
      Tel est le destin d'ici-bas.

Chante, chante toujours ! Garde longtemps encore
      Ta franche gaîté, ta fraîcheur ;
Puisse le ciel pour toi conserver cette aurore,
      Pure auréole de ton cœur.

Abandonne tes jours au bonheur sans mélange ;
      Tes nuits aux songes les plus doux,
Et, gracieuse enfant, qu'à ton réveil un ange
      Te les redise à deux genoux.

            [publié le dimanche 13 mai 1866]

Le Jasmin

   À Mme L. S...

Lélia D... t [Adolphe Duhart]

Jasmin, fleur préférée
De ma chaste adorée,
Viens sur mon triste cœur ;
Viens de mon espérance
Ouïr la confidence.
Oh ! viens, ma blanche fleur !

Écoute, je t'en prie,
Ma molle rêverie
Et mon amour discret ;
Ô ma fleur odorante,
De mon âme souffrante
Écoute le secret.

It is the dream of love. In this hour grown quiet,
        Your breast quivers ever so gently.
All smiles on you, both life and hope so sweet;
        For you all things shine brilliantly.

Enjoy the spring, when happiness has wings;
        If it flees, it never returns;
Tears and pain are the only eternal things.
        For such are fate's concerns.

Sing, forever sing! And keep while you can
        Your youthful bloom and gaiety.
May heaven grant to you the purest dawn
        To adorn your heart's purity.

Abandon your days to uncorrupted bliss.
        Your nights to dreams exquisite,
And then, fair child emerging from sleep's abyss,
        May they be retold by an angel come to visit.

        [published Sunday, 13 May 1866]

Jasmine

   For Madame L. S——

LÉLIA D——T [Adolphe Duhart]

Jasmine, flower whose allure
Enchants my darling, chaste and pure,
Come nigh my heart in plight;
Come nigh and hear the confession
Of my deepest hope's expression.
Come nigh, oh flower of white!

Prithee, listen carefully
To both my mellow reverie
And my love, ever discreet;
Oh flower full of fragrance,
Of my suffering soul's torments
Listen to the secret.

Viens, viens ! Je veux encore
De celle que j'adore
Confier en ton sein
Le nom cher à mon âme,
Son nom divin, cinname,
Doux comme toi, jasmin.

Oh ! viens tarir mes larmes,
De mes vives alarmes
Chasser le chagrin noir...
Ô fleur, vois ma tristesse ;
Viens me rendre à l'ivresse,
Viens me donner espoir !...

Jasmin, fleur préférée,
De ma chaste adorée,
Viens sur mon triste cœur ;
Viens de mon espérance
Ouïr la confidence.
Oh viens, ma blanche fleur !

[publié le dimanche 20 mai 1866]

Amaritudo

À M. L. Mansion

LÉLIA D... T [Adolphe Duhart]

> Un froid mortel en mon sein vient de naître !
> Mon front pâlit et je me sens faiblir...
> — A. Lanusse

Je ressens dans mon cœur une tristesse amère ;
Dans mes yeux presque éteints roulent de brûlants pleurs,
Et de ma fièvre aiguë une molle chimère
Jamais n'a calmé les douleurs.

    Pourtant j'avais cru dans mon âme
    Sentir une secrète flamme,
    — Mystique et céleste dictame —
    Venir enfin cautériser
    Ma profonde et large blessure ;
    Mais toujours elle me pressure,
    Et sa livide meurtrissure
    Ne pourra se cicatriser.

Come near, come near! I wish
To place the name I cherish
Onto your bosom's shrine,
The name so dear to my soul,
Divine like cinnamon's smell,
As sweet as you, oh jasmine.

Oh! come to quench my tears,
To chase the gnawing fears
That cause my heart to mope ...
Behold my black chagrin;
Give me joy once again:
Oh flower, let me hope!

Jasmine, flower whose allure
Enchants my darling, chaste and pure,
Come nigh my heart in plight;
Come nigh and hear the confession
Of my deepest hope's expression.
Come nigh, oh flower of white!

[published Sunday, 20 May 1866]

Amaritudo [86]

For Mr. L. Mansion [87]

LÉLIA D——T [Adolphe Duhart]

> A deathly cold has just been born in my breast!
> My brow grows pale, and I feel myself grow weak.[88]
> — A. Lanusse

I feel a bitter sadness within my breast;
My eyes have nearly drowned in burning tears,
No gentle illusion has granted any rest
From the fiery pangs of these fevers.

I thought I felt inside my soul
The flame sparked of a secret coal
— a mystic balm that restoreth whole —
Administered to cauterize
My wound, gaping deep and wide;
But still the pain afflicts my side,
For this awful gash will not abide
Any attempt to cicatrize.

86. Latin for "bitterness."

87. The poet Lucien Mansion.

88. Duhart takes his epigraph from a Lanusse poem about a dying daughter ("La jeune agonisante," which originally appeared in *Les Cenelles*). Many of Duhart's poems published in *La Tribune* in 1866 show evidence of his grief over the 1864 deaths of three small daughters: see, e.g., pp. 270–75 ("Berthe! ... Lucie! ... Marie! ...").

Ainsi que la pure rosée
Qu'un ange pieux a posée
Au sein de la rose irisée
Pour la ranimer, pauvre fleur ;
Ainsi cette flamme, — doux rêve
Qu'en Éden une vierge achève —
Vint porter une faible trêve
À ma violente douleur...

Mais hélas ! quand l'ardente brise
Passe rapide, brûle et brise :
La pauvre fleur, pâle, surprise,
Frémit et meurt fatalement...
Cette douce trêve, comme elle,
Ressentit l'étreinte mortelle,
Et s'envola, froide infidèle,
Alors loin de mon cœur aimant.

❖

Ce souffle impur des morts a passé sur ma lyre,
Et l'a voilée, hélas !... d'un long crêpe de deuil...
Et de vagues terreurs tout bas semblent prédire,
À mon cœur abattu par le sombre délire,
   Le silence... le noir cercueil...

Oh ! je sens se presser de sinistres pensées
Dans ma tête inclinée, en mon sein plein de fiel !
Comme un spectre hideux loin des routes tracées,
Comme un ange maudit, de mes heures passées
   L'avenir veut aigrir le miel...

Je marche toujours seul... et ma plainte étouffée
De nul n'est entendue en ce monde trompeur ;
Et quand la fièvre intense en mon âme échauffée
Vient me bleuir le corps, comme une bonne fée,
   Non !... nul n'en vient calmer l'ardeur.

❖

Oh ! n'aurai-je jamais dans mon ciel triste et sombre
   Une lueur, un pur rayon ?
N'entendrai-je jamais dans l'ouragan, dans l'ombre
   Les cris plaintifs de l'alcyon ?

Just as the purest drops of dew
That a pious angel comes to strew
Onto a rose, arrayed in hue,
To resuscitate this piteous flower,
This flame — a dream like none so sweet
That a virgin in Eden happens to meet —
With meekness has come to entreat
My pain to abate its violent power.

Alas! When heaves the heat-kissed breeze
Burning and breaking all it can seize,
The pitiful flower, sunk to its knees,
Shudders, then unto death does depart.
This sweet reprieve, turning its face,
Now feels the force of the fatal embrace
And, unfaithful, flies away, apace,
Far too far from my fawning heart.

❖

The rotten breath of the dead has blown o'er my lyre,
And concealed it — alas! — in a long pall of mourning...
Meanwhile, vague terrors, portending the most dire,
Impart to my heart all the dread they can inspire:
  Silence... A dark coffin's forewarning...

Oh! What somber and sinister thoughts have been placed
In my head, into my bosom awash in bile!
Like a ghastly ghost from traveled highways chased
Or an angel damned, the future will spoil the taste
  Of the honey of days enjoyed erstwhile.

I always walk alone... and my muffled cry
Is heard by none in this world ruled by deceit;
When fever, fiery to some unknown degree,
Like a kindly fairy, begins to burn my body,
  No one comes to soothe its heat!

❖

Oh! Shall I never see a slice of sunshine
  Across my sad and somber skies?
Shall I never hear, amidst the hurricane
  Or the shadows, the halcyon's plaintive cries?

J'ai pleuré !... j'ai souffert une douleur mortelle,
    Et jamais un ange des cieux
N'abrita mon amour à l'ombre de son aile
    Et ne me sourit, gracieux...

Non !... Mon cœur n'eût jamais une molle chimère...
    Je ne connus que des sanglots...
Et bientôt mon esquif, battu sur l'onde amère,
    Va disparaître au fond des flots !...

Nouvelle-Orléans, le 25 mai 1866

        [publié le dimanche 27 mai 1866]

Ange du ciel

  À Mlle E. B...n

Lélia D... t [Adolphe Duhart]

Vous que tout bas j'appelle en ma prière,
Ange du ciel, rêve du Paradis,
Comme un rayon du divin sanctuaire
Jetez les yeux sur mon cœur solitaire...
Priez pour moi !... car mes jours sont maudits !...

Pour adoucir mon destin triste et sombre,
Ange du ciel, fille aux douces vertus,
Conduisez-moi sur les écueils sans nombre
Jetés, hélas ! sur mon chemin dans l'ombre...
Veillez sur moi !... car je n'espère plus !...

L'ombre me glace et vainement je pleure ;
Mon front pâli de la mort est couvert...
Ange du ciel, dans la froide demeure,
Venez parfois prier un jour, une heure,
Dans le parvis de mon tombeau désert...

        [publié le dimanche 17 juin 1866]

I've wept! ... Despite my mortal suffering,
    Never has any heavenly angel
Sheltered my love beneath the shade of her wing,
    Or granted me her gracious smile ...

No! With a lifetime of sobs I've paid the cost ...
    My heart has drunk no chimerical potion ...
And soon my skiff, by the waves relentlessly tossed,
    Will disappear beneath the ocean!

New Orleans, 25 May 1866

    [published Sunday, 27 May 1866]

Angel from Heaven

   To Miss E. B——n

LÉLIA D——T [Adolphe Duhart]

You to whom gently I whisper a prayer,
You heaven-sent Angel, by Paradise dreamed,
As a sunbeam, divine, falls down through the air,
Please cast your eyes on my heart's despair ...
Please pray for me! For my days are damned!

To soften my fate, so somber and joyless,
You heaven-sent Angel, by sweet virtues crowned,
Come guide me now through the obstacles, endless,
That litter, alas, my path plunged in darkness ...
And watch over me — for no hope can be found!

By shadows chilled, I weep in vain;
Death shrouds my brow, grown pale with gloom ...
You heaven-sent Angel, come now and then
For a day or an hour, to this cold, lonely den,
To pray in the forecourt of my forlorn tomb ...

    [published Sunday, 17 June 1866]

Souvenir

Lélia D... t [Adolphe Duhart]

Suave comme une lumière,
Molle clarté des cieux ;
Suave comme la prière
Que dit un ange radieux...
Tel s'offre en une souvenance
Ce regard trop vite effacé,
C'était pour mon cœur l'espérance...
Ce doux regard... il est passé.

Suave comme la surprise
Des aveux naïfs, consolants ;
Suave aussi comme la brise
Parfumée et pleine de chants...
Tel s'offre en ma souvenance
Ce soupir trop vite effacé.
C'était pour mon cœur l'espérance...
Ce doux soupir... il est passé.

Suave comme un brûlant rêve,
Rêve d'amour et de bonheur ;
Suave enfin comme une trêve
Laissée à la vive douleur...
Tels s'offrent en ma souvenance
Ces pleurs, pleurs trop vite effacés
C'était pour mon cœur l'espérance,
Et ces tendres pleurs sont passés.

[publié le dimanche 24 juin 1866]

A Memory

LÉLIA D——T [Adolphe Duhart]

As soft as a gentle light
Illuminating the skies;
As soft as a prayer in flight
On a radiant angel's sighs ...
Like a memory we cherish,
As fleeting as the dawn,
It was my heart's only wish ...
But this gentle glance ... is gone.

As soft as the sudden surprise
Of naïve, consoling confessions;
As soft as the fragrant breeze
Perfumed by musical expressions ...
Thus shall I ever recall
This sigh too soon withdrawn,
My hoping heart did hear its call,
But this sigh so sweet ... is gone.

As soft as a feverish dream,
A dream of love and bliss;
As soft as a reprieve can seem
Amidst pain's ugliness ...
Thus shall I ever recall
These tears ... too soon withdrawn ...
My hoping heart did hear their call,
But these tender tears are gone.

[published Sunday, 24 June 1866]

« La fleur de mars — Chanson » (1835), par Henri Blaze,
recopié et publié dans *La Tribune* sous le titre :

La fleur indiscrète

À Mlle Nathalie Formento

[attribué dans *La Tribune* à « Antony » (Victor Eugène Macarty)]

À l'heure où dans les eaux la lune se reflète
Je suis venu m'asseoir près d'une violette ;
Douce fleur du printemps que de petits gazons
Paraissaient abriter des inondations
Et du soleil trop chaud et de la brise vive.
Or, elle demeurait immobile et pensive,
Et comme j'étendais la main pour la cueillir,
Je ne l'ai vue alors ni trembler ni pâlir ;
Elle a levé sur moi son œil mélancolique
Puis, ayant murmuré le salut angélique,
M'a dit en s'agitant sur sa tige en émoi :
« Salut, je te connais, jeune homme, approche-toi,
« Et causons à cette heure où le vent me balance. »
Et moi, tout glorieux de cette confiance,
Je me suis incliné vers son calice bleu,
Ainsi que j'aurais fait pour lui faire un aveu,
Et me suis mis alors à lui dire à voix basse
Le nom, et les vertus, et le charme, et la grâce
De la dame que j'aime, et sa molle pudeur,
Tandis qu'avec ma main de la petite fleur
J'éloignais avec soin les herbes curieuses
Qui, pour savoir aussi mes peines amoureuses,
Tendaient leur col charmant avec précaution.
Or, ayant raconté de cette passion
Tout ce que je renferme en mon âme inquiète,
J'ai baisé sur le front la pâle violette,
Et me suis éloigné, lui recommandant bien
De garder mon secret et de n'en dire rien
Aux brins d'herbe nombreux qui croissent autour d'elle ;
Et la vierge a promis de me rester fidèle.

❖

Mais hélas ! c'est péché d'ouvrir ainsi son cœur,
Même à la violette, à la plus douce fleur,
Et j'aurais dû savoir que cette fleur chérie
Aime trop ardemment ses sœurs de la prairie,
Et sent trop le besoin de leur faire plaisir,
Pour ne pas employer ses heures de loisir
À leur conter, la nuit une si douce chose.

"The Flower of March: Song" (1835), by Henri Blaze,
copied and republished in *La Tribune* as:

The Indiscreet Flower

For Miss Nathalie Formento[89]

[attributed in *La Tribune* to "Antony" (Victor Eugène Macarty)]

At the hour when the waters reflect the moonlight,
I came to sit beside a violet —
The sweet flower of spring whom, sparing no pains,
The shrubs seemed to shield from the flooding rains,
The scorching sun, and the bracing breeze.
Unmoving, she kept at contemplative ease.
Attempting to pick her, I started to stretch out my hand.
Neither trembling nor growing pale, she continued to stand
And upon me set her melancholy eye;
Then, with a greeting murmured angelically,
She said as atop her stem she shook eagerly,
"Hello, I know you, young man, come closer to me,
And let us converse in this hour when I'm tossed and swayed
By the wind." Intensely proud of the trust she'd displayed,
I gently bent down toward her calyx of blue,
Just as to make a confession I might do,
And, lowering my voice, I began to proclaim
The virtues, the charm, the grace — the very name
Of the woman I love, and her gentle modesty,
As I pushed aside ever so carefully
The grasses, full of curiosity,
That, to learn of my heart's infelicity,
Had stretched their necks toward me with furtive care.
After I'd had occasion to declare
The passion that my worried soul begat,
I kissed the brow of the pallid violet,
And started to leave, respectfully requesting
That my secret not be revealed, even in jesting,
To the numerous strands of grass that around her grew.
And the virgin promised to stay forever true.

❖

But alas! It is a sin to open one's heart,
To even the sweetest of flowers impart
A secret; I should have been able to foresee
That the violet loved her sisters from the prairie
And wanted far too much to give them pleasure
For her not to while away her moments of leisure
By telling them at night a thing so sweet.

---

89. On the literary hoax involving the poet "Antony," see pp. 31–35. The *Tribune* version adds a fictitious date of composition and has been dedicated to Nathalie Formento (on Formento, see p. 189n63 ["The Weeping Willow"]). Interestingly, the physical copy of *La Tribune* from which this poem was transcribed (the only known paper copy still extant, located at the American Antiquarian Society) was originally sent to Formento by a friend, Élodie Mansion (daughter of Lucien Mansion), who left a handwritten message above the masthead: "À Nathalie Formento, de la part de son amie Élodie Mansion. 25 juillet 1866."

La violette a dit mon secret à la rose,
Qui l'a dit à son tour à la fraise des bois ;
Et mon secret, ainsi porté de voix en voix,
Est venu jusqu'au lys qui, sous son diadème,
S'est épris des beautés de la dame que j'aime,
Et pour les raconter aux tiges de sa cour
A suspendu ses chants de prière et d'amour ;
Et voilà qu'à présent les fleurs de la vallée
Savent toutes le nom de cette Immaculée.

Avril 1866

[publié le dimanche 22 juillet 1866]

L'amour

À Mlle Louise C...

BERTHE D... [possiblement Adolphe Duhart]

> What is love ? — An inexpressible thing ; a volume in a word ;
> an ocean in a tear ; a whirlwind in a sigh.
> — Anonymous

L'amour ? — L'amour, vois-tu, c'est un doux sentiment
Qui, sans réflexion, se forme dans notre âme,
S'en empare soudain, l'attache uniquement
Et la fait rayonner d'une secrète flamme.

C'est un foyer ardent... C'est une passion
Qui se nourrit d'espoir, de folle illusion
Et des rêves brillants d'une indicible ivresse,
Par qui tout se colore et par qui tout caresse.
C'est une passion qui rend indifférent,
Jaloux, capricieux, cruel ; désespérant
Tout autre qui n'est pas l'objet de notre culte :
C'est que son amour seul nous embellit la vie !
— Mystique vision de toute âme asservie
Qui répand à jamais et toute joie au cœur,
Et purs ravissements, et délice et bonheur...

L'amour ! — Mais sans amour que serait l'existence ?
C'est que l'amour est tout !... frénésie... avenir...
Suave émotion... éternel souvenir !
Mais l'amour c'est la Foi, c'est la molle Espérance.

[publié le dimanche 16 septembre 1866]

To the rose did the violet first divulge my secret;
The latter went to tell the wild strawberry,
And my secret, which other voices began to carry,
Arrived at the lily who under his crown did learn
About the woman I love and then in turn
Became entranced with her beauty; so as to apprise
The stems of his court, all songs of love did cease.
At present all the flowers of the valley
Do know the name of this Immaculate Lady.

April 1866

[published Sunday, 22 July 1866]

Love

For Miss Louise C——

BERTHE D—— [possibly Adolphe Duhart][90]

> What is love? — An inexpressible thing; a volume in a word;
> an ocean in a tear; a whirlwind in a sigh.
>
> — Anonymous[91]

What's Love? Love, you see, is a feeling most sweet;
Without forethought, it forms within our soul
And suddenly seizes it, binding its hands and feet,
And makes it glow like a hidden, burning coal.

It is a blazing hearth ... It is a passion
Which feeds on hope, the folly of illusion,
And dreams that gleam with unspeakable drunkenness,
Coloring all things, inhabiting each caress.
It is a passion that renders indifferent,
Capricious, jealous, and cruel — inducing dejection
In all who are not the object of our affection,
For that love alone can make our life beautiful!
— A mystical vision for any subdued soul,
Discharging into the heart an endless bliss
And ecstasies pure, pleasure and happiness.

Oh Love! For, lacking love, what life have we?
For love is everything! Excitement ... the future ...
Emotion so tender ... memories forever!
But, truly, Love is Faith; 'tis Hope come softly.

[published Sunday, 16 September 1866]

90. Berthe Duhart, daughter of Adolphe and Odilia, died before the age of three, on 28 July 1864.

91. This quotation, popular in the nineteenth century, is an adaptation of a passage from "Of Love," a poem by the English writer Martin F. Tupper (1810–89).

Berthe!... Lucie!... Marie!...

Lélia D...t [Adolphe Duhart]

Dolor !

Maintenant que tout est silence
Autour de leur petit berceau,
Et que je puis sur leur tombeau
Sceller mes regrets, ma souffrance ;

Et puisque je puis de leur nom
Épeler les lettres de flamme
Et, sans pâlir, en ma pauvre âme
En entendre le divin son ;

Puisque sur mes lèvres de mère
Aucun blasphème n'a jailli,
Et que mon cœur n'a pas failli
En sa douleur profonde, amère ;

Maintenant je puis vers le ciel
Élever mon humble prière ;
Les pleurs, enfin, sous ma paupière
Ont tari leur source de fiel...

Débile et penchée en la brume,
Mon âme, conservant sa foi
Peut répandre, Seigneur, vers toi
Son calice plein d'amertume.

Je viens, courbée, à deux genoux,
T'apporter toutes mes alarmes,
Tous mes chagrins, toutes les larmes
Que je versais en ton courroux.

Quel crime avais-je pu commettre ?
Mon bonheur n'était pas le tien :
C'était de mes jours le soutien,
Pourquoi me l'avoir pris, ô Maître ?

C'étaient de la nuit et du jour
Les fleurs de l'Éden de ma vie,
Ma seule joie inassouvie,
Ces enfants — trinité d'amour ! —

Berthe!...Lucie!...Marie!...[92]

LÉLIA D——T [Adolphe Duhart]

Dolor! [93]

Now that all has fallen to silence
Around their little cradle,
And upon their tomb I'm able
To seal my regrets, my torments;

And since of their names I can spell
Each and every fiery letter,
And, my sad soul, without a shudder,
Still hears their sound like a bell.

Since from my motherly lips
No sacrilege has e'er been pinched,
And my heart has never once flinched,
Even in deep pain's bitter grips.

Toward the sky I now am able
To lift my humble prayers;
Beneath my eyelids, at last my tears
Have dried their springs of bile...

Enfeebled and hunched in the fog's dimness,
My soul, in its faith steadfastly moored,
Can discharge toward you, Oh Lord,
Its chalice full of bitterness.

On bended knee, I come before
You, to bring my concerns and cares —
All of my sorrows and all the tears
That onto your wrath I'd begun to pour.

Of what crime could I have been guilty?
Your will and mine were not in accord,
Though this was my life's only support:
Oh Master, why did you take it from me?

They were, by day and by night,
The flowers of my life's Eden,
A trinity of love — these children! —
My only joy unsatisfied.

[92]. The poem is named for three of Adolphe and Odilia Duhart's daughters: two infants and a toddler, who all passed away in quick succession over the summer of 1864.

[93]. "Pain" in Latin.

C'était l'iris de mon aurore,
Rayon, épanouissement,
L'étoile d'or du firmament
Qui dans mon sein venait d'éclore...

Et penché sur l'immensité,
Tu m'as tout pris !... Ton ciel sans ombre
N'a-t-il pas des anges sans nombre
Et l'azur et l'Éternité ?...

N'avais-je donc pas fait mon heure
Et travaillé mon dur sillon,
Pour que mon œil soit sans rayon
Et vide mon humble demeure ?...

L'Éther n'avait rien de si beau,
Rien qui pût donc te satisfaire,
Puisqu'en notre stérile sphère
Tu vins chercher dans le berceau ?

Quoi !... toutes trois, l'une après l'autre,
Elles ont pris leur triste essor
Vers les sommets bleus du Thabor,
[texte illisible]

Quoi !... malgré toutes mes sueurs,
Malgré mes angoisses étranges,
Il te fallait encor leurs langes
Parmi la myrrhe et les lueurs...

❖

Quand j'entendis les chants funèbres
Vibrer autour de leur cercueil,
Un nuage couvrit mon œil
Comme un long voile des ténèbres...

Morne, le front plein de pâleurs,
Je me demandais, moi qui souffre :
Pourquoi tant de pleurs au noir gouffre,
Tant d'épines aux blanches fleurs ?

Pourquoi donc ce sombre mystère :
Le bonheur mêlé de sanglots,
Le ciel, et l'abîme aux grands flots,
L'amour dans le cœur solitaire ?...

They were the iris of my morn,
A ray of light, a blossoming,
A golden star in heaven's ring
That in my breast had just been born.

O'erlooking this immensity,
You took it all from me! Are not your skies
Already full of countless angels' sighs
And azure and eternity?

Haven't I already done my time,
And ploughed enough my stony row —
So that my eye would lose its glow
And empty become my humble home?

Was there nothing, for Heaven's sake,
As lovely as they up there in the Ether,
Such that down here, in our sterile sphere,
From the cradle you had to take?

What! All three, each one in turn,
Have taken wing in their sad flights
Toward the blue summits of Tabor's heights
[text illegible]

What! In spite of all my sweat,
Despite my load of strange distress,
You needed still their swaddling dress
Amidst your myrrh and gleams of light . . .

❖

When I heard the song from the funeral
Around their coffins resound,
Instantly a cloud came down
To shroud my eyes like a long, dark veil.

Doleful, my face full of gloom,
I asked myself, pale with anguish,
Wherefore such tears in this black abyss,
Such thorns on these white blooms?

Why this somber mystery —
Sobs all mixed with happiness,
The sky, the wave-washed abyss,
And love in a heart so solitary?

Puis j'ai gémi... pleuré longtemps
Ces enfants qui, blanches colombes,
Vont chercher, au-delà des tombes
D'autres étés... d'autres printemps...

❖

Maintenant que me font la lyre,
Les chants des oiseaux le matin ?
Mon cœur, brisé par le destin,
À leurs chants ne sait plus sourire...

Que me font les parfums des fleurs ?...
Je suis comme un roseau qui ploie :
Mon unique et suprême joie,
C'est d'être seule avec mes pleurs.

Oh ! que ferai-je, ainsi farouche,
Sans ces enfants, anges aux cieux,
Sans le doux regard de leurs yeux
Et sans les baisers de leur bouche ?

À quoi bon le nid sans l'oiseau,
L'âtre où ne brille l'étincelle,
L'arbre où ne s'arrête aucune aile,
Enfin sans l'enfant, un berceau ?

[publié le dimanche 7 octobre 1866]

Au cimetière

LÉLIA D... T [Adolphe Duhart]

Dies iræ, dies illa.

C'est l'heure de la prière ;
Peuple, à genoux et prions
Avec ceux qui sur la pierre
Regrettent leurs doux sillons.
Prions pour ces destinées
Qui, pauvres fleurs inclinées,
N'ont pas connu de printemps ;
Prions surtout avec celle
Dont le cœur tremble et chancelle
Pour avoir pleuré longtemps...

And then I moaned, long lost in my weepings
For children who, just like white doves
Fly off to seek, beyond their graves,
Other summers ... other springs.

❖

How now can my lyre be worth its while?
What good are the songs of birds in the morn?
My heart, by fate to pieces torn,
At their songs no longer can smile.

What use are the fragrances of flowers?
For like the reed that bends am I:
My joy supreme, my one and only,
Is to be alone with my tears.

Oh! What shall I do, gone wild like this,
Without these children, now angels in the skies,
Without the soft gaze from their eyes
And from their mouths, their little kisses?

What good is the nest without the bird,
The hearth where shines no spark,
The tree where no wing comes to park,
And without the child, a baby's bed?

[published Sunday, 7 October 1866]

At the Cemetery

LÉLIA D——T [Adolphe Duhart]

Dies iræ, dies illa. [94]

The hour of prayer is come;
Ye people, get down on your knees
And pray with those for whom
Regrets are as wide as the seas.
For all who'll never know,
Like flowers bended low,
The magic of spring's rebirth,
Let's pray, and also for her
Whose heart does quake and quiver
As its tears waters the earth ...

[94]. "A day of wrath is this day." Most of the Latin passages interspersed throughout are taken from the liturgy of the Catholic funeral mass, or requiem. There are some slight deviations from the traditional text of the requiem.

Requiem æternam dona eis, Domine, et lux perpetua luceat eis.

À genoux ! à genoux ! — Prie
Pour qui sont allés aux ports
De la céleste Patrie.
Peuple ! c'est le jour des morts !
Bien des fosses sont désertes
Et de mousses sont couvertes...
Nul n'y porte plus ses pas :
L'humide et sombre ossuaire
Cache en son triste suaire
Tous les secrets du trépas...

Ne irascaris, Domine, ne ultra meminis iniquitatis.

Peuple, à ces sinistres fosses
Qui scellent dans le cercueil
Tant d'âmes pures ou fausses,
Jette un long voile de deuil.
Laisse sur leur froide cendre
De ton cœur ému descendre
Quelques regrets, quelques pleurs ;
Car, qui sait ce que les larmes
Peuvent effacer d'alarmes
Et de cruelles douleurs ?

Huic ergo, parce, Domine.

Il en est qui, sous la nue,
Dans le gouffre spacieux,
Gardent une âme inconnue,
Oubliée au fond des cieux,
Pauvre âme sans funérailles,
Tombée au choc des mitrailles,
Dont il ne reste rien après ;
Pour qu'elle brille et rayonne,
Peuple, apporte une couronne
De lauriers et de cyprès.

Absolve, Domine, animas omnium fidelium defunctorum,
ab omni vinculo delictorum.

Puis d'autres — sombres mystères —
Couvrent des restes maudits
Dont les âmes solitaires
Errent hors du Paradis.
[texte illisible] l'homicide

Requiem æternam dona eis, Domine, et lux perpetua luceat eis. [95]

95. "Give them eternal rest, Lord, and may a perpetual light shine upon them."

On your knees, on your knees! Pray
For those who've gone to stay
In the ports of their heavenly Home.
The day of the dead is come,
Ye people! Many a tomb
Has been left to its lonely gloom ...
For no one pays their respects:
The afterlife's secrets have slipped
Into the lightless crypt
Where death's decay collects.

Ne irascaris, Domine, ne ultra meminis iniquitatis. [96]

96. "Do not be angry, Lord, and remember our wickedness no longer." This line is not from the requiem mass but from a hymn based on Isaiah 64.9.

To cover these dismal holes
Which inside the coffin seal
Both honest and treacherous souls
Ye people, cast a long veil.
From your tender heart dispense
Onto their ashen remnants
A few tear-borne regrets;
For who can really doubt
That such concern abates
Our pains within and without?

Huic ergo, parce, Domine. [97]

97. "Spare him therefore, Lord."

Some souls that choose to dwell
In the heights of heaven's space,
Have bade their final farewell,
Forgotten, without a trace.
Sad soul by no funeral blessed,
Whom bullets laid to rest
And who has no more to tell!
So that it shall shine down,
Ye people, bring a crown
Woven of cypress and laurel.

*Absolve, Domine, animas omnium fidelium defunctorum,
ab omni vinculo delictorum.* [98]

98. "Absolve, Lord, the souls of all the deceased faithful from every bond of their sins."

Other mysteries from yonder
Enclose accursèd remains
Whose lonely souls do wander
Outside Heaven's domains.
[text illegible] homicide,

Morne et livide suicide
Brisé par un lourd fardeau...
Pour ceux-là fais ta prière,
Car pour eux le cimetière
N'a ni pitié, ni flambeau...

Pie Jesu Domine, dona eis requiem.

Prions : tout tend à la tombe :
Gloire, honneur, ivresse, amour ;
Tout fatalement y tombe
Et disparaît en un jour...
Du Maître trois fois auguste,
C'est la loi suprême et juste !...
Jeunesse ! — Vœux superflus !
Vers qui notre cœur s'élance,
Doit laisser dans le silence
Un peu de cendre de plus...

2 novembre 1866

[publié le dimanche 4 novembre 1866]

Vision

À Mlle Cecilia B. [16]

YACOUB [Joseph Mansion]

N'es-tu pas un fantôme égaré sur la terre
      Pour un jour ?
Ange à qui j'ai donné ma vie et ma prière,
      Mon amour.

Du Seigneur n'es-tu pas envoyé dans ce monde,
      Mon enfant ?
Pour calmer le malheur qui sur ma tête gronde
      Par moment.

Du Céleste séjour n'es-tu pas cette étoile
      Qui me fuit ?
N'es-tu pas cette enfant qui se couvre d'un voile
      Dans la nuit ?

16. Joseph Mansion and Marie Cecilia Boyer were married in January 1868, a little over a year after this poem was published.

A gloomy, livid suicide
With heavy burden weary ...
Do pray for all of them;
For neither mercy nor flame
Will light the cemetery ...

Pie Jesu Domine, dona eis requiem. [99]

[99]. "Pious Lord Jesus, give them rest."

Let's pray; the tomb takes all:
Glory and fame, love and delight —
Therein all things will fall
And vanish as into the night ...
'Tis the law, supreme and just,
Of our Master, thrice august!
Oh youth! Your wasted wishes,
Whereto our heart is bent,
Will offer, ever silent,
Another heap of ashes.

2 November 1866

[published Sunday, 4 November 1866]

A Vision

For Miss Cecilia B.

YACOUB [Joseph Mansion]

Are you not a ghost who, lost on earth, appears
    Then returns above?
An angel to whom I've given my life, my prayers,
    And my love?

By the Lord were you not sent down into this world,
    Child of mine,
To soothe the misfortunes that upon me are unfurled
    From time to time?

Up there in Heaven's Realm, are you not that star
    Who flees my sight?
Are you not that child who under a veil takes cover
    In the night?

J'ai cherché vainement dans ma douleur amère
À connaître le nom que je te donnerai ;
Oh ! reviens près de moi, toujours je t'aimerai
Ange mystérieux, vision éphémère.

Je suis, dit l'inconnue, une Vierge du Ciel
        Qui pardonne ;
Dans mon cœur j'ai gardé pour toi le divin miel
        Que Dieu donne.

Je suis l'ange gardien qui veille, quand tu dors,
        Sur ton âme ;
Je suis l'astre brillant qui réchauffe ton corps
        De sa flamme.
Je suis dans la nuit sombre un feu follet brillant
        Qui s'envole ;
Sur mes ailes de feu j'emporte bien souvent
        Ta parole.

Quand vient la fin du jour, que ton âme s'endort,
Dans tes rêves du soir j'occupe ta pensée :
Le matin près de toi tu me revois encor ;
Ami, ne suis-je pas ta chère fiancée !

Novembre 1866

                [publié le dimanche 11 novembre 1866]

Méditations

   À M. Armand Lanusse

YACOUB [Joseph Mansion]

Quand la brume du soir a déchiré son voile,
À l'heure où dans la nuit apparaît une étoile
        Dans un ciel argenté ;
Avez-vous entendu cet étrange murmure
Que répètent ces voix de toute la nature
        Dans notre immensité ?

Oh ! que j'aime à vous voir quand dans ma solitude ;
Vous vous enveloppez, brillante multitude,
        De vos robes de feu.
J'aime à vous voir courir dans l'horizon immense,
Semblable au feu follet qui s'échappe et s'élance
        Pour remonter vers Dieu.

I've tried in vain, despite my bitter pain,
To know the name that upon you I'll confer.
Oh! Return to me here; I'll love you forever,
Mysterious angel, evanescent vision.

"I am," said the unknown one, "a Heavenly Virgin
      Who forgives;
In my heart I keep for you that honey most divine
      That only God gives.

"I am the guardian angel who, while you sleep,
      Does shield your soul.
I am the gleaming star that with its flame does keep
      Your body from the cold.
"In the somber night, a will-o'-the wisp am I;
      As I fly away,
On my fiery wings I often carry with me
      The words you say.

"When the day is done and your soul has found its rest,
In your evening dreams, your thoughts come my way;
In the morning, you see me again upon your breast:
My friend, am I not your belovèd fiancée!"

November 1866

        [published Sunday, 11 November 1866]

Meditations

For Mr. Armand Lanusse

Yacoub [Joseph Mansion]

When the evening mist has rent its veil, at the hour
At which in the midst of the night appears a star
      Upon a silvery sky.
Have you happened to hear, perchance, the strange murmur
Repeated by all the chorus of voices of nature
      Before our immensity?

How I love to see you when, in my solitude,
You wrap yourselves, a shining multitude,
      In your robes of fire;
I delight to see you along the vast horizon,
Just like the will o' the wisp does leap and run
      Soaring toward God, ever higher.

Oh ! qu'elle est belle alors ; c'est l'heure où le poète
Écoute tous ces chants que le désert répète,
      Concert triste ou joyeux,
Que forment dans la nuit ces voix mystérieuses
Qui se mêlent toujours à ces âmes heureuses
      Qui s'envolent aux cieux.

Et vous, vaste océan, immensité perdue,
Qui semble quelquefois dans sa large étendue
      Étaler sa grandeur,
Gouffre toujours béant, intarissable abîme,
Vous êtes noble et fier !... car vous êtes sublime
      Au poète rêveur.

J'aime à vous contempler à l'heure où la nuit sombre
Étend son voile noir, et que l'on voit une ombre
      S'envoler en riant.
J'aime entendre le chant de votre voix plaintive,
Que rapporte l'écho sur le bord de la rive
      Au voyageur priant.

J'ai vu la vaste mer s'élancer dans l'espace,
Puis se tordre et tomber comme un aigle qui passe
      Frappé d'un coup mortel.
Puis je l'ai vue encor dans sa fureur extrême
Se courber et fléchir devant l'Être Suprême
      [texte illisible]

Alors je méditai dans ma pensée intime,
Tout ce qu'avait mis Dieu de grand et de sublime
      Dans ce concert touchant.
Je sentis tout à coup s'humecter ma paupière,
Puis je m'agenouillai pour offrir ma prière,
      Au Maître Tout-Puissant.

Le 3 décembre 1866

      [publié le dimanche 16 décembre 1866]

How lovely it is! This is the hour when poets
Come listen to songs that the wilderness repeats,
      Some sad, some happy,
Composed in the night by voices mysterious
Prepared to join those souls, ever joyous,
      That away to heaven fly.

And you, vast ocean, endlessly immense,
At times you seem, through your boundless expanse,
      Your greatness to exhibit;
A yawning gulf, an abyss of infinity,
How proud and noble are you! For you are truly
      Sublime to the dreaming poet.

How I love to behold you just at the hour when night
Opens its somber veil, and a shadow takes flight,
      Letting resound its laughter.
How I love the song of your plaintive voice to hear
As it carries the echo back from the edge of the shore
      To the praying traveler.

I watched the sea attempt to fly to space
Only to writhe and fall like an eagle does race
      When struck by a mortal blow.
In its extreme fury, I saw it again, bowing
On bended knee before the Supreme Being,
      [text illegible]

Within my inner thoughts I meditated
Upon the sublime grandeur that God created
      For this stirring ensemble.
Suddenly feeling my eyes begin to water,
I then knelt down to offer up my prayer,
      To the Almighty Master of all.

3 December 1866

      [published Sunday, 16 December 1866]

La sensitive

À Mlle Nat… F…

L. M. [Lucien Mansion]

À la fin du printemps pendant un beau matin,
Alors qu'un doux zéphyr explorait le jardin,
Sous un épais buisson une humble sensitive
Déplorait hautement de sa voix expansive
Les coups réitérés qu'un destin trop jaloux
Dans sa mauvaise humeur laisse tomber sur nous ;
Sans songer à son sort, aux embûches sans nombre
Qu'on rencontre ici-bas dans ce passage sombre,
La charmante rêveuse avait encor le don
De relever les cœurs réduits à l'abandon ;
Elle plaignait surtout la rose printanière
Qu'on voyait autrefois si pédante et si fière,
Aujourd'hui délaissée, en proie au désespoir
N'espérant du repos que dans le frais du soir.
La violette aussi dans un coin confinée
Attirait ses regards, sur sa tige inclinée ;
Un éclair flamboyant par le ciel allumé
Avait décoloré son beau front parfumé,
Et sa tête penchée à présent sur la terre
Attestait le chagrin dans ce gai caractère.
Le lis immaculé, qui vantait sa blancheur,
Perdit en un instant sa pudique fraîcheur ;
Une araignée immonde épandant sa souillure
Avait laissé des traits sur sa blonde figure.
La tâche ineffaçable excitait le dédain
Qu'on éprouvait déjà pour cet esprit hautain.
Le petit réséda passait toute sa vie
À prouver que sa belle était la plus jolie ;
Il aimait la pensée, aimable fleur des champs,
Qui se bouchait l'oreille à ses accents touchants,
Et semblait, on dirait, se poser en coquette
Pour un grand dahlia qui lui tournait la tête.
Un gros jasmin de l'Inde, esprit peu délicat,
Avait voué, dit-on, ses jours au célibat,
Espérant rencontrer dans cette âpre existence
Un bonheur qui fuyait devant sa persistance,
Quand le dégoût survint dans ce débordement
Et lui fit regretter son matin si charmant.
Enfin ces maux divers réunis en présence
Trouvaient incontinent une douce assistance,
Des soins affectueux chez la sensible fleur

The Sensitive Plant[100]

For Miss Nat—— F——

L. M. [Lucien Mansion]

Near the final days of spring, on a lovely morning,
As a gentle zephyr ran through my garden, exploring,
Beneath a shrub, a humble sensitive plant
Expressed in terms effusive her complaint
Against the blows which fate, ever jealous,
Succumbing to ill will, lets befall us.
Thinking neither of herself nor the constant perils
Which we encounter throughout our mortal travels,
This charming dreamer still possessed the gift
Of casting a lifeline to hearts cut adrift.
She especially pitied the rose that blooms with spring,
Once proud, pretentious, and spurning everything,
Forsaken now, caught in the grips of despair,
Her sole respite: the cool evening air.
To the violet, drooping and limp, to a corner restricted
The rose's attention was nonetheless attracted.
A fiery flash, which from the sky had strayed,
Had caused her lovely, perfumed brow to fade,
And her head, bent low to the ground in submission
Revealed the sadness in her sunny disposition.
The flawless lily, once having vaunted her whiteness,
Immediately lost that virginal brightness;
A filthy spider, spattering its foul trace,
Had left unsightly stains upon her face.
The indelible smudge could only enhance the scorn
Which, thanks to her haughtiness, she had always borne.
The mignonette was determined to spend his life
Convincing others he'd win the most beautiful wife;
He loved the pansy, fair flower o' the meadows,
Who plugged her ears at the tender sound of his prose
And busied herself with batting her coquettish eyes
For a tall dahlia she judged a more worthy prize.
A jasmine of India, anything but gentle,
As a youth had committed an error quite fundamental
In hoping to sweeten the bitter pill of existence
With future bliss that eluded his persistence,
Till self-disgust eventually took its course
And left him tasting little but remorse.
These miseries, gathered in each other's presence,
At last discovered a possible source of assistance:
The affectionate care supplied by that sensitive flower,

100. "Sensitive plant" is another name for *Mimosa pudica*, a flowering plant whose leaves fold inward and droop when touched or disturbed. On Nathalie Formento, to whom the poem is dedicated, see p. 189n63 ("The Weeping Willow").

Qui s'était dévouée, il paraît, au malheur ;
Cette âme charitable — expression sincère
De la pure amitié sur cette ingrate terre —
Sacrifiait ses jours sereins et précieux
À secourir le faible et le cœur vertueux.
Mais, Dieu ! quel contretemps ! un foudroyant orage
Vient d'éclater soudain dans notre voisinage,
La pauvre sensitive, hélas ! dès ce moment,
De frayeur, inclina son front pur tristement.

[publié le dimanche 27 octobre 1867]

L'ange en exil

À Mlle J...e F...er

LÉLIA D...T [Adolphe Duhart]

> Vous que Dieu couronna d'une ardente auréole,
> Femmes, sachez toujours comprendre votre rôle,
> ....
> Seules, vous pouvez consoler notre exil.
> — D. Rouquette

Esprit divin, que viens-tu faire
Au milieu des faibles humains ?
Que viens-tu chercher sur la sphère
Des ronces et des durs chemins,
Où tu blesseras tes pieds d'ange ?
Pourquoi quittes-tu ton beau ciel,
Tes félicités sans mélange
Et les chœurs sacrés d'Ariel ?

C'est que toute âme veut son âme,
C'est que tout cœur cherche son cœur,
C'est qu'au ciel l'ange est une femme,
— Foyer d'amour et de bonheur —
Que Dieu, sur notre triste voie,
Comme un espoir, comme un trésor,
Dans sa miséricorde envoie
Pour nous parler des cieux encor.

Sœur du printemps, chaste créole,
Brunie aux baisers du soleil,
Bel ange à la blanche auréole,

Devoted, it seems, to uprooting suffering's power.
This charitable soul — the embodiment
Of finest friendship, through any predicament —
Sacrificed her days, otherwise calm,
To help the weak and pour on hearts her balm.
No, God! Catastrophe strikes! A sudden storm
Over our neighborhood took frightening form.
Alas, the poor little sensitive plant, thereafter
Alarmed, bent down her head in the face of disaster.

          [published Sunday, 27 October 1867]

The Angel in Exile

For Miss J——e F——er

LÉLIA D——T [Adolphe Duhart]

    Crowned by God with a fiery aureole,
    Women, always seek to know your role,
    ....
    For ye alone our exile can console.
                    — D. Rouquette [101]

Divine spirit, just why are you here,
Amidst us humans whom weakness corrodes?
What do you seek upon this sphere
Of thorny briars and stony roads
Too eager to bruise your angelic feet?
For what reason have you left the sky,
Its ecstasies so pure and sweet,
And Ariel's holy choirs on high?

It's true: each soul desires its soul,
And every heart seeks out its heart,
And truly, woman is heaven's angel
— The point where love and happiness start —
That God does send, like a ray of hope
To shine upon our path of sorrow,
A merciful gift to help us cope
By showing us the skies of tomorrow.

Oh sister of spring, virtuous Creole
With tawny skin by sunlight kissed,
Angel crowned with an aureole,

[101]. The Louisiana French poet François-Dominique Rouquette (1810–90), author of *Les Meschacébéennes* (1839) and *Fleurs d'Amérique* (1856). He and his brother, the poet and priest Adrien Rouquette (1813–87), were among the best-known Louisiana francophone writers of the mid-nineteenth century.

Exilé du dôme vermeil,
Laisse tomber sur le poète
Un doux rayon de tes beaux yeux ;
Sa lyre alors, longtemps muette,
Reprendra ses refrains joyeux.

20 décembre 1866

[publié le dimanche 22 décembre 1867]

Idéalisme. — Matérialisme.

Imitation

Lélia D...t [Adolphe Duhart]

Au bal. — Minuit sonnait. — Elle était brune et rose,
Ses cheveux étaient noirs et ses grands yeux d'azur,
Souple comme un roseau son corps avait la pose
Que donna Raphaël à la vierge au front pur.

Sa voix avait les sons d'une flûte sonore.
Telle qu'une grenade entrouverte au soleil
Et qui semble sourire au rayon qui la dore,
Sa bouche sensuelle avait l'éclat vermeil.

Et moi, tremblant, ému, je n'osais pas lui dire
De mon cœur palpitant la vive passion :
Je craignais d'encourir son dédain ou son ire,
Ou qu'elle disparût comme une vision.

Cependant je lui dis : — Oh ! Je t'aime, doux ange !
Comme savent aimer les esprits dans le ciel,
De cet amour brûlant, majestueux, étrange
Que pour Marie avait l'archange Gabriel.

Laisse tomber sur moi ton beau regard limpide
Pour que je croie encore à mon ange gardien.
— Ah ! Fit-elle en bâillant, mon cher que t'es stupide !
Paie un *gombo* plutôt, vrai ! Ça me f'ra plus d'bien !

[publié le dimanche 19 janvier 1868]

From the crimson dome now banished,
Let fall, I pray, upon the poet
A tender ray from your lovely eyes;
Then from his lyre, for too long quiet,
Refrains of joy again will rise.

20 December 1866

[published Sunday, 22 December 1867]

Idealism. — Materialism.

Imitation

Lélia D——t [Adolphe Duhart]

At the dance. — Midnight rang. — She was brown and pink;
Her hair was black, her wide eyes of azure,
And, supple like a reed, her body made one think
Of the pose of Raphael's virgin, of brow so pure.

Her voice possessed the sounds of a lively flute.
Like a pomegranate opened under the sun,
Offering up to its rays a smiling salute,
Her sensual mouth with ruby brilliance shone.

And I, touched and trembling, dared not explain
The passion stirring within my fluttering heart:
I feared provoking either wrath or disdain,
Or that like a vision she'd suddenly depart.

Yet I told her, "Oh! I love you, sweet angel,
As strongly as spirits do in the heavens above,
Just as for Mary the archangel Gabriel
Did feel a burning, strange, and majestic love.

"Grace me, I pray, with your gaze, lovely and clear,
So that once again I'll believe in my guardian angel."
"Ah!" she yawned, "How stupid you are, my dear!
Buy me a *gumbo* instead! That'll do good for real!"

[published Sunday, 19 January 1868]

Une dépêche télégraphique

JOANNI [Joanni Questy]

   Marie, on dit que la reine d'Espagne
   Loin de Madrid, de son royaume, a fui
Très bien décournnée ; et puis que Marfori,
Est, de tous ses sujets, le seul qui l'accompagne.

   On dit encor, qu'elle a déjà vendu
   Tous ses joyaux, son brillant diadème,
Et qu'elle a donné tout à cet homme qu'elle aime :
Bien ! l'ex-reine Isabelle a fait ce qu'elle a dû !

Cela me fait penser qu'il vous faudrait, Marie,
Vous résoudre à choisir, entre tous vos sujets,
Que je vois, maintenant à vous plaire engagés,
Un compagnon fidèle, un ami pour la vie.

Vous descendrez du trône en prenant un époux ?
Mais, donnant votre cœur à cet objet unique,
Vous serez plus heureuse au foyer domestique :
Mariez-vous, Marie, et faites cent jaloux !

     [publié le dimanche 24 janvier 1869]

La couronne d'amour

 À Mlle E. M.

L. M. [Lucien Mansion]

L'enfant offre à la Vierge une blanche couronne
   Dans les beaux jours de mai ;
Son cœur de chérubin jouit de ce qu'il donne,
   Car il se sent aimé.

Quand, du Christ, s'exhalaient ces paroles divines :
   « Père, pardonnez-leur ! »
Les bourreaux attachaient la couronne d'épines
   Sur son front de Sauveur.

À genoux à l'autel, l'humble communiante,
   Accomplit un doux vœu,
En détachant les fleurs de sa tête charmante
   Pour les remettre à Dieu.

A Telegraphic Dispatch

JOANNI [Joanni Questy]

> They say, Marie, that the queen of Spain,
>   From Madrid, from her kingdom, was forced to flee,
> Completely uncrowned; and also that Marfori [102]
> Was the only subject she managed to retain.

> They tell, as well, that she did part
>   With her jewels and sparkling diadem;
> Ex-queen Isabella followed her heart:
> She loved this man and surrendered all to him!

This makes me think that you might need, Marie,
To choose, among the mass of your devotees,
All of whom seem equally eager to please,
A faithful companion, a friend on life's journeys.

But you'd give up your throne if you deigned to take a spouse?
Should some lucky subject receive your heart,
You'll be happier in the kingdom of the hearth.
Get married, Marie, and make a hundred men jealous!

[published Sunday, 24 January 1869]

102. Carlos Marfori y Callejas (1821[?]–92), a Spanish politician and the confidant of Queen Isabella II of Spain, who had recently been forced into exile during the Revolution of 1868.

The Crown of Love

For Miss E. M. [103]

L. M. [Lucien Mansion]

In the loveliest days of May, the child offers
    To the Virgin a crown of white;
For her love, his cherubinic heart prefers
    To enjoy giving's delight.

When Christ, divinely turning his cheek to their scorns,
    Exclaimed, "Forgive them, Father!"
His persecutors placed a crown of thorns
    Upon the brow of our Savior.

The communicant, before the altar led,
    Fulfills a wish, humble and sweet,
By lifting the flowers from her lovely head
    To lay them at God's feet.

103. Élodie Mansion, the poet's daughter.

Un peuple confiant, dans sa douce espérance,
    S'il veut nommer un roi,
De sa main le couronne et respecte en silence
    L'arbitre de la loi.

La jeune fiancée à l'âme pure et bonne
    Rit d'un destin jaloux,
Quand elle vient poser sa pudique couronne
    Aux pieds d'un tendre époux.

Le mortel vertueux à l'âme sympathique,
    Qui nous laisse ici-bas,
Emporte sur son front la couronne civique
    À l'heure du trépas.

À cette aimable enfant, timide fleur cachée
    Loin des rayons du jour,
Je veux donner ici de mon cœur détachée
    La couronne d'amour.

Puisse-t-elle toujours écarter de son âme
    Tout contact vénéneux ;
Puis activer aussi l'édifiante flamme,
    De son cœur vertueux.

        [publié le dimanche 31 janvier 1869]

Dors !

À Élode [17]

JOANNI [Joanni Questy]

17. It is likely that the *i* was accidentally omitted from the name Élodie.

    La femme de Raymond était de la nation des visages pâles.
      (*Traduction indienne*)

Dors, mon enfant, sur le sein de ta mère !
Le temps est sombre ; et puis, là-bas,
Le vent mugit à travers la pinière ;
Bien des chasseurs reviennent à grands pas !
    Déjà l'orage,
  Sur notre toit, passe en grondant ;
Le lac est noir, et le pêcheur prudent,
    Qui lit dans le nuage,
Reprend ses carrelets et revient au rivage :
    Dors, mon enfant,
    Sur le sein de ta mère !

A hopeful people, full of confidence
        And wishing to name a king,
Will coronate him, then respect in silence
        This sovereign of their making.

With pureness of soul, the young fiancée
        Will laugh at fate, ever jealous,
When comes the day her modest crown to lay
        Before her gentle spouse.

Possessed of kindly soul, the virtuous mortal
        Who abandons us down here
Will carry his civic crown toward heaven's portal
        When the hour of death draws near.

To this lovely child, a shy and hidden flower
        From the daylight set apart,
I wish to give the crown of love to wear,
        For it's taken from my own heart.

May she always protect from poison of any kind
        Her soul's precious virtue,
As well as light the fire within her mind
        That keeps her heart ever true.

        [published Sunday, 31 January 1869]

Sleep!

For Élode

JOANNI [Joanni Questy]

        Raymond's wife was of the nation of the pale faces.
        (*Indian translation*)[104]

Go to sleep, my child, upon your mother's breast!
The day grows dark, and a ways away
The wind comes howling through the piney forest;
The men hurry home after hunting all day.
        Already, the storm,
    Rumbling over our roof, passes by.
    The lake is black, and the fisherman's watchful eye
        Examines the cloud's contour;
He draws up his nets and begins to return to shore.
        Sleep, my child; find rest
    Upon your mother's breast.

104. The source of the poem's epigraph and tale is not clear. Questy may have been told a story like it or may have invented it himself. There is a tradition of writing "Indian legends" in Louisiana French literature, as there is in US anglophone literature.

Le vent mugit à travers la pinière ;
Bien des chasseurs reviennent à grands pas
Portant, chacun, leur fusil sous le bras :
Et la pluie a voilé déjà, sur leur passage,
Les sentiers sillonnés par les pieds du sauvage,
Puis bientôt, sous ses eaux,
Cachera le plantain et les jeunes rameaux
Du grenadier sauvage
Que couvre de son vert feuillage
Le solitaire sassafras.

Le vent mugit à travers la pinière :
Dors, mon enfant, sur le sein de ta mère !

Bien des chasseurs reviennent à grands pas,
Et Raymond, ô mon Dieu, Raymond ne revient pas !
Il allait se livrer au plaisir de la chasse ;
Ce matin, j'ai porté son beau fusil bronzé
Jusqu'au tronc de ce pin que l'orage a brisé
Et près duquel le bayou passe
En faisant un détour.

« Quand le soleil aura répandu sa lumière
« Sur la moitié de sa carrière,
« Tu salûras, disait-il, mon retour. »

L'heure a sonné pourtant ! Et, dans cette demeure
Que l'ouragan assiège, inquiète, je pleure,
Je tremble et je me sens mourir ;
Mais dors, mon pauvre enfant, en attendant ton père ;
Bientôt Raymond va revenir :
Dors, dors sur le sein de ta mère !

Raymond ne revient pas. — Un jeune Talapous,
Quand la lune éclaira des pins la cime altière,
À pas précipités traversa la pinière :
Il rapportait la carnassière
Du malheureux époux :
« Ouvre de ton wigwam la porte hospitalière,
« Dit-il, ô fleur de magnolia !
« Triste épouse de mon goula,
« Raymond va s'éloigner pour toujours de la terre ;
« Il va bientôt chasser aux célestes forêts,
« Aux forêts où les fleurs ne se fanent jamais,
« Il s'en va, nénuphar miné par les racines,
« Refleurir et t'attendre aux lagunes divines.

    The wind comes howling through the piney forest;
    The men hurry home after hunting all day,
    Their weapons under their arms while finding their way.
The rain has covered, where they made their passage,
The paths and trails traversed by the feet of the savage,
        And soon, beneath its flood,
The plantain will hide, and the pomegranate will shroud
        Its tender branches
    Veiled by the verdant foliage
        Of the outcast sassafras.

    The wind comes howling through the piney forest;
    Go to sleep, my child, upon your mother's breast!

    After hunting all day the men are hurrying home
And Raymond, dear God, Raymond continues to roam!
To enjoy the thrill of the hunt he chose to go.
That morning I brought his gun, handsome and brown
To the trunk of the pine that a storm had once brought down
        And close to which the bayou
            Pursues a lazy turn.

"By the time the sun has spread its light
        To the halfway point of its daily flight,
    You will hail," he had said, "my return."

The hour has rung, alas! And in this dwelling
That the hurricane assaults, I weep, worrying;
        I tremble and shake as I feel myself die.
But sleep, my poor child, while waiting for your father;
        The return of Raymond surely is nigh:
        So sleep, go to sleep on the breast of your mother.

But Raymond has not returned. — When the moon illumined
The treetops, a youth of the Tallapoosa band[105]
With speedy steps traversed the pine-covered land,
        A hunting pouch in hand:
            It belonged to the ill-fated husband.
He cried, "Open your wigwam's welcoming door,
        Oh magnolia blossom!
        Sad wife of my goula,[106] come!
For Raymond has gone from the earth forevermore
And soon he will hunt in those heavenly forests
Where the flowers never wilt; he rests,
Or rather, like a rootless lily, floats away
To bloom again for you in God's lagoon.

105. Group of Upper Creeks, native to Alabama, who belonged to the Muscogee Confederacy before forced Indian removal by the US government in the 1830s.

106. "Goula" is a corruption of the name of a Muscogee tribe, variously mistranslated since the nineteenth century, when it was generally (erroneously) thought to mean "people."

« Viens ! Viens voir ton époux ! Là-bas sur le chemin
        « Qui mène à la savane,
« Je l'ai trouvé gisant à l'ombre d'un platane ;
« C'est là que son fusil s'est brisé dans sa main.
     « Près de fermer ses yeux à la lumière,
       « Frappé par un éclat fatal,
« Raymond, le beau chasseur, le tireur sans égal
« Désire te donner l'accolade dernière. »

Mais nul ne vint ouvrir au jeune Talapous
     Qui rapporta la carnassière
        Du malheureux époux.

Depuis ce soir on dit que, quand le temps est sombre,
Quand la nuit, sur le lac, a répandu son ombre,
        On entend quelque fois
        Une plaintive voix
Murmurer tristement à travers la pinière :
Dors, dors, dors, mon enfant, sur le sein de ta mère !

                [publié le dimanche 7 février 1869]

S... à L...

STÉNIO [pseudonyme d'un auteur inconnu]

Tu ne le savais pas ? Oui, quelquefois, le soir,
Quand tous mes souvenirs alors faisaient silence,
Ton image, en mon cœur, brillait comme un miroir
Qu'un doux rayon du jour caresse en confidence.

Je contemplais longtemps ton œil limpide et noir ;
Tout se transfigurait autour de ta personne ;
Sur ton modeste front souvent je croyais voir
Les lettres de mon nom se poser en couronne.

Et pendant que, captif dans ton rayonnement,
De l'amour je goûtais les délices suprêmes,
Tremblant, je m'écriais, dans mon ravissement :
Oh ! dis-moi, s'il est vrai, s'il est vrai que tu m'aimes !

I beg you, come! Come to see your husband!
       On the path to the prairie,
I found him lying under the shade of a plane tree;
That's where his gun lay broken in his hand.
   Prepared for the light to depart his face,
     Struck down by a blow soon fatal.
The handsome Raymond, a hunter without equal,
Desires to impart to you a final embrace."

But no one answered the youth from the Tallapoosa band
     With hunting pouch in hand,
          Retrieved from the ill-fated husband.

They say that since that evening, whene'er the sky grows dark,
When the shadow of night covers the lake, if you hark,
          At times you just might hear
          A melancholy murmur,
A mournful voice throughout the piney forest:
Sleep, sleep, sleep, my child, upon your mother's breast!

            [published Sunday, 7 February 1869]

S—— to L——

STÉNIO [pseudonym of unknown author]

You didn't know? Why yes, sometimes, at night
When silence fell upon my memories,
Within my heart, your image glimmered bright
Like a mirror that sunlight caresses in secrecy.

At length I'd gaze into your dark and limpid eye;
All was transfigured around your lovely frame;
Upon your brow, I often thought I saw
Set, like a crown, the letters of my name.

And while held captive by your radiance,
While tasting love's supreme delights anew,
I cried out, trembling in my raptured trance,
"Oh, tell me! Do you love me? Is it true?"

Cette illusion d'or tout à coup s'effaçait,
Et puis, de temps en temps, encor reparaissait.

Je n'osais point pourtant révéler à personne
            Ces merveilles d'amour ;
          Mais, voici qu'un beau jour,
       À l'amitié je m'abandonne :
Mon secret qui dormait, tranquille dans mon cœur,
Déjà rendu public, sera, d'un ris moqueur,
            Accueilli par vous-même ;
Et puis, feignant aussi de ne rien deviner
À ces vers, où vos yeux viennent de s'incliner,
Vous-même, vous direz : Quelle est celle qu'il aime !

         [publié le dimanche 21 février 1869]

This golden illusion would vanish all of a sudden
And then, from time to time, appear again.

I dared not tell a single soul about
                Love's magical sway;
              But then, it happened one day:
        Trusting a friend, I let the secret out:
The truth, which in my heart slept peacefully,
Made public now, with a mocking laugh will be
                By you received.
And then, inducing yourself to be deceived
About the lines your eyes have read above,
You'll ask yourself, "Whomever does he love?"

        [published Sunday, 21 February 1869]

Biographical Notes on Known Authors

Adolphe Duhart

La Tribune's most prolific poet, Pierre-Adolphe Duhart (1830–1908), was born in New Orleans on 1 February 1830, to Louis-Adolphe Duhart, a native of Havana with roots in Saint Domingue, and Françoise Palmyre Brouard, originally from Saint Domingue (*Alphabetical Birth Indexes*; Woods and Nolan 133).

He grew up in a household deeply involved in the development of the community of free people of color. His father, a gunsmith by trade, maintained some ties with Haiti, as shown by the 11 October 1838 issue of *L'Union: recueil commercial et littéraire* (a newspaper based in Port-au-Prince), which lists Louis-Adolphe as stockholder in that country's Banque agricole (9). Interestingly, according to the 1850 census, the Duhart family, which included eight children at that time, lived with eighty-year-old Pointe-du-Jour Daragneinte, born in Saint Domingue (most likely a servant or family member), whose presence would have provided a living link with colonial-era Haiti. Louis-Adolphe served on the board of the foundation that established the Institution catholique des orphelins indigents, where his wife taught as well, and his son, who frequently omitted "Pierre" and went simply by "Adolphe," would dedicate much of his own career to this school.[1]

Adolphe's sister Lélia (christened Marie Lélia, in keeping with the francophone Catholic tradition of affixing a saint's name before the actual name to be used in daily life) was born on 3 August 1853 (*Alphabetical Birth Indexes*). Her death as a child would inspire her brother to take the name Lélia as pseudonym, a choice doubtless inspired by his Spiritualist convictions.

As a young man, Duhart worked as a mason. Rodolphe Desdunes's biographical sketch indicates that he studied in France, completing the educational opportunities that would allow him to give back to the community through the Institution catholique. His brother Armand, a printer by trade, also served on the school's board.[2] Adolphe participated in Afro-Creole intellectual radicalism by engaging in the Spiritualist movement from the late 1850s onward; he frequently took part in séances hosted by Henry Louis Rey and others, and he held some in his own home (Bell, *Revolution* 215; Emily Suzanne Clark 27–30).

Adolphe Duhart and Odilia Boyer were married in late July 1856. Their first child, Marie Alice, was born the following year. Tragedy would strike their family repeatedly: three other daughters — Louise Berthe, born 1862, and twins Lucie and Marie, born

1864 — would all pass away in the summer of 1864. By 1870 their children Alice, 12; Odilia, 10; a younger Odilia, 3; and infant George, were growing and healthy.³

Like other *gens de couleur*, Duhart enlisted in the pro-Confederacy Native Guards at the outbreak of the war. He subsequently devoted himself to the Union cause after federal occupation, as expressed in his editorial "Un mot des Natifs," in the 25 October 1862 issue of *L'Union*.

By all evidence, Duhart's literary endeavors began in earnest in the mid-1860s, after the founding of *La Tribune*. On the heels of his first poems signed "Lélia D...t," published in late 1864, he submitted two short stories, both of which tackle racial themes. "Simple histoire," dedicated to L. C. Roudanez for the "work of regeneration" that he had undertaken through the newspaper, recounts the family background of one of the Haitian Revolution's first antislavery martyrs. A longer work, "Trois amours," appeared in late summer 1865; this poignant tale of forbidden love between a young white Creole, Charles Beaufort, and the *mulâtresse* Lydia ends in the acceptance of their relationship by Lydia's adopted mother, albeit on the apparent condition of Lydia's origins remaining secret. Both stories highlight the hypocrisy of racial ideologies.⁴

An actor as well as a writer, Duhart appeared in French plays at the Théâtre d'Orléans. These performances included a fundraiser for the Republican Central Executive Committee.⁵ Duhart also penned a drama, the text of which has not survived but whose title indicates that the theme of his short stories had been further developed: *Lydia ou la victime du préjugé*. Another writer-activist, Victor Eugène Macarty, played a leading role, presumably opposite the title character. Announcements in *La Tribune* specify that the drama consisted of three acts, entitled "Le déshonneur" ("Dishonor"), "L'enlèvement" ("The Kidnapping"), and "Le pardon" (which could be translated as "The Pardon" or as "Forgiveness" — lack of the original text makes it impossible to know). *Lydia* premiered at the Théâtre d'Orléans on 10 June 1866, as part of an evening of theatrical entertainment touted as a benefit event for "Lélia D...t," i.e., Adolphe himself, suggesting some sort of hardship of which the community would have been aware.⁶

Upon the death of Joanni Questy, in 1869, Duhart succeeded him as principal of the Institution catholique. Moreover, he maintained his political activism after the demise of *La Tribune*. In 1873 he joined the ranks of the Unification movement, a short-lived centrist political coalition for racial reconciliation, undertaken by a bipartisan Committee of One Hundred whose primary organizers included Louis Charles Roudanez as well as the former Confederate general P. G. T. Beauregard. Later city directories through 1891 give Duhart's profession as printer, as was his brother Armand.⁷

Sporadic writing by Duhart continued to appear in city newspapers such as the bilingual *Louisianian*, which in September 1881 featured two pieces written by "Lélia": "Une légende" (a short story about the Sainte-Chapelle in Paris) and a prose monologue, "La pluie" ("The Rain") (Fabre, "New Orleans Press" 46). "La pluie," though not about a political topic, includes a trenchant passage describing New Orleans as a city "where assassins and thieves are considered gentlemen, where policemen indiscriminately use poor blacks as targets for their revolvers, where a stolen pig has more value than the life of any citizen" ("où les assassins et les voleurs sont considérés comme des gentlemen, où les policemen prennent, à tort et à travers, de pauvres noirs comme de points de cible pour leurs revolvers, où un cochon volé a plus de valeur que la vie de n'importe quel citoyen"; *Weekly Louisianian*, 17 Sept. 1881, p. 1).

Nevertheless, all evidence indicates that by the 1880s, despite the magnitude of his contributions to the ideological battles of the Civil War era, the defeat of Reconstruction dissuaded Duhart from continuing the fight. The 1880 census specifies the race of his family as white, with Adolphe having given his first name as Pierre; he is also white on the 1900 census, where he is listed as a widower, Odilia having passed on the year before. It would seem that he ultimately chose to opt out of the struggle against segregation that his comrades continued to wage through the Comité des citoyens and its organ the *Crusader*.[8]

Duhart died in New Orleans on 10 January 1908 (*L'Abeille de la Nouvelle-Orléans*, 11 Jan. 1908).

Jean-Sylvain Gentil

A freethinking republican journalist in France during the turbulent years of the Second Republic and the rise of Napoléon III, Jean-Sylvain Gentil (1829–1911) came to Louisiana to escape further persecution after a brief imprisonment. Arriving from London in 1853, he made his living as a teacher and tutor in St. James Parish until the war's disruption closed most schools. In August 1865, he founded the newspaper *Le Louisianais* (Tinker, *Les Écrits* 245–48).

In its sixteen-year existence, Gentil's St. James Parish–based weekly offered a colorful take on politics, culture, and a wide, unpredictable range of other topics. His anticlericalism angered local clergy on more than one occasion. In the face of unrelenting political turmoil and a climate of partisan patronage, *Le Louisianais* maintained an independent voice. When the Republican government pressured the parish to withdraw the paper's status as official publication, *Le Louisianais* added a sarcastic and defiant subtitle to its nameplate: *Journal non Officiel de la Paroisse Saint-Jacques*. Though his criticism spared neither radical Republicans nor reactionary Democrats, Gentil always opposed slavery on the grounds of classic liberalism. In 1872, he wrote (in French),

> What we need, for morality to rise to the level of Christian civilization, are men who are truly free and respected as such, not would-be slaves or despicable valets. And if the great plantation, the last refuge of slavery, acts as a scarecrow to free labor and to the laborer — because it never was, as its flatterers claim, intelligent hospitality — then the great plantation, now an immense pasture and an unproductive wilderness, must be divided up for the sake of national wealth and the particular good of the classes. Not too many rich, nor too many poor, but a people of well-off folks; that is the goal to be achieved. (*Le Louisianais*, 31 Aug. 1872)

Witty irreverence drenches his editorial pieces, while whimsy characterizes his endless stream of literary pieces. Edward Larocque Tinker estimates that works by Gentil published in *Le Louisianais* include 750 full-length articles, 750 poems, and 35 serial novels (*Les Écrits* 248–49).

In late Reconstruction and afterward, Gentil held a number of administrative positions in St. James Parish, including president of the Parish Board of School Directors in 1877 and police juror in 1888. In 1889, Governor Francis T. Nicholls named Gentil honorary commissioner to the Exposition universelle in Paris. Though he was suggested by the local press as a representative to the 1898 state constitutional convention, his name does not appear among the delegates.[9]

In the years before his death, he lived in St. James Parish with his wife, Oscalie (née Vavasseur); their daughter, Blanche; and Blanche's three daughters.[10] Tinker would later come to meet Blanche, who gave him her father's entire collection of newspapers, now housed at the American Antiquarian Society.

Auguste Girod

Little documentation exists that can be authoritatively linked to Auguste Girod. Apparently unrelated to the well-known family of Nicolas Girod, mayor of New Orleans during the War of 1812, Girod immigrated from France to Louisiana in 1867, settling in New Iberia (*Louisiana Naturalization Records*). Among persons of the same name found in European records, an Auguste Girod appears as the author of the lyrics to a song entitled "Le vieux tuteur" ("The Old Guardian"), published in the French serial *Le Siècle chantant* (17 Apr. 1865, p. 364). In the 1870s he is listed among the agents of Jean-Sylvain Gentil's weekly *Le Louisianais*, based in St. James Parish (*Louisiana Naturalization Records*).

ÉMILE HONORÉ

Not known as a writer outside of his poems in *La Tribune*, Émile Honoré (1837–1905), the likely author of the pieces signed "E. H.," was a free, mixed-race planter from Pointe Coupée Parish. He became involved in the Republican Party after the war, ultimately ascending to the office of secretary of state.

The Honoré family traces its roots to the Destréhans, settlers during the French colonial era. Émile Honoré's great-great-great-grandmother, Geneviève Bienville, had been enslaved to Jean-Baptiste d'Estréhan de Beaupré, who arrived from France in 1721, at age twenty-one, with the position of royal treasurer. Geneviève's daughter with Jean-Baptiste, Catiche (or Catalina) Destréhan, married an enslaved man, Pompé, who took his wife's surname. Their son Jean-Baptiste Honoré Destréhan (1750–1845) obtained his freedom; he and Marie-Félicité Gravier, *femme de couleur libre*, were joined in matrimony at St. Louis Cathedral in June 1789. It was their second son, Jean-François (1789–1842), who preferred Honoré as a last name and settled in New Roads (Chemin neuf), Pointe Coupée Parish, where he married a mixed-race woman, Marie-Céleste Decuir (1795–1842). Émile's father, Jean-François Honoré *fils* — referred to as Honoré *fils* on census enumeration and other official documents — followed in his own father's footsteps as a planter.

Émile's mother, Euphémie Tounoir (1809–47), was born enslaved to her own father, a condition in which she remained until age seven. Married to Honoré *fils* in 1840, she had eight children by him between 1833 and 1847, the year of her death, presumably in childbirth.[11]

Born in 1837 after brothers Joseph and Ovide, Émile grew up in a slaveholding household. According to the Slave Schedules for Pointe Coupée Parish, his father held sixteen people in slavery in 1850 and thirteen in 1860. We can assume that they would have been domestics as well as field hands and skilled workers. Since no occupation is given for the adult Honoré children on the 1860 census, it appears that all contributed to the operation and management of the plantation until the war.[12] Émile would likely have received his education — a bilingual one that included the poetry of Robert Burns, as we know from his poem "Le droit de suffrage des noirs" ("Blacks' Right to Vote") — from a private tutor.

The war came to Pointe Coupée after the siege of Port Hudson in spring 1863 and during the Red River Campaign of 1864. Since New Roads is not far from Port Hudson, Honoré would have been aware of the fighting and would have heard firsthand accounts of the battle in which André Cailloux lost his life. Though the Honoré family initially expressed allegiance to the Confederacy, they supplied animals and significant quantities of food to federal troops encamped in the area (United States, Congress 89–90).

Belonging to an influential political family in Pointe Coupée, Honoré was elected to the Louisiana House of Representatives in 1868; during his first term, he served on the Ways and Means Committee. From 1870 to 1872, he was the first black sheriff of Pointe Coupée Parish. Honoré served a second term in the legislature from 1874 to 1876, then accepted the nomination as secretary of state under Governor Stephen B. Packard. Honoré broke with the Republican Party after the political crisis of 1877 and the return of Democratic dominance under Francis T. Nicholls.[13]

He returned to Pointe Coupée, significantly impoverished, with wife Adorea (née Décuir, 1841–1915), whom he had married in 1862. He was a farmer until his death, in 1905. Three years later, the federal government awarded Adorea $9,550 in compensation for the supplies provided to the US military during the Civil War.[14]

Armand Lanusse

A pioneer in education and, as editor of *Les Cenelles* (1845), one of the founding figures of both Louisiana French and African American literature, Armand Lanusse (1812–68; born Jean Armand Lanusse) served as a mentor to a number of Creole intellectuals of the nineteenth century.

Despite his influential stature, there exists some uncertainty regarding Lanusse's family origins and early life. Since there is no record of his belonging to the only known Lanusse family of color in New Orleans, it is likely that his father was a white Frenchman; it is also probable that his mother was Euphrosine Wiltz, free woman of color, since she was named as the mother of his brother, Numa, when the latter was indentured in 1822 to learn the trade of cabinetmaker. Numa, also a poet, would die at age twenty-six from a fall from a horse.[15]

Though Armand surely began his schooling in Louisiana, there is disagreement as to where he completed his studies. Tinker claims that he attended the École polytechnique in Paris, while, according to Rodolphe Desdunes, Lanusse "visited France only through the prism of his imagination" (Tinker, *Les Écrits* 272; R. Desdunes, *Our People* 13). Whatever the case, his erudition impressed his contemporaries, especially his love of the grammatical and stylistic particulars of the French language.

Lanusse's literary activities in the 1840s demonstrate an acute awareness of the racial hierarchy as well as the willingness to denounce its harmful effects. Appearing in *L'Album littéraire: journal des jeunes gens, amateurs de littérature* (1843), his short story "Un mariage de conscience" calls attention to the ill treatment awaiting women of color taken as lovers or concubines by white men, as would his "Épigramme" in *Les Cenelles*. *Les Cenelles* features seventeen of his poems; it and the literary journal *L'Album littéraire* showcase Lanusse's intellectual and cultural leadership among the *gens de couleur*. While his initiative in *Les Cenelles* has long been recognized, Tinker believed as well that Lanusse — not Jean-Louis Marciacq, as is generally assumed — was also the real driving force behind *L'Album littéraire*, and that Marciacq's status as a white man was used to validate the journal's radical content (*Les Écrits* 298).

Lanusse held a strong belief in the power of education as a force for uplift and betterment; in the preface to *Les Cenelles*, he argues that "a good education is a shield which dulls the arrows cast upon us by disdain and calumny" ("Preface" 13). He offered his services in the establishment of the Institution catholique and succeeded its first principal, Félicie Cailloux, in 1849; in 1852, once construction of the Institution's permanent facilities had been completed, the school's directors granted him the position indefinitely (see Christian). As Desdunes reports, "It was he who created the program of studies, it was he who put this program into action, and it was he who taught his faculty how to proceed" (*Our People* 22).

With his career on firm footing, Lanusse married Aglaé Robin de Logny in the summer of 1855; of their five children born over the next several years, only one son lived to adulthood. Aglaé would survive her husband by almost three decades.[16]

Lanusse's course of action during the early days of the Civil War occasioned some controversy. In the days following the battle of Fort Sumter, in April 1861, he took a leading role in organizing the Confederate Native Guards, addressing a meeting of nearly two thousand *hommes de couleur* at the Institution catholique. Lanusse was quickly promoted to captain, though Confederate authorities never sent Louisiana's Native Guards into battle. Shortly after federal occupation, Lanusse pushed his defense of his home state to the extreme of refusing to fly the American flag over the Institution catholique, in disobedience of an order from General Benjamin Butler. By all accounts, he soon came to feel deep regret for his rash act of defiance.[17]

Following this incident, Lanusse joined the vanguard of radical *gens de couleur*. Indeed, his first poem in *L'Union*, "Étrange coïncidence" ("A Strange Coincidence"), published on 19 May 1863, was accompanied by a lengthy diatribe against the racist attitudes encountered while serving under the Confederate banner. In 1865, Lanusse took part in the Convention of Universal Suffrage, and, relinquishing his work at the Institution catholique in 1866, accepted a seat on the city's Board of Police Commissioners, alongside Victor Eugène Macarty.[18]

Desdunes devotes lengthy passages of *Nos hommes et notre histoire* to Lanusse's character and intellectual temperament. In addition to praising his exemplary generosity and dedication to others, Desdunes offers this remark on his former principal's concept of identity: "One may say Lanusse never boasted of being an American. His pride in being Creole was more dear to him than his being a Louisianian, or than anything else pertaining to his origin. All his preferences and resentments stemmed from this" (*Our People* 21).

Upon Lanusse's unexpected passing on 16 March 1868, the Board of Police Commissioners convened that evening to plan the official response to the death of their "worthy, esteemed, and honorable colleague," in whose honor the major, chief, and lieutenants of police and twenty-five officers were to attend his funeral and offer condolences to his family (*New Orleans Republican*, 17 Mar. 1868).

Victor Eugène Macarty

While Victor Eugène Macarty (1821–81) did not himself write the poems associated with him in this collection, he remains a key figure in the Afro-Creole community, and the literary hoax in which he participated (see pp. 31–35) is embedded in the poetic discourse of *La Tribune*. Considered by some, according to Rodolphe Desdunes, as "the only real artist among the Creoles" of the nineteenth century, Macarty combined his talents as composer, pianist, vocalist, actor, and writer with intense political activism (*Our People* 84). The son of Eugène Theodore de Macarty, a white New Orleans financier, and Héloïse Croy, a free woman of color who had fled the Haitian Revolution, Victor Eugène (sometimes called Eugène Victor) was born into "a numerous, acquisitive, and far from straight-laced clan."[19] Prominent among the Creole elite, the extended family included both a mayor of New Orleans, Augustin Macarty, and the infamous torturer Delphine Macarty Lalaurie, who fled to France by 1835, after the exposure of her crimes against enslaved persons (Long, part 1, p. 101).

After beginning piano instruction under J. Norres, Macarty left Louisiana at age nineteen to study voice and composition at the Conservatoire de Paris. When he eventually returned to New Orleans, he earned his living as a music teacher, composer, and performer, often alongside his friends Basile Barès and Samuel Snaër. Having lost his wife, Louise Galland, in 1855, as well as their three young children, he would have two more life partners: wife Lucie Lee, with whom he had three children before her death, in 1874, and Rosalie Hugon, also the mother of three children (Long, part 2, 206–07).

As a musician, Macarty styled himself the "Pianist of the fashionable Soirées of New Orleans" (*Fleurs*, title p.); on the stage, claims Desdunes, leading roles were "bestowed on him by common consent" (*Our People* 84). These roles would include the eponymous character of Alexandre Dumas's *Antony*, which Macarty played from October 1865 through the year 1867 — the period during which he signed at least four poems as "Antony" in *La Tribune* and another as "A." As discussed in the introduction (pp. 31–34), these poems ("Combat de l'Aigle Républicain et du Copperhead," "À Théodule Delassize," "Il est," "La fleur indiscrète," and "Les trois perles"), plagiarized from French Romantic-era sources, constitute a literary hoax — possibly a mere caprice on the part of the perpetrator(s), but also serious, given the weighty subject matter of some of the texts.

The postwar years saw Macarty take part in a number of charity events; for example, the 9 May 1865 issue of *La Tribune* indicates he was slated to participate in the musical portion of a reading by Louise de Mortie (a benefit for a home for orphans of freedmen) on 10 May and in a fundraiser for musicians of color the following month.

Concurrently, Macarty answered the call of public service under successive Reconstruction governments. By all appearances, the massacre of 30 July 1866, which Macarty witnessed firsthand from inside the Mechanics' Institute, stimulated increased political involvement on his part (Horne 507–08). In late 1866, he was elected to the Central Committee of the Republican Party, in which capacity he worked to found the Fifth Ward Republican Club. In 1867, he served on the parish's Board of Police Commissioners. By 1870, Macarty would win elected office in the state legislature. Throughout these years, he was sought out as an orator, giving speeches around the state in favor of civil rights. He would continue to do so through much of the following decade (Horne).

Macarty threw himself onto the front lines of the fight against racial segregation after he was expelled from viewing a performance of *The Barber of Seville* on 19 January 1869. Despite his very fair complexion, some patrons had complained of the presence of a man of color in the audience, and the manager of the New Orleans Opera House had acquiesced. Macarty sued for fifteen hundred dollars; the case was never settled. His later work for the school board, during the Reconstruction-era desegregation of public schools in Louisiana, drew the enmity of the conservative faction, to such a point that he suffered a vicious assault in 1875 (Horne).

After settling in Baton Rouge in 1878, he taught school. Macarty passed away at his son's home in New Orleans on 25 June 1881, leaving behind "a number of friends to mourn his loss" ("Obituary," *Weekly Louisianian*, 2 July 1881).

Joseph Lucien Mansion

The son of the poets Lucien Mansion (also featured in this volume) and Elizabeth Francis, Joseph Lucien Mansion (1839–1912) served in the Louisiana House of Representatives from 1868 to 1872, in addition to other political activities and public service beginning during the Civil War.

Born on 8 November 1839, Joseph was the eldest child in his father's family with Elizabeth. (Lucien had families with two longtime partners at the same time.) As a young man, he followed in Lucien's footsteps in the cigar business, as would his brothers Gaston (born 1837) and Numa (born 1851) and half-brother Léo Placide (born 1850). In later years, Joseph had a career as an undertaker, operating a funeral parlor on Bourbon Street.[20]

Following the publication in *La Tribune* of Joseph's poem "Méditations," dedicated to Armand Lanusse and signed "Yacoub," Lanusse replied in the paper with the following message, which allows us to identify Joseph Mansion as "Yacoub":

À Mr. J. Mansion

Monsieur et ami — C'est avec un véritable plaisir que j'ai lu dans la *Tribune* d'hier la charmante pièce de vers que, sous le pseudonyme significatif de Yacoub, vous m'avez fait l'honneur de m'adresser. Cette pièce, comme toutes celles que j'ai lues de vous, se recommande par l'exactitude de la versification, la noblesse des sentiments et la preuve que vous nous donnez que l'étude que vous avez ardemment faite de nos grands maîtres vous a été très fructueuse. Bravo, mon jeune collègue, les lauriers que vous cueillez maintenant comme poète valent ceux qui ont dernièrement couronné vos efforts sur la scène. Croyez que je suis heureux et fier de voir un compatriote et le fils d'un de mes anciens amis se distinguer dans deux arts dont la culture offre tant de déboires. Puisse votre exemple donner de l'émulation à la plupart de ceux qui appartiennent à la même génération que vous, et permettez-moi, je vous prie, de leur crier bien haut ici:

Les vieux s'en vont, les vieux s'en vont; c'est à vous, jeunes esprits, de les remplacer avec avantage; il ne vous faut pour cela qu'une volonté ferme et constante. (23 Dec. 1866)

To Mr. J. Mansion

Sir and friend — It was with real pleasure that I read in yesterday's *Tribune* the delightful piece of verse that, under the meaningful pseudonym of Yacoub, you paid the honor of addressing to me. This piece, like all of yours that I have read, is to be commended for the exactitude of its versification, the nobility of feeling, and the evidence you've given us that your fervent study of the great masters has proven very fruitful. Bravo, my young colleague, the laurels that you now gather as a poet are worth those that have, of late, crowned your efforts on the stage. Know that I am happy and proud to see a compatriot and the son of one of my old friends distinguish himself in two arts whose cultivation produces so many mishaps. Would that your example might inspire emulation in the majority of those of the same generation as you, and allow me, I pray, to cry out loud and clear to them here:

> The old ones are departing, the old ones are departing; it is up to you, young minds, to replace them advantageously; for that you will only need firm and constant willpower.

One of Joseph's theatrical endeavors was a comic opera entitled *Les deux aveugles* (*The Two Blind Men*), which he cowrote and presented as part of a benefit event held at Economy Hall for the Association louisianaise pour le bénéfice des orphelins indigents. His talents as a violinist were also appreciated (Trotter 348).

Joseph Mansion and Marie Cecilia Boyer were married in January 1868. The couple had two sons, Lucien (christened Joseph Lucien, born 1868) and Charles Victor (born 1869), and two daughters, Henriette (born 1871) and Marie Hortensia (born 1874).[21]

Elected to the state legislature as a representative from Orleans Parish's Fifth District, Joseph Mansion served on the Education Committee during his first term (1868–70), helping to oversee desegregation efforts. In July 1868, during a hiatus in publication of *La Tribune* owing to fallout from the recent conflict over the governor's race, he introduced a resolution to promote the Republican Party's official organ, the *New Orleans Republican*, in the House. During his second term (1870–72), he was chairman of the seven-member Enrollment Committee. Starting in April 1870, he was commissioned as a tax assessor for the state (alongside Henry Louis Rey), a position he held for several years. Having distanced himself from the radical faction of his party, Joseph Mansion supported — as did Louis Charles Roudanez and other prominent Creoles — the Unification movement of 1873. The so-called Unification Party would have granted black people equal political rights with white people in exchange for conservative fiscal measures; Joseph served as one of a number of the group's vice presidents.[22]

Well after the defeat of the Reconstruction governments, Joseph involved himself in another effort intended to improve the condition of black people in New Orleans: he served as vice president of the colored men's meeting for the North, Central, and South American Exposition, held in New Orleans from November 1885 through March 1886 in the wake of the mammoth World's Industrial and Cotton Centennial Exposition. In October 1885, he helped organize a convention at Economy Hall, the meeting place and social club of the Société d'Économie, an important Creole fraternal organization. This particular gathering was designed to present to the public the preparations for the exposition and was thematically devoted to advancing racial harmony.

The *Tribune* founder Paul Trévigne, one of the guests, delivered "an eloquent speech in French, speaking of the progress the colored man had made and how his handiwork would be seen in the Southern exhibits." The assembly also resolved to invite Frederick Douglass to attend New Orleans's next Emancipation Day celebration (*Daily Picayune*, 29 Oct. 1885).

Perhaps because of his profession as undertaker, Joseph Mansion seems to have witnessed a number of tragic incidents that were reported in the press. As an example: in April 1891, the *Daily Picayune* reported that Joseph had received a letter from Alfred Jourdain, a friend, Republican Party activist, and officer in the Société d'Économie, as well as a barber by trade, stating that Jourdain, having separated from his wife, intended to commit suicide. Joseph rushed out to seek the letter writer and eventually located him in Congo Square, just in time to see Jourdain shoot himself with a .38 revolver. As horrified acquaintances of the barber looked on, Joseph took the dying man into his arms (*Daily Picayune*, 14 Apr. 1891).

In the final years of his life, Joseph and Cecilia lived with their son Lucien (a plasterer by trade) and the family of their daughter Marie and her husband, George St. Avid.[23] Joseph Mansion passed away on 22 February 1912 (*L'Abeille de la Nouvelle-Orléans*, 24 Feb. 1912).

Lucien Mansion

Lucien Mansion (1812–94), father of the poet Joseph Mansion (also featured in this volume) and called by the nickname "Lolo," rose to prominence as the successful owner of a cigar factory. Though Lucien wrote poetry throughout his life, sharing his writings in his social circle, little of it was published outside *La Tribune*.

A free man of color, Lucien Mansion claimed to be "the natural son of a Mr. Mansion, a Frenchman who abandoned him in infancy."[24] For many years, he lived with Elizabeth Francis, a free black woman from New York State. It is to their daughter, Élodie (born 1842), their third child of six after brothers Gaston (born 1837) and Joseph (born 1839), that several of the poems in *La Tribune* are addressed. Lucien had a second life partner, Marie Aline Palao, *femme de couleur libre*, with whom he enjoyed a family as well. Of their six children, born between 1841 and 1859, only daughter Aménaïde (born 1841) and son Léo (born 1850) would live to adulthood.[25] (These aspects of Lucien's personal life stand in contrast to the normative vision of the patriarchal family that he projects in his lengthy poem "Hommage au sexe" ["Homage to the Fairer Sex"]).

For many years, his cigar factory operated at 44 Orleans Street. Lucien also helped to establish his nephew George Alcès, whose factory would come to employ some two hundred workers. Lucien's sons Gaston, Léo, and Numa also took up the trade. In 1848, Lucien had built on Pauger Street a home that still stands out in the New Orleans neighborhood known today as the Faubourg Marigny: a striking three-bay cottage whose "Greek revival door surround and [...] hall reveal Anglo-American influence."[26]

His business's prosperity permitted him to lend philanthropic support to various causes. In 1855, in reaction to the mounting hostility against free people of color, Lucien funded the emigration of a few hundred of his fellow citizens to Haiti and Mexico (R. Desdunes, *Our People* 65); the descendants of those who settled in Mexico still live in the Veracruz region (Gehman).

Lucien Mansion enjoyed lifelong friendships with François Boisdoré, a Republican Party activist from a distinguished Creole family, and Joanni Questy. Lucien's daughter Élodie married Questy's nephew Jean Questy, the son of Lucien's brother Paul, in 1873.[27]

Sometime in the 1870s, Lucien separated from Elizabeth Francis to live with Marie Aline Palao in the house he had purchased for her on Bagatelle Street in New Orleans. It was there that he resided in the final years of his life.[28]

Lucien's progeny made significant contributions to black political and intellectual life. Joseph's career is discussed above. Numa helped found the Comité des citoyens, the civil rights group whose bold challenge to racial segregation would ultimately be decided by the Supreme Court in *Plessy v. Ferguson* (1896). One of Lucien's great-grandsons, the historian Charles Barthelemy Roussève, wrote the influential study *The Negro in Louisiana: Aspects of His History and His Literature* (1937).

A later poem, "La folle," appeared in 1886 in the journal of the Athénée louisianais (*Comptes-rendus de l'Athénée louisianais*), a New Orleans–based learned society founded by the white Creole physician, novelist, and French-language activist Alfred Mercier. Noting the general lack of coordination among differently racialized Creoles in the late nineteenth century, Rodolphe Desdunes remarks ironically that Lucien Mansion's "name was saved from oblivion only through the sympathetic consideration of a group completely unknown to the population of color" (*Our People* 65).

Joanni Questy

A devoted educator who spent his entire life in New Orleans, Joanni Questy (1817–69) taught modern languages at the Institution catholique, taking over as principal upon Armand Lanusse's death, in 1868. He was a key collaborator in the two literary initiatives by *gens de couleur* of the 1840s, *L'Album littéraire* and *Les Cenelles*. He served as associate editor of *La Tribune* from 1865 until his death.

Joanni Questy was born Giovanni Questiz, named after his father Giovanni Questiz (1780–1833), an immigrant from Ragusa, Sicily, who came to New Orleans around 1795 before eventually settling in Iberville Parish. Questy's mother was Annette Catoir, a free woman of color from New Orleans, sometimes called Annette Dominique, who also bore Joanni's older brother, Paul (1813–50), and a sister, Henriette. In July 1850, when Questy was still in his early twenties, his brother Paul committed suicide.[29] The incident surely affected Questy deeply and suggests a personal connection to some of the tragic elements in his work.

Questy enjoyed a long-term romantic partnership with Marie Beaulieu, herself a *femme de couleur libre*. The couple had two sons, Jacob (born 16 May 1844) and Charles (born 18 July 1846). As an adult, Jacob became a marble cutter and resided next door to Victor Eugène Macarty. Questy also shared a close relationship with his late brother Paul's son Jean Questy, who would eventually marry Élodie Mansion (daughter of Questy's friend Lucien Mansion) in 1873.[30]

The author of Questy's obituary in the French edition of *La Tribune* (most likely Paul Trévigne or Adolphe Duhart) claims that Questy founded *L'Album littéraire: journal des jeunes gens, amateurs de littérature*. The first issue of *L'Album littéraire*, appearing on 1 July 1843, featured a lament to a dead lover, "Essai poétique" by Questy, and the 1 August issue included his short story "Le chêne du chemin du bayou" ("The Oak of the Bayou Road"). Two years later, three of his poems were published in *Les Cenelles*: "Une larme sur William Stephen" ("A Tear for William Stephen"), "Vision" (dated Sept. 1841), and "Causerie" ("A Chat"). According to the obituary's author, Questy's contemporaries held him in high regard for his literary talent: "A Louisianian first and foremost, he is one of the rare poets of our country who has always made a point of observing local color in his compositions. He wrote with astounding ease, and I have seen him write more than one lovely piece in verse without crossing out a word."[31] Another postmortem homage noted the difficulty that Questy encountered in seeking publication for his works, "[o]wing to the prejudice attached to color" ("Joanni Questy," *Weekly Louisianian*, 4 Dec. 1875).

In addition to teaching French and Spanish at the Institution catholique, Questy held the position of assistant principal under Armand Lanusse. Rodolphe Desdunes later recalled, "Mr. Questy enjoyed a wide popularity because of his amiable and sympathetic disposition. All the children knew him as Mr. Joanni" (*Our People* 26). Desdunes's brother, Pierre-Aristide, later composed "Homage to My Esteemed Teacher Joanni Questy," the first stanza of which conveys the admiration he inspired:

> Ami, si comme toi disciple de Virgile,
> Je pouvais du Parnasse atteindre la hauteur,
> Ma muse au ciel irait, d'une aile alors agile,
> Ravir ces notes d'or pour chanter mon bonheur. (99)

> Friend, if only, just like you, a disciple of Virgil,
> I could attain the glorious heights of Parnassus,
> My muse to heaven would fly with wing so agile
> As to steal its golden notes to sing of my bliss.

Questy's obituary praises his pedagogical talent: "As a teacher, he had few equals in Louisiana. He seemed to have received from heaven the ability to impart to others whatever he wanted to teach them. The numerous students whom he educated over two generations are there to attest to this." Continuing his legacy, many of them went on to wage the struggle for equal rights.

Questy became a devotee of Spiritualism in the 1850s. He regularly attended séances hosted by Henry Louis Rey, though the last meeting held before the outbreak of the Civil War was conducted in Questy's home (Daggett, *Spiritualism* xiii).

In the fall of 1861, he was mustered into the Confederate Army, in the Savary Guards company of the Louisiana Native Guards, under the command of Captain Joseph Joly.[32] Later, eager to commit himself to the Union cause, Questy joined the regular staff of *La Tribune*, contributing articles and columns as well as literary pieces. According to Neil L. O'Brien, Questy had emigrated to Mexico when *La Tribune* was founded (28). He corresponded with the paper and became its associate editor on his return to New Orleans in 1865.[33]

In addition to the poems republished in this volume, Questy also penned a noteworthy novella, *Monsieur Paul*, which appeared in *La Tribune* in 1867 (25 Oct. through 3 Nov.; republished in Michaelides 167–86). Taking place in 1860 and 1861, the story tells of a tragic friendship between the narrator, a New Orleanian of color, and a white Frenchman, the eponymous Monsieur Paul. After Paul is killed in a duel in a rivalry over his companion (a woman of color), the narrator discovers that Georges, a young man enslaved to Paul, is in fact Paul's nephew. As the Civil War begins, Georges emigrates to Haiti rather than serve in the Confederate Army. This highly politicized work of fiction addresses interracial relationships while highlighting the revolutionary universalism of Haiti, depicted as morally superior to US values. The novella's postscript denounces Louisiana society's materialism, suggesting that Questy's brother Paul, whose suicide was driven by financial distress, was on the author's mind.

Stricken by a sudden illness, Questy passed away on 26 August 1869, in the home he shared with Marie Beaulieu. His contemporaries indicate that he left behind a considerable trove of unpublished manuscripts.[34]

Given Questy's status as a visionary writer, it is not surprising that the Spiritualist medium Henry Louis Rey recorded otherworldly "communications" from Questy after his death. In one message, Questy supposedly lauded "the great and sublime figure of Lincoln" and "the majestic form" of John Brown, the abolitionist activist who led the Harpers Ferry revolt of 1859. In another, he is reported to have wished for young progressive activists to take their place in politics (Emily Suzanne Clark 143, 132).

Henry Louis Rey

As a store clerk and an educator, a soldier and a Spiritualist medium, a poet and a politician, Henry Louis Rey (1831–94) traveled a career trajectory that embodied several intersecting aspects of the struggle for civil rights during the Civil War and Reconstruction.

Both of Rey's parents, Louis Barthélemy Rey and Rose Agnès Sacriste, were free *gens de couleur* born in the Caribbean; they were married in 1829 in New Orleans. His father (who went by Barthélemy), a tailor who embarked on a career as a real estate broker, took part in the establishment and the management of the Institution catholique. Barthélemy was also a slaveholder, owning eight individuals in 1850. Henry Louis, the Reys' second child, was to have four sisters and two brothers; in the process of praising all three sons, Rodolphe Desdunes would describe Henry Louis and his brother Hippolyte as "worthy men who zealously occupied themselves with the fate of their people."[35]

Educated in New Orleans, Henry Louis Rey worked as a young man as a bookbinder and as a clerk in a hardware store. In 1857, he and Adèle Crocker, the daughter of family friends, were wedded at St. Augustine Church. The couple spent their first years together at a home on Columbus Street in the Faubourg Tremé. Adèle gave birth to two children before the war, daughter Lucia Rose (born 7 Feb. 1859) and son Henry Joseph (born 14 Apr. 1860), and two more sons after federal occupation, Albert Louis (born 28 Nov. 1864) and Placide Augustin (born 3 Sept. 1866); the youngest died as a toddler.[36]

Rey first experienced otherworldly communications after the death of his father in 1852. Subsequently becoming a disciple of the French immigrant Joseph Barthet, an influential advocate of Spiritualism in the United States, Rey converted to Spiritualism and eventually became one of the religion's primary exponents in New Orleans, both before and after the war. Having interrupted his activities as a medium during the war, in 1867 Rey founded the Cercle harmonique, a group that would meet twice a week until 1875; during its heyday, the Cercle harmonique counted among its members a number of Creole radicals and thinkers, including fellow poets Joanni Questy and Adolphe Duhart. After its dissolution, Rey continued to record communications received in solitude until 1877. His records form the seven-thousand-page collection of Spiritualist registers that René Grandjean, son-in-law of one of Rey's séance companions, would donate to the University of New Orleans in the 1970s.[37]

When *L'Union* published his poem "L'Ignorance" on 27 September 1862, Rey was serving in the Union Army as a captain in the First Regiment of the Native Guards; his brothers Octave and Hippolyte were lieutenants with the Second and Third Regiments, respectively. Like Armand Lanusse, he had enthusiastically joined the Confederate Native Guards at the war's outbreak, then had played a significant role in the formation of the Union units after the federal occupation of New Orleans (Hollandsworth, *Louisiana* 6, 17–18). Indeed, Desdunes claims that Henry and Octave composed half of the four-man committee that met with General Butler and thus were among "the first to give the example of loyalty to the cause of the Union" (*Our People* 118). Throughout the fall of 1862, Rey sent dispatches to *L'Union* from his station on Bayou Lafourche. Illness forced him to resign from the army in April 1863, several weeks before the offensive against Port Hudson.

Rey's political involvement began in earnest when he joined the Central Executive Committee of the Friends of Universal Suffrage, which met in September 1865 to found the Republican Party of Louisiana. In 1868, he was elected as a representative to the state's General Assembly and, following the constitutional measure integrating schools, was appointed chairman of the Committee on Education, holding both offices until 1870. His attempts to improve conditions at the Institution catholique, which had fallen on hard times, met with only partial success. From 1870 to 1872, Rey served as assessor for the city's Third District, and from 1873 to 1877, he was a member of the Orleans Parish School Board ("Members of the General Assembly," *New Orleans Republican*, 25 June 1868; Daggett, *Henry Louis Rey* 39–40, 52, 56).

The end of Reconstruction and the years to follow were scarred by hardship. The family home having burned down in 1875, Rey returned to work at a hardware store. His request for a war pension was ultimately denied, and Adèle passed away in 1890. Rey himself was struck down by anthrax on 19 April 1894 (Daggett, *Henry Louis Rey* 57, 60–61).

Henry Train

The author of the poem "Washington et Lincoln," Henry Train (1818–?) was a white attorney from Martinique who served as a judge during Reconstruction.

During the campaign of 1868, a conservative country newspaper would accuse him of being "like most all of the carpetbaggers, [...] a man of desperate political fortunes." Train, however, had been living in Louisiana since age twenty-two at the latest (quite possibly earlier). In 1850, he and Delphine Philibert Moreno, a native of Alabama, had married in New Orleans, and a few years later he had moved his law practice upriver to St. Charles Parish. He had returned to New Orleans sometime before the war, establishing his firm in the famed Pontalba buildings on Jackson Square, with his partner Josiah Fisk. Train and Fisk supported *La Tribune* by advertising regularly in the paper.[38]

Train represented the Fifth District of Orleans Parish, alongside the Creole activists Aristide Mary and Théodule Delassize (on the poem Victor Eugène Macarty plagiarized and retitled "For Théodule Delassize," see p. 203n71), at the 1865 Convention of Universal Suffrage, and also served on its Central Executive Committee.

By 1868, he had accepted a position as district judge in the city of Houma (in Terrebonne Parish). He would later serve in St. Mary Parish, where he would settle for several years. Train encountered resistance from reactionary local attorneys, notably in 1873, when lawyers in Franklin, Louisiana, refused to recognize his authority. His judicial career continued through Reconstruction.[39]

NOTES

FOREWORD

1. While there exists an excellent and growing scholarly literature on New Orleans's Afro-Creoles, their historical and literary contributions are rarely integrated into textbooks or courses that focus on the US as a whole. Instead, Afro-Creoles' contributions are more likely to be limited to syllabi or courses that specialize in Louisiana history. The scholarship is there, but it often it does not reach a broader audience.
2. For more on some Afro-Creoles' differentiation of themselves from the Anglo-black population, see Gaudin, esp. ch. 1; and Parham, esp. ch. 4.
3. Bruce notes this ambivalence in the introduction when he cites an editorial that, while declaring allegiance with recently freed black people, also insists that "one cannot, without being unfair, confuse the new freedmen with our intelligent population who, by its industry and education, has rendered itself as useful to society and to the country as any other class of citizens."
4. For a contemporary account of the fire, see *Last Journal of the Rt. Rev. George Burgess*, the journal of an Anglican missionary who arrived in Port-au-Prince just before the fire raged through the city. The outsider status of the writer is clear, and his disparaging remarks about the lack of local organization mirrors that of the international press, which in some ways blamed the fire on Haitian people themselves. For a recent account that provides critical reflection on this international critique and places the reaction to the 1866 fire in dialogue with reactions to post-Katrina New Orleans, see Brickhouse.

INTRODUCTION

1. For a detailed account of the military operations of 1862, see Chester G. Hearn, *The Capture of New Orleans, 1862*. Though I will refer to a number of excellent works on Reconstruction-era Louisiana, I draw primarily, for general context and major events, from Joe Gray Taylor, *Louisiana Reconstructed, 1863–1877*, and Ted Tunnell, *Crucible of Reconstruction: War, Radicalism, and Race in Louisiana, 1862–1877*. For the broader national perspective, Eric Foner's *Reconstruction: America's Unfinished Revolution, 1863–1877* proves extremely useful, while important analytical insights regarding race and class are offered by W. E. B. Du Bois, *Black Reconstruction in America, 1860–1880*.
2. The twentieth-century incarnation, though otherwise unrelated to the original, was founded with the idea of "speak[ing] to the issues of today as eloquently and as forcefully as Roudanez did then" ("About Us").
3. Underrepresented in anthologies of Louisiana French literature, the corpus from *L'Union* and *La Tribune* has been partially republished in only one modern edition, now out of print: *La Marseillaise noire et autres poèmes français des Créoles de couleur de la Nouvelle-Orléans (1862–1869)*, edited by James Lorenz Cowan. It also bears adding that many excerpts translated in scholarly works

and historical studies deviate from the originals in ways that seem attributable less to interpretive choice than to misunderstandings of the French.

4. Kein, "Introduction" xv. For a thorough examination of the Creole-definition controversy from the perspective of legal anthropology, see Domínguez.

5. In a nineteenth-century context, the descriptor "mulatto" cannot be strictly equated with "mixed race": "mulatto" (*mulâtre*) was a distinct social category of the day, recognized in Louisiana and elsewhere, and legal definitions and cultural understandings of who was considered mulatto varied. This volume uses *mulatto* or *mulâtre* when a historical social category is meant.

6. For a brief critique of Bell's failure to account for proslavery attitudes of free black people, see S. Johnson 107–08, 225.

7. Statistics taken from United States, Bureau of the Census, *US Federal Census Collection* (hereafter abbreviated as USFCC), *Eighth Census of the United States* (1860). The 1860 census also lists significant (largely French-speaking) free communities of color in central Louisiana, in the parishes of St. Landry (965 free people of color), Pointe Coupée (721), and East Baton Rouge (532); and in northern Louisiana, in Natchitoches Parish (959). For an introductory look at other Creole populations of the region, see the essays in Dormon.

8. For a list of slave voyages to Louisiana during the French colonial period, see Hall, *Africans* 381–97.

9. For a succinct overview of the African presence in early colonial Louisiana, see Klingler 3–24. See also *Le Code noir, ou Édit du Roy servant de règlement pour le gouvernement et l'administration de la justice, police, discipline et le commerce des esclaves nègres dans la province et colonie de la Louisianne* (published in 1727), esp. articles 6, 10, 50, 52, 53, and 54.

10. For more extensive treatment by Hanger, see her volume *Bounded Lives, Bounded Places: Free Black Society in Colonial New Orleans, 1769–1803*.

11. On the militias of free men of color during the Territorial Period and the Battle of New Orleans, see Bell, *Revolution*; Berlin 114–30; McConnell; and Everett.

12. See Berry; and Hollandsworth, *Louisiana*, esp. chs. 1 and 2.

13. For a classic study on the Haitian Revolution in the US political imagination, see Hunt.

14. See biographical note on Adolphe Duhart.

15. For details, see Duplantier 160–61.

16. Among the expatriates in France were the composer Edmond Dédé, the writers Victor Séjour and Camille Thierry, and the inventor Norbert Rillieux.

17. The decree was spearheaded by another longtime abolitionist, Victor Schœlcher, though Lamartine was often given the credit. On the influence of Romanticism in nineteenth-century Louisiana and admiration for Victor Hugo and Lamartine, including later remembrances by Trévigne, see Bell, Introduction 25–33.

18. Qtd. in King 345. Gayarré is taking aim at the portrayals of race relations in the works of George Washington Cable, whose essays and fiction, beginning with *Old Creole Days* (1879), offended white Creole pride.

19. In her examination of pre–Civil War travel narratives and fiction, Emily Clark attributes the legend of the "luxuriously kept quadroon women" in New Orleans to "the projection of male fantasy leavened with just enough gossip and

sightings at the ballroom and the theater to make the legend as plausible to the men whose writing disseminated it as it was to the reading public titillated by it" (*Strange History* 170). Clark goes on to dismantle the sexualized, specifically interracial understanding of *plaçage*, noting the term's roots in Haiti, where the practice did not necessarily entail different races or a power imbalance but encompassed extralegal marital unions between people who could not legally marry for any number of reasons.

20. Paul Lachance offers several examples of the term *privileged* applied to free people of color by historians of the past few decades ("Limits" 428).

21. Quote taken from Shirley Elizabeth Thompson's discussion of the plantation owner and real estate dealer Francis Ernest Dumas, who was worth some $250,000 and whose family actively maintained ties with France (162). Having served as a major in the Native Guards and having organized a military unit composed of individuals formerly enslaved to him, Dumas would receive the backing of *La Tribune* in his (ultimately unsuccessful) 1868 campaign for lieutenant governor.

22. Lack of an existing emancipation record suggests Cailloux's mother may have died before she was legally freed (Ochs 45).

23. For examples, see Sterkx 161–65.

24. The Northern abolitionist press reported the events that ensued when a newspaper run by a French immigrant, *Le Libéral*, tested the censorship law by advocating for voting rights for free people of color: publication was suspended, and the editor left the state (Reilly 20–21).

25. Viatte's original text is in French. Here and throughout, translations from the French are my own unless otherwise indicated.

26. For an overview in English of Louisiana's francophone literature of the nineteenth century, see Brosman.

27. For a study of the transatlantic literary dynamic in Louisiana serial fiction of the 1840s, see Bruce, "Caught between Continents."

28. Though some later scholars interpreted "cenelles" to refer to holly berries (e.g., Edward Larocque Tinker, in his 1953 book *Creole City* [268]), Jerah Johnson has reminded contemporary readers that Lanusse's title takes its name from the bright red fruit of the hawthorn bush, or mayhaws. Jelly made from mayhaws, difficult to gather, was much prized in Louisiana kitchens. Comparing the Creole poets' works to these berries "subtly and poetically evoked the image of small, uniquely flavored, and rare local delicacies that struggled for life in surroundings so hostile as to make the very gathering of them a dangerous travail, but one worth the risk because of the richness of the reward" (J. Johnson 410).

29. For an overview of the 1850s crisis on the national level, see Berlin, ch. 11. Roussève describes the period from the standpoint of the *gens de couleur* (44–49). On the kidnapping of free people of color, see Schafer 115–28. One case that deserves further attention is the lawsuit that Jean Montaigne — better known as the famous New Orleans Vodou healer Doctor John, himself a native of what is now Senegal — filed in 1862 against Bertrand Saloy, claiming that Saloy had sold his daughter into slavery even though she had been emancipated in Ohio (see "A Voudou Doctor Claiming Damages," *Daily Picayune*, 21 Feb. 1874, p. 2).

30. The most voluminous manuscript source of Louisiana Spiritualist communications is the collection of séance registers in the René Grandjean Collection, housed at the Earl K. Long Library of the University of New Orleans. The registers record the activities of Rey's Cercle harmonique and are discussed in Daggett's 2017 study, *Spiritualism in Nineteenth-Century New Orleans*.

31. A translated excerpt of a poem in this introduction will not always match the complete translated poem as it appears in this volume. In this essay, where discussion centers on individual word choice and the literal meaning of a few extracted words, excerpts from the poems are occasionally translated word for word. In contrast, translations of complete poems in this anthology do not necessarily offer word-for-word equivalents of the French texts, but seek rather to create equivalent poems in English. Equivalency of a complete poem involves, in part, transposing French versification using the resources of meter and rhyme in English. For further explanation, see "Note on the Translation."

32. For a helpful overview of both newspapers' editorial stances, see Rouzan. For the publication details of the papers, see the accurate information collected by David C. Rankin in his introduction to Jean-Charles Houzeau's *My Passage at the New Orleans* Tribune, which ends some longstanding scholarly confusion (19–20).

33. The petition and memorial were reprinted in the *Liberator* (based in Boston) on 1 Apr. 1864. In reference to a message sent immediately by the president to Louisiana governor Michael Hahn, Eric Foner indicates that, though "[h]ardly a ringing endorsement, [. . .] Lincoln's letter nonetheless represented his first quasi-official statement on black voting" ("Rights" 868).

34. The biblical name Cham — rendered "Ham" in English — had racial connotations. The descendents of Noah's son Ham were believed to have populated Africa and to have suffered the so-called curse of Ham — interpreted by some as the origin of black skin and used to justify the institution of slavery. For details of Houzeau's life, see Rankin, "Introduction"; and Houzeau 69–78.

35. E.g.: *New York Herald*, 14 June 1867, p. 5, and 24 Nov. 1868, p. 7; *New York Times*, 2 Dec. 1867, p. 2, and 24 Nov. 1868, p. 1; Philadelphia *Evening Telegraph*, 7 Aug. 1866, 3rd ed., p. 1; *Philadelphia Inquirer*, 4 Dec. 1865, p. 4, and 21 Aug. 1866, p. 2; *Liberator*, 1 Sept. 1865, p. 3; *Chicago Tribune*, 31 Aug. 1866, p. 2, and 2 Sept. 1866, p. 1.

36. "Notice," *New Orleans Republican*, 8 July 1868; "Notice," *New Orleans Republican*, 18 Oct. 1870. Some scholars list 1871 as the year the paper ceased publishing, but the 18 Oct. 1870 notice reads, "The press and material of the New Orleans Tribune has been purchased by the Christian Republican Printing Association, and the first number of the 'Christian Republican' will be issued on *Thursday*, the twenty-second instant."

37. "Allégeance et confiscation," *L'Union*, 1 Oct. 1862. Native Guard militia under the Confederacy included the poets Adolphe Duhart, Armand Lanusse, Joanni Questy, and Henry Louis Rey.

38. "Negro Soldiers—The Question Settled and Its Consequences," *New York Times* 11 June 1863, p. 4. For an account of Cailloux's role and death during the siege of Port Hudson, see Ochs 137–52.

39. Poems about Cailloux included both heartfelt dirges and reactionary satires; see Ochs 155–63.
40. In New Orleans, an early issue of the *Black Republican* (a short-lived competitor to *La Tribune*) offered both a well-known translation of "La Marseillaise" — to be sung by "soldiers at Camp Walker [located just outside New Orleans, in Metairie] being desirous of learning the words" — and the home-penned "Song of the Black Republicans" (29 Apr. 1865).
41. The present-day address is 527 Conti Street, just around the corner from The Historic New Orleans Collection's Williams Research Center. In 2018 the location was marked with a historical plaque explaining the site's significance.
42. For further details on Rey's involvement in the political arena of the Reconstruction era, see Daggett, *Spiritualism* 78–94, 116–135.
43. USFCC, Population Schedules and Slave Schedules of the *Seventh Census of the United States* (1850), St. Bernard Parish.
44. Edward Larocque Tinker (who would have spoken in the early twentieth century with New Orleanians familiar with Macarty) does not explicitly address the Antony-Macarty equation but simply assumes it: he skips discussion of the pseudonym and directly attributes to Macarty the Antony poem "La fleur indiscrète" (22 July 1866; see Tinker, *Les Écrits* 294–95). This poem, as I explain in the preface to this volume, was long believed to be lost until I located the text in a folder at the American Antiquarian Society. The plagiarized source text is "La fleur de mars — Chanson" ("The Flower of March: Song"), by Henri Blaze, first published in 1835 in *La Revue des deux mondes*.
45. In analyzing "Combat de l'Aigle Républicain et du Copperhead," Horne notes that "Macarty derived the entire poem from Alexandre Soumet's *Jeanne d'Arc*, which had originally run as a play while he was studying in Paris" (511). This remark prompted me to investigate the origin of the other poems signed "Antony."
46. For an in-depth account of the events of summer 1866, see Hollandsworth, *Absolute*.
47. The full content of Sheridan's telegraph is given in his testimony in the *Report of the Select Committee on the New Orleans Riots* (Select Committee 351).
48. The testimony of Houzeau, who used the name Charles Dalloz in his work with the *Tribune*, is recorded under the name "Charles Dallas" (Select Committee 73–76). While there has been some scholarly confusion on the matter of names, McCrary (331n52) and others have persuasively argued that Houzeau and Dalloz/Dallas are one and the same.
49. See the preface to this volume, which is adapted from my article "Discovering the Lost 1866 Issues of the *New Orleans Tribune*," in the Winter 2018 issue of *64 Parishes*.
50. I have located the first part (2 Aug.) reprinted on 7 Aug. in a Northern newspaper, Philadelphia's *Evening Telegraph*, while the second installment, both in English and French ("Notes pour servir à l'histoire du massacre de la Nouvelle-Orléans") is featured in the 3 Aug. 1866 issue, in the holdings of the American Antiquarian Society.
51. Responding to traditionalist historiography shaped by strong biases against the Republican cause, Du Bois highlights in *Black Reconstruction in America*

the complicity of municipal authorities, a stance shared more recently by Foner (*Reconstruction*). Rather than a concerted plot per se, Reynolds blames an "explosion of blind rage" on "a fundamental inability of the whites to accept the emancipation of slaves and its revolutionary implications" (27). Vandal, a Canadian historian, expresses dissatisfaction with Reynolds's assessment and, analyzing the economic status and class origins of the rioters alongside the public discourse leading up to the massacre, blames the fear held by whites, including police, of losing their economic standing due to the rising fortunes of African Americans. According to Hollandsworth, the massacre resulted from "complex and interrelated" causes, namely "the postwar struggle for political control of the state government, the uncertain authority of the Union army of occupation, the deterioration of social restraint [. . .], the inconsistent and confusing intervention of federal authority from Washington, the persistent and aggressive efforts of many Louisianans to rehabilitate the doctrine of white supremacy, and the emergence of a vocal and well-organized protest movement made up primarily of black citizens" (*Absolute* 3). Likewise taking a circumspect approach, James K. Hogue believes that the recourse to violence was prepared by racially charged clashes on the battlefields of the Civil War, leading to "a much broader pattern of vigilante violence across racial lines" (51).

52. Daniels's poem appears on the English page of the *Tribune*, 30 July 1867, while Maistre's sermon is summarized in the 1 Aug. 1867 issue; the speeches by Waples and Smith are reprinted in the *New Orleans Republican*, 31 July and 1 Aug. 1867, respectively.

53. Taylor 151. For the debates surrounding the adoption of the 1868 constitution as well as its implications, see Taylor (146–55) and Tunnell (116–53).

54. *Constitution Adopted by the State Constitutional Convention of Louisiana, March 7, 1868* (New Orleans: The *Republican* Office, 1868).

55. In his classic work on colonial Saint Domingue, the white jurist M. L. E. Moreau de Saint-Méry catalogued 128 combinations of racial types, in nine groups; a number of those terms remained in use in Louisiana well into the nineteenth century. See Moreau de Saint-Méry 71–75.

56. For Horne, the "Macarty affair," involving an *homme de couleur* whose fair complexion showed no visible difference from that of a "white" man, "embodied the social and political turmoil of Reconstruction Louisiana" (497).

57. For an overview of relations between francophone Creoles of color and African Americans, see Logsdon and Bell.

58. The *races-places* rhyme has not been reproduced as "race" and "place" in the translation, because the French word *place* is not an exact match with the English word "place." The two are false cognates with some overlap in meaning. Here, *places* refers to stations in life and opportunities for betterment. The metaphor in the English version conveys the very American ideal of rising above one's previous condition.

59. Nemo, "Our Port Hudson Correspondence," *New York Times*, 13 June 1863, p. 1.

60. According to Daggett, Victor Lacroix's father, the real estate mogul François Lacroix, also a cofounder of the Institution catholique, attended séances of the Cercle harmonique in an attempt to make otherworldly contact with

his deceased son. Moreover, the elder Lacroix and Henry Louis Rey's father, Barthélemy, , had been longtime friends (*Spiritualism* 130–31).

61. See Fatima Shaik's *Economy Hall* for a detailed examination of how one of these organizations, the Société d'Économie et d'Assistance Mutuelle (Economy and Mutual Assistance Society), served to constantly reinforce familial, social, and economic bonds. Shaik demonstrates that from its founding in 1836, the society sought to enact such ideals as fraternity, unity, and charity within their community of free people of color. Drawing inspiration from the French and Haitian Revolutions, throughout the nineteenth century they pushed for liberté and égalité for themselves as well as for freedmen during the Civil War and Reconstruction.

62. *La Tribune*, 23 Dec. 1866. My translation of Lanusse's letter is reproduced in full in the biographical note on Joseph Mansion in this volume.

63. Besides Adolphe Duhart's pseudonym Lélia D——t, the only other woman's name listed as the author of a poem is Berthe D——, who is credited with writing "L'amour" ("Love"). The poet may indeed be a woman, but it is also possible that the poem was written by Duhart, who may have diverged from his usual practice of using his sister's name and assumed instead the name of his daughter, Berthe Duhart, who died before the age of three. Duhart's poem "Berthe!... Lucie!... Marie!...," about Berthe and her two very young sisters (all of whom died in 1864), was published in 1866, only a few weeks after the poem attributed to Berthe D——.

64. For details and documentary sources, see the biographical note for Lucien Mansion in this volume.

65. Haiti does feature prominently in short stories by Duhart and Questy. The relative scarcity of explicit references to Haiti in the poetry is curious (the poets, after all, would have been well aware that the cry of *Liberté, égalité, fraternité* was central to the Haitian Revolution) and invites further study.

66. On 26 Jan. 1868, *La Tribune* responded to insinuations of "Franco-African inferiority" by exclaiming, "Alex. Dumas! The great Dumas! [. . .] Why, he's another Franco-African, that one! [. . .] Has not the whole world devoured his works? Have not all the races — in paying them the honor of translation — more or less mutilated them, the Anglo-Saxons even more than the others?" ("Alex. Dumas! le grand Dumas! [. . .] c'est encore un franco-africain, celui-là! [. . .] [L]e monde entier n'a-t-il pas dévoré ses œuvres? Toutes les races — leur faisant l'honneur de la traduction — ne les ont-elles pas plus ou moins mutilées, les Anglo-Saxons plus que les autres?").

NOTE ON THE TRANSLATION

1. Qtd. in Honig 155. The idea of creating "with different means, analogous effects" is taken by Paz from the French poet Paul Valéry.

2. For successful examples of an alternative strategy of translating nineteenth-century Louisiana French poetry — namely, that of translating in stricter imitation of English-language poetry of the period — see Shapiro.

3. Boileau-Despréaux 173–74. A few years earlier, in 1668, the poet John Dryden

(1631–1700) had famously asserted in his "Essay of Dramatic Poesy," "Rhyme is incapable of expressing the greatest thoughts naturally, and the lowest it cannot with any grace: for what is more unbefitting the Majesty of Verse, than to call a Servant, or bid a door be shut in Rhyme" (198).

BIOGRAPHICAL NOTES ON KNOWN AUTHORS

1. United States, Bureau of the Census, *US Federal Census Collection* (hereafter abbreviated as USFCC), *Seventh Census of the United States* (1850), New Orleans, Municipality 3, Ward 1; R. Desdunes, *Our People* 21; Bell, *Revolution* 124–25.
2. USFCC, *Seventh Census of the United States* (1850), New Orleans, Municipality 3, Ward 1; R. Desdunes, *Our People* 68.
3. New Orleans Justices of the Peace; *Alphabetical Birth Indexes*; *Louisiana Vital Records*. A death notice for Louise Berthe Duhart, giving her parents' names, appears in *L'Abeille de la Nouvelle-Orléans*, 29 July 1864.
4. "Simple histoire" and "Trois amours" have been republished in Michaelides (81–85, 101–45).
5. For details on some of Duhart's performances at the Théâtre d'Orléans, see editions of *La Tribune* from 13 Feb. 1866 and 11 Apr. 1866.
6. *La Tribune*, 7 June 1866 (at the American Antiquarian Society). Desdunes and others give the play's title as *Lélia*. While it is possible that a different play entitled *Lélia* exists, and that Desdunes and others have misremembered which play was performed at the benefit, it is more likely that the title Lydia and the name Lélia have been confused. Though the reason for the benefit remains unclear, Duhart's father, Louis-Adolphe, is listed in city papers in July 1866 for unpaid taxes.
7. City directories consulted on microfilm at the Louisiana Room of the New Orleans Public Library. For Duhart's involvement in New Orleans's Committee of Fifty-One (formed in 1872 in an attempt to establish a reform political party), see Nystrom 119.
8. The names of other family members on the 1880 enumeration confirm Duhart's identity. By contrast, his brother Armand continued to be listed as black.
9. Lusher 159; *Donaldsonville Chief*, 18 Oct. 1879; *Official Journal* 458; Secretary of State 80; *Lafayette Gazette*, 27 Nov. 1897.
10. USFCC, *Thirteenth Census of the United States* (1910), St. James Parish, Louisiana, Police Jury Ward 2, District 53.
11. Genealogical information condensed from Haydel and Greenlee.
12. USFCC, Population Schedules and Slave Schedules of the *Seventh Census of the United States* (1850); and USFCC, *Eighth Census of the United States* (1860), Pointe Coupée Parish.
13. Vincent, *Black Legislators* 74, 82, 234; *New Orleans Republican*, 3 Dec. 1870 and 17 Mar. 1872; *New Orleans Daily Democrat*, 4 July 1878.
14. The 1880 census gives Honoré's occupation in Pointe Coupée as "laborer" and shows that the Honorés had taken a boarder (USFCC, *Tenth Census of the United States* [1880], Pointe Coupée, Ward 3). Information about his later occupation

and government compensation comes from USFCC, *Twelfth Census of the United States* (1900), Pointe Coupée, Ward 3; and United States, Congress 89–90.

15. Armand Lanusse's birth does not appear in Woods and Nolan's *Sacramental Records of the Roman Catholic Church of the Archdiocese of New Orleans*. For a glimpse of the genealogy of the Lanusse (also spelled Lanus) family from Saint Domingue, see Emily Clark 230. On Numa's indenture, see New Orleans Office of the Mayor, *Indentures 1809–1843*; Numa's death is described in R. Desdunes, *Our People* 50.

16. See Moore. Armand and Aglaé's marriage is recorded in the card index of *Orleans Parish Justices of the Peace Marriage Records, 1846–1880* (New Orleans Justices of the Peace). The death notice for Aglaé Robin de Logny, widow of Armand Lanusse, appears in the *Times-Picayune*, 28 Apr. 1895.

17. "Meeting of the Free Colored Population," in *Gazette and Sentinel* (Iberville Parish, LA), 27 Apr. 1861; R. Desdunes, *Our People* 22–23.

18. The proceedings of the Convention of Universal Suffrage list Lanusse as a delegate from the Seventh District (Republican Party of Louisiana, *Proceedings* 16–17). Lanusse's and Macarty's names are mentioned in notices regarding the Board of Police Commissioners in issues of the *Daily Picayune* from 1867 and 1868.

19. Long, part 1, p. 101. William Horne notes that "all three of Eugène Theodore's long-term mistresses were free women of color" and observes that the "most famous of the three, Eulalie Mandeville de Marigny, was perhaps more powerful than her lover and even helped finance his business ventures" (500).

20. *Alphabetical Birth Indexes*; USFCC, *Eighth Census of the United States* (1860), New Orleans, Ward 5; *Edward's* 271. For more on Mansion's siblings, see biographical note for Lucien Mansion.

21. *Alphabetical Birth Indexes*; USFCC, *Tenth Census of the United States* (1880), New Orleans.

22. Vincent, *Black Legislators in Louisiana during Reconstruction*, 83, 86; *Times-Democrat*, 22 July 1868; *Daily Picayune*, 20 Apr. 1870 and 16 July 1873.

23. USFCC, *Thirteenth Census of the United States* (1910), New Orleans, Ward 5.

24. Deposition of François Boisdoré (Succession Papers of Lucien Mansion, image 314). Curiously, the 1850 census indicates that Mansion's household included seventy-one-year-old Joseph Mansion, black, whom one would assume to be Lucien's father; further research may elucidate that relationship (USFCC).

25. *Alphabetical Birth Indexes*; Succession Papers of Lucien Mansion, image 639.

26. *Soards* 461; Roussève 46; quotation from Toledano 57.

27. Succession Papers of Lucien Mansion, image 314; R. Desdunes, *Our People* 65; *Louisiana Vital Records*.

28. USFCC, *Ninth Census of the United States* (1870), New Orleans, Ward 5; USFCC, *Tenth Census of the United States* (1880), New Orleans, Ward 6; Succession Papers of Lucien Mansion, image 639.

29. Last Will and Testament of Giovanni Questi; Affidavit of Citizenship for John Questiz. The tragic loss of Questy's brother occurred in a particularly distressing manner, according to the account in the press: in an episode of depression

brought on by financial hardship, Paul, "a well-known newspaper carrier," shot himself through the mouth in front of his wife ("The Last Suicide," *New Orleans Weekly Delta*, 29 July 1850).

30. Last Will and Testament of Joanny Questy; *Alphabetical Birth Indexes*; USFCC, *Ninth Census of the United States* (1870), New Orleans, Ward 5; *Louisiana Vital Records*.

31. Questy's obituary appeared in *La Tribune de la Nouvelle-Orléans* on 27 or 28 Aug. 1869. I thank Caryn Cossé Bell for sharing with me her copy of this clipping.

32. See United States, Record and Pension Office, *Compiled Service Records of Confederate Soldiers Who Served in Organizations from the State of Louisiana*, US National Archives and Records Administration, M320, roll 95.

33. "Joanni Questy," *Weekly Louisianian*, 4 Dec. 1875. Houzeau's memoir makes no mention of Questy.

34. Obituary for Joanni Questy, *La Tribune de la Nouvelle-Orléans*, 27 or 28 Aug. 1869, Charles B. Roussève Papers, Amistad Research Center, Tulane Univ.; Death notice for Joanni Questy, *L'Abeille de la Nouvelle-Orléans*, 27 Aug. 1869.

35. R. Desdunes, *Our People* 114. Biographical information comes from Woods and Nolan 18: 343; Daggett, *Henry Louis Rey* 13, 17; USFCC, Population Schedules and Slave Schedules, *Seventh Census of the United States* (1850), New Orleans, Municipality 3, Ward 1.

36. New Orleans Justices of the Peace; Daggett, *Henry Louis Rey* 19–21; *Gardner's* 372; *Alphabetical Birth Indexes*.

37. For a well-documented account of Rey's Spiritualist activities in biographical perspective, see Daggett, *Henry Louis Rey*. Emily Suzanne Clark's *A Luminous Brotherhood* offers contextualized analysis of the content of the Grandjean Spiritualist registers. For an ideological history of radical Spiritualism in New Orleans, see Bell, *Revolution*, esp. 215–20.

38. *The Planters' Banner*, 4 Apr. 1868; USFCC, Population Schedules of the *Seventh Census of the United States* (1850); New Orleans Justices of the Peace; *Le Meschacébé*, 5 July 1855; *Gardner's* 432; *L'Union*, 28 June 1864 and other issues.

39. Republican Party of Louisiana, *Proceedings* 10; *New Orleans Republican*, 7 Apr. 1868; *Le Courrier des Opelousas*, 12 Apr. 1873.

Bibliography

ARCHIVAL REPOSITORIES

American Antiquarian Society, Worcester, MA
Amistad Research Center, Tulane University, New Orleans, LA
Boston Athenaeum
The Historic New Orleans Collection
Louisiana and Special Collections Department, Earl K. Long Library, University of New Orleans
Louisiana Division / City Archives and Special Collections, New Orleans Public Library

ONLINE DATABASES AND DIGITAL REPOSITORIES

Ancestry, Ancestry.com
Chronicling America: Historic American Newspapers, Library of Congress, chroniclingamerica.loc.gov
FamilySearch, www.familysearch.org
Gallica, Bibliothèque nationale de France, gallica.bnf.fr
International Association for the Preservation of Spiritualist and Occult Periodicals, www.iapsop.com
Louisiana Digital Library, louisianadigitallibrary.org
Louisiana Vital Records Index, Louisiana Secretary of State, www.sos.la.gov/HistoricalResources/ResearchHistoricalRecords/Pages/OnlinePublicVitalRecordsIndex.aspx
Marcus Christian Collection, Louisiana and Special Collections Department, Earl K. Long Library, University of New Orleans (available at *Louisiana Digital Library*, louisianadigitallibrary.org/islandora/object/uno-p15140coll42:collection)
Newspapers.com by Ancestry, newspapers.com
Tulane Digital Library, Tulane University, digitallibrary.tulane.edu
US Federal Census Collection, United States Bureau of the Census, 1790–1940 (available at *Ancestry*, search.ancestry.com/search/group/usfedcen)
The USGenWeb Archives Project: Alphabetical Birth Indexes for Orleans Parish, 1796–1900, www.usgwarchives.net/la/orleans/birth-alpha.htm

NEWSPAPERS CONSULTED

L'Abeille de la Nouvelle-Orléans / New Orleans Bee (available at Jefferson Parish Library, Metairie, LA)
Black Republican, New Orleans, LA (available at *Newspapers.com by Ancestry*)
Chicago Tribune (available at *Chronicling America*)
Cleveland Daily Leader (available at *Newspapers.com by Ancestry*)
Le Courrier de la Louisiane / Louisiana Courier, New Orleans, LA (available at Louisiana State University, Baton Rouge, LA)

Le Courrier de Opelousas / Opelousas Courier, Opelousas, LA (available at *Chronicling America*)

Daily Picayune, New Orleans, LA (available at *Newspapers.com by Ancestry*)

Donaldsonville Chief, Donaldsonville, LA (available at *Chronicling America*)

Evening Telegraph, Philadelphia, PA (available at *Chronicling America*)

Gazette and Sentinel, Iberville Parish, LA (available at *Chronicling America*)

Lafayette Gazette (available at *Chronicling America*)

Liberator, Boston, MA (available at *Newspapers.com by Ancestry*)

Le Louisianais / The Louisianian, Convent, LA (available at *Chronicling America*)

Le Meschacébé, Bonnet Carré, LA (available at *Chronicling America*)

New Era, Washington, D.C. (available at *Newspapers.com by Ancestry*)

New Orleans Daily Democrat (available at *Newspapers.com by Ancestry*)

New Orleans Republican (available at *Chronicling America*)

New Orleans Weekly Delta (available at *Newspapers.com by Ancestry*)

New York Herald (available at *Chronicling America*)

New York Times (available at *Newspapers.com by Ancestry*)

Philadelphia Inquirer (available at *Newspapers.com by Ancestry*)

Planters' Banner, Franklin, LA (available at *Chronicling America*)

Le Spiritualiste de la Nouvelle-Orléans, New Orleans, LA (available at *International Association for the Preservation of Spiritualist and Occult Periodicals*)

Times, London, United Kingdom (available at *Newspapers.com by Ancestry*)

Times-Democrat, New Orleans, LA (available at *Chronicling America*)

Times-Picayune, New Orleans, LA (available at *Chronicling America*)

La Tribune de la Nouvelle-Orléans / New Orleans Tribune (available at New Orleans Public Library; American Antiquarian Society, Worcester, MA; Boston Athenaeum)

L'Union: mémorial politique, littéraire et progressiste / The Union: Political, Literary, and Progressive Record, New Orleans, LA (available at New Orleans Public Library)

L'Union: recueil commercial et littéraire, Port-au-Prince, Haiti (available at *Gallica*)

Weekly Louisianian, New Orleans, LA (available at *Chronicling America*)

WORKS CONSULTED

"About Us." *New Orleans Tribune,* 2017. www.theneworleanstribune.com/main/about-us/. Accessed 19 Dec. 2018.

"An Act Relative to Slaves and Free Colored Persons." *Acts Passed by the Second Legislature of the State of Louisiana, at Its Second Session, Held and Begun in the Town of Baton Rouge, on the 15th January, 1855.* New Orleans, Émile La Sère, 1855.

Acts Passed at the Second Session of the Ninth Legislature of the State of Louisiana. Donaldsonville, C. H. Duhy, 1830.

Affidavit of Citizenship for John Questiz. 29 Sept. 1807. *Proofs of Citizenship Used to Apply for Seamen's Protection Certificates for the Port of New Orleans, Louisiana, 1800, 1802, 1804–07, 1809–12, 1814–16, 1818–19, 1821, 1850–51, 1855–57,* National Archives and Records Administration, M1826, roll 3.

Ancestry, U.S., Citizenship Affidavits of US-born Seamen at Select Ports, 1792–1869, Louisiana Certificates, M1826, roll 3. Image 289.

Alphabetical Birth Indexes for Orleans Parish, 1796–1900. The USGenWeb Archives Project / Darnell Marie Brunner-Beck, 2008, www.usgwarchives.net/la/orleans/birth-alpha.htm.

Amelinckx, Frans C. Introduction. *Michel Séligny: homme libre de couleur de la Nouvelle-Orléans*, by Michel Séligny, PU Laval / Centre international d'études françaises, 1998, pp. 13–39.

Aslakson, Kenneth Randolph. *Making Race: The Role of Free Blacks in the Development of New Orleans' Three-Caste Society, 1791–1812*. 2007. U of Texas, Austin, PhD dissertation.

Bell, Caryn Cossé. "The Common Wind's Creole Visionary: Dr. Louis Charles Roudanez." *South Atlantic Review*, vol. 73, no. 2, Spring 2008, pp. 10–25.

———. Introduction. P. Desdunes, pp. 8–87.

———. *Revolution, Romanticism, and the Afro-Creole Protest Tradition in Louisiana, 1718–1868*. Louisiana State UP, 1997.

Béranger, Pierre-Jean de. *Œuvres complètes de Béranger*. Vol. 3, Paris, H. Fournier aîné, 1839.

Berlin, Ira. *Slaves without Masters: The Free Negro in the Antebellum South*. Pantheon Books, 1974.

Berry, Mary F. "Negro Troops in Blue and Gray: The Louisiana Native Guards, 1861–1863." *Louisiana History*, vol. 8, no. 2, Spring 1967, pp. 165–90.

Blassingame, John W. *Black New Orleans, 1860–1880*. U of Chicago P, 1973.

Blaze, Henri. "Le cygne — À M. Sainte-Beuve." *Revue de Paris*, vol. 28, 1841, pp. 290–91. *Gallica*, gallica.bnf.fr/ark:/12148/bpt6k5805050c/f1.item.r.

———. "La fleur de mars — Chanson." *La Revue des deux mondes*, 4th series, vol. 4, 1 Oct. 1835, pp. 766–67.

Boileau-Despréaux, Nicolas. *Art poétique*. 1674. *Œuvres poétiques de Boileau Despréaux*, edited by N. A. Dubois, Paris, Jules Delalain et fils, 1875.

Brickhouse, Anna. "'L'Ouragan de Flammes' ('The Hurricane of Flames'): New Orleans and Transamerican Catastrophe, 1866/2005." *American Quarterly*, vol. 59, no. 4, Dec. 2007, pp. 1097–127.

Brosman, Catharine Savage. *Louisiana Creole Literature: A Historical Study*. U of Mississippi P, 2013.

Brown, James. Letter to Henry Clay. 26 Feb. 1810. Hopkins, pp. 452–55.

Bruce, Clint. "Caught between Continents: The Local and the Transatlantic in the French-Language Serial Fiction of New Orleans's *Le Courrier de la Louisiane*, 1843–1845." *Transnationalism and American Serial Fiction*, edited by Patricia Okker, Routledge, 2012, pp. 12–35.

———. "Discovering the Lost 1866 Issues of the *New Orleans Tribune*." *64 Parishes*, Winter 2018, p. 64.

Burgess, George. *Last Journal of the Rt. Rev. George Burgess, D.D., Bishop of Maine, from December 27, 1865, to April 20, 1866*. Introduced by Alfred Lee, Boston, E. P. Dutton, 1866. *Project Canturbury*, anglicanhistory.org/usa/gburgess/journal1866.html.

Cable, George Washington. *Old Creole Days*. New York, Scribner, 1879.

Casanova, Pascale. *Le République mondiale des lettres.* Éditions du Seuil, 1999.

Céré-Barbé, Hortense. "L'existence de Dieu." *La France littéraire*, vol. 2, 1832, pp. 646–47. *Gallica,* gallica.bnf.fr/ark:/12148/bpt6k5747304n?rk=64378;0.

Chaumette, J. *Les droits de l'homme....* New Orleans, 1865. American Antiquarian Society, call no. G850 C497 D865.

Christian, Marcus. "Negro Education." *The Negro in Louisiana*, by Marcus Christian and Dillard Unit of Louisiana Writers' Project, 1942, ch. 20. *Marcus Christian Collection*, U of New Orleans Library, 2011. *Louisiana Digital Library*, louisianadigitallibrary.org/islandora/object/uno-p15140coll42%3A49.

Clark, Emily. *The Strange History of the American Quadroon: Free Women of Color in the Revolutionary Atlantic World.* U of North Carolina P, 2015.

Clark, Emily Suzanne. *A Luminous Brotherhood: Afro-Creole Spiritualism in Nineteenth-Century New Orleans.* U of North Carolina P, 2016.

Le Code noir, ou Édit du Roy, servant de règlement pour le gouvernement et l'administration de la justice, police, discipline et le commerce des esclaves nègres dans la province et colonie de la Louisianne. Paris, Imprimerie royale, 1727. *Gallica,* notice no. FRBNF33836228, gallica.bnf.fr/ark:/12148/btv1b86086055?rk=21459;2.

Connor, William P. "Reconstruction Rebels: *The New Orleans Tribune* in Post-War Louisiana." *Louisiana History*, vol. 21, no. 2, Spring 1980, pp. 159–81.

Conrad, Glenn R., editor. *A Dictionary of Louisiana Biography.* Louisiana Historical Association, 1988. 2 vols.

Constitution Adopted by the State Constitutional Convention of Louisiana, March 7, 1868. New Orleans, The *Republican* Office, 1868.

Cowan, James Lorenz. *La Marseillaise noire et autres poèmes français des Créoles de couleur de la Nouvelle-Orléans (1862–1869).* Éditions du Cosmogone, 2001.

Daggett, Melissa. *Henry Louis Rey, Spiritualism, and Creoles of Color in Nineteenth-Century New Orleans.* 2009. U of New Orleans, MA thesis.

———. *Spiritualism in Nineteenth-Century New Orleans: The Life and Times of Henry Louis Rey.* UP of Mississippi, 2017.

Derrida, Jacques. *Positions.* Translated by Alain Bass, U of Chicago P, 1981.

Desdunes, Pierre-Aristide. *Rappelez-vous concitoyens! La poésie de Pierre-Aristide Desdunes.* Introduced and annotated by Caryn Cossé Bell, Éditions Tintamarre, 2010.

Desdunes, Rodolphe Lucien. *Nos hommes et notre histoire. Notices biographiques accompagnées de réflexions et de souvenirs personnels.* Arbour and Dupont, 1911.

———. *Our People and Our History: Fifty Creole Portraits.* 1911. Translated and edited by Dorothea Olga McCants, Louisiana State UP, 1973.

Dessens, Nathalie. *From Saint-Domingue to New Orleans: Migration and Influences.* UP of Florida, 2007.

Domínguez, Virginia R. *White by Definition: Social Classification in Creole Louisiana.* Rutgers UP, 1986.

Dormon, James H., editor. *Creoles of Color of the Gulf South.* U of Tennessee P, 1996.

Dryden, John. "An Essay of Dramatic Poesy." 1668. *Classic Writings on Poetry*, edited by William Harmon, Columbia UP, 2003, pp. 159–206.

Dubois, Laurent. "The Haitian Revolution and the Sale of Louisiana; or, Thomas Jefferson's (Unpaid) Debt to Jean-Jacques Dessalines." *Empires of the Imagination: Transatlantic Histories of the Louisiana Purchase*, edited by Peter J. Kastor and François Weil, U of Virginia P, 2009, pp. 93–116.

Du Bois, W. E. B. *Black Reconstruction in America, 1860–1880*. 1935. Introduction by David Levering Lewis, Free Press, 1998.

Dumas, Alexandre. *L'Alchimiste: drame en cinq actes, en vers*. Paris, Dumont, 1839.

Duplantier, Jean-Marc Allard. *"Nos frères d'outre-golfe": Spiritualism, Vodou and the Mimetic Literatures of Haiti and Louisiana*. 2006. Louisiana State U, PhD dissertation.

Edward's New Orleans Directory, vol. 17, 1872. New Orleans, Southern Publishing, 1872.

Everett, Donald E. "Emigres and Militiamen: Free Persons of Color in New Orleans, 1803–1815." *The Journal of Negro History*, vol. 38, no. 4, Oct. 1953, pp. 377–402.

Fabre, Michel. "New Orleans Creole Expatriates in France: Romance and Reality." Kein, *Creole*, pp. 179–95.

———. "The New Orleans Press and French-Language Literature by Creoles of Color." *Multilingual America: Transnationalism, Ethnicity, and the Languages of American Literature*, edited by Werner Sollors, New York UP, 1998, pp. 29–49.

Fanon, Frantz. *Peau noire, masques blancs*. Seuil, 1952.

Foner, Eric. *Reconstruction: America's Unfinished Revolution, 1863–1877*. Harper and Row, 1988.

———. "Rights and the Constitution in Black Life during the Civil War and Reconstruction." *The Journal of American History*, vol. 74, no. 3, Dec. 1987, pp. 863–83.

Gardner's New Orleans City Directory for 1861. New Orleans, Charles Gardner, 1861.

Gates, Henry Louis, Jr. *Loose Canons: Notes on the Culture Wars*. Oxford UP, 1993.

Gaudin, Wendy Ann. *Autocrats and All Saints: Migration, Memory, and Modern Creole Identities*. 2005. New York U, PhD dissertation.

Gehman, Mary. "The Mexico-Louisiana Creole Connection." *Louisiana Cultural Vistas*, vol. 11, no. 4, Winter 2001–02, pp. 68–75.

Gruesz, Kirsten Silva. *Ambassadors of Culture: The Transamerican Origins of Latino Writing*. Princeton UP, 2002.

Guillemin, Henri. *Le Jocelyn de Lamartine: étude historique et critique avec des documents inédits*. Slatkine Reprints, 1967.

Hall, Gwendolyn Midlo. *Africans in Colonial Louisiana: The Development of Afro-Creole Culture in the Eighteenth Century*. Louisiana State UP, 1995.

———. "The Formation of Afro-Creole Culture." Hirsch and Logsdon, pp. 58–87.

Hanger, Kimberly S. *Bounded Lives, Bounded Places: Free Black Society in Colonial New Orleans, 1769–1803*. Duke UP, 1997.

———. "Origins of New Orleans Free Creoles of Color." Dormon, pp. 3–27.

Hankins, Laurel. "What the Folk Printed: Verse Culture and the Black Press in 1865 New Orleans." *African American Review*, vol. 45, no. 4, Winter 2012, pp. 527–40.

Haydel, Belmont F., and Gina C. Greenlee. "Who Are the Louisiana Honorés? A Synthesis of Mixed-Race Relations." *New Orleans Genesis*, vol. 51, no. 201, Jan. 2013, pp. 1–15.

Hearn, Chester G. *The Capture of New Orleans, 1862*. Louisiana State UP, 1995.

Hirsch, Arnold R., and Joseph Logsdon, editors. *Creole New Orleans: Race and Americanization*. Louisiana State UP, 1992.

Hogue, James K. *Uncivil War: Five New Orleans Street Battles and the Rise and Fall of Reconstruction*. Louisiana State UP, 2006.

Hogue, W. Lawrence. "Radical Democracy, African American (Male) Subjectivity, and John Edgar Wideman's 'Philadelphia Fire.'" *MELUS*, vol. 33, no. 3, Fall 2008, pp. 45–69.

Hollandsworth, James G., Jr. *An Absolute Massacre: The New Orleans Race Riot of July 30, 1866*. Louisiana State UP, 2001.

———. *The Louisiana Native Guards: The Black Military Experience during the Civil War*. Louisiana State UP, 1995.

The Holy Bible, New International Version. Biblica, 2011. *BibleGateway*, www.biblegateway.com/versions/New-International-Version-NIV-Bible/.

Honig, Edwin. *The Poet's Other Voice: Conversations on Literary Translation*. U of Massachusetts P, 1985.

Hopkins, James F., editor. *The Papers of Henry Clay. Vol. 1: The Rising Statesman*. U of Kentucky P, 1959.

Horne, William I. "Victor Eugène Macarty: From Art to Activism in Reconstruction-Era New Orleans." *The Journal of African American History*, vol. 103, no. 4, Fall 2018, pp. 496–525.

Houzeau, Jean-Charles. *My Passage at the New Orleans* Tribune: *A Memoir of the Civil War Era*. Edited by David C. Rankin, translated by Gérard Denault, Louisiana State UP, 1984.

Hunt, Alfred. *Haiti's Influence on Antebellum America: Slumbering Volcano in the Caribbean*. Louisiana State UP, 1988.

Janvier, Louis-Joseph. *Les Constitutions d'Haïti (1801–1885)*. Paris, C. Marpon and E. Flammarion, 1886.

Johnson, Jerah. "*Les Cenelles*: What's in a Name?" *Louisiana History*, vol. 31, no. 4, Winter 1990, pp. 407–10.

Johnson, Sara E. *The Fear of French Negroes: Transcolonial Collaboration in the Revolutionary Americas*. U of California P, 2012.

Kadish, Doris Y., and Deborah Jenson. Introduction. *Poetry of Haitian Independence*, edited by Kadish and Jenson, translations by Norman R. Shapiro, foreword by Edwidge Danticat, Yale UP, 2015, pp. xxi–xliii.

Kein, Sybil, editor. *Creole: The History and Legacy of Louisiana's Free People of Color*. Louisiana State UP, 2000.

———. Introduction. Kein, *Creole*, pp. xiii–xxiv.

Kelley, William D. *Remarks of [H]on. William D. Kelley, of Pennsylvania, in Support of His Proposed Amendment to the Bill "Guaranty to Certain States Whose Governments Have Been Usurped or Overthrown a Republican Form of Government."* Washington, DC, 1865. *HathiTrust*, babel.hathitrust.org/cgi/pt?id=miun.adh0299.0001.001.

King, Grace. *New Orleans: The Place and the People*. Macmillan, 1917.

Klingler, Thomas A. *If I Could Turn My Tongue Like That: The Creole Language of Pointe Coupée Parish, Louisiana*. Louisiana State UP, 2003.

Lachance, Paul. "The 1809 Immigration of Saint-Domingue Refugees to New Orleans: Reception, Integration and Impact." *The Road to Louisiana: The Saint-Domingue Refugees, 1792–1809*, edited by Carl Brasseaux and Glenn R. Conrad, Center for Louisiana Studies, 1992, pp. 245–84.

———. "The Limits of Privilege: Where Free Persons of Color Stood in the Hierarchy of Wealth in Antebellum New Orleans." Vincent, *African American*, pp. 428–46.

Lamartine, Alphonse de. *Des destinées de la poésie*. Paris, C. Gosselin / Furne, 1834.

Lanusse, Armand, editor. *Les Cenelles: choix de poésies indigènes*. 1845. Text established by Mia D. Reamer, Éditions Tintamarre, 2003.

———. "Épigramme." Lanusse, *Les Cenelles*, p. 21.

———. "Un mariage de conscience." Michaelides, pp. 75–80.

———. Preface. Lanusse, *Les Cenelles*, pp. 13–15.

Last Will and Testament of Giovanni Questi. July 1833. *Ancestry*, Louisiana, Wills and Probate Records, 1756–1894, Iberville Parish, Wills, 1818–1927, no. 32, image 61.

Last Will and Testament of Joanny Questy. Filed 31 Aug. 1869. *Ancestry*, Louisiana, Wills and Probate Records, 1756–1984, Orleans Parish, Will Book, vol. 15, 1867–71, pp. 318–19, images 367–68.

Leavens, Finnian Patrick. L'Union *and the* New Orleans Tribune *and Louisiana Reconstruction*. 1966. Louisiana State U, MA thesis.

Lefevere, André. *Translating Poetry: Seven Strategies and a Blueprint*. Van Gorcum, 1975.

Logsdon, Joseph, and Caryn Cossé Bell. "The Americanization of Black New Orleans." Hirsch and Logsdon, pp. 201–61.

Long, Carolyn Morrow. "The Macarty Family in Orleans Parish" (Parts 1 and 2). *New Orleans Genesis*, issue 202, Apr. 2013, pp. 101–18; issue 203, July 2013, pp. 201–13.

Louisiana Naturalization Records, 1831–1906. National Archives and Records Division, Southwest Region. *FamilySearch*, www.familysearch.org.

Louisiana Vital Records Index. Louisiana Department of State, 2018, www.sos.la.gov/HistoricalResources/ResearchHistoricalRecords/Pages/OnlinePublicVitalRecordsIndex.aspx.

Lusher, Robert M. *Annual Report of the State Superintendent of Public Education, Robert M. Lusher, to the General Assembly of Louisiana, for the Year 1877*. New Orleans, Office of the *Democrat*, 1878.

Macarty, Victor Eugène, composer and publisher. *Fleurs de Salon: Two Favorite Polkas*. 1854. *Tulane University Digital Library*, digitallibrary.tulane.edu/islandora/object/tulane%3A18751.

Majors, Monroe A. *Noted Negro Women: Their Triumphs and Activities*. Donohue and Henneberry, [1893]. *HathiTrust*, babel.hathitrust.org/cgi/pt?id=emu.10002350120&view=1up&seq=1.

Marshall, Bill. *The French Atlantic: Travels in Culture and History*. Liverpool UP, 2009.

McConnell, Roland C. "In the Battle of New Orleans." Vincent, *African American*, pp. 312–27.

McCrary, Peyton. *Abraham Lincoln and Reconstruction: The Louisiana Experiment*. Princeton UP, 1978.

Melançon, Kristi Richard. *An African American Discourse Community in Black and White: The* New Orleans Tribune. 2011. Louisiana State U, PhD dissertation.

Michaelides, Chris, editor. *Paroles d'honneur: écrits de créoles de couleur néo-orléanais*. Éditions Tintamarre, 2004.

Mitchell, Mary Niall. *Raising Freedom's Child: Black Children and Visions of the Future after Slavery*. New York UP, 2008.

Moore, David W. "Armand Lanusse." Conrad, vol. 1, p. 483.

Moreau de Saint-Méry, M. L. E. *Description topographique, physique, civile, politique et historique de la partie française de l'isle Saint-Domingue*. Vol. 1, Philadelphia, M. L. E. Moreau de Saint-Méry / Paris, Dupont, 1797. *Gallica*, gallica.bnf.fr/ark:/12148/bpt6k111179t?rk=21459;2.

Neidenbach, Elizabeth C. "'Mes dernières volontés': Testaments to the Life of Marie Couvent, a Former Slave in New Orleans." *Transatlantica*, no. 2, 2012, transatlantica.revues.org/6186.

Nero, Charles. *"To Develop Our Manhood": Free Black Leadership and the Rhetoric of the* New Orleans Tribune. 1991. Indiana U, PhD dissertation.

New Orleans Justices of the Peace. *Orleans Parish Justices of the Peace Marriage Records, 1846–1880*. Louisiana Division / City Archives, New Orleans Public Lib.

New Orleans Office of the Mayor. "Indenture of Numa Lanusse with Jean Rousseau, sponsored by Euphrosine Wilz," *Indentures 1809–1843*, vol. 3, no. 302, 18 Sept. 1822. Louisiana Division / City Archives, New Orleans Public Lib.

Noirot, Adolphe. "Correspondance — Lettre de M. le rédacteur en chef de la *Tribune de la Nouvelle-Orléans*, à M. Melvil-Bloncourt." *Revue du monde colonial, asiatique et américain*, vol. 13, Oct. 1864, pp. 486–87.

Nystrom, Justin A. *New Orleans after the Civil War: Race, Politics, and a New Birth of Freedom*. John Hopkins UP, 2010.

O'Brien, Neil L. *The* New Orleans Tribune *and the Genesis of Black Unity in Occupied Louisiana*. 1984. Florida State U, MA thesis.

Ochs, Stephen J. *A Black Patriot and a White Priest: André Cailloux and Claude Paschal Maistre in Civil War New Orleans*. Louisiana State UP, 2000.

Official Journal of the Senate of the State of Louisiana at the Regular Session Begun and Held in the City of Baton Rouge, May 14th, 1888. Baton Rouge, Leon Jastremski, 1888.

Parham, Angel Adams. *American Routes: Racial Palimpsests and the Transformation of Race*. Oxford UP, 2017.

Pommier, Amédée. "Les trois perles — Élégie." *Recueil de l'Académie des Jeux Floraux*, Toulouse, Imprimerie de Jean-Matthieu Douladoure, 1832, pp. 248–50.

Questy, Joanni. "Monsieur Paul." *New Orleans Tribune / La Tribune de la Nouvelle-Orléans*, 25 Oct. –3 Nov. 1867. Michaelides, pp. 167–68.

Raffel, Burton. *The Art of Translating Poetry*. Pennsylvania State UP, 1988.

Rankin, David C. "Introduction." Houzeau, pp. 1–67.

———. "The Origins of Black Leadership in New Orleans during Reconstruction." *The Journal of Southern History*, vol. 40, no. 3, 1974, pp. 417–40.

Reed, Emily Hazen. *Life of A. P. Dostie; or, the Conflict in New Orleans*. New York, W. P. Tomlinson, 1868.

Reilly, Timothy F. "*Le Libérateur*, New Orleans' Free Negro Newspaper." *Gulf Coast Historical Review*, vol. 2, no. 1, Fall 1986, pp. 5–24.

Republican Party of Louisiana. *Official Report of the Proceedings, Addresses and Resolutions of the Republican State Convention of Louisiana, Held in Turner Hall, New Orleans, August 9 and 10, 1871*. New Orleans, Office of the Republican, 1871.

———. *Proceedings of the Convention of the Republican Party of Louisiana Held at Economy Hall, New Orleans, September 25, 1865, and of the Central Executive Committee of the Friends of Universal Suffrage of Louisiana, Now the Central Executive Committee of the Republican Party of Louisiana*. New Orleans, *New Orleans Tribune* Office, 1865.

Rey, Henr[y] Louis. "Communications spiritualistes." Michaelides, pp. 189–210.

Reynolds, Donald E. "The New Orleans Riot of 1866, Reconsidered." *Louisiana History*, vol. 5, no. 1, Winter 1964, pp. 5–27.

Roach, Joseph R. *Cities of the Dead: Circum-Atlantic Performance*. Columbia UP, 1996.

Roudané, Mark Charles. "Discovering Dr. Louis Charles Roudanez." *South Atlantic Review*, vol. 73, no. 2, Spring 2008, pp. 7–9.

Roussève, Charles Barthelemy. *The Negro in Louisiana: Aspects of His History and His Literature*. Xavier UP, 1937.

Rouzan, Laura. "The Genesis of the Black Press in New Orleans: *L'Union* and the *New Orleans Tribune*." *Gumbo People*, rev. ed., edited by Sybil Kein, Margaret Media, 1999, pp. 135–73.

Schafer, Judith Kelleher. *Becoming Free, Remaining Free: Manumission and Enslavement in New Orleans, 1846–1862*. Louisiana State UP, 2003.

Secretary of State. *Report of the United States Commissioners to the Universal Exposition of 1889 at Paris*. Washington, D. C., Government Printing Office, 1890.

Select Committee on the New Orleans Riots. *Report of the Select Committee on the New Orleans Riots.* Washington, D.C., Government Printing Office, 1867. *HathiTrust*, babel.hathitrust.org/cgi/pt?id=loc.ark:/13960/t3320cwof&view=1up&seq=150.

Senter, Caroline. "Creole Poets on the Verge of a Nation." Kein, *Creole*, pp. 276–94.

Shaik, Fatima. *Economy Hall*. The Historic New Orleans Collection, forthcoming.

Shapiro, Norman R., translator. *Creole Echoes: The Francophone Poetry of Nineteenth-Century Louisiana*. Introduction and notes by M. Lynn Weiss, U of Illinois P, 2004.

Smith, Jesse Carney, editor. *Notable Black American Women, Book 2.* Gale Research, 1996.

Soards' New Orleans Directory, Vol. 6. New Orleans, L. Soards, 1879.

Soumet, Alexandre. *Jeanne d'Arc: trilogie nationale.* Paris, Didot Firmin Frères, 1846.

Sterkx, H. E. *The Free Negro in Antebellum Louisiana.* Fairleigh Dickinson UP, 1972.

Succession Papers of Lucien Mansion. Filed 17 Dec. 1894. *Ancestry,* Louisiana, Wills and Probate Records, 1756–1984, Orleans Parish Civil District Court, 1893–95, Case Papers nos. 44539–750, images 299–317, no. 44598, images 639–40.

Swift Riginos, Alice. "The Wounding of Philip II of Macedon: Fact and Fabrication." *The Journal of Hellenic Studies,* vol. 114, 1994, pp. 103–19.

Taylor, Joe Gray. *Louisiana Reconstructed, 1863–1877.* Louisiana State UP, 1974.

Thompson, Shirley Elizabeth. *Exiles at Home: The Struggle to Become American in Creole New Orleans.* Harvard UP, 2009.

Tinker, Edward Larocque. *Creole City: Its Past and Its People.* Longmans, Green, 1953.

———. *Les Écrits de langue française en Louisiane au XIXe siècle: essais biographiques et bibliographiques.* Honoré Champion, 1932.

Toledano, Roulhac. *The National Trust Guide to New Orleans.* Preservation Press / John Wiley and Sons, 1996.

Trotter, James M. *Music and Some Highly Musical People.* Boston, Lee and Shepard / New York, Charles T. Dillingham, 1880.

Trouillot, Michel-Rolph. *Haiti, State against Nation: The Origins and Legacy of Duvalierism.* Monthly Review Press, 1990.

Tunnell, Ted. *Crucible of Reconstruction: War, Radicalism, and Race in Louisiana, 1862–1877.* Louisiana State UP, 1984.

United States, Bureau of the Census. *US Federal Census Collection.* 1790–1940. Ancestry.com Operations, 2004–18, search.ancestry.com/search/group/usfedcen.

———, Congress, Senate Committee on Claims. *Allowance of Certain Claims Reported by Court of Claims under Bowman and Tucker Acts, to Accompany House Report 15372.* Government Printing Office, 1908. 60th Congress, 1st session. House Report 382. *Internet Archive,* archive.org/details/allowancesofcert00unit/page/n1.

———, Record and Pension Office. *Compiled Service Records of Confederate Soldiers Who Served in Organizations from the State of Louisiana.* United States National Archives and Records Administration, M320. *Ancestry,* www.ancestry.com/search/collections/confederatesoldiersindexescsrs/.

Vandal, Gilles C. *The New Orleans Riot of 1866: Anatomy of a Tragedy.* Center for Louisiana Studies, 1983.

Venuti, Lawrence. *Translation Changes Everything: Theory and Practice.* Routledge, 2013.

Viatte, Auguste. *Histoire littéraire de l'Amérique française des origines à 1950.* PU Laval, 1954.

Vincent, Charles, editor. *The African American Experience in Louisiana, Part A: From Africa to the Civil War.* Center for Louisiana Studies, 1999. Louisiana Purchase Bicentennial Series in Louisiana History 11.

———. *Black Legislators in Louisiana during Reconstruction.* Rev. ed., Southern Illinois UP, 2011.

Warmoth, Henry Clay. *War, Politics, and Reconstruction: Stormy Days in Louisiana.* Macmillan, 1930.

Wesling, Donald. *The Chances of Rhyme.* U of California P, 1980.

Williams, George Washington. *History of the Negro Race in America from 1619 to 1880.* Vol. 2, G. P. Putnam's Sons, 1883. *Project Gutenberg,* www.gutenberg.org/files/21851/21851-h/21851-h.htm.

Wilson, Joseph Thomas. *The Black Phalanx: A History of the Negro Soldiers of the United States in the Wars of 1775–1812, 1861–65.* Hartford, American Publishing, 1890.

Wolfson, Susan J., editor. *Felicia Hemans: Selected Poems, Letters, Reception Materials.* By Felicia Hemans, Princeton UP, 2000.

Woods, Earl C., and Charles E. Nolan. *Sacramental Records of the Roman Catholic Church of the Archdiocese of New Orleans.* Archdiocese of New Orleans, 1987–2003. 19 vols.

Lists of Poems by Title

POEMS ALPHABETIZED BY FRENCH TITLE

! / !   *Adolphe Duhart*   168
Le 13 avril / The 13th of April   *Adolphe Duhart*   124
Amaritudo / Amaritudo   *Adolphe Duhart*   258
L'amour / Love   *Adolphe Duhart [possible]*   268
Ange du ciel / Angel from Heaven   *Adolphe Duhart*   262
L'ange en exil / The Angel in Exile   *Adolphe Duhart*   286
L'astre s'est levé ! / The Star Has Risen!   *Armand Lanusse*   100
À Théodule Delassize / For Théodule Delassize
   "Antony" [Victor Eugène Macarty, copying text by Henri Blaze]   202
À toi / To You   *"Aster"*   104
Au cimetière / At the Cemetery   *Adolphe Duhart*   274
À une enfant / For a Child   *Adolphe Duhart*   250
Au Père Chocarne / To Father Chocarne   *"Pierre (l'Hermite)"*   164
Aux conservateurs / To the Conservatives   *Joanni Questy*   134
L'avenir / The Future   *Lucien Mansion*   218
Berthe !... Lucie !... Marie !... / Berthe! . . . Lucie! . . . Marie! . . .
   Adolphe Duhart   270
Le capitaine André Caillou et ses compagnons d'armes / Captain André
   Caillou and His Comrades-in-Arms   *Émile Honoré*   116
Le chien et le chat / The Dog and the Cat   *Adolphe Duhart*   148
Combat de l'Aigle Républicain et du Copperhead / The Clash of the
   Republican Eagle and the Copperhead   *"A." [Victor Eugène Macarty,*
   copying text by Alexandre Soumet]   132
Communication d'outre-tombe / Message from beyond the Grave   *"J. B."*   152
La couronne d'amour / The Crown of Love   *Lucien Mansion*   290
Un cri de l'alcyon / The Halcyon's Cry   *Adolphe Duhart*   160
Une dépêche télégraphique / A Telegraphic Dispatch   *Joanni Questy*   290
Des baisers / On Kisses   *Adolphe Duhart*   236
Deux novembre / The Second of November   *Adolphe Duhart*   214
Dors ! / Sleep!   *Joanni Questy*   292
Le droit de suffrage des noirs / Blacks' Right to Vote   *Émile Honoré*   158
L'échelle de l'amour / The Ladder of Love   *Adolphe Duhart*   242
Épître familière / A Familiar Epistle   *Henry Louis Rey*   186
Espérance / Hope   *Adolphe Duhart*   102
Étoile du soir / Evening Star   *Adolphe Duhart*   246
Étrange coïncidence / A Strange Coincidence   *Armand Lanusse [probable]*   146
Fiat Lux ! / Fiat Lux!   *Adolphe Duhart*   98
La fleur blessée / The Wounded Flower   *Adolphe Duhart*   252
La fleur et le papillon / The Flower and the Butterfly   *Ernest de la Valette*   200
La fleur indiscrète / The Indiscreet Flower
   "Antony" [Victor Eugène Macarty, copying text by Henri Blaze]   266
La guerre et l'avenir / The War and the Future   *"L. de P."*   110
Guzla / Gusle [1865]   *Adolphe Duhart*   244

Guzla / Gusle [1866] *Adolphe Duhart* 254

Hommage au poète / Homage to the Poet *Henry Louis Rey* 90

Hommage au sexe / Homage to the Fairer Sex *Lucien Mansion* 228

Idéalisme. — Matérialisme. / Idealism. — Materialism. *Adolphe Duhart* 288

L'Ignorance / Ignorance [1862] *Henry Louis Rey* 176

L'Ignorance / Ignorance [1865] *Henry Louis Rey* 180

Il est / He Is *"Antony" [Victor Eugène Macarty, copying text by Hortense de Céré-Barbé]* 194

Il n'est pas / He Is Not *Armand Lanusse* 196

Le Jasmin / Jasmine *Adolphe Duhart* 256

Lettre à Nath / Letter to Nath *Joanni Questy* 220

Maris Stella / Maris Stella *Adolphe Duhart* 178

La Marseillaise noire : chant de paix / The Black Marseillaise: Song of Peace
   "Camille Naudin" 166

Méditations / Meditations *Joseph Mansion* 280

Le moqueur / The Mockingbird *Adolphe Duhart* 180

Ode aux martyrs / Ode to the Martyrs *"Camille Naudin"* 136

Une page de Hebel / A Page from Hebel *Adolphe Duhart* 192

Pensée / Pansy *Adolphe Duhart* 240

La poésie / Poetry *Joseph Mansion* 94

Poésie ! Vox Dei ! / Poetry! Vox Dei! *Adolphe Duhart* 96

Le poète / The Poet *Adolphe Duhart* 84

Pot-pourri / Potpourri *Jean-Sylvain Gentil* 140

Pour les incendiés de Saint-Domingue / For the Victims
   of the Saint Domingue Fire *Adolphe Duhart* 154

La rébellion du Sud en permanence / The South's Unending Rebellion
   Henry Louis Rey 128

Résignation / Resignation *Henry Louis Rey* 184

Rêve / Dream *Adolphe Duhart* 248

S… à L… / S—— to L—— *"Sténio"* 296

Le saule pleureur / The Weeping Willow *Adolphe Duhart* 188

La sensitive / The Sensitive Plant *Lucien Mansion* 284

Sonnet / Sonnet [1865] *Adolphe Duhart* 242

Sonnet / Sonnet [1867] *"Pierre (l'Hermite)"* 210

Souvenir / A Memory *Adolphe Duhart* 264

Le souvenir des morts / Remembrance of the Dead *"Camille Naudin"* 212

Stanza [À M. A. P…] / Stanza [For Mr. A. P——] *Adolphe Duhart* 82

Stanza [À M. Th. J. Durant] / Stanza [For Mr. Th. J. Durant] *Adolphe Duhart* 150

Le triomphe des opprimés / The Triumph of the Oppressed *Anonymous* 146

Tristesse / Sadness *Adolphe Duhart* 206

Les trois perles / The Three Pearls
   "Antony" [Victor Eugène Macarty, copying text by Amédée Pommier] 204

Les tyrans au tribunal de l'histoire / Tyrants before
   the Judgment of History *Anonymous* 82

La vie en rêve / The Dream of Life *Auguste Girod* 222

Vision / A Vision *Joseph Mansion* 278

Votre temps est passé ! / Your Time Has Passed! *Anonymous* 118

Washington et Lincoln / Washington and Lincoln *Henry Train* 128

POEMS ALPHABETIZED BY ENGLISH TITLE

! / ! *Adolphe Duhart* 169
The 13th of April / Le 13 avril *Adolphe Duhart* 125
Amaritudo / Amaritudo *Adolphe Duhart* 259
Angel from Heaven / Ange du ciel *Adolphe Duhart* 263
The Angel in Exile / L'ange en exil *Adolphe Duhart* 287
At the Cemetery / Au cimetière *Adolphe Duhart* 275
Berthe! … Lucie! … Marie! … / Berthe !… Lucie !… Marie !… *Adolphe Duhart* 271
The Black Marseillaise: Song of Peace / La Marseillaise noire : chant de paix *"Camille Naudin"* 167
Blacks' Right to Vote / Le droit de suffrage des noirs *Émile Honoré* 159
Captain André Caillou and His Comrades-in-Arms / Le capitaine André Caillou et ses compagnons d'armes *Émile Honoré* 117
The Clash of the Republican Eagle and the Copperhead / Combat de l'Aigle Républicain et du Copperhead *"A." [Victor Eugène Macarty, copying text by Alexandre Soumet]* 133
The Crown of Love / La couronne d'amour *Lucien Mansion* 291
The Dog and the Cat / Le chien et le chat *Adolphe Duhart* 149
Dream / Rêve *Adolphe Duhart* 249
The Dream of Life / La vie en rêve *Auguste Girod* 223
Evening Star / Étoile du soir *Adolphe Duhart* 247
A Familiar Epistle / Épître familière *Henry Louis Rey* 187
Fiat Lux! / Fiat Lux ! *Adolphe Duhart* 99
The Flower and the Butterfly / La fleur et le papillon *Ernest de la Valette* 201
For a Child / À une enfant / For a Child *Adolphe Duhart* 251
For Théodule Delassize / À Théodule Delassize *"Antony" [Victor Eugène Macarty, copying text by Henri Blaze]* 203
For the Victims of the Saint Domingue Fire / Pour les incendiés de Saint-Domingue *Adolphe Duhart* 155
The Future / L'avenir *Lucien Mansion* 219
Gusle / Guzla [1865] *Adolphe Duhart* 245
Gusle / Guzla [1866] *Adolphe Duhart* 255
The Halcyon's Cry / Un cri de l'alcyon *Adolphe Duhart* 161
He Is / Il est *"Antony" [Victor Eugène Macarty, copying text by Hortense de Céré-Barbé]* 195
He Is Not / Il n'est pas *Armand Lanusse* 197
Homage to the Fairer Sex / Hommage au sexe *Lucien Mansion* 229
Homage to the Poet / Hommage au poète *Henry Louis Rey* 91
Hope / Espérance *Adolphe Duhart* 103
Idealism. — Materialism. / Idéalisme. — Matérialisme. *Adolphe Duhart* 289
Ignorance / L'Ignorance [1862] *Henry Louis Rey* 177
Ignorance / L'Ignorance [1865] *Henry Louis Rey* 181
The Indiscreet Flower / La fleur indiscrète *"Antony" [Victor Eugène Macarty, copying text by Henri Blaze]* 267
Jasmine / Le Jasmin *Adolphe Duhart* 257
The Ladder of Love / L'échelle de l'amour *Adolphe Duhart* 243

Letter to Nath / Lettre à Nath   *Joanni Questy*   221

Love / L'amour   *Adolphe Duhart [possible]*   269

Maris Stella / Maris Stella   *Adolphe Duhart*   179

Meditations / Méditations   *Joseph Mansion*   281

A Memory / Souvenir   *Adolphe Duhart*   265

Message from beyond the Grave / Communication d'outre-tombe   *"J. B."*   153

The Mockingbird / Le moqueur   *Adolphe Duhart*   181

Ode to the Martyrs / Ode aux martyrs   *"Camille Naudin"*   137

On Kisses / Des baisers   *Adolphe Duhart*   237

A Page from Hebel / Une page de Hebel   *Adolphe Duhart*   193

Pansy / Pensée   *Adolphe Duhart*   241

The Poet / Le poète   *Adolphe Duhart*   85

Poetry / La poésie   *Joseph Mansion*   95

Poetry! Vox Dei! / Poésie ! Vox Dei !   *Adolphe Duhart*   97

Potpourri / Pot-pourri   *Jean-Sylvain Gentil*   141

Remembrance of the Dead / Le souvenir des morts   *"Camille Naudin"*   213

Resignation / Résignation   *Henry Louis Rey*   185

Sadness / Tristesse   *Adolphe Duhart*   207

The Second of November / Deux novembre   *Adolphe Duhart*   215

The Sensitive Plant / La sensitive   *Lucien Mansion*   285

Sleep! / Dors !   *Joanni Questy*   293

Sonnet / Sonnet [1865]   *Adolphe Duhart*   243

Sonnet / Sonnet [1867]   *"Pierre (l'Hermite)"*   211

The South's Unending Rebellion / La rébellion du Sud en permanence
    Henry Louis Rey   129

Stanza [For Mr. A. P——] / Stanza [À M. A. P...]   *Adolphe Duhart*   83

Stanza [For Mr. Th. J. Durant] / Stanza [À M. Th. J. Durant]   *Adolphe Duhart*   151

The Star Has Risen! / L'astre s'est levé !   *Armand Lanusse*   101

S—— to L—— / S... à L...   *"Sténio"*   297

A Strange Coincidence / Étrange coïncidence   *Armand Lanusse [probable]*   147

A Telegraphic Dispatch / Une dépêche télégraphique   *Joanni Questy*   291

The Three Pearls / Les trois perles   *"Antony" [Victor Eugène Macarty,
    copying text by Amédée Pommier]*   205

To Father Chocarne / Au Père Chocarne   *"Pierre (l'Hermite)"*   165

To the Conservatives / Aux conservateurs   *Joanni Questy*   135

To You / À toi   *"Aster"*   105

The Triumph of the Oppressed / Le triomphe des opprimés   *Anonymous*   147

Tyrants before the Judgment of History / Les tyrans
    au tribunal de l'histoire   *Anonymous*   83

A Vision / Vision   *Joseph Mansion*   279

The War and the Future / La guerre et l'avenir   *"L. de P."*   111

Washington and Lincoln / Washington et Lincoln   *Henry Train*   129

The Weeping Willow / Le saule pleureur   *Adolphe Duhart*   189

The Wounded Flower / La fleur blessée   *Adolphe Duhart*   253

Your Time Has Passed! / Votre temps est passé !   *Anonymous*   119

Index

Note: Page numbers in italics indicate figures. Titles marked with *indicate uncertain authorship; those marked with **indicate plagiarized works republished under pseudonyms of Victor Eugène Macarty.

! ("!") (Duhart), **168–73**
"Le 13 avril" ("The 13th of April") (Duhart), 57–59, 75, **124–29**

A. (pseudonym), 33, **132–33**. *See also* Antony (pseudonym); Macarty, Victor Eugène
abandonment, theme of, 13
L'Abeille de la Nouvelle-Orléans / New Orleans Bee, 39, **140–41**, 141n37
abolition, 28
abolitionism, 9, 14, 316
    Northern, 56, 3214n24
    punishable in Louisiana, 11
abolitionist press, 8. *See also specific publications*
    Northern, 321n24
activism, xv, 10, 14, 32, 35, 45, 52, 53, 56, 316
Adams, Lucien, **198–99**, 199n67
African American community, Creole *gens de couleur* among, 2–3
African American history, 61
African Americans, violence against, 61
African Methodist Episcopal Church, 45–46
Africans, enslaved, 5
Afro-Creole. *See also* Creole *gens de couleur*
    as ideological orientation, 4
    use of the term, 3, 4
Afro-Creole activists, 10, 45. *See also* activism
Afro-Creole community, contributions to US history and politics, xv
Afro-Creole elite
    editorials by, 46–47
    racial solidarity and, 45–46
Afro-Creole heritage, 3
Afro-Creole intellectuals, 11
Afro-Creole intellectual tradition, 4–12
Afro-Creole leadership, 23
Afro-Creole literature, 12
Afro-Creole poetics, 13, 70–73, 77
Afro-Creole poetry
    arrangement of this collection, 60–61
    discursive practices, 53–54
    French Romantic poetry and, 12, 32–35, 70–73, 77
    incorporation of language used in political debates, 30–31
    linguistic practices, 54–55
    Mechanics' Institute massacre and, 39, 42
    thematic classification of, 60–61
    translation of, 70–76
    twenty-first-century relevance of, 61
Afro-Creole political discourse, 12
Afro-Creole protest tradition, 4, 11, 28
Afro-Creole radical discourse, 12–15, 17–18
Afro-Creole radicals
    egalitarianism and, 34–35
    Freemasonry and, 15
    Spiritualism and, 15, 17–18
Afro-Creoles
    Anglo-black community and, xiv
    called *nègre* (negro), 45
    emigration to France, 8
    emigration to Haiti, 8
    emigration to Mexico, 8
    as enslavers, 4, 10, 11, 44, 71
    familial structures of, 56
    freedmen and, 319n3
    as *gens de couleur* under state law, 44
    oppression of, 11
    race and, 44–45
    rest of black population and, 45
    rights of, 11
    scholarly literature on, 319n1
    self-identified as *Créoles*, 44
    status of, 11
    ties with Haiti, 8
    voting rights and, 11
    with white French fathers, 8
L'Album littéraire: journal des jeunes gens, amateurs de littérature (Lanusse and Questy), 12–13, 314
Alcyone, **160–61**
alexandrine (verse form), 72, 73
allegiances, 28
allusions, 54
Américains, vs. *ancienne population*, 7

American Antiquarian Society (AAS), xvii–xviii, 38, 60, 267n89, 304, 323n44, 323n50
American Register, 23
"L'amour" ("Love") (Duhart)*, **268–69**, 325n6
ancienne orthographe, 65–66
ancienne population, vs. *Américains*, 7
Anglo-Americans, 5
    dominance of, 12
Anglo-black community, Afro-Creoles and, xiv
anonymous works
    "Le triomphe des opprimés" ("The Triumph of the Oppressed"), **146–49**
    "Les tyrans au tribunal de l'histoire" ("Tyrants before the Judgment of History"), xiii–xiv, 18, *64*, 72, 74, **82–83**
    "Votre temps est passé !" ("Your Time Has Passed!"), 27, **118–25**
anticolonialism, 61–62
Antilles, political representatives from, 10
antiracism, 56, 70
antislavery convictions, 11–12. *See also* abolitionism
Antony (pseudonym), 9, 31–35, 39, 54–55, 60, 133n24, **194–97**, **196–99**, **202–03**, **204–07**, **266–69**, 309, 323n44. *See also* Macarty, Victor Eugène
archival research, 59–60
Ariel (archangel), **96–97**, **286–87**
artistes engagés (politically engaged artists), 32, 35
L'Art poétique (Boileau-Despréaux), 70–71
assonance, 74
Aster (pseudonym), "À toi" ("To You"), **104–07**
"L'astre s'est levé !" ("The Star Has Risen!") (Lanusse), 62, **100–01**
"À Théodule Delassize" ("For Théodule Delassize") (attributed to Macarty)**, 32, 33, **202–03**, 203n71
"Au Père Chocarne," ("To Father Chocarne") (Pierre l'Hermite), 47–48, **164–65**
"Au public" (editorial by Trévigne), 19
the *Aurore*, 5
authorship, issues of, 31–35, 55, 60, **194–97**, 195n66, **202–07**, 203n71, 205n72, **266–69**, 323n44
"Aux conservateurs" ("To the Conservatives") (Questy), 31, 48–49, 73, **134–37**

"Aux Louisianais" (anonymous essay), 13
Averin, John B. (Valmour), 15

Banks, Nathaniel P., 27, **118–19**
Barthet, Joseph, 15, 17, 317
"battle for the black man," 2
Battle of New Orleans, 6, 23
Beaulieu, Marie, 314, 316
Beauregard, P. G. T., 302
Bell, Caryn Cossé, 4, 328n31
Benjamin (biblical figure), **238–39**
Béranger, Pierre-Jean de, 17, 71, **152–55**, 153n49
"Berthe!… Lucie!… Marie!…" (Duhart), 259n88, **270–75**
Bertonneau, Arnold, 19, 21
Bight of Benin, 5
binary thinking, 48–49. *See also* racial binary
black ancestry, 3
black canon, 13
"black codes," 29. *See also* Code noir
black identity, 44, 48–52
black literatures of the Americas, 59
"The Black Marseillaise: Song of Peace" ("La Marseillaise noire : chant de paix") (Naudin), xiv, 28, 53, 74, 76, **166–69**, 319–20n3
blackness, 48–52
    appropriation of by Creole poets, 49
    as political identity, 48–49, 76
black people. *See also* enslaved people; free black people; free people of color; people of color
    Afro-Creole people and, 3, 19, 45
    anglophone, 45
    attitudes of *gens de couleur* toward, 10
    civil rights struggle of 1860s, xv, 2
    in Civil War, 23, 25, *26*, *27*
    as enslavers, 4, 10, 11, 44, 71
    Haitian Revolution, 6, 8, 48
    literature of, 3, 59
    Mechanics' Institute massacre, xvii, 35, 50–51, 323–24n51
    police violence, 303
    postwar rights of, xv, 32, 311
    racial identity, xiv–xv, 3–4, 44, 45–52, 66, 326n8
    treatment of, 13
    La Tribune and, 21–22
black press, 8

the *Black Republican*, 323n40

"Blacks' Right to Vote" ("Le droit de suffrage des noirs") (Honoré), 74, **158–61**, 305

black suffrage, xvii, 19, 21, 28, **158–61**

black troops

    in Civil War, 2, 6, 8, 11, 19, 23–28, *24*, 25, *26*, 35, 302, 307, 315, 317

    in Confederate army, 6, 23, 25, 302, 307, 315, 317

    discrimination against, 25

    inferior pay and, 25

    manual labor and, 25

    in Union army, 6, 8, 11, 19, 23, 25, 27, 35, 317

    veterans assaulted at Mechanics' Institute, 35

    in War of 1812, 19

blanc-noir dichotomy, 49–52. *See also* racial binary

Blaze, Henri, 60

    "Le cygne — À M. Sainte-Beuve" ("The Swan: For Mr. Saint-Beuve"), **202–03**

    "La fleur de mars — Chanson" ("The Flower of March: Song"), **266–69**, 323n44

"Bleeding Kansas," 14

Boileau-Despréaux, Nicolas, 69

    L'Art poétique, 70–71

Boisdoré, François, 313

    "Considérations," 46

    "La liberté," 46

Boston Athenaeum, 60

Boyer, Marie Cecilia, 278n16, **278–81**, 311, 312

Boyer (Duhart), Odilia (wife of Adolphe Duhart), **178–79**, 179n60, 269n90, 271n92, 301, 303

Breaux, Octave, 39

Brickhouse, Anna, 57

Britain, emancipation and universal male suffrage in, 9–10

brotherhood, xiv, xvii, 15, 53–59, 60

Brouard, Françoise Palymyre, 7

Brown, John, **140–41**, 316

Brown, Sarah, 52

Bruce, Clint, xiii, xiv, 321n27

Bunker Hill, Boston, Massachusetts, **112–13**

Burns, Robert, 74, **158–59**, 159n51

    "Is There for Honest Poverty" ("A Man's a Man for A' That"), 74

Butler, Benjamin F., 25, 27, 307, 317

Caesar, Julius, **122–23, 150–51**

Cailloux, André, 11, 14, 27–28, 49–50, 51–52, **116–19**, 305

    death of, 27–28

    funeral of, 28, *29*

    physical qualities of, 50

Cailloux, Félicie, 14, 307

"La campagne de 1814–15" ("The Campaign of 1814–15") (Castra), 6

"Le capitaine André Caillou et ses compagnons d'armes" ("Captain André Caillou and His Comrades-in-Arms") (Honoré), 11, 27–28, 49–50, **116–19**

capitalization, 66

the Caribbean, 1, 11. *See also specific countries*

Casanova, Pascale, 70

Castra, Hippolyte (pseudonym), "La campagne de 1814–15" ("The Campaign of 1814–15"), 6

Catholic Church, 15, 42

Catholic universalist ethic, 4

Catoir, Annette, 314

Les Cenelles: choix de poésies indigènes (*The Mayhaws: Selected Indigenous Poetry*) (Lanusse and Questy), xv, 12–14, 55, 70, 306, 307, 314, 321n28

censorship, 321n24

Central Executive Committee of the Republican Party of Louisiana, 29–30, 309, 317, 318

Cercle harmonique ("Harmonic Circle"), 15, 51, 315, 317, 322n30, 324–25n60

Céré-Barbé, Hortense de, "L'existence de Dieu" ("The Existence of God"), 39, 55, **194–95**, 195n66

Chalon, Gabriel, **146–47**

Cham (biblical name), 322n34

Charles IX, king of France, **136–37**, 137n29

Chaumette, J., **90–93**

Chicago Tribune, 22

Chocarne, Bernard, **164–65**

Christ. *See* Jesus Christ

Cirnaire, Marie Justine (Marie Couvent), 11, 13–14

citizenship, 22
civil rights, xv, 35, 44, 52, 60. *See also specific rights*
    during Reconstruction, 56
    struggle during 1860s, 2, 23
civil society, 53, 55, 325n61
Civil War, 1, 2, 4, 60
    black troops in, 2, 6, 8, 11, 19, 23–28, *24, 26*, 35, 302, 307, 315, 317
    debates over racial issues, 10
    free black people serving in, 6
    hommes de couleur in, 2, 23, 25
    legacy of, 61
    La Tribune during, 18–44
    L'Union during, 18–44
Clark, Emily, 13, 17, 320–21n19
Clark, Emily Suzanne, 15, 328n37
"The Clash of the Republican Eagle and the Copperhead" ("Combat de l'Aigle Républicain et du Copperhead") (attributed to Macarty)**, 32–34, **132–33**
class, 6, 28–29
coalition-building, 21
Code noir, 5, 14, 29
"colored aristocracy," 10
Columbus, Christopher, **176–77**, **182–83**
"Combat de l'Aigle Républicain et du Copperhead" ("The Clash of the Republican Eagle and the Copperhead") (attributed to Macarty)**, 32–34, **132–33**
"Communication d'outre-tombe" ("Message from beyond the Grave") (J. B.), 17, **152–55**
community, articulations of, 53–59
Confederacy, 21
    Copperhead Party and, 34
    gens de couleur and, 25
    monuments to, 61
Confederate army, 1, 27–28
    black troops in, 6, 23, 25, 302, 307, 315, 317
    free black people serving in, 6
    Native Guards in, 23, 25, 302, 307, 315, 317
Confederate rebels, 43–44, 51, **136–37**
    Mechanics' Institute massacre and, 35, 38
    return to power, 28, 29–30
confrérie, 54

Congressional Reconstruction, 38, 161n53. *See also* Reconstruction
Cononge, Louis-Placide, 143n39
conservatives, benefits of alliance with, 45
"Considérations" (essay by Boisdoré), 46
consonance, 74
Constantine, **100–01**
Conti Street, *30, 31*, 61, 323n41
Convention of Universal Suffrage, 307, 318, 327n18
Copperhead Party, 34, *34*, 133n24
Corps d'Afrique, in Union army, 25
corpus, presenting the, 59–62
Couvent, Bernard, 11
Couvent, Marie (Marie Justine Cirnaire), 11, 13–14
Couvent school. *See* Institution catholique des orphelins indigents
Cowan, James Lorenz, *La Marseillaise noire et autres poèmes français des Créoles de couleur de la Nouvelle-Orléans (1862–1869)*, 59, 319–20n3
Creeks, **294–95**, 295n105
Creole, use and racial implications of the term, 3
Creole culture, African element in, 3
Creole *gens de couleur*, 1–3, 23, 52. *See also gens de couleur*
    African American community and, 2–3
    Afro-Creole intellectual tradition and, 4–12
    political leadership of, 3
Creole identity, in Louisiana, 3–4
Creole languages, 3
Creole Louisiana, race in, 6
Creole mores, 1
Creole poetics, 13
Creole poets, francophone worldview of, 2
Creole radicals, 55–56
Creoles, 5
    emigration movement and, 5
    sense of superiority, 45
Creole society, slavery and, 71
Crocker, Adèle, 316, 318
Croy, Héloïse, 32, 308
Cuba, Saint Dominguan refugees in, 7
"Le cygne — À M. Sainte-Beuve" ("The Swan — To M. Sainte-Beuve") (Blaze), **202–03**
Cythera, **242–43**

Daggett, Melissa, 15, 324–25n60
Daily Picayune, 5
Dalloz, Charles (Charles Dallas). *See* Houzeau (de Lahaie), Jean-Charles
Daniels, Cora L. V., 42
Dante Alighieri, xiv
Daragneinte, Pointe-du-Jour, 7–8
Davis, Jefferson, 51, **140–41**
Davis, Theodore R., *The Riot in New Orleans*, 36, 37
Davy de la Pailleterie, Thomas-Alexandre, 59
Déclaration des droits de l'homme et du citoyen (Declaration of the Rights of Man and of the Citizen), 6–7
dedications, 53, 54
Defenders of the Native Land, 23
Delacroix, Eugène, 233n79
Delassize, Louis Théodule, 32, 33, **202–03**, 203n71, 318
DeLille, Henriette, 55
Democrats, Northern, 34
de Mortie, Louise, 60, **242–45**, 243–45n82, 309
de P., L. (pseudonym),"La guerre et l'avenir" ("The War and the Future"), **110–17**
"Une dépêche télégraphique" ("A Telegraphic Dispatch") (Questy), 56, **290–91**
Derrida, Jacques, 49, 50
Desdunes, Pierre-Aristide, 8, 314–15
Desdunes, Rodolphe Lucien, 8, 22, 301, 306, 307, 308, 309, 313, 314–15, 316, 317
  Nos hommes et notre histoire (Our People and Our History), 6, 308
desegregation, 35
Dessalines, Jean-Jacques, 48
"Des destinées de la poésie" (essay by Lamartine), 18
"Deux novembre" ("The Second of November") (Duhart), 53, **214–17**
diacritics, 66–67
Diana (Roman goddess), **180–81**
direct address, 53–54
discrimination, 10, 52
discursive practices, 53–54
Dominican immigrants, 44
Don Juan, **232–33**
Douglass, Frederick, 22, 312
"Dream" ("Rêve") (Duhart), 60, **248–49**

Dred Scott v. Sandford, 14
"Le droit de suffrage des noirs" ("Blacks' Right to Vote") (Honoré), 74, **158–61**, 305
Dryden, John, 325–26n3
Du Bois, W. E. B., 21, 38, 323–24n51
the *Duc du Maine*, 5
Duhart, Adolphe, 2, 7, 14, 15, 17, 25, 47, 54, 179n60, **218–19**, 301–03, 314, 317, 325n65, 326n6. *See also* Duhart, Adolphe, works of
  black identity and, 52
  blackness in, 49
  born Pierre-Adolphe Duhart, omits Pierre, 301
  intertextual borrowing by, 59
  Lélia D——t used as pseudonym, 54, 301–03, 325n63
  poems dedicated to, 54, **94–95**, **100–01**, **218–19**
Duhart, Adolphe, works of
  "!," **168–73**
  "Le 13 avril" ("The 13th of April"), 57–59, 75, **124–29**
  "Amaritudo" ("Amaritudo"), **258–63**
  "L'amour" ("Love")*, **268–69**, 325n63
  "Ange du ciel" ("Angel from Heaven"), **262–63**
  "L'ange en exil" ("The Angel in Exile"), **286–89**
  "Au cimietière" ("At the Cemetery"), **274–79**
  "À une enfant" ("For a Child"), **250–51**
  "Berthe!... Lucie!... Marie!...," 259n88, **270–75**
  "Le chien et le chat" ("The Dog and the Cat"), **148–51**
  "Un cri de l'alcyon" ("The Halcyon's Cry"), **160–63**
  "Des baisers" ("On Kisses"), **236–39**
  "Deux novembre" ("The Second of November"), 53, **214–17**
  "L'échelle de l'amour" ("The Ladder of Love"), **242–43**
  "Espérance" ("Hope"), **102–05**
  "Étoile du soir" ("Evening Star"), **246–47**
  "Fiat Lux !," **98–99**
  "La fleur blessée" ("The Wounded Flower"), **252–55**
  "Guzla" ("Gusle") [1865], **244–47**

Duhart, Adolphe, works of (*continued*)
"Guzla" ("Gusle") [1866], **254–57**
"Idéalisme. — Matérialisme." ("Idealism. — Materialism."), 60, **288–89**
"Le Jasmin" ("Jasmine"), **256–59**
"Maris Stella" ("Maris Stella"), **178–79**
"Le moqueur" ("The Mockingbird"), **180–81**
"Un mot des Natifs" (editorial), 302
"Une page de Hebel" ("A Page from Hebel"), **192–93**
"Pensée" ("Pansy"), **240–41**
"Poésie ! Vox Dei !" ("Poetry! Vox Dei!"), 49, **96–99**
"Le poète" ("The Poet"), 18, 54, **84–91**
"Pour les incendiés de Saint-Domingue" ("For the Victims of the Saint Domingue Fire"), xv, 33, 57, 74, **154–59**
"Rêve" ("Dream"), 60, **248–49**
"Le saule pleureur" ("The Weeping Willow"), **188–91**
"Sonnet" [1865], 60, **242–45**
"Souvenir" ("A Memory"), **264–65**
"Stanza" [À M. A. P...] ("Stanza" [for Mr. A. P——]), **82–85**
"Stanza" [À M. Th. J. Durant] ("Stanza" [For Mr. Th. J. Durant]), **150–53**
"Tristesse" ("Sadness"), **206–11**
Duhart, Armand, 301, 302
Duhart, Berthe, **268–69**, 269n90, **270–75**, 271n92, 325n63
Duhart, Lélia (sister of Adolphe Duhart), 301
name used as pseudonym by Duhart, 54, 301– 03, 325n63
Duhart, Louis-Adolphe (father of Adolphe Duhart), 7, 14, 301, 326n6
Duhart, Lucie, **270–75**, 271n92
Duhart, Marie, **270–75**, 271n92
Duhart, Odilia (name of two daughters of Adolphe Duhart), 302. *See also* Boyer (Duhart), Odilia (wife of Adolphe Duhart)
Duhart, Pierre-Adolphe. *See* Duhart, Adolphe
Dumas, Alexandre (*père*), 32–33, 325n66
L'Alchimiste, 58–59
Antony, 32–33, 309
Dumas, Francis E., 44, 321n21
Durant, Thomas Jefferson, **151–52**

Échelle de progression (*Ladder of Progression*) (Rey), *16*
economic development, 21
Economy and Mutual Aid Society (Société d'Économie et d'Assistance Mutuelle), 325n61
education, 13–14
Edward Larocque Tinker Collection of Louisiana History and Literature at the American Antiquarian Society, 38
egalitarianism, 4, 8–9, 28, 34–35, 48–49, 74
égalité, xiv, xvii, 2, 6, 15, 53, 74, 325n61
elegy, 74, 75
emancipation, 2, 5, 19, 45, 323–24n51
in Britain, 9–10
in France, 9–10
Emancipation Proclamation, 19
empathy, 55, 57
Empyrean (l'Empyrée), **96–97**
English poetic tradition, 72–73
enslaved people, 2–5, 7
arming of, 23–25
discrimination against, 10
emancipation of, 2
held by *gens de couleur libres*, 4, 10, 11, 44, 71
literacy and, 11–12
manumission of, 11, 14
in Saint Domingue, 6–7, 11
suits for freedom based on residence in France, 8
teaching of, 11–12
enslavement, 50
Époque (newspaper), **140–43**, 143n41
equality, xiv, xvii, 2, 6, 15, 53, 74, 325n61. *See also* egalitarianism; racial equality
"L'esclavage" (editorial by Trévigne), 19
Escobar y Mendoza, Antonio, **122–23**
"Étrange coïncidence" ("A Strange Coincidence") (Lanusse)[*], **146–47**, 307
exile, theme of, 13
"L'existence de Dieu" ("The Existence of God") (Céré-Barbé), 39, 55, **194–97**, 195n66. *See also* "Il est" ("He Is") (attributed to Macarty)[**]

Fabre, Michel, 8
familial structure, 56

Fanon, Frantz, 61–62
Farragut, David D., 1
February Revolution, 9
federal census, racial categories on, 44
female poetic voice, 55
femmes de couleur, 55–56, 325n61
    libres, 56
Ferrier, Alphonse, **146–47**
Fifteenth Amendment, 22
Fisk, Josiah, 318
"La fleur de mars — Chanson" ("The Flower of March: Song") (Blaze), **266–69**, 323n44
"La fleur et le papillon" ("The Flower and the Butterfly") (la Valette), **200–01**
"La fleur indiscrète" ("The Indiscreet Flower") (attributed to Macarty)**, 32, 33, 60, **266–69**
Foner, Eric, 319n1, 322n33, 323–24n51
Fontainebleau, **238–39**
Formento (Populus), Nathalie, 33, **188–91**, 189n63, **220–23**, 221n77, **266–69**, 267n89, **284–87**
"For Théodule Delassize" ("À Théodule Delassize") (attributed to Macarty)**, 32, 33, **202–03**, 203n71
"For the Victims of the Saint Domingue Fire" ("Pour les incendiés de Saint-Domingue") (Duhart), xv, 33, 57, 74, **154–59**
Fort Sumter, 307
Fourier, Charles, 15, **182–83**
Fourteenth Amendment, 22
France, **112–13**, **122–23**. *See also* French Revolution
    Afro-Creole emigration to, 8
    egalitarianism and, 8–9
    emancipation in, 9–10
    ends slavery in all territories, 9
    February Revolution in, 9
    immigrants from, 12
    integration of nonwhites into French political life, 10
    leftist uprising of February 1848, 9–10
    Louisiana Creole literature published in, 12
    political liberals fleeing from, 12
    Second Republic, 9
    slavery and, 5, 8, 9–10
    as a *terre de liberté*, 8
    universal male suffrage in, 9–10
Francis, Elizabeth, 56, 310, 312
francophone literature
    in Louisiana, 12–13, 319–20n3
    poetry, 54–55
francophone population, 7, 10, 45–46. *See also* Afro-Creoles; Creoles
Francs-Amis, 53, **214–15**, 215n76
fraternité, xiv, xvii, 15, 53–59, 60
free black labor, 19, 21
free black militias, 5–6, 23, 25. *See also* black troops
free black people, xvii, 28, 31, 45, 46, 325n61
    Afro-Creoles and, 319n3
    arming of, 23–25
    Johnson declares himself "Moses" of, 31
    labor policies and, 19
    La Tribune and, 48
    violence against, 29
    voting rights of, 35
freedmen and freedwomen, xvii, 28, 31, 45, 46, 325n61
    Afro-Creoles and, 319n3
    arming of, 23–25
    Johnson declares himself "Moses" of, 31
    labor policies and, 19
    La Tribune and, 48
    violence against, 29
    voting rights of, 35
Freedmen's Aid Association, 45–46
freedom. *See* liberty
freedom of assembly, 11, 14
freedom of movement, 11, 14
freedom of speech, 11, 71
freedwomen, violence against, 29
Freemasonry, 15, 53
free people of color, xvii, 1–4, 4, 5, 7, 45, 58
    arming of, 23–25
    in Civil War, 6
    denied rights of citizenship in *Dred Scott* decision, 14
    dire situation in 1850s, 14–15
    emigration to Haiti, 15
    emigration to Mexico, 15
    erosion of rights of, 14–15
    free people of color communities, 11
    gens de couleur and, 46
    increasing population of, 7

free people of color (*continued*)
    kidnapping of, 321n29
    of Louisiana, 4–5
    martial tradition of, 5–6
    opportunities available to, 10
    perceived as "privileged" caste, 10
    possession of enslaved people and, 10–11
    prejudiced attitudes of light-skinned, 10
    as privileged, 321n20
    property ownership and institution-building, 11
    purchase of relatives by, 11
    rights of, 14–15
    serving in Confederacy, 6
    socioeconomic achievements of, 10
    sold into slavery, 321n29
    threat of kidnapping and, 15
    violence against, 15, 35, 38, 321n29
    voting rights of, 19, 21. *See also* voting rights
"Free State" Constitution, 28
French Creole culture, 7
French Imprimerie nationale, 67
French language
    spelling and vocabulary, 65–66
    standardization of, 65
    as "universal language," 54–55
French-language press, 12
French poetics, 70–73
French regime, 5
French Revolution, 4, 6–7, 9, 53, **136–37**, 325n61
French revolutionary motto: *Liberté, égalité, fraternité*, 2, 17, 42, 55, 325n65
French revolutionary tradition, 30
French Romantic movement, 9, 12–13, 33–35, 70, 73, 320n17
French Romantic poetry, 12, 32–35, 70–73, 77
friendship, 60
Friends of Universal Suffrage of Louisiana, convention of, 29

Gabriel (archangel), **288–89**
Galileo Galilei, **176–77**, **180–81**
Galland, Louise, 308
Garrison, William Lloyd, 22
Gates, Henry Louis, Jr., 13, 70
Gayarré, Charles, 10

gender normativity, 55–56
gender propriety, 13
gens de couleur. *See* people of color
gens de couleur libres. *See* free people of color
Gentil, Jean-Sylvain, 60, 303–04
    "Pot-pourri" ("Potpourri"), 60, **140–43**
Germantown, Pennsylvania, **112–13**
Girod, Auguste, 304–06
    "La vie en rêve" ("The Dream of Life"), **222–25**
Girod, Nicolas, 304
Glissant, Édouard, 57
Grandjean, René, 317
Grant, Ulysses S., 35, 38, 203n71

Haiti, xiv–xv, 5, 8, 12, 57, 325n65
    Afro-Creole emigration to, 8
    Afro-Creoles' ties with, 8
    blackness as political identity in, 48
    discrimination based on skin color in, 10
    emigration of free people of color to, 15
    fire in Port-au-Prince, 57, 74, **154–59**, 319n4
    founding of, 7
    Haitian Revolution, 4, 6–8, 48, 53, 302, 325n61
    immigrants from, 7, 44
    literature of, 12
    ongoing exchange with, 8
    race in, 44–45
"Un Haïtien n'agit pas de la sorte" (song), **116–19**, 117n17
Hall, Gwendolyn Midlo, 3–4
Harpers Ferry, 316
Hebel, Johann Peter, **192–93**, 193n65
"He Is" ("Il est") (attributed to Macarty)**, 32, 33, 39, 55, 60, **194–97**
"He Is Not" ("Il n'est pas") (Lanusse), 31, 33, 39, 42, 60, 195n66, **196–99**
Hemans, Felicia, 253n85
Henderson, John, **138–39**
Henry (pseudonym). *See* Rey, Henry Louis
Heurtelou, Eugène, 19
Hire, William Henry, 38
historical fact, vs. propaganda, 71
historicity, 73
The Historic New Orleans Collection (THNOC), xvii, xviii, 323n41

352   AFRO-CREOLE POETRY

hoax. *See* literary hoax; Macarty, Victor Eugène
Hogue, James K., 323–24n51
Hollandsworth, James G., Jr., 323–24n51
"Hommage au sexe" ("Homage to the Fairer Sex") (Lucien Mansion), 56, **228–37**, 312–13
hommes de couleur, 5–6, 59. *See also* people of color
    in Civil War, 6, 23, 25
    literature by, 13
Honoré, Émile
    "Le capitaine André Caillou et ses compagnons d'armes" ("Captain André Caillou and His Comrades-in-Arms), 11, 27–28, 49–50, **116–19**
    "Le droit de suffrage des noirs" ("Blacks' Right to Vote") 74, **158–61**, 305
Honoré, Jean-François, 305
Horne, William I., 9, 32, 33–34, 309, 323n45, 324n56, 327n19
Horton, Jotham W., **138–39**
Houzeau (de Lahaie), Jean-Charles, 4, 21, *22*, 23, 44, 45, 47, 323n48
    becomes editor-in-chief of *La Tribune*, 21–22
    Congressional testimony under the name Charles Dallas, 323n48
    editorials in *La Tribune*, 21
    flees to Mexico, then Philadelphia, 21
    leaves *La Tribune*, 23
    Louisiana Republican Party and, 30
    Mechanics' Institute massacre and, 38
    memoir of, 45
    prosuffragist stance of, 56
    same person as Charles Dalloz/Dallas, 323n48
    socialist outlook of, 21
Hugo, Victor, 12, 19, 73, 320n17
Hugon, Rosalie, 308
humanistic universalism, 54–55
humanité, 74
human rights, 60

iambic poetry, 72–74
idealism, 2–3, 4, 30
"Idéalisme. — Matérialisme." ("Idealism. — Materialism.") (Duhart), 60, **288–89**
ideology, 6
    revolutionary, 6–7

"L'Ignorance" ("Ignorance") [1862] (Rey), 1, 2, 17, 19, **176–79**, 317
"L'Ignorance" ("Ignorance") [1865] (Rey), 74, **180–83**
"Il est" ("He Is") (attributed to Macarty)**, 32, 33, 39, 55, 60, **194–97**
"Il n'est pas" ("He Is Not") (Lanusse), 31, 33, 39, 42, 60, 195n66, **196–99**
immigrants, 5, 7, 12
India, **284–85**
Indigenous peoples of the US
    anglophone and francophone tradition of writing "Indian legends," 293n104
    "Goula" (corruption of name of a Muscogee tribe), **294–95**, 295n106
    Muscogee Confederacy, 295n105
    Tallapoosa group of Upper Creeks, **294–97**, 295n105
"The Indiscreet Flower" ("La fleur indiscrète") (attributed to Macarty)**, 32, 33, 60, **266–69**
individuality, 12
injustices, in Louisiana, 13
Institution catholique des orphelins indigents (Couvent school), 14, 301, 302, 307, 313–14, 316, 317, 324–25n60
institutions, participation in, 5
integration, 35
interracial marriage, 35, 52
    illegality of, 56
interracial unity, 50, 51
Isabella II, queen of Spain, 291n102
"Is There for Honest Poverty" ("A Man's a Man for A' That") (Burns), 74

Jackson, Andrew, 6
Jacob (biblical figure), **238–39**
J. B. (pseudonym), 17, 153n49
    "Communication d'outre-tombe" ("Message from beyond the Grave"), 17, **152–55**
Jeanne d'Arc : trilogie nationale (*Joan of Arc: National Trilogy*) (Soumet), 34, **132–33**, 323n45
Jeremy (biblical prophet), **104–05**
Jesus Christ, 51, 58, **104–05**, **122–23**, **126–27**, **164–65**, **182–83**, **238–39**, **244–45**
Jim Crow segregation, 52, 53
Joan of Arc, 34, **176–77**, **182–83**
Johnson, Andrew, 28, 31, 38, **198–99**, 199n68

Joly, Joseph, 315
Jourdain, Alfred, 312
Judas, **136–37, 238–39**

Kein, Sybil, 3
Kelley, Benjamin Franklin, **100–01,**101n11
Kelley, William D., 22
Kościuszko, Tadeusz, **124–25**, 125n23
Kress, Dana, xviii

labor policies, 19, 21
labor rights, 21
Lachance, Paul, 10, 321n20
Lacroix, François, 50, 139n32, 324–25n60
Lacroix, Victor, 50–52, **138–39, 140–41,** 324–25n60
Ladder of Progression (*Échelle de progression*) (Rey), *16*
Lafayette, marquis de (Gilbert du Motier), **124–25**
Laizer, J. Clovis, 23
Lalaurie, Delphine Macarty, 308
Lamartine, Alphonse de, 9, 12, 15, 57, **168–69,** 320n17
  "Des destinées de la poésie," 18
Lamennais, Félicité Robert de, 15
  Paroles d'un croyant (*Words of a Believer*), 15
land distribution, 21
language, mastery of, 71
Lanusse, Armand, 2, 8, 14, 23, 33, 39, 54–55, 60, **84–85, 98–99, 194–95, 258–59,** 259n88, **280–83,** 306–08, 310–11, 313–14, 317. *See also* Lanusse, Armand, works of
  death of, **168–73,** 169n57
  education and, 13–14
  Louisiana Republican Party and, 30
  poems dedicated to, 54, **84–85, 98–99, 168–73, 194–97, 280–83**
  as principal of Institution catholique des orphelins indigents, 14
Lanusse, Armand, works of
  L'Album littéraire: journal des jeunes gens, amateurs de littérature, 12–13, 314
  "L'astre s'est levé !" ("The Star Has Risen!"), 62 , **100–01**
  Les Cenelles: choix de poésies indigènes (*The Mayhaws: Selected Indigenous Poetry*), xv, 12–14, 55, 70, 306, 307, 314, 321n28

  "Épigramme," 13
  "Étrange coïncidence" ("A Strange Coincidence")*, **146–47**, 307
  "Il n'est pas" ("He Is Not"), 31, 33, 39, 42, 60, 195n66, **196–99**
  "Un mariage de conscience," 13, 306–07
Lanusse, Numa, 8, 306
Latin Catholic cultures, three-tiered racial hierarchy of 7, 52
la Valette, Ernest de, "La fleur et le papillon" ("The Flower and the Butterfly"), **200–01**
La Vallière, Louise de, **238–39**, 239n80
Lazarus, **126–27**
L. de P. (pseudonym), "La guerre et l'avenir" ("The War and the Future"), **110–17**
Lee, Lucie, 308
Legouvé, Ernest, **228–29**, 229n78
Lélia D——t (pseudonym). *See* Duhart, Adolphe; Duhart, Lélia (sister)
Lemoine, Gustave, 153n48
Lexington, Massachusetts, **112–13**
Le Libéral, 321n24
liberation struggles, 59
the *Liberator*, 22
liberté. *See* liberty; *see also* freedom
"La liberté" (essay by Boisdoré), 46
"La liberté et l'esclavage" ("Freedom and Slavery") (Pécatier), 59
liberty, xiv, 53, 60, 74, 325n61. *See also* freedom
  dual commitment to human and creative, 9
libres de couleur, 45–46. *See also* free people of color
Lincoln, Abraham, 58, 75, **104–05, 124–29,** 316
  assassination of, 2, 18, 28, **124–29**
  conciliatory approach to readmitting Louisiana to the Union, 28
  legacy of, 58, 75
  meeting with Roudanez and Bertonneau, 19, 21
  messianic impact of, 58
line arrangements, 66–67
literacy, 11–12
literary hoax, 31–35, **132–33, 194–97, 202–03, 204–07, 266–69**. *See also* Macarty, Victor Eugène
literary journals, 12–13
Logny, Aglaé Robin, 307

Louise, Sister, 15
Louisiana, 33
    abolishment of slavery in, 19
    "black codes" in, 29
    "colored aristocracy" in, 10
    communities of color in, 320n7
    consequences of Haitian Revolution in, 7–8
    Creole identity in, 3–4
    demographics on eve of Civil War, 4–5
    discrimination based on skin color in, 10
    francophone literature in, 12–13
    French-language press in, 12
    injustices in, 13
    legislature of, 29
    racial hierarchy in, 10
    readmitted to the Union, 28
    Reconstructed Constitution of the State of Louisiana, 43–44
    rights of free people of color in, 14–15
    Saint Dominguan refugees in, 7–8
    state constitution of 1868, 61
    state elections in, 29, 44
    US possession of, 5–6
Louisiana constitutional conventions
    1864, 35
    1866, xvii, 35, 135n25, 137n30
    1868, 43–44, *43*, 304
Louisiana Creole identity, 12
Louisiana Creole literature, published in France, 12
Louisiana francophone literature, 12–13, 319–20n3
Louisiana House of Representatives, 310
Le Louisianais (newspaper), **140–43**, 141n36, 303, 304
Louisiana Native Guards. *See* Native Guards (Confederate army); Native Guards (Union army)
Louisiana Purchase, 7
Louisiana Republican Party, 9, 29–30, 161n53, 317
    La Tribune and, 44
Louis-Napoléon, 9
Louis-Philippe, 9
Louis XIV, king of France, **238–39**
Loup, Constance, **136–37**
Louverture, Toussaint, 7, **168–69**

Louvre, **136–37**
"Love" ("L'amour") (Duhart)*, **268–69**, 325n63

Macarty, Augustin, 308
Macarty, Eugène Theodore de, 32, 308
Macarty, Victor Eugène, 8, 31–35, 39, 60, 243–43n82, 302, 307–09, 318. *See also* Macarty, Victor Eugène, works falsely attributed to
    "Antony" as pseudonym of, 9, **194–97**, 195n66, **202–03**, 203n71, **204–07**, 205n72, **266–69**, 309, 323n44
    as *artiste engagé* (the politically engaged artist), 32
    beating of, 33
    lawsuit against Opera House, 32, 45, 309
    literary hoax and, 31–33
    Louisiana Republican Party and, 30
    Mechanics' Institute massacre and, 309
    Republican Party and, 32
    residence in France, 9
Macarty, Victor Eugène, works falsely attributed to
    "À Théodule Delassize" ("For Théodule Delassize")**, 32, 33, **202–03**, 203n71
    "Combat de l'Aigle Républicain et du Copperhead" ("The Clash of the Republican Eagle and the Copperhead")**, 32, **132–33**
    "La fleur indiscrète" ("The Indiscreet Flower")**, 60, **266–69**, 323n44
    "Il est" ("He Is")**, 32, 33, 39, 55, 60, **194–97**
    "Les trois perles" ("The Three Pearls")**, **204–07**
Maistre, Paschal, 42
Mammon, **120–21**
manhood, 55–56
"A Man's a Man for A' That" ("Is There for Honest Poverty") (Burns), 74
Mansion, Élodie, 267n89, 291n103, **290–91**, **292–97**, 312, 314
Mansion, Joseph Lucien, 2, 54, 56, 278n16, 310–12
    "Méditations" ("Meditations"), 54, **280–83**
    "La poésie" ("Poetry"), 54, **94–95**
    "La sensitive" ("The Sensitive Plant"), **284–87**
    "Vision" ("A Vision"), **278–81**

Mansion, Lucien, 8, **102–03**, **258–59**, 310, 312–13
    "L'avenir" ("The Future"), **218–19**
    "La couronne d'amour" ("The Crown of Love"), **290–91**
    "Hommage au sexe" ("Homage to the Fairer Sex"), 56, **228–37**, 312–13
manumission, 11, 14
Marciacq, Jean-Louis, 12–13, 307
Marfori y Callejas, Carlos, **290–91**, 291n102
"Un mariage de conscience" (short story by Lanusse), 306–07
Mars, **158–59**
"La Marseillaise" (song), 323n40
"La Marseillaise noire : chant de paix" ("The Black Marseillaise: Song of Peace") (Naudin), xiv, 28, 53, 74, 76, **166–69**, 319–20n3
La Marseillaise noire et autres poèmes français des Créoles de couleur de la Nouvelle-Orléans (1862–1869) (Cowan), 59, 319–20n3
Mary (Virgin Mary), 179n59, **288–89**
Mary, Aristide, 318
Mary Magdalene, **228–29**
masculine bias, 55–56
Massachusetts Fifty-Fourth Regiment, 25
Mechanics' Institute massacre, xvii–xviii, 33, 35, *36*, *37*, 38, 39, 60, **134–35**, **138–39**, 309, 323–24n51
    Afro-Creole poets and, 39, 42
    anniversary of, 42
    commemoration of, 42
    La Tribune reportage of, xvii–xviii, 38–39, *40*, *41*
"Méditations" ("Meditations") (Joseph Lucien Mansion), 54, **280–83**
Melançon, Kristi Richard, 56
Mélot, Félicia, 189n63
Melvil-Bloncourt, Sainte-Suzanne, 23
Mercier, Alfred, 12, 313
Mesmer, Franz Anton, 15
"Message from beyond the Grave" ("Communication d'outre-tombe") (J. B.), 17, **152–55**
Mexico
    Afro-Creole emigration to, 8, 315
    emigration of free people of color to, 15, 313

Mintz, Sidney, 44–45
Mississippi River, 3, 5
Mississippi Valley, Saint Dominguan refugees in, 7–8
Mitchell, Mary Niall, 14, 46
mixed race, difference from the term *mulatto*, 320n5
Monroe, John T., **134–35**
Monsieur Paul (novella by Questy), 71, 315
Montaigne, Jean, 321n29
Mont-Carmel, **84–85**
monuments, 61
Moreau de Saint-Méry, M. L. E., 324n55
Moreno, Delphine Philibert, 318
Morgan, Thomas J., 25
Moses (biblical figure), **198–99**
"Un mot sur la population de couleur" ("A Word on the Population of Color") (editorial by Trévigne), 46
Mount Tabor, **90–91**
mulatto (*mulâtre*), use of the term, 320n5
"mulatto" people, 44, 46, 48, 59, 302, 320n5
multiracial heritage, 3
Muscogee Confederacy, **295–96**, 295nn105–06
mysticism, 15

Napoléon Bonaparte, 7
Nast, Thomas
    The Escaped Slave in the Union Army, 24
    A Negro Regiment in Action, 24
national community, search for, 44
National Equal Rights League, Louisiana branch of, 29
national unity, struggle for, 57–59
Native Americans. *See* Indigenous peoples of the US
Native Guards (Confederate army), 23, 25, 147n45, 302, 307, 315, 317
Native Guards (Union army), 6, 8, 11, 19, 25, *26*, *27*, 317
Naudin, Camille (pseudonym), 47
    "La Marseillaise noire : chant de paix" ("The Black Marseillaise: Song of Peace)," xiv, 28, 53, 74, 76, **166–69**, 319–20n3
    "Ode aux martyrs" ("Ode to the Martyrs"), 42, 50–52, 76, **136–41**

"Le souvenir des morts" ("Remembrance of the Dead"), **212–15**
Neidenbach, Elizabeth C., 11
Nerval, Gérard de, 58–59
New Orleans, Louisiana
    Comité des citoyens, 52, 313
    Conti Street, 30, *31*, 61, 323n41
    exclusion of children of color from schools in, 13
    Faubourg Marigny neighborhood, 14
    "free colored" population of, 4–5
    liberation of, 6
    Saint Dominguan refugees in, 7–8
    Tremé neighborhood, 15, 215n76
    War of 1812 and, 6
    as zone of cultural convergence, 6
New Orleans Bee / L'Abeille de la Nouvelle-Orléans, 39, **140–43**, 141n37
New Orleans Crescent, **140–43**, 143n42
New Orleans Opera House, segregation of, 9, 32, 45, 309
New Orleans Republican, 44, **140–43**, 143n44, 311
New Orleans Tribune (original newspaper, extant 1864–70). *See La Tribune de la Nouvelle-Orléans / New Orleans Tribune*
New Orleans Tribune (periodical founded in 1985), 2, 319n2
newspapers, positions of, 28. *See also specific newspapers*
New York Herald, 22
New York Times, 22, 27, 50
Nicholls, Francis T., 304, 306
"noir," identification as, 49
Nos hommes et notre histoire (*Our People and Our History*) (Desdunes), 6, 308
nouvelle orthographe, 65–66
Nystrom, Justin, 28

O'Brien, Neil L., 315
octavon (octaroon), 45
"Ode aux martyrs" ("Ode to the Martyrs") (Naudin), 42, 50–52, 76, **136–41**
organizations in Afro-Creole community, 53, 55, 325n61
orthography, 65–66
Ouidah, Benin, 5

Our Colored Troops at Work: The First Louisiana Native Guards Disembarking at Fort Macombe, 26
Our Colored Troops: The Line Officers of the First Louisiana Native Guards, 26

Packard, Stephen B., 306
Palao, Marie Aline, 56, 312, 313
parallelism, 74
Parham, Angel Adams, 52, 319n2
Paroles d'un croyant (*Words of a Believer*) (Lamennais), 15
"passing," 52–53
patriarchy, 13, 55, 56
Patrice, **146–47**
Paul (biblical figure), **182–83**
Paz, Octavio, 69
Pécatier, Adolphe, 59
Pelletan, Eugène, 211n74
people of color, 1–4, 31, 44, 45, 46
    anglophone, 45–46
    arming of, 23–25
    in Civil War, 6
    Confederacy and, 25
    denied rights of citizenship in *Dred Scott* decision, 14
    discrimination based on skin color among, 10
    as enslavers, 4, 10, 11, 44, 71
    erosion of rights of, 14–15
    of Louisiana, 4–5
    martial tradition of, 5–6
    opportunities available to, 10
    political rights of, 9–10
    required to carry passes, 14
    sense of worth and dignity, 10
    serving in Confederacy, 6
    subordinate condition of, 13
    transnational experiences and international awareness of, 9–10
    traveling in Haiti, 8
    violence against, 35, 38
    voting rights of, 19, 21, 35
Peri (figure from Persian folklore), **180–81**
Peter (biblical figure), **136–37**
Peter of Amiens, **164–65**, 165n55, **210–11**

Peter the Hermit (Pierre l'Hermite) (pseudonym)
"Au Père Chocarne" ("To Father Chocarne"), 47–48, **164–65**
"Sonnet" [1867], **210–11**
Petrarca, **248–49**, 249n84
Philadelphia Inquirer, 22
Philip II, king of Macedon, **104–05**, 105n14
philosophical poetry, 60
Phrygia (kingdom), **136–37**
the *Picayune*, **140–43**, 141n38
Pickets of the First Louisiana "Native Guard" Guarding the New Orleans, Opelousas and Great Western Railroad, 27
Pierre l'Hermite (Peter the Hermit) (pseudonym)
"Au Père Chocarne" ("To Father Chocarne"), 47–48, **164–65**
"Sonnet" [1867], **210–11**
Pindemonte, Ippolito, **252–53**, 253n85
plaçage, *placées*, 10
challenging the legend of, 320–21n19
Lanusse's conception of, 13
plagiarism, 31–35, 55, 60, **194–97**, 195n66, **202–07**, 203n71, 205n72, **266–69**, 323n44. *See also* Macarty, Victor Eugène
Plessy, Homer, 52
Plessy v. Ferguson, xv, 52, 313
"La poésie" ("Poetry") (Joseph Lucien Mansion), 54, **94–95**
poésie engagée, 28
"Poésie ! Vox Dei !" ("Poetry! Vox Dei!") (Duhart), 49, 54, 95n6, **96–99**
"Le poète" ("The Poet") (Duhart), 18, 54, **84–91**
poetic community, constitution of, 53–59
poetic dialogues, 54, 60
poetic exchanges, 60–61
poetic form, Afro-Creole poets' relation to, 70–73, 77
poeticity, 73
poetic meter, difference in French and English conventions, 72–73
poetry
philosophical, 60
politically committed, 28
as prophecy, xiii–xiv, 17–18, 60
translation of, 70–75
political action. *See* activism
political commentary, oblique, 31–32

political debates, incorporated into Afro-Creole poetry, 30–31
political empowerment, 9–10
political identity, blackness as, 76
politically committed poetry, 28
Pommier, Amédée, "Les trois perles, élégie" ("The Three Pearls, Elegy"), 34–35, **204–07**
population de couleur, 46–47
Populus, Nathalie. *See* Formento (Populus), Nathalie
Port-au-Prince, Haiti, fire in, 57, 74, **154–59**, 155n50, 319n4
Port Hudson, Louisiana, campaign at, 25, 27–28, **116–19**, 117n16, 305, 317
"Pot-pourri" ("Potpourri") (Gentil), 60, **140–43**
"Pour les incendiés de Saint-Domingue" ("For the Victims of the Saint Domingue Fire") (Duhart), xv, 33, 57, 74, **154–59**
Presidential Reconstruction, 28. *See also* Reconstruction
the press. *See also* newspapers
abolitionist press, 8, 321n24. *See also specific publications*
black press, 8
French-language press, 12
propaganda, vs. historical fact, 71
Le Propagateur catholique (newspaper), **140–43**, 141–43n39
prophecy, poetry as, xiii–xiv, 17–18, 60
proslavery apology, 8
proslavery Southerners, 14
pseudonyms, 325n63. *See also* Antony (pseudonym); de P., L. (pseudonym); Duhart, Adolphe; Henry (pseudonym); J. B. (pseudonym); Naudin, Camille (pseudonym); Peter the Hermit (pseudonym); Sténio (pseudonym); Yacoub (pseudonym)
public schools, children of color excluded from, 13
Puget, Loïsa, 153n48
punctuation, 66–67

quadroon balls, 10, 320–21n19
Quadroon Bill, 45
quarteron (quadroon), 45
Questiz, Giovanni, 314, 327–28n29. *See also* Questy (Questi), Joanni

Questy, Jean, 314
Questy (Questi), Joanni, 2, 15, 47, 56, 302, 313–17, 322n37, 325n65, 327–28n29
    L'Album littéraire: journal des jeunes gens, amateurs de littérature, 12–13, 314
    "Aux conservateurs" ("To the Conservatives"), 31, 48–49, 73, **134–37**
    Les Cenelles: choix de poésies indigènes (*The Mayhaws: Selected Indigenous Poetry*), 12–14, 55, 70, 306, 307, 314, 321n28
    "Une dépêche télégraphique" ("A Telegraphic Dispatch"), 56, **290–91**
    "Dors !" ("Sleep!"), **292–97**
    "Lettre à Nath" ("Letter to Nath"), **220–21**
    Monsieur Paul, 71, 315–16
    as principal of Institution catholique des orphelins indigents, 14
Questy, Paul, 314, 315, 327–28n29

race
    in Creole Louisiana, 6
    in Haiti, 44–45
    permeability of race relations, 4
    race-based oppression, 4
    race-based solidarity, 28–29
    as sociopolitical construct, 3
racial ambiguity, 52–53
racial binary, 7, 45, 48–50, 52
racial categories, 44–45, 320n5, 324n55
racial difference, 48–50
racial duality, 51
racial equality, xiv, 15, 35, 43, 48–49, 60
    fight for, 6
    legal recognition of, 2
    movement for, 23
racial hierarchy, 4
    attempts to challenge, 4
    effects of, 13
    in Louisiana, 10
    as obstacle to political empowerment, 10
    three-tiered, in Latin Catholic cultures, 7, 52
racial identity, 3
racial justice, 30
"racial palimpsest," 51–52
racial poetics, crafting a, 44–52
racial prejudice, 21
racial solidarity, Afro-Creole elite and, 45–46
racial structures, 51–52
racism, damage of, 61–62
radicalism, 4, 301
radical newspapers, 4
Radical Reconstruction, 23, 38, 52, 161n53. *See also* Reconstruction
Radical Republicans, 34, 42–43
Raffel, Burton, 76
Ramsey, JR, xvii
Raphael (painter), **288–89**
rationalism, 15
reactionaries, xvii, 22, 28. *See also* Confederate rebels; white supremacy
"La rébellion du Sud en permanence" ("The South's Unending Rebellion") (Rey), 29, **128–31**
Reconstructed Constitution of the State of Louisiana, 43–44, *43*
Reconstruction, 1, 2, 12, 43–45, *43*, 52, 58, 60–61, 304, 323–24n51
    civil rights during, 56
    Congressional Reconstruction, 38, 161n53
    negation of, 53
    politics of, 28, 53–54
    Presidential Reconstruction, 28
    Radical Reconstruction, 23, 38, 52, 161n53
    La Tribune during, 18–44
    L'Union during, 18–44
Reconstruction Acts, 161n53
Reconstruction Amendments, 38
Reconstructionist politicians, 31
Reconstructionists, **134–35**
Redemption movement, 52
refugees, **196–97**
    from Saint Domingue, 7–8, 44
relationships, social and personal, 60
La Renaissance louisianaise (newspaper), **140–43**, 141–43n40
républicanisme, 30
Republican Party, 14, 23, 29–30, 32, 317
"Rêve" ("Dream") (Duhart), 60, **248–49**
revolutionary ideology, 6–7, 30
Revue du monde colonial, asiatique et américain, 23

Rey, Barthélemy, 14, 316, 324–25n60
Rey, Henry Louis, 2, 14–15, 18, 23, 25, 51, 153n49, 301, 311, 315–18, 324–25n60. *See also* Rey, Henry Louis, works of
    as *artiste engagé* (the politically engaged artist), 32
    as captain in First Regiment, 25
    Cercle harmonique ("Harmonic Circle") and, 322n30
    Louisiana Republican Party and, 30
Rey, Henry Louis, works of
    Échelle de progression (*Ladder of Progression*), 16
    "Épître familière" ("A Familiar Epistle"), **186–89**
    "Hommage au poète" ("Homage to the Poet"), **90–93**
    "L'Ignorance" ("Ignorance") [1862], 1, 2, 17, 19, **176–79**, 317
    "L'Ignorance" ("Ignorance") [1865], 74, **180–83**
    "La rébellion du Sud en permanence" ("The South's Unending Rebellion"), 29, **128–31**
    "Résignation" ("Resignation") **184–85**
Rey, Hippolyte, 316
Rey, Louis Barthélemy. *See* Rey, Barthélemy
Rey, Octave, 25, 317
Reynolds, Donald E., 323–24n51
rhyme, 70–71, 72, 73–74, 75
rights, xv, 21, 60. *See also* civil rights; human rights; suffrage; voting rights; *specific freedoms*
    of Afro-Creoles, 11
    of free people of color, 14–15
right to bear arms, 11, 23–25
"riot" of 30 July 1866. *See* Mechanics' Institute massacre
Rochambeau, count (Jean-Baptiste Donatien de Vimeur), **124–25**
Romanticism, 9, 12–13, 33–35, 70, 73, 320n17
Romantic literature, 12–13
Romantic philosophy, 4
Roudané, Mark Charles, 52
Roudanez, Jean-Baptiste, 1, 19, 21, 23, 44
    letter from Douglass to, 22
    Louisiana Republican Party and, 30
Roudanez, Louis Charles, 1, *9*, 23, 52, 302, 311
    residence in France, 8–9

Rouquette, Adrien, 12, 287n101
Rouquette, François-Dominique, **286–87**, 287n101
Rousseau, Jean-Baptiste, **158–59**, 159n52
Roussève, Charles Barthelemy, 2, 313

Sacriste, Rose Agnès, 316
Sade, Marquis de, 201n70
Saint Dominguan refugees, 7–8
Saint Domingue, xiv–xv, 6–7, 44, 59, **154–59**
    enslaved people in, 6–7, 11
    racial categories in, 324n55
    racial structure of, 10
    refugees from, 7–8, 32, 33, 44
    slavery in, 6–7
Saloy, Bertrand, 321n29
Le Salut (newspaper), **140–43**, 143n43
Sardanapalus (Assyrian king), **232–33**, 233n79
Schœlcher, Victor, 320n17
school desegregation, 35, 43
séances, 15, 324–25n60
secession, 25
"The Second of November" ("Deux novembre") (Duhart), 53, **214–17**
Second Republic, 9
segregation, 9, 32, 35, 45, 52, 53, 309
self-purchase (*coartación*), 5
Senegambia, 5
Senter, Caroline, 48
"separate but equal" doctrine, 52, 53
sexual mores, 10, 13
Shaik, Fatima, 325n61
Sheridan, Philip, 35, 38
Sisters of the Holy Family, 55
sizain hétérométrique, 75
skin color, 44–45
slavery, 1, 5, 30, 46
    abolished throughout Louisiana in 1864, 19
    Creole society and, 71
    denounced in *L'Union*, 19
    ended in France, 9
    fight against, 6
    gens de couleur libres and, 10–11
    legacy of, 61
    in Saint Domingue, 6–7
    sectional conflict in 1850s, 14–15
slaves. *See* enslaved people

slave ships, 5
Smith, J. B., 42
social equality, 32, 35
social harmony, concept of, 15
social integration, 28
Société d'Économie et d'Assistance Mutuelle (Economy and Mutual Assistance Society), 325n61
Socrates, **176–77**, **182–83**
solidarity, 28–29
"Sonnet" [1865] (Duhart), 60, **242–45**
"Sonnet" [1867] (Pierre l'Hermite), **210–11**
Soulé, Pierre, 9
Soumet, Alexandre, *Jeanne d'Arc : trilogie nationale* (*Joan of Arc: National Trilogy*), 34, **132–33**, 323n45
"The South's Unending Rebellion" ("La rébellion du Sud en permanence") (Rey), 29, **128–31**
Spain, 7, 291n102
Spanish regime, 5
Spiritualism, 15, *16*, 17–18, 51, **152–55**, **176–81**, 315–17, 322n30, 324–25n60
Le Spiritualiste de la Nouvelle-Orléans, 17
Spiritualist messages, 17–18, 51
Spiritualist periodicals, 17
Staël, Germaine de, 253n85
"The Star Has Risen!" ("L'astre s'est levé !") (Lanusse), 62, **100–01**
St. Augustine Church, 316
St. Bartholomew's Day Massacre, 38, 42, **136–37**
Sténio (pseudonym), "S... à L..." ("S—— to L——"), **296–99**
St. James Parish, 303, 304
"A Strange Coincidence" ("Étrange coïncidence") (Lanusse)*, **146–47**, 307
suffering, 55, 57
suffrage, 21, 29–30, 35, 45
    black suffrage, 19, 21, 28
    Convention of Universal Suffrage, 307, 318, 327n18
    universal male suffrage, 9–10, 21, 22, 29–30, 31, 35
    women's suffrage, 56
Sumner, Charles, **100–01**, 101n11
"The Swan — To M. Sainte-Beuve" ("Le cygne — À M. Sainte-Beuve") (Blaze), **202–03**
Swedenborg, Emanuel, 15, 17, **176–77**, **182–83**

Taliaferro, James G., 23, 44
Tallapoosa people, **294–97**
"A Telegraphic Dispatch" ("Une dépêche télégraphique") (Questy), 56, **290–91**
Testut, Charles, 15
Thersites (fictional character), **106–07**
THNOC (The Historic New Orleans Collection), xvii, xviii, 323n41
Thompson, Shirley Elizabeth, 13, 57, 321n21
"The Three Pearls" ("Les trois perles") (attributed to Macarty)**, 32, 33, 34–35, **204–07**
"The Three Pearls, Elegy" ("Les trois perles, élégie") (Pommier), 34–35, **204–07**
the *Times*, **142–43**
the *Times* of London, 28
the *Times-Picayune* / *New Orleans Advocate*, **140–43**, 141n38
Tinker, Edward Larocque, xviii, 304, 306, 321n28, 323n44
"To Father Chocarne" ("Au Père Chocarne") (Peter the Hermit), 47–48, **164–65**
"To the Conservatives" ("Aux conservateurs") (Questy), 31, 48–49, 73, **134–37**
Tounoir, Euphémie, 305
Train, Henry, 4, 318
    Louisiana Republican Party and, 30
    "Washington et Lincoln" ("Washington and Lincoln"), **128–29**
transatlantic literary relations, 33–34
translation, 69–70, 322n31, 324n58
    domestication and, 76
    poetic form and, 70–75
    translation theory, 77
Trenton, New Jersey, **112–13**
Trévigne, Paul, 1, 21, 243–45n82, 312, 314
    "Au public," 19
    "L'esclavage," 19
    letter to Sainte-Suzanne Melvil-Bloncourt, 23
    Louisiana Republican Party and, 30
    "Un mot sur la population de couleur" ("A Word on the Population of Color"), 46
    threats against his life, 21
La Tribune de la Nouvelle-Orléans / *New Orleans Tribune*, xiii–xv, xvii–xviii, 2, 9, 13, 21, 33, *40*, *41*, 45, 52–55, 59, 325n66
    application of "Afro-Creole" to, 4
    availability of, 3

La Tribune de la Nouvelle-Orléans / New Orleans Tribune (*continued*)
 as bilingual endeavor, 19
 briefly reopens in 1868, 44
 challenges of, 65
 during the Civil War, 18–44
 commemoration of anniversary of Mechanics' Institute massacre, 42
 Conti Street address, *30*, *31*, 61
 contributions to civil rights struggles of 1860s, 23
 demographic composition of staff, 7–8
 discourse of, 56
 discredited after election rivalries, 42–44
 dissension in, 23
 Douglass's praise of, 22
 editorials by Afro-Creole elite in, 47
 election crisis and, 43–44, 55
 first black daily in US, 21
 formation of Louisiana Republican Party and, 29–30
 founding of, 302
 fractured coalition of, 44
 freedmen and, 48
 Haiti and, 8, 57
 impact of, 2
 international readership of, 23
 issues published after Mechanics' Institute massacre, xvii–xviii, 38–39, *40*, *41*
 issues sent to the North by Unionists, 38
 lauded in speech in Congress, 22
 legacy of, 2
 "lost" issues of, xvii–xviii, 38–39, *40*, *41*, 60
 Louisiana Republican Party and, 44
 Mechanics' Institute massacre and, xvii–xviii, 35, 38–39, *40*, *41*
 nineteenth-century poetic conventions and, 70
 offices of, *30*
 "Official Journal of the United States Government," 22
 as "official organ" of Republican Party, 30
 outreach to anglophone black people, 45–46
 "Pages for a Narrative of the New Orleans Massacre," 39
 at "pinnacle of prestige and influence," 35
 plagiarized poetry in, 32–34
 poets of, 8, 15, 17–18
 potential of, 21–22
 prestige of, 22
 radical discourse of, 57
 readership of, 23
 Reconstruction and, 18–44, 48
 "Religious Department," 45–46
 run of, 61
 scarcity of issues, 65
 schism of 1868 and, 44
 shuts down temporarily in 1868, 23
 staff of, 14
 suspends publication in 1868, 44
"Les trois perles" ("The Three Pearls") (attributed to Macarty)**, 32, 33, 34–35, **204–07**
"Les trois perles, élégie" ("The Three Pearls, Elegy") (Pommier), 34–35, **204–07**
Trouillot, Michel-Rolph, 10
Tunnell, Ted, 28
Tupper, Martin F., 269n91
"Les tyrans au tribunal de l'histoire" ("Tyrants before the Judgment of History") (anonymous), xiii–xiv, 18, *64*, 72, 74, **82–83**

Unification Party, 311
Union army, 1
 black troops in, 6, 8, 11, 19, 23, 25, 27, 35, 317
 black veterans of, 35
 Corps d'Afrique in, 25
 First Regiment, 25, 27
 Native Guards in, 6, 8, 11, 19, 25, 317
Unionism, conservative, 28
L'Union : mémorial politique, littéraire et progressiste (*The Union: Political, Literary, and Progressive Record*), xiii–xv, xvii–xviii, 1–2, 13, *20*, 53, 59, *64*
 adds English-language edition, 19
 advocacy for black troops in war effort, 19
 advocacy for emancipation, 19
 advocacy for voting rights, 19
 application of "Afro-Creole" to, 4
 availability of, 3
 as bilingual endeavor, 19
 challenges of, 65

during the Civil War, 18–44
closes after threats to Trévigne's life, 21
contributions to civil rights struggles of 1860s, 23
demographic composition of staff, 7–8
editorials by Afro-Creole elite in, 23, 25, 46–47
English translations of, 3
first publication of, 6
free black troops and, 23, 25, 27
Haiti and, 8, 57
inaugural issue of, 18–19, *20*
nineteenth-century poetic conventions and, 70
poets of, 15, 17–18
radical discourse of, 57
during Reconstruction, 18–44
scarcity of issues, 65
Spiritualist messages in, 17
staff of, 14
United States
    blackness as political identity in, 48–49
    Louisiana Purchase and, 5–6, 7
    racial binary in, 7, 45, 48–49, 52
L'Univers (newspaper), **140–43**, 141–43n39
universalism, 54–55, 56–57, 74
universality, 12
universal male suffrage, 9–10, 21, 22, 29–30, 31, 35
US Congress, 22, **154–55**
    investigation into Mechanics' Institute massacre, 39
    testimony about Mechanics' Institute massacre before, 38
US House of Representatives, 22
US Supreme Court, 14, 52, 313
    Dred Scott v. Sandford, 14
    Plessy v. Ferguson, xv, 52

Valet, Etienne Dufroisin, 201n69
Valmour (John B. Averin), 15
Vandal, Gilles C., 323–24n51
Venuti, Lawrence, 76
vernacular speech, 74
Veuillot, Louis, **140–41**, 143n39
Viatte, Auguste, 12

Vimeur, Jean-Baptiste Donatien de (count Rochambeau), **124–25**
violence, 15, 29, 42, 61. *See also* Mechanics' Institute massacre
Virgil, *Aeneid*, 205n73
Virgin Mary, 179n59, **288–89**
voting rights, 11, 19, 21, 35, 321n24. *See also* suffrage
"Votre temps est passé !" ("Your Time Has Passed!"), 27, **118–25**

Waples, Rufus, 42
Warmoth, Henry C., 23, 44
War of 1812, 6, 19, 304
Washington, George, **112–13**, **124–29**
wealth gap, between whites and free people of color, 10
Wells, James Madison, 29
Wesling, Donald, 73
whiteness, 3, 48–52
white people, 7
    doubts about black people's ability to bear arms, 23–25
    fear of common interests between enslaved people and *libres de couleur*, 12
    feeling threatened by free black militias, 5–6
    Saint Dominguan refugees, 7–8
white supremacy, xv, 50, 323–24n51
    resistance to, 15
    restoration of, 52
Williams Research Center at The Historic New Orleans Collection, xvii, 323n41
Wiltz, Euphrosine, 306
women, 55–56, 325n61
    investments in human property and, 11
    quadroon balls and, 10, 320–21n19
    roles of, 56
women poets, 55–56
women's rights, 56
women's suffrage, 56

Yacoub (pseudonym), 54, **94–97**, **278–83**, 310–11. *See also* Mansion, Joseph Lucien
Yorktown, New York, **112–13**
"Your Time Has Passed!" ("Votre temps est passé !") (anonymous), 27, **118–25**

CLINT BRUCE is assistant professor at Université Sainte-Anne, in Nova Scotia, where he holds the Canada Research Chair in Acadian and Transnational Studies. His research focuses on the Acadian diaspora and transnational Acadia, on francophone identities in Louisiana, and on the francophone Atlantic world. He holds a doctorate in francophone studies from Brown University, a master's degree in education from the City University of New York, Lehman College, and two bachelor's degrees from Centenary College of Louisiana. His work has appeared in *Nineteenth-Century French Studies*; *Francophonies d'Amérique*; *Minorités linguistiques et société*; *Histoire engagée*; *Transatlantica, revue d'études américaines*; and *Romance Studies*, among other publications, and his previous translations include works by T. Mayheart Dardar, Caryn Cossé Bell, and Jean Arceneaux.

CLINT BRUCE est professeur adjoint à l'Université Sainte-Anne en Nouvelle-Écosse, où il est titulaire de la Chaire de recherche du Canada en études acadiennes et transnationales. Ses recherches portent sur la diaspora acadienne et l'Acadie transnationale, sur les identités francophones en Louisiane et sur le monde atlantique francophone. Il possède un doctorat en études francophones de Brown University, une maîtrise en éducation de la City University of New York, Lehman College, ainsi que deux baccalauréats de Centenary College of Louisiana. Ses travaux ont paru dans *Nineteenth-Century French Studies*; *Francophonies d'Amérique*; *Minorités linguistiques et société*; *Histoire engagée*; *Transatlantica, revue d'études américaines*; et *Romance Studies*, parmi d'autres revues scientifiques, et ses traductions antérieures comprennent des textes de T. Mayheart Dardar, de Caryn Cossé Bell et de Jean Arceneaux.

MUSEUM · RESEARCH CENTER · PUBLISHER

BOARD OF DIRECTORS

Drew Jardine, *Chair*
John Kallenborn, *Vice Chair*
E. Alexandra Stafford
Hilton S. Bell
Bonnie Boyd
Lisa H. Wilson
G. Charles Lapeyre
John E. Walker, *Emeritus*

Daniel Hammer, *President and CEO*

very Laborer His Due:
EQUITABLE SALARY.
Hours a Legal Day's Work.

issues of yesterday and day be
ve been exhausted, notwithstand-
e large number of copies that
en struck off. Most of the matter
e to the massacre will be found
weekly edition, which will ap-
n Saturday morning. Thousands
BUNES have been taken by our
ists to be sent at the North.

Rebels Ashamed and
t Out of Countenance.

continue to copy W. H. C.
dispatches to the N. O. Times.
ing, as we stated yesterday, is—
y and politically—a fair speci-
f the Johnson men of New
ns.

will first give the telegram, and
make some remarks:

ASHINGTON, August 1, 1866.—The
als are making a great outcry
t the President, charging him
eing the cause of the riots. On
her hand developments will soon
fully establishing the fact that
for inciting the riot were con-
in this city.

is reported that Mr. Hahn went
w Orleans fully prepared to in-
ate measures which would lead to
mmission of violence.

or-General Baird is loudly cen-
and his course does not meet
he approval of the Administra-
With a full knowledge of what
likely to transpire, it is charged
fter the mass meeting and pro-
n of negroes he took no prevent-
ps until too late, and his every
nmistakably proved him in full
thy with the Convention people.
is failure to immediately recog-
he order sent to Attorney Gen-
Ierron, has been met with a re-
and very decided demand.

ov. Wells is denounced by every-
—Radicals and Conservatives.
None so poor to do him reverence."

is quite likely his functions will
pended until impeachment takes

He can only save himself by
ing. This is positive.

ov. Wells and Gen. Baird are re-
d as the authors, aiders, and
rs of the rioters.

he President fully comprehend-
uation, and highly colored dis-
es, no matter from what source,
derstood and regarded at their
r value.

Who will be made to believe that they are now in a state of disobedience to the orders of the Executive, and in the position of rebels to their Government? This is, indeed, too obviously absurd to be credited, and was even too coarse an invention to be published in any respectable or in any sensible paper.

We know what tremendous pres sure the rebels tried to bear on President Johnson to do away not only with the military power, but before all with the Investigation. But the very dispatch of King shows that the facts were so bad and that the indignation in the North ran so high that the President shrunk from the responsibility of a second massacre, and had—although, perhaps, unwillingly—to set aside, at least for a while, the Heron's scheme of Government.

There is another point very curious. The rebels at Washington say that Gov. Hahn concocted there the plan of the riot. Every body knows what Gov. Hahn "concocted." It was the reassembling of the Convention of 1864. This was no mystery indeed. It was not done through any underground means. It was advocated in public meetings, discussed in the press of the city and State. The Convention was called by proclamations of the Governor and of Judge Howell, Chief Justice of Louisiana. Whether the call was legal, it was a question for the judiciary to decide. The meeting of a Convention is not an act of violence, it is not a riot. The Convention, when dispersed by the assassins, had done nothing, not even a bare quorum was present; therefore no act whatever could be charged against them, besides the mere fact of having met pursuant to the call of the Governor.

"High colored dispatches" cannot controvert this simple assumption of facts.

Now it is said that Ex-Governor Hahn wished violence and blood shed. If so, the rebels of New Orleans have been terribly "green"—to use a somewhat vulgar but expressive word—since they played in his hand like unsophisticated school boys. If Gov. Hahn wished for violence, the rebels gave him more perhaps than he had desired. If, on the contrary, as the

the Philadelphia Johnson Conventio
and the rebel delegation, composed
most exclusively of out and out rebe
will be accepted. Let the Northe
men see what kind of " patriots" wa
to reconstruct the Union, after fighti
against its flag, and showing all possib
contempt for it.

To THE N. O. TIMES.—The Tim
asks why we call the rioters and the
abettors *rebels*. Because, after I
Dostic had been shot and was co
sidered dead, said rioters gather
around him, and hurrahed three tim
for Jeff. Davis. Will the Times c
this the utterance of a loyal sentime
by good reconstructed friends of t
Union? Witnesses to the above m
tioned fact are now before the Inves
gation Board.

V. LACROIX.—We deny *in toto* t
narrative of the N. O. Times in re
tion to that gallant young man. A
is imaginary in that narrative, fr
beginning to end, as evidence w
prove.

NEWS FROM THE WOUNDE

At the Marine Hospital there
now about one hundred and fi
wounded, most colored. Rev. J.
Horton is still alive, but no hope is
tertained of his recovery.

At the Hotel Dieu, Dr. Dostie see
to be more cheerful, but his conditi
remains very critical. S. S. Fish is i
proving. Also Dr. Hire. Rev. R.
Jackson is improving slowly, but
recovery remains doubtful.

Central Executive Commi
tee.

SESSION OF AUGUST 2.

At the usual hour, the Commit
met, pursuant to adjournment. At r
call there being no quorum present
motion to adjourn was put and carri

PAGES FOR A NARRATIVE O
THE NEW ORLEANS MASSACR

II.

While the rebel papers were high
clamoring for their rights and the
mission of their representatives to C
gress, we, the union men, were atta
ed by them in our most sacred right